THE CURSE OF
THE MISBEGOTTEN

.

Eugene O'Neill

THE CURSE OF
THE MISBEGOTTEN

*A Tale of
the House of O'Neill*

═══

by

CROSWELL BOWEN

with the assistance of

SHANE O'NEILL

═══

RUPERT HART-DAVIS
SOHO SQUARE LONDON
1960

This book is dedicated to
Cathy Givens O'Neill and Oona O'Neill Chaplin
and to
Eugene O'Neill's ten grandchildren
Maura, Sheila, Ted, and Kathleen O'Neill;
Geraldine, Michael John, Josephine,
Victoria, Eugene, and Jane Cecile Chaplin,

with the sure knowledge they have all
escaped the curse of the misbegotten

Printed in Holland by L. Van Leer & Co, of London & Amsterdam.

CONTENTS

ILLUSTRATIONS

PREFACE

The first time I saw Eugene O'Neill was in the fall of 1946. It was in the offices of the Theatre Guild, a great stone mansion on Fifty-third Street near Fifth Avenue. O'Neill, who had been away from New York for more than ten years, had just returned to attend rehearsals of his latest play, *The Iceman Cometh*. It was the first play he had allowed to go into production since *Ah, Wilderness!* and *Days Without End* in 1933 and 1934.

I had come to the Guild offices to get material for an article on O'Neill for *Picture News*, a New York Sunday newspaper supplement. When I arrived rehearsals were already in progress in a large, high-ceilinged ballroom on the second floor. I paused at the top of the winding marble staircase and noticed Lawrence Langner, the head of the Theatre Guild, and his wife, Armina Marshall, talking with Joe Heidt, the Guild's press agent. I also saw Theresa Helburn, a Guild executive; Carlotta Monterey O'Neill, the dramatist's third wife; and a number of my colleagues of the press. All around the place there was much talking and hurrying and scurrying.

Suddenly, a hush descended over the entire group. The tall, spare figure of Eugene O'Neill, his handsome face cast slightly downward, strode through the hallway into the rehearsal room. I had seen his picture many times, and now I felt that I was looking at a familiar face—the mustache and the wry, sardonic smile crossing his lean, lantern-jawed, ascetic features. And I felt that his glowing eyes took in the entire hallway and everyone in it.

Later, I peered into the ballroom and saw O'Neill sitting at a table with Eddie Dowling, the play's director, listening to the actors read their lines. Again I felt the strange, almost religious mood which enveloped O'Neill and those around him. O'Neill was the creator of an entire world—the world of his magnificent and terrifying plays. The characters he had brought to life were, it had been said, souls speaking to one another, souls whose bodies lived, suffered and died. A literary statistician had ascertained that in the world of Eugene O'Neill's plays there had been twelve murders, eight suicides, twenty-three other deaths, and seven cases of insanity.

It seemed to me that I had lived and suffered and died with O'Neill's characters in *Strange Interlude, The Hairy Ape, Desire un*

der the Elms, *Mourning Becomes Electra* and the other great dramas.
I was not a drama critic, just a reporter, but O'Neill's people and his
plays were a part of my life. Perhaps I had never fully analyzed and
evaluated these plays, but I had experienced them.

I did not attempt to speak to O'Neill that day, but rather I
decided to go first to the place he had come from, the place he had
spent most of his youth—New London, Connecticut. There I talked
to friends of his family, people who had known him in his youth, and
the O'Neill family lawyer. From old Thomas Fortune D'Orsey, James
O'Neill's friend and New London real estate adviser, I discovered
the theme of my piece. "Young Eugene," he told me, "was the gloomy-
type Irishman, brooding, always readin' books—a black Irishman!"

Then I drove over to Wallingford to visit the Gaylord Farm
tuberculosis sanitarium. I wanted to see and feel for myself the place
about which O'Neill wrote *The Straw* and where he experienced the
awakening of his artistic spirit. In New York, I talked with Neysa
McMein, the artist; Barrett Clark, O'Neill's official biographer; Saxe
Commins, his friend and editor; and Eugene junior, O'Neill's eldest
child.

Young Eugene, a brilliant, charming classical scholar, was then
on leave from a teaching position at Yale University. He had just
edited and translated a volume of Greek dramas, and I thought he
had the whole world before him. At that time I did not sense Eugene's
inner torture, the torture that drove him to suicide just a few years
later.

Eugene junior approved of the "black Irishman" theme I was
pursuing in my article about his father. In fact, he recalled that O'Neill
had once told him that "the critics have missed the most important
thing about me and my work—the fact that I am Irish." At one point
I remarked to Eugene that we (and our generation) were much more
optimistic than his father. "No," he said, "my father's seemingly tragic
view of life covers a deep-seated idealism, a dream of what the world
could be 'if only. . . .' My father not only is the most sensitive man
I have ever known but also possesses the highest idealism of any man
who ever lived."

At about this time I also met O'Neill's other son, Shane, and,
during a dress rehearsal of *The Iceman Cometh*, Carlotta Monterey
O'Neill. She was sitting, dressed entirely in black, at the very top of
the highest balcony in the Martin Beck Theatre. She was very beautiful. In the course of my interview with her, Mrs. O'Neill cautioned

me not to interpret anything her husband said, or any of his work, in political terms. Art was the only important thing, she said.

Finally, I found Eugene O'Neill himself in the wings of the stage. I spent a long time with him and experienced the same fascination so many other writers apparently had felt before me. I remember that I wanted to become his disciple; I wanted to defend him against the world. His sad, intense eyes seemed to be piercing right into me. They haunted me for days after.

The title of the long profile that I wrote was "Black Irishman," as I had known it would be almost from the start. That article was not the end of my interest and concern in the O'Neills; it was just the beginning.

During the next ten years I watched the tragedy of Eugene O'Neill. I maintained my friendship with Eugene junior, and now and then I would see Shane hurrying through the darkened streets of Greenwich Village. Perhaps because of my Irish blood, I became obsessed with the idea that here was a family on whom a terrible curse rested, and I wanted to search out the lives of the O'Neill family and learn about that curse. But nobody at that time seemed to be interested in Eugene O'Neill or his plays.

In 1956, three years after the playwright's death, there was a substantial revival of interest in Eugene O'Neill, largely as a result of the successful off-Broadway production of *The Iceman Cometh* and the widely acclaimed Broadway presentation of *Long Day's Journey into Night,* which won a Pulitzer prize and the New York Drama Critics' Circle award. I continued my pursuit of the story of the O'Neills and their curse, interviewing hundreds of people and rereading the plays. Early in the winter of 1958 I learned that Shane O'Neill and his wife and four children were living at Point Pleasant, New Jersey. Although *Long Day's Journey into Night* was a great success, they were living on less than twenty-five dollars a week. Shane was ill and unemployed, and I asked him if he would collaborate with me on a book about his father. Shane was puzzled; he could not really believe that anyone would be interested in his father and his family. He said he would not himself write about his father but would contribute any letters or documents he had, tell me anything he could remember, and read and correct what I wrote.

In Ireland there exists an ancient belief that when ill fortune consistently plagues a family it is the result of a curse. Some ancestor may have done some terrible deed, and generation after generation must suffer retribution. Someone who had been harmed by a member of the family might have uttered the curse, or it might have been God's curse, the most terrible of all. This is one of the famous Irish curses:

> *May the grass grow at your door and the fox build his nest on your hearthstone. May the light fade from your eyes, so you never see what you love. May your own blood rise against you. May you die without benefit of clergy. May there be none to shed a tear at your grave, and may the hearthstone of hell be your best bed forever.*

Of course, I have never found even a hint of a story about the placing of any curse on the O'Neill family, but I did come across a wonderful Irish legend about an O'Neill. In the sixteenth century, there was a famous Irish king, Shane O'Neill, called Shane the Proud. Eugene O'Neill, I know, liked to think of himself as descended from the great Shane O'Neill, and he named his second son after him. O'Neill especially enjoyed the story of Shane's swimming across a lake in competition with another Irish warrior for the hand of a beautiful princess. It was specified that the swimmer whose hand first touched the far shore would win the fair lady. After Shane had swum three-quarters of the distance across the lake, he realized his opponent was going to win. Thereupon, he took a dagger from his belt, cut off one of his hands at the wrist and flung it to the far shore—winning the race and the princess.

I once mentioned my preoccupation with a possible O'Neill curse to Saxe Commins. "I know what you mean," he said, "but it's not so simple as a curse. It's a mystic thing." Perhaps I had been foolish to entertain such a notion for so long, but I have always half believed that the bad things that happen to one, the bad luck, are decreed by some evil force. O'Neill himself was troubled by this feeling. Our destinies are ruled by the incidental, the accidental, the fated, he used to say. If one believes in the doctrine of original sin, as I was brought up to believe and as O'Neill was brought up to believe, then one may feel that a curse rests on all mankind.

Working on the closing pages of my manuscript and looking back over its long dark journey through the lives of Eugene O'Neill and his family, I suddenly realized that what I had been searching for had been apparent all along and I had not had eyes to see it. Or perhaps I had feared to come to a conclusion too similar to one I had arrived at before in seeking to account for tragedy in others' lives—a lack of love, or the inability to give and receive love.

In the case of the O'Neills there was something still more complex and elusive. Most of them seemed people with a great capacity for feeling deep love. But something invariably conspired to keep each one forever alone and apart. As Clifford Odets wrote me, one always felt that if one or two little moves had been made, the O'Neills could have lived happy lives together. The tragedy of the O'Neill family was not the lack of love but the lack of communication of their love. In a sense, this was the theme of so many of O'Neill's plays—man's agonizing loneliness, his feeling of not belonging, of wanting and not wanting to belong, of being cursed to remain alone, above, and apart.

Croswell Bowen

Chappaqua, New York

ACKNOWLEDGMENTS

First of all I want to express my gratitude to Shane O'Neill; elsewhere I have detailed his contribution to this book. I am also indebted to Cathy Givens O'Neill, Shane's wife, who was of immense help. Shane's mother, Agnes Boulton Kaufman, and her husband, Mac Kaufman, know how grateful I am to them not only for information but for actual food and lodging.

As always, fellow writers were more than generous, particularly Marc Brandel, Bessie Breuer, Elizabeth Shepley Sergeant, Russel Crouse, Stark Young, Robert Manning, Jane Burnside, Peggy Baird Conklin. I am grateful to drama critics John Mason Brown, Walter Kerr, and John Chapman for their advice and information. To Brooks Atkinson I am indebted not only for his observations in a quarter century of reviews of O'Neill's plays but also for the material he gave me by letter and in person. I want to give special thanks also to the patient editors, Bob Gutwillig, Ed Kuhn, and Ed Schneider, who worked on the book at my publisher's.

Attorney Joseph Trachtman, of Ridgefield, Connecticut, sent me to see Silvio Bedini, who had played with Shane at Brook Farm in Ridgefield when they were little boys. Silvio and his mother were, of course, helpful with information. Frederick P. Latimer, Jr., whose father had been an intimate friend of Eugene O'Neill in New London, was helpful, as was his sister, Mrs. Daniel Fairchild Porter, of Darien. I am grateful to Mrs. Samuel Green and Mrs. Eugene Northrup; and to Mrs. Barrett H. Clark, of Briarcliff, New York, and Mrs. Clayton Hamilton, of New York City, both widows of distinguished drama authorities. Mrs. Clark was particularly generous with letters and papers belonging to her late husband. James Light and Susan Jenkins were especially helpful on O'Neill's Provincetown days. In my own town of Sherman, Connecticut, Muriel and Malcolm Cowley were helpful in a number of directions. In the theater Florence Eldridge, Fredric March, Gusti Huber, Lawrence Langner, and the late Mary Welch, helped and encouraged me. Although Dr. Merrill Moore of Boston died before I was able to visit him, we carried on an extensive correspondence.

The libraries were especially important in this project and it is fortunate that so many of them have shown foresight in assembling

O'Neill materials. At Princeton, Alexander Clark, Curator of Manuscripts, made a special effort to help me with the George Tyler letters. Marcus A. McCorison, Chief, Rare Books Department of the Baker Library at Dartmouth College, did similar yeoman service for me with the Landauer Collection of O'Neilliana. William L. Lucey, S.J., Librarian of the College of the Holy Cross, arranged for me to see the Michael Earls, S.J., Collection of O'Neill and Richard Dana Skinner letters located in the Dinand Library. At the Library of Congress Robert H. Land, Acting Chief, Manuscript Division, and Frederick R. Goff, Chief of the Rare Book Division, helped greatly. Marion McCandless, Secretary Emeritus of Saint Mary's College at Notre Dame, Indiana, Ella Quinlan O'Neill's alma mater, provided me with reams of material. Sister Mary Madeleva, distinguished poet and president of the college, helped in my research and wrote me continually. I thank May Davenport Seymour, curator of the theater and music collections of the Museum of the City of New York. The Berg Collection, the manuscript division, and the theater collection at the New York Public Library all provided help. I am especially grateful to Donald Gallup, Curator of American Manuscripts, and James Babb, Director, of the Sterling Memorial Library at Yale University.

Allen V. Heely, headmaster of the Lawrenceville School, and a number of his faculty members helped in re-creating Shane's prep school days. Art McGinley, staff writer for the *Hartford Times,* was most generous in supplying information about O'Neill, with whom he grew up in New London and whom he continued to see until the early 1930s. Sophus Keith Winther, of the University of Washington, was helpful with material concerning O'Neill's life on the West Coast.

To the late Saxe Commins I am especially grateful for reading the entire manuscript and saving me from some bad errors, and to Dorothy Commins, his wife, who supplied both information and strength to carry on. I want to thank William Glover, Associated Press drama writer, who also read the manuscripts and recommended corrections. Dr. Doris Alexander of Staten Island College was most generous despite the fact that she is in process of writing her own book on O'Neill. Dr. Alexander Renner, who knew O'Neill in China, was helpful. So were Helen P. Duffy, Secretary of St. Mary's Cemetery in New London, and Mrs. Eva Chang, Secretary of the Euthanasia Society of America.

To Winfield Aronberg and his wife Mary, I am grateful for a variety of things too numerous to list here.

In Chappaqua, I am grateful to Bob Aylesworth, who let me use part of his office to write the book, and Janet Scilipoti and Florence Smith who spent so many hours typing the manuscript.

As for the contribution of Hamilton Basso, I cannot adequately express my gratitude not only for letting me see his working notes made during his O'Neill interviews, but for aid and encouragement throughout the project. Mary Heaton Vorse spent several afternoons at the Overseas Press Club giving me her recollections of O'Neill and Provincetown and letting me record them on tape. When he was a senior at Dartmouth College and for a time after he was graduated, Carl W. Schmidt gave invaluable service as interviewer and researcher. Others who helped were Betty and Carl Carmer, Bennett Cerf, the late Samuel Hopkins Adams, and Pauline Turkel.

I know I have failed to mention others to whom I am grateful, and I ask their forgiveness.

Because such complete bibliographies have been done on O'Neill and his work and because an up-to-date bibliography would be out of date when this book is published, I see no point in publishing another one at this time. I am now compiling complete footnotes to all materials contained in this book and hope to print this in later editions.

REFERENCES

Basso, Hamilton, from "The Tragic Sense," *The New Yorker*, February 28, March 6, and March 13, 1948. By permission of Hamilton Basso and *The New Yorker*. Bodenheim, Maxwell, from "Profile," *The New Yorker*, 1926.   Clark, Barrett H., *Eugene O'Neill: The Man and His Plays*. Copyright 1926, 1929 by Barrett H. Clark. Copyright 1947, by Barrett H. Clark (revised version). By permission of Dover Publications, Inc.   Cowley, Malcolm, from "A Weekend with Eugene O'Neill," *The Reporter*, September 5, 1957. By permission of *The Reporter* & Malcolm Cowley. Deutsch, Helen and Hanau, Stella, *The Provincetown: A History of the Theatre*. 1931, Farrar & Rinehart, Inc. By permission of Helen Deutsch and Stella Hanau.   Langer, Lawrence, *The Magic Curtain*. Copyright 1951, by Lawrence Langner. By permission of Lawrence Langner.

Mullett, Mary B., from "The Extraordinary Story of Eugene O'Neill," *The American Magazine*, November, 1922. By permission of The Crowell-Collier Publishing Company.   Nathan, George Jean, *The World of George Jean Nathan*, edited and with an introduction by Charles Angoff, 1952. By permission of Alfred A. Knopf, Inc.   O'Neill, Eugene Gladstone, *Ile, Strange Interlude, Marco Millions, The Great God Brown, Ah, Wilderness!, The Iceman Cometh, Moon for the Misbegotten, The Emperor Jones, The Straw*, and *Lazarus Laughed*. By permission of Random House, Inc.   O'Neill, Eugene Gladstone, Jr., "Poem," from *The Helicon*, 1930. By permission of Yale University.   Prideaux, Tom, from "Eugene O'Neill," *Life*, October 14, 1946. Copyright by Time, Inc. By permission of *Life* Magazine.

Quinn, Arthur Hobson, from *History of American Drama from the Civil War to the Present Day*, vol. 2, 1927. By permission of Harper & Brothers.   Skinner, Richard Dana, from *Eugene O'Neill; A Poet's Quest*, 1935. By permission of Longman's, Green & Company.   Vorse, Mary Heaton, from *Time and the Towne: A Provincetown Chronicle*.

Copyright 1942 by the author and used by permission of the publisher, The Dial Press, Inc. Wolfe, Thomas, from *Look Homeward, Angel,* 1929. By permission of Charles Scribner's Sons. Young, Stark, from "Eugene O'Neill: Notes from a Critic's Diary," *Harper's Magazine,* June, 1957. By permission of Harper & Brothers.

From *The New York Times:* Atkinson, J. Brooks, quotations from reviews of *The Fountain, Desire under the Elms, Mourning Becomes Electra, The Iceman Cometh,* and *Long Day's Journey into Night.* Daniel, Clifton: description of Oona Chaplin's arrival in London, September, 1952. Obituary of James O'Neill, August 12, 1920. Story on O'Neill's will, December 25, 1953. Kalodyne, Louis, "O'Neill Lifts the Curtain on His Early Days," December 21, 1924. Shriftgiesser, Karl, *The Iceman Cometh,* October 6, 1946. S. J. Wolf, from "Eugene O'Neill Returns after Twelve Years," September 15, 1946. Woolcott, Alexander, 1920. By permission of *The New York Times.*

From *The New York Herald Tribune:* Karsner, David, "O'Neill at Close Range in Maine," August 8, 1926. Young, Marguerite, interview with O'Neill. Watts, Richard, Jr., "Realism Doomed, O'Neill Believes," February 5, 1928. By permission of *The New York Herald-Tribune.*

From *The New York News:* Pasley, Fred, "Odyssey of Eugene O'Neill—the Ulysses of the Drama," January 24–30, 1932. Reynolds, Ruth, interview with Oona O'Neill, July, 1942. By permission of *The New York News.*

From *The New York Post:* Wilson, Earl, interview with O'Neill. Copyright, 1946, New York Post Corporation. Dudar, Helen, interview with Shane O'Neill. Copyright 1956, New York Post Corporation. By permission of *The New York Post.*

From *The New York World:* Vorse, Mary Heaton, "Eugene O'Neill's Pet Saloon Is Gone," May 4, 1930. Weaver, John V. A., "I Knew Him When—," February 21, 1926. News story on O'Neill's divorce, March 25, 1929. By permission of Jackson, Nash, Brophy, Barringer, & Brooks.

Unpublished letters and papers of Eugene Gladstone O'Neill, by permission of Yale University Library.

The pictures on the jacket are used by permission of Culver Service, Robert Aylesworth, and European Picture Service.

PROLOGUE

໙

HOMECOMING

On a Sunday in May, 1931, Eugene O'Neill stood on the deck of the Holland-America liner *Statendam* as the ship neared the United States. Beside him was his third wife, the beautiful and reportedly rich actress Carlotta Monterey. They were returning from an exile of three years, after a courtship that had extended over half the globe. The playwright's figure was straight and slender; his face was lean, the features finely drawn; his eyes were dark and probing.

As for Carlotta, the artist Neysa McMein described her then as "possessing the beauty of all women, of all races, of all time. Even another woman was aware of that. She was so beautiful that she made you suddenly afraid." Within a year the great photographers of the thirties—Nicholas Muray, Ben Pinchot, and others—filled the society and fashion pages with portraits of this royal couple of the arts.

O'Neill was forty-two. He had been honored in the United States as a great literary figure whose plays had revitalized the American theater, his work was being performed in South America, in France

and in Germany, and the Kamerny Theater of Russia had toured
Europe with several of his plays in its repertory. His output had been
impressive. To date, he was the author of nineteen full-length plays.
He had published six one-act plays while still in his twenties. Three
times during the past decade he had been awarded the Pulitzer Prize
for Drama. Yale University had conferred on him an honorary degree
and had placed a bronze bust of him in its Drama School. He had
been elected to the American Academy of Arts and Letters.

Now, in 1931, he told drama critic George Jean Nathan, he was
happy for the first time in his life. Talking with Nathan in London, he
said his new-found happiness had "stood tests which would have
wrecked it, if it wasn't the genuine article." He added, "I feel as if
I had tapped a new life."

No one seeing the couple together could doubt that O'Neill's
exaltation stemmed from his happy marriage with Carlotta Monterey.
When they celebrated their second wedding anniversary two months
later he gave her a copy of his new play, *Mourning Becomes Electra,*
with this moving inscription:

> I have known your love with my love even when I have
> seemed not to know; I have seen it even when I have appeared
> most blind; I have felt it warmly around me always (even in
> my study in the closing pages of an act!)—sustaining and com-
> forting, a warm, secure sanctuary for the man after the author's
> despairing solitude and inevitable defeats—a victory of love-in-
> life. Mother and wife and collaborator! I love you!

On that Sunday in May, after the liner docked, O'Neill and his
wife checked into the Hotel Madison on East Fifty-eighth Street.
There was nothing, seemingly, on the horizon to mar this homecoming. He told a friend that he felt he was just at the right age to "begin
to learn." In addition, he had everything to back him up now—love,
security, peace and fame. He said he looked forward with confidence
to years of undisturbed hard work and of giving himself up to the joy
of living. Now he could even pick up the loose ends of his past life.

He had made arrangements through his friend and lawyer, Harry
Weinberger, to bring his two children by his second wife—Oona,
then five, and Shane, twelve—into New York to visit him. His anger
at their mother, Agnes Boulton, occasioned by the divorce suit, was
ended. He sent word to Shane to tell her that he was sorry, sincerely
sorry, and to say that all the bitterness had got burned out of him

when he was in a hospital in the Far East. The future years would prove this, he said. He also planned to see Eugene junior—his son by his first wife—who was completing his third year at Yale. Eugene, a brilliant student who showed promise as a poet, had made Phi Beta Kappa and had been tapped for the most exclusive of Yale's senior societies, Skull and Bones.

Confident of himself and his future, O'Neill had agreed to appear at a press conference at the offices of the Theatre Guild the following Thursday afternoon; but, as always, his address and phone number were a guarded secret. The occasion for the interview was the forthcoming production of the new O'Neill play, *Mourning Becomes Electra.*

On Wednesday, May 20, just a block south of where O'Neill and Carlotta were staying, Ralph Barton, a celebrated *New Yorker* magazine caricaturist, composed a note for the newspapers. On the bed before him was a photograph of his former wife and a book of cartoons entitled *Suburbia.* In the flyleaf of the book was an inscription she had written while they were still married— "To Ralph sometime on a certain Friday or was it Saturday?" It was signed "Carlotta."

> I have run from wife to wife [Barton wrote], from house to house and from country to country in a ridiculous effort to escape from myself. . . . In particular, my remorse is bitter over my failure to appreciate my beautiful lost angel, Carlotta, the only woman I ever loved and whom I respect and admire above all the rest of the human race. I do hope that she will understand what my malady was and forgive me a little. I kiss my dear children and Carlotta.

Then Barton shot himself in the head.

Harold Ross, editor of *The New Yorker* and an intimate friend of both O'Neill and Barton, broke the news to the O'Neills. It was Carlotta who first received the word, and her reaction clearly indicated that she didn't envision her involvement in the publicity that would be given to the suicide. However, she soon found her name brought into the newspaper stories about the case, when Homer Barton, the artist's brother, told the press that Ralph had visited the O'Neills shortly before he killed himself.

"My brother was still in love with his third wife, Carlotta Monterey," Homer told *The New York Times,* "and the realization that he had lost her broke his heart. It was a matter of impulse, I am sure, for Ralph was very impulsive. When Mr. and Mrs. O'Neill came to New York, he paid them a friendly visit."

To the O'Neills this was a most unpleasant development, and they wondered whether they should even acknowledge the statement by issuing a denial. They consulted with Harry Weinberger and they decided that they would not meet the press to discuss the matter. O'Neill, of course, was committed to a press conference later that week at the Theatre Guild; he would keep that engagement, but he would make no comment there on the Barton suicide. On that matter the O'Neills' answer would be confined to a formal statement issued to the press by Weinberger:

> Mr. and Mrs. O'Neill have asked me to state that contrary to newspaper reports of statements by Homer Barton, brother of Ralph Barton, they have not seen Mr. Ralph Barton since their return to the United States and Mrs. O'Neill, the former Carlotta Monterey, desires to state that she never saw or heard from Mr. Barton since her divorce more than five years ago.

The newspapers made the most of this dramatic situation. On the day of the funeral, the New York *Journal* said that Barton had had ninety-two girls in his life but "no one came to mourn him today. Of these, he loved one. She was not there for a final look at the man she once held tightly in her arms."

Homer Barton persisted in drawing attention to the O'Neill aspect of his brother's suicide. "If Carlotta won't see him," Homer told reporters, "nobody shall see him. It is the O'Neill influence that has kept Carlotta from this final farewell to Ralph."

On Thursday afternoon, O'Neill arrived at the Guild Theatre on West Fifty-second Street. Surrounded by some thirty reporters, he agreed to being questioned by one of them in the presence of the others. Joseph Heidt, press agent for the Guild, called on John Chapman, then a reporter on the drama desk of the *Daily News,* to act as spokesman for the group.

"O'Neill was pallid and shaking and sweating when he faced me," Chapman, now the drama critic of the *News,* has recalled. "For that matter, so was I."

O'Neill talked freely about *Mourning Becomes Electra,* but this was not what the reporters wanted to hear. At the end of the theater part of the interview, Chapman said, "We're sorry, Mr.

O'Neill, to have to ask you some personal questions, but our desks have ordered us to."

To all of Chapman's questions about Barton's suicide O'Neill replied that he had no comment to make. He pointed out that his attorney had issued a statement emphatically denying that he or his wife had seen Barton. Chapman called attention to Homer Barton's statements, and finally O'Neill volunteered a possible explanation.

"We hadn't seen him since our arrival on Sunday," he said. "As far as I know, I never met Ralph Barton. He did not call on us. I do not question his brother's sincerity, for Mr. Barton might have told him he called. He was in a very peculiar mental state. I know that he had made no effort to see Mrs. O'Neill."

Barton's body was cremated and his ashes were shipped to Kansas City, where he had been born and raised. The incident was soon forgotten, but in casting the shadow of tragedy over the jubilation of a happy homecoming it exemplified the recurrent theme of paradox in the playwright's life—private disaster linked with public triumphs, pain with joy, beauty with ugliness and light with darkness. Perhaps no other artist has ever "lived" the emotional content of his material so directly, or expressed it with such awesome truthfulness, as did this man who experienced and created the haunted world and haunted life of Eugene O'Neill.

CHAPTER

ONE

ଊଊ

THE COUNT AND
THE CONVENT GIRL

Any way you spell O'Neill—with or without an O, with Mac or Mc, with Niall or Neale or Nihill—the name means *champion* in Gaelic. James O'Neill, the father of Eugene O'Neill—who always addressed him as "Governor" and referred to him as "Monte Cristo"—was born in 1846 in Thomastown, Kilkenny County, Ireland. James's father was probably the Thomas O'Neill who in 1851 held several acres of land and a house in the hamlet of Grennan, a part of Thomastown. James O'Neill used to tell his publicity men that he came from yeoman parents and his sons that he came from a family which raised horses.

The O'Neill family left Ireland following the potato famine years of the middle nineteenth century. Poverty-stricken, they sailed to the New World by steerage about 1854. James used to say that a coil of rope served as his bed on that voyage. The family landed in New York and soon afterward journeyed upstate to settle in Buffalo. James had two older brothers, who left the family and struck out for themselves not long after they arrived in the United States. He also had two older sisters and five younger brothers and sisters. In their new home the family again found only utter poverty. Soon the father decided that if he stayed any longer he would die of the "white plague" —tuberculosis, which in those days was considered the curse of the Irish, because so many of them, weakened by years of malnutrition, succumbed to it. So Thomas, who was remembered by his son James as superstitious and impetuous, left his wife and eight children and went back to Ireland, where, it is thought, he died of the disease he had tried to run away from.

As the oldest remaining male after his father left, James became head of the family and had to go to work to help support it. Only ten years old, with but a few years' schooling, he settled for a job as clerk in a store. The mother worked as a domestic and the two older sisters worked as seamstresses. It was a harsh existence. Twice, James afterward remembered, his mother and the children were evicted from the hovels in which they lived. One Christmas his mother received an extra dollar, and she at once spent it for food; it was the first full meal the family had ever enjoyed.

When the chance came along, James quit his job as clerk and went to work in a machine shop for a bigger salary—fifty cents a day. He spent his few hours of recreation in a pool hall next door to a theater. When theatrical companies came to Buffalo, the stage manager would walk into the pool hall and hire his supernumeraries on the spot. James was always available. The reward was high—a dollar a night. His first appearance on the stage as a super was in the company of Edwin Forrest in 1865. Fascinated, he began to think about becoming an actor.

James O'Neill became friends with some of the actors and talked to them about going on the stage. One of them—it was a family tradition that it was either Lawrence Barrett, who was playing Cassius in *Julius Caesar,* or Edwin Booth in *Hamlet*—encouraged him. "If you want to be an actor," he was told, "get rid of that Irish accent and learn how to talk. Learn something from Shakespeare, and when we come here next year I'll listen to you."

The following year James recited a soliloquy from *Hamlet* in an audition and he was added to the Forrest troupe.

He made his debut as a member of the company in the National Theatre in Cincinnati. He continued with the company on a barnstorming tour of the country, until it became stranded—an occupational hazard of the theatrical profession in those days—somewhere in the hinterland.

James somehow made his way back to Cincinnati, got a small part in the company of a "Colonel" Bob Miles and was soon promoted to the position of "walking gentleman." He then went on to Ford's Theatre in Baltimore where he played leading juvenile parts. In Cleveland he joined the company of Edwin Forrest again, filling important roles in *Macbeth*. In 1871 he played in McVicker's Theatre, Chicago, in a company that included Charlotte Cushman and Adelaide Neilson. He alternated with Edwin Booth in playing Othello and Iago. One night, as O'Neill played Othello, Booth turned to the theater manager and said, "That young man is playing the part better than I ever did." The manager told James, who was so pleased that he insisted it be written down. He carried the paper around in his wallet for years and showed it, with perhaps pardonable pride, wherever he went.

In 1873 he joined Hooley's Stock Company in Chicago, playing Hamlet and Richelieu, then went on to San Francisco. The following year he joined the stock company of A. M. Palmer at the Union Square Theatre in New York City. For two seasons he played with Charles R. Thorne, Jr., taking the parts of the Prince in *The Danchieffs*, Jean Renaud in *A Celebrated Case,* and Pierre in *The Two Orphans*. His portrayal of the last-named part was said to have been one of the greatest pieces of character acting ever seen on the American stage.

James O'Neill was a devout Catholic—in his youth he had even thought for a time that he had the calling for the priesthood—and he always went to Mass on Sunday, even when he was on tour. At one period early in his theatrical career, however, he lapsed in the strict observance of his Church's commandments and became the father of an illegitimate child. The mother was an actress, presumably a member of a troupe to which O'Neill belonged. The extent of her emotional involvement is not recorded, but it is of some significance that the child, a boy, was given the name James O'Neill, Jr. Understandably, the whole episode remained a secret shared by a very small number of persons, the details have nowhere been completely recorded, and the boy himself died in early childhood. But it was not a casual or momentary relationship that had existed between the two principals. Whatever the circumstances of its ending, O'Neill did assume at least some of the responsibilities of a parent. Even afterward James O'Neill was to be troubled recurrently by the moral implications of his participation in the affair.

It was some time after the ending of that liaison, apparently, that he met the father of the girl who later was to become his bride. While coming out of church one Sunday morning in Cleveland, where he was performing at that time, he struck up an acquaintance with Thomas J. Quinlan, a prosperous wholesale grocer. He invited his new friend to come backstage after a performance, and the two Irishmen became warm friends—so warm, in fact, that Quinlan wrote to his eighteen-year-old daughter, then in a convent at South Bend, Indiana, that when she came home for the Easter vacation he would take her to see his friend the famous actor James O'Neill in one of his plays. Later, he added, he would take her backstage to meet this friend *in person*.

Ella Quinlan, who was to become Eugene O'Neill's mother, was born in New Haven, Connecticut, in 1857. The family later moved to Cleveland. An only child, she entered St. Mary's Academy at South Bend in September, 1872, when she was fifteen. St. Mary's, founded in 1844, was run by the Sisters of the Holy Cross, a French order. It later became St. Mary's College and is today one of the most distinguished Catholic women's colleges in the country. The academy accepted girls of any faith, and only about fifty per cent of them were Catholic. The girls were taught Latin, modern languages, art, science, and music, including the harp, violin, voice, and piano. Ella studied the piano and became an accomplished performer. She played at the commencements of 1874 and 1875.

One of her most intimate friends was Ella Nordlinger, the mother of George Jean Nathan, a lifelong champion of the plays of Eugene O'Neill and one of the dramatist's most intimate friends. Nathan said his mother told him that Ella Quinlan was very beautiful and one of the most pious girls in the convent.

In the winter of her senior year at the convent, Ella went through an experience many an adolescent Catholic girl has known. She received the calling—or what she thought was the calling—to become a nun. She had a vision; she felt, as she knelt before the statue of the Blessed Virgin standing in the lake, that it had come alive, and the Virgin smiled on her, she afterward said, as though in approval. She took the matter up with the Mother Superior, for whom she had formed a deep attachment, and whom she loved more than she did her own mother.

When she had heard Ella's tale, the Mother Superior told her that the vision was not enough, that the girl must make sure that she really had the calling. She advised Ella to put herself to a test, after graduation, by going to dances and parties with young men. If she still felt the same in a year or two, they would discuss it again. In *Long Day's Journey into Night* Eugene O'Neill fictionalized his mother's vision. He visualized this scene as taking place in the grotto of the Catholic boarding school that he himself attended as a young boy.

During the Easter vacation Ella was taken by her father to a performance of *A Tale of Two Cities.* When she saw James O'Neill thrust into prison in his handsome nobleman's costume, she wept bitterly. Afterward, when she told about this, she used to say that she was mighty sorry that she had cried, for she was sure her eyes and nose were red when she went backstage with her father.

The actor and the convent girl were immediately attracted to one another—or so they told each other and everyone else in the years that followed. She returned to St. Mary's, where the following year, on June 23, 1875, she was graduated with honors, including a gold medal. But her dream of becoming a nun was over.

She was in love.

In 1875 James O'Neill was a likely man for any girl to fall in love with. He was the John Barrymore of his day, but with a reputation for steadiness and good morals—he was known to be a devout and practicing Catholic. A contemporary described him at the time he married Ella Quinlan as "a quiet gentleman of medium height, well-proportioned figure, square shoulders, and standing very erect. He has black hair, black eyes, rather dark complexion, a black mustache, and a fine set of teeth, which he knows how to display to advantage. He dresses with taste on and off the stage."

It is reported also that he kept himself somewhat aloof from the general run of actors and actresses, who never felt free to approach him as an equal. On the other hand, he was said to be very kind and helpful to actors just starting out on their careers. It was acknowledged that no actor in the world could walk down a stage stairway, especially a winding one, like James O'Neill. The way he touched the balustrades, the hesitant or forthright step, the sideways glance, the tilt of the chin—every movement, gesture and look added to the characterization he was portraying. His voice was remarkably fine and resonant. Wilton Lackaye, one of his colleagues, said that "James O'Neill's voice is a gift of God."

Although it was said that James O'Neill "took his wife out of a convent," actually there was a discreet two-year interval between their first meeting and their marriage. In 1875 he went to San Francisco, where he joined Hooley's Comedy Company, opening at Maguire's Opera House, later known as the Standard Theatre, on Bush Street.

Back in Cleveland, Ella had two years to think over her decision. No doubt the Quinlans were hesitant about letting their daughter marry an actor, even if he was James O'Neill. But since her meeting with O'Neill, Ella lived in a dream. She told her friends that her betrothed was handsome, different from ordinary men, and like someone from another world.

When Ella Quinlan and James O'Neill were married in New York City June 14, 1877, the Quinlans "did it up right." Ella had the finest bridal gown that money could buy. It was a beautiful dress of white shimmering satin trimmed with duchesse lace and pulled into a bustle at the back. The basque was boned and very tight. She wore white slippers and there were orange blossoms on her misty white veil.

Ella kept her wedding dress all her life and lived in the hope that she would have a daughter who would one day wear the dress at her own wedding. It was kept in the attic of their New London cottage and Eugene grew up aware of its presence in the house. He had it brought out to appear in *Long Day's Journey into Night*.

After the wedding, James and Ella O'Neill went to San Francisco, where he joined E. J. Baldwin's company. Ella did not mingle with the actors and actresses because she thought a well-bred girl should not associate with stage people. She was beginning what was to become a lonely existence, and it was to get lonelier as time went on—the hotel existence of an actor's wife.

Along toward Christmas of 1877 Ella knew that she was pregnant. Her first child, whom Eugene O'Neill was to portray as the hero of *A Moon for the Misbegotten,* was born in San Francisco on September 11, 1878. He was christened James O'Neill II. The

"II" was James senior's tacit—and perhaps penitent—acknowledgement of his illegitimate son.

It was in San Francisco that O'Neill assumed the role of the Christus in an adaptation of the Oberammergau Passion Play. In later years he always seemed most proud of having played this part, claiming to have been the "only actor on the English-speaking stage who has impersonated our Saviour."

The production was staged by David Belasco. It appeared to be scheduled for a long run but "the ragged-edge preachers"—as James O'Neill called the vocal Protestant clergy—"not the important clergymen of the city," inveighed against the play as the profanation of a sacred theme. One night a policeman came to James O'Neill's dressing room, arrested him and took him to jail in a cab. The rest of the cast were also arrested and jailed. The next day O'Neill was bailed out and some days later fined fifty dollars. The Passion Play closed.

As late as 1918, James O'Neill still felt very strongly about the desirability of putting on this play. He declared that "it would be a relief after all the filth we get on the stage, and especially in vaudeville and the movies. People have seen so much lewdness on the stage that they have become nauseated with it."

In 1882, the impresario John Stetson offered him the part of Edmond Dantes in *The Count of Monte Cristo* at Booth's Theatre in New York City. The role and the play were decisive in the life and fortunes of James O'Neill. It brought him wealth and fame; but, paradoxically, it embittered not only his own life but the life of his dramatist son. For James O'Neill wrecked his character along with his career on the glittering shoal of this immense success. According to one report, he played the part of Dantes six thousand times. He told his son Eugene that the play had been his "curse"; that because of it he had taken the easy (money) way out, and ruined what might have been an impressive theatrical career. But in 1882 at Booth's Theatre, he sensed that the play was his fortune and at once proceeded to purchase the dramatization rights, and later the entire production.

In December, 1883, Ella became pregnant a second time. A second son was born in September, 1884, and they named him Edmund Dantes O'Neill. The O'Neills were now suddenly prosperous, but they paid a heavy price for their wealth. The play was constantly on tour, and Ella insisted on accompanying her husband. Jamie had been cradled in the bureau drawers of hotel rooms; now there was another baby to care for.

The family traveled back and forth across the United States. There was a nurse to help Ella, but the protracted tours, with their one-night stands, were to take their toll on the sensitive mind of the convent-bred wife. As she persistently refused to join in any kind of social life with the actors and actresses in her husband's company, she was often desperately alone. One of the things that most distressed her on these tours was that, as the wife of an actor, she was not welcome in the home of girls she had known at St. Mary's.

"She was deeply hurt," Eugene O'Neill told his second wife, Agnes Boulton, "that girls from wealthy families she had known in school dropped her after she married my father."

In March of 1885, while on tour with his parents, little Edmund contracted measles and died. O'Neill's sons later chided him for the "cheap hotel quacks" he used when members of his family became ill. Edmund was buried in St. Mary's Catholic Cemetery in New London, Connecticut, where James O'Neill had purchased a plot thirty-two feet square for a family burying ground. The grave was marked only by a headstone, but in 1930 Eugene O'Neill purchased an expensive monument for the plot. In *Long Day's Journey into Night* O'Neill chose Edmund—the name of the infant brother he had never known—as the name of the character representing himself.

Following the death of Edmund, the O'Neills sent Jamie, as he was called by the family, off to boarding school. They chose the elementary school then being conducted at Notre Dame University, which also maintained a high school on the campus. The younger boys were known as "minims," probably a contraction of the Latin word *minimus* (smallest). There were also "lifers"—a child could be dropped at Notre Dame and left until virtually grown up. Jamie was to stay at Notre Dame nine years.

Ella's third child, it was said repeatedly in the family, was conceived "to replace Edmund." For now, once again at Christmas time, in 1887, Ella Quinlan O'Neill was pregnant.

CHAPTER

TWO

୭ଥ

THE EARLY YEARS

Eugene Gladstone O'Neill was born October 16, 1888, in a third-floor corner room of Barrett House, a family hostelry at Forty-third Street and Broadway with a view of Times Square. It was a mile and a half from the northern limits of the theater district, which then centered around Fourteenth Street; but in a few years O'Neill's birthplace was to be surrounded by theaters, some of which would present his tragedies. The uptown march of the theaters was beginning in the year of his birth, when the New Broadway Theatre opened on the southwest corner of Broadway and Forty-first Street, with Fanny Davenport playing the lead in Sardou's *La Tosca*.

In 1888, New York was essentially a sprawling collection of easygoing, intimate little communities. But on Broadway life seemed to be leaping forward and reaching out impatiently toward the future. One by one the dignified brownstone family homes were giving way to garish new business buildings. On the sidewalks pedestrians swarmed and streamed in controlled disorder. Out in the street smart carriages behind fast-stepping pacers darted in and out among the lumbering drays and horsecars. All about was movement and bustle, a chattering of wheels and a jangle of bells as the turbulent stream surged up and down in confused purposefulness. And as nighttime came, myriad flickering gaslights flared out to hold back the dark and make their own bright day in a Great White Way.

In 1888, Benjamin Harrison, a Republican, was elected President of the United States even though his opponent, Grover Cleveland, received a larger popular vote. New York got a Tammany mayor, Hugh J. Grant, who succeeded the respectable Mayor Hewitt, candidate of the reform Democrats. The Metropolitan Museum of Art, far uptown on Eighty-second Street, opened its south wing. The spires of St. Patrick Cathedral on Fifth Avenue had just been completed. The New York State Legislature passed a bill that criminals sentenced to death would no longer be hanged but electrocuted.

It was the year the venerable Edwin Booth, who had helped to launch James O'Neill on his theatrical career, purchased the Valentine Hall mansion at 16 Gramercy Park. He remodeled it and willed it to the "Players," a gentlemen's club used by "actors and friends of the drama." At its bar Eugene's father would one day boast about the playwriting talents of his son.

The birth of Eugene O'Neill proved to be a difficult one, and his mother was ill for some time. The child was given the middle name Gladstone because, as his father was fond of explaining, the British Prime Minister was the only Englishman with a brain in his head. Gladstone went down to defeat trying to get Parliament to pass a home rule bill for Ireland. A hotel doctor, apparently not understanding the nature of her illness, prescribed morphine. That, at least, was the story young Eugene grew up with and eventually wove into *Long Day's Journey into Night*. But many patent medicines of the day contained narcotics (the Federal Food and Drug Act had not yet come into being) and his mother's drug habit may have originated in them, as was the case with hundreds of Americans of that era.

Eugene was taken on tour with his parents. His earliest recollection was of feeding the squirrels in the park in Memphis, Tennessee. "My first seven years," O'Neill has written, "were spent mainly in the larger towns all over the United States—my mother accompanying my father on his road tours in *Monte Cristo* and repertoire, although she was never an actress and had rather an aversion for the stage in general. A child has a regular, fixed home, but you might say I started in as a trouper. I knew only actors and the stage. My mother nursed me in the wings and in dressing rooms."

A Scottish nurse, with Eugene until he was seven, entertained him with horrible tales and "sordid episodes, from the latest murder to the farthest terror that her whimsey could contrive."

Eugene often recalled these years as a succession of one-night stands, of perpetual waiting in the wings, dirty dressing rooms, stuffy trains and shoddy hotels. Yet the elder O'Neill was the idol of the American stage all the time his son was growing up. People never tired of seeing Monte Cristo rip the sack in which he had been thrown into a canvas ocean.

"I can still see my father," Eugene recalled, "dripping with salt and sawdust, climbing on a stool behind the swinging profile of dashing waves. It was then that the calcium lights in the gallery played on his long beard and tattered clothes, as with arms outstretched as he declared that the world was his. That was the signal for the house to burst into deafening applause that overwhelmed the noise of the storm manufactured backstage."

Young Eugene grew to hate the world of false sentiment which his father's play represented. Later, he knew that what he had seen merely reflected the times—"an age ashamed of its own feeling. The theater reflected its thoughts. Virtue always triumphed and sin always got its just deserts. It accepted nothing halfway; a man was either a hero or a villain, and a woman was either virtuous or vile."

James O'Neill tried to imbue his two sons with the romance and glory of the stage, and his greatest ambition was to see them follow in his footsteps as actors. But Eugene was to look back on this as an almost inhuman attempt to bend them to his will. "It reminds me," he was to say years later, "of the oppression of the Jesuits and of the saying, 'Give me a child until he is seven and then you can have him.' They meant, of course, that he would be true to the faith."

The elder O'Neill's desire to build a theatrical dynasty is understandable in the light of the fact that his acting—whatever his sons thought of its artistic merit—provided an excellent livelihood. He was earning up to $40,000 a year.

Eugene grew up in the golden age of the American theater. Towns with a population of no more than two thousand saw Shakespeare presented by professionals; billboards throughout the country were heralding Edwin Booth as Hamlet, Mary Anderson as Juliet, Lawrence Barrett as Cassius and Clara Morris as Camille. Between

1880 and 1900 there were more touring companies in the country than at any other time. The number of actors increased from five thousand to fifteen thousand. (Some of them must have turned in substandard performances. A Minnesota drama critic wrote: "Thompson's *Uncle Tom's Cabin* appeared at the opera house last night. The dogs were poorly supported.")

When the time came for Eugene to go to school, his parents chose the boarding school conducted by the Sisters of Charity at Mount St. Vincent-on-Hudson at Riverdale, New York. Here he received his first formal Catholic indoctrination and acquired the Catholic conscience that runs strongly through his plays. He learned that despite the redemption of man through Christ's suffering, man possessed free will and freedom of choice; but he also learned that God knows the future of all His creatures. The conflict between predestination and free will was an essential element in the development of O'Neill as a playwright. Ultimately he came to believe that man is doomed, that free will or no, he moves inexorably to destruction.

When Eugene was twelve and in the sixth grade, he was deemed ready to receive his first Holy Communion. His father at the time was taking a respite from his perennial playing of Monte Cristo and was starring in an adaptation of another Dumas novel, *The Three Musketeers,* in New York City. Eugene was given free passes and he invited three of his classmates to go along. One of the sisters at Mount St. Vincent was so horrified at their going to the wicked theater that she refused to let Eugene and his friends receive Communion the next morning. It was a shattering experience for Eugene, not only because he felt that he had done nothing wrong, but because the sister's form of punishment suggested that his father was wicked in the eyes of the Church. The experience undoubtedly added to his lifelong feeling of unworthiness. He had already been made aware that he had been ushered into the world to replace Edmund. Soon he would be told that his birth had been the cause of his mother's illness, that she had used morphine for the first time to alleviate her pain, and that, in effect, he was responsible for his mother's addiction to drugs.

Eugene always retained an affection for the boys he knew at Mount St. Vincent. He roomed with a boy named John A. McCarthy who shared his enthusiasm for Kipling's *Jungle Book*. They were kept in line by Sister Mariti and Sister Gonzaga, who, Eugene recalled in later years, "used to knuckle us on the bean." Another class-mate was Stephen Philbin, later a distinguished New York attorney, who has recalled that his contemporaries were conscious that Eugene was the son of "a famous actor, but otherwise he was like any of the other boys."

In 1900, after his three years at Mount St. Vincent, Eugene entered De La Salle Institute on Fifty-ninth Street in New York City as a day student, and the following year he became a boarder there. In the fall of 1902 he transferred to Betts Academy in Stamford, Connecticut, as a boarder. Betts, now out of existence, was a typical New England prep school, whose primary purpose was to get boys into an Ivy League college. O'Neill fell quickly into the role of a prep-school boy of that era. He wore a boater straw hat with his school colors on it, put great effort into dressing well, and was almost immaculate. He was giving evidence, at this time, of being studious. "His nose is always in a book," his father liked to say.

Eugene told Lawrence Langner that he read a great deal about Bernard Shaw when he was a student at Betts. In his last year there he read *Quintessence of Ibsenism* and underlined in red ink the passages wherein he agreed with Shaw. At the end of the year, he said, almost the entire text was underlined.

"Whenever Gene indulged in an argument [at Betts]," Langner wrote, "he would slay his opponents by quoting Shaw, and, indeed, he gained a reputation for being Mephistophelean among the other boys by his apt quotations."

While at Betts, Eugene was apparently able to get into New York a good deal. His brother Jamie, who had vague notions of becoming a newspaperman, was by this time a recognized habitué of all the saloons on Broadway. He had a large acquaintance among chorus girls and took it upon himself to instruct his brother in the way of the world. "Gene learned sin," Jamie told a friend, "more easily than other people. I made it easy for him," he added.

"While most boys my age were in love with a pure girl," Eugene once said, "or shivering into a fit of embarrassment at the mere thought of a show girl, I really was a Broadway wise guy."

Eugene was graduated from Betts Academy in June, 1906, with marks sufficiently high to permit him to be admitted to Princeton. He was not yet eighteen, and like many other eighteen-year-olds he had no idea what he wanted to do with his life. But unlike most of his contemporaries, Eugene was rootless. Except for the O'Neills' summer place in New London, the family had no permanent home. Even there he experienced the mild ostracism which the local Yankees accorded not only summer people but also, and especially, theatrical people; and, to make matters worse, many of the townspeople knew that his mother was a drug addict.

Academically, Eugene was well prepared for college; emotionally he was ill prepared. Certainly Princeton, which at that time cherished a strong tradition of drinking and general hell-raising in the local taverns, was unready for the problems of Eugene O'Neill.

CHAPTER

THREE

ᖇᖇ

THE FIRST MARRIAGE

AND DIVORCE

O'Neill made little or no impression on Princeton. And, conversely, Princeton made little or no impression on him. Eugene chose to do as little studying as possible and to engage in heavy drinking with his classmates, who nicknamed him "Ego" because he took himself so seriously. O'Neill was restless and temperamentally unfit for settling down and studying.

Only one major incident emerges from O'Neill's freshman year at Princeton. He had gone to Trenton with a group of undergraduates to spend an evening in the taverns there. Shortly after midnight, while walking the trolley tracks back to college, the students amused themselves by throwing stones at the glass insulators on telegraph poles. Evidence suggests that they were not drunk, certainly not *very* drunk, for along their ten-mile route they managed to hit a great number of the insulators. But, despite his apparent innocence —of drunkenness—Eugene was suspended for two weeks. He had just about made up his mind to withdraw from the university and, despite the dean's urging that he reconsider, he submitted his resignation.

Out of this episode a legend grew, apparently fostered by O'Neill himself, who had such a flair for publicity that he got it even when he didn't want it. He told the poet John V. A. Weaver, a fellow student at Harvard in 1914, that his exodus from Princeton was caused by his "shying a beer bottle through Prexy Wilson's dormer window." O'Neill told much the same story to his old friend George Jean Nathan and then spent the rest of his life denying it. Over the years, the beer bottle was turned into a whisky bottle, psychiatrists and *Time* magazine pondered the significance of it all, and Princeton University issued an official denial. O'Neill's final denial came in 1947, six years before his death. "I wouldn't have done anything like that for anything in the world even if I'd been swimming in a sea of vodka," he said. "I liked President Wilson."

Years later, O'Neill said of his brief stay at Princeton, "I am perhaps excusing myself for the way I loafed and fooled and got as much fun and as little work as I could out of my one year at Princeton, but I think that I felt there, instinctively, that we were not in touch with life or on the trail of the real thing, and that was one consideration that drove me out. Or perhaps I was merely lazy."

At the end of his freshman year, in 1907, Eugene took an apartment on West Eighty-fifth Street in New York City with his friend Frank Best. O'Neill's parents were staying nearby, at the Lucerne Hotel on Amsterdam Avenue and Seventy-eighth Street.

The elder O'Neill said it was now up to his son to settle down and go to work. He arranged for him to take a job in a mail-order house in which he had invested some of his wife's money—the New York-Chicago Supply Company. Eugene was given the courtesy title of secretary to the president. The firm sold, he recalled, "ten-cent jewelry, giving an alleged phonograph record as a premium to children and seminary girls who disposed of the shabby baubles." Eugene hated the job. His salary was very small. In later years he admitted he hadn't worked very hard. He was reading—now it was everything by Jack London, and his dream was to be a soldier of fortune in faraway places.

Suddenly he fell in love. The girl, who was living with her divorced mother on the upper West Side, was named Kathleen Jenkins. Her mother was a member of an old New York family, one of her grandfathers having been among the founders of the New

York Stock Exchange. Mrs. Jenkins also claimed descent from a long line of Corsican aristocrats, and one of her ancestors, she said, was the first white girl to live on Manhattan Island.

Kathleen was an extraordinarily beautiful girl. She was tall and well-proportioned and "had a complexion that was like honey. Her hair was dark, she had beautiful eyes." In fact, Kathleen was so attractive that she worked as an artist's model before she met O'Neill. This was rather unusual for a girl who had attended a fashionable finishing school, but the family was no longer rich.

Eugene went around with a set of boys from Princeton and other Ivy League colleges and some "nice" girls in New York. He met Kathleen through his roommate, Frank Best. Eugene was known for his wildness, and Frank and other friends urged him to marry Kathleen because "she was a nice girl and we felt it might make him settle down." Apparently O'Neill wanted very much to marry her, but when he told his parents they objected vigorously. He was not making enough money to support a wife, the girl was not a Catholic, and her parents were divorced. Jamie, too, was against the marriage on the grounds of Eugene's youth.

Although Mrs. Jenkins strongly disapproved of a marriage, the very handsome Eugene evidently was irresistible to Kathleen, for in the summer of 1909 they went across the river to Hoboken, New Jersey, the Gretna Green of the day, and were married by the Reverend William Bernard Gilpin at Trinity Episcopal Church on Washington Street. When they returned to New York and told their parents of the marriage, James and Ella and Mrs. Jenkins were all furious. If the children lived together in marriage they did not do so for many weeks, for not long afterward Eugene left on a gold-mining expedition to Honduras. It is not really known whether this was his scheme or his father's. Gene hoped to make his fortune and then come back and settle down. At any rate, whether intended or not, this flight signaled the end of his first attempt at marriage.

Eugene O'Neill sailed for Central America from San Francisco early in October, 1909, with a Mr. and Mrs. Earl C. Stevens. Apparently he had a very nebulous financial arrangement with them, for he later wrote to his father to ask if the Stevenses were going to pay him, adding that he hoped he wasn't enduring the hardships of the trip for love. O'Neill was to say of Stevens, a mining engineer, that "this chap had the grant of a river from the Honduran Government. He was going to boom [dynamite] it—something they don't allow in civilized countries. It was my first trip on my own. I expected to do a lot of jungle shooting. I wore a bandoleer slung from my right shoulder and carried a 30–30 Winchester and a machete."

When Eugene left the United States his father had gone on tour with a production of *The White Sister*. Jamie, too, was on tour, starring in a play; and, as usual, he was drinking heavily. From time to time he sent his younger brother a postcard. Eugene was homesick and wrote his parents many letters. He said he had never known how much he could miss his mother, his father, and home. In one of his letters he asked his father to thank John, a barkeeper of his acquaintance, for writing to him.

O'Neill found the life of a soldier of fortune something of a disappointment. He suffered intensely from flea bites. He hated the food, which was largely fried rice and salty dried meat—also fried, and as tough as leather. He liked to say, later on, that he was sure God got his inspiration for hell after He created Honduras. The natives, he said, were the laziest, lowest, most ignorant bunch of two-footed animals who ever polluted a land. He spent Christmas Day in the town of Guahuiniquil and termed it the most depressing and dismal day he had ever endured. His Christmas dinner consisted of beans, fried tortillas, one egg, and tea brewed from lemon leaves.

Nevertheless, it turned out to be an adventurous trip. Eugene and the Stevens couple went into parts of the country that few white men had ever visited before. They traveled by muleback into the interior for more than a hundred miles, living on iguana, wild pig, monkey, and "hope." Then they started prospecting.

"All I bagged was a lizard—no gold," Eugene has said with a smile. But on that expedition the smell and feel and taste of the jungle were caught and were preserved in his memory so that when he came to write the stage directions for *The Emperor Jones* he was able to re-create the tropical background:

> The forest is a wall of darkness dividing the world. Only when the eye becomes accustomed to the gloom can the outlines of separate trunks of the trees be made out, enormous pillars of deeper blackness. A somber monotone of wind, lost in the leaves, moans in the air. Yet this sound serves but to intensify the impression of the forest's relentless immobility, to form a background throwing into relief its brooding, implacable silence.

After six months of brooding, implacable silence with only the Stevens couple and a few friendly Indian guides, Eugene tired of the Central American wilderness. He also came down with malaria. With one of the guides, Eugene rode muleback for ten miles through the jungle to Tegucigalpa, the capital. When the bedraggled pair arrived in town they found that there was a fiesta scheduled for the next day and that all the hotels were full. Eugene, behaving like any American tourist, made for the United States consulate. The consul insisted that he go to bed immediately in his own house, where he underwent the usual violent malarial chills and fevers. The chills were difficult to withstand because Tegucigalpa is at an altitude of more than 3,000 feet, making the nights extremely cold. As the consul didn't have enough blankets, he covered his young patient with American flags.

"I looked just like George M. Cohan," O'Neill recalled later.

On May 5, 1910, while Eugene was in Honduras, Kathleen bore him a son, whom she named Eugene Gladstone O'Neill, Jr. According to Mrs. Jenkins, Ella and James O'Neill came up to her apartment and held their first grandchild in their arms. But, whatever their emotions over the baby were, they did not relent. When they had first heard about the marriage they tried to have it annulled. Because they were such ardent Catholics, it is quite possible that they felt their son's Episcopal ceremony did not constitute a real wedding. But Kathleen's mother has reported that the elder O'Neill presented a different argument in a heated talk with his daughter-in-law— "What do you want to be married to Eugene for, anyhow? He's nothing but a no-good drunken bum!"

A few weeks after his son was born, Eugene returned to New York. He was completely broke and his father, mother and brother were all on tour. He was twenty-one and he had failed at everything —Princeton, his New York job, his gold-prospecting adventure, even his recent marriage. Completely down and out, he took a room at "Jimmy the Priest's," a waterfront saloon at Fulton Street and the North River. According to a story his grandmother told Eugene junior, his father came uptown when Kathleen was out and asked Mrs. Jenkins if he could see his son. O'Neill held the child in his arms and cried. But he did not try to see Kathleen.

Eugene junior was also to hear this story from his father, who amplified it. O'Neill told him that he left the Jenkins apartment and walked all the way down to the Battery. There he sat on a bench trying to decide what he should do. He could not support his wife, and his family was against the marriage. "It was the lowest moment of my life," he told his son. He contemplated suicide. Finally he bought some veronal, went to his room at Jimmy the Priest's, took an overdose of the sleeping medicine and lay down to die.

O'Neill apparently told the same story to his friend Nathan. "Certain emotional misfortunes in an encounter with Cupid," Nathan wrote, "weighed on O'Neill's mind and—now it may be told—a month or so after James Beith (a friend of O'Neill's) took his life, the man who was to become the first of American dramatists attempted, with an overdose of veronal, to follow suit." The next afternoon, when O'Neill did not turn up at the bar, some of his friends went to his room. Failing in their attempts to rouse him, they summoned an ambulance. He was taken to Bellevue Hospital and, while his friends looked on solicitously, two interns worked over him for an hour until he showed signs of life. When it appeared that O'Neill would recover, his friends left, saying that they would return.

Some time later, according to Nathan's version, they reappeared, hilariously drunk. They had wired James O'Neill that his son was ill and fifty dollars was needed to pay his hospital bill.

"You dirty bums," Eugene said. "How much have you got left?"

"Thirty-two dollars," they admitted.

"All right, divide," O'Neill ordered. His pals complied. Then, Nathan wrote, he tucked his sixteen dollars under the covers, rolled over, and went to sleep. Nathan reported the incident some years after the event, and he put it in a humorous light; but that period must have been one of the most wretched in O'Neill's life. In this suicide attempt O'Neill was giving positive expression to an inner drive that was to be noted by others at many stages in his life— a drive which Freudian analysts have called the "death instinct" and which Brooks Atkinson, a few years after O'Neill's death, so nicely described as an "infatuation with oblivion."

It is reasonably certain that Eugene did not see Kathleen after his return from Honduras. His parents, as well as Kathleen's mother, were bitter about the marriage, and everyone wanted to end it. Mrs. Jenkins financed the divorce.

Since adultery was the only ground for divorce in New York

State, O'Neill agreed to be caught in *flagrante delicto*. The time chosen
for the little divorce playlet, an often-repeated judicial joke played
on New York State's Supreme Court, was the evening of December
29, 1911. Edward Ireland, a Princeton friend, and O'Neill had
dinner together at Ireland's studio at 120 West 104th Street. Afterward they went to the Campus, a nearby barroom, where they met
James Warren, a friend of Kathleen's and her mother's, and two other
men, Edward Mullen and Frank Archibold. After a few drinks Ireland
made his exit, leaving O'Neill with the others. The four went downtown to the Garden Restaurant on Fiftieth Street, then to two bars on
Forty-fifth Street, having a few drinks at each one. Finally O'Neill and
his three companions went to a house at 140 West Forty-fifth Street.

"We were in there for a short time," Mullen later testified in
court, "and Mr. O'Neill saw some girl there that attracted him, and
he left us and went upstairs with this girl."

After some time, Mullen and Archibold sent word up to O'Neill
that they were leaving. O'Neill sent a maid downstairs to tell them
"to come up and have a drink before we departed. And we went upstairs into this room and saw Mr. O'Neill and this woman in bed
together. They were both undressed." The three men and "a woman
whose name is unknown to the plaintiff," as the court record puts it,
had a drink together and then the men went on their way, leaving
O'Neill and the unknown woman in bed.

Sufficient evidence of O'Neill's alleged act of adultery having
been obtained by Kathleen's lawyers, they arranged to have O'Neill
served with a summons to answer an "action for absolute divorce on
the grounds of adultery." He did not appear at the divorce suit hearing, which was held in the Supreme Court at White Plains on June
10, 1912, nor did he contest the action.

The divorce was granted, and it became final October 11, 1912.
Kathleen was to have "exclusive care, custody and control of Eugene
O'Neill, Jr." No provision was made for his support by O'Neill.
Kathleen did not ask for alimony and received none.

Thus ended one of the strangest and least understood episodes
in the life of Eugene O'Neill. One can only conjecture why Eugene
and Kathleen were ever married at all. Were they really in love or
was the whole thing a "mistake," as O'Neill once said years later?
Certainly Eugene was ill equipped for marriage. He was a very handsome, restless, unstable young man, not ready to settle down. In fact,

Eugene O'Neill was never to settle down. And of the Kathleen of this period? All one knows is that she was beautiful, patrician and "a nice girl."

In 1915 Kathleen married George Pitt-Smith, an accountant in a large New York advertising agency, and moved to Douglaston, Long Island. Eugene junior was brought up in the belief that he was Pitt-Smith's son. He also believed that his stepbrother, George Pitt-Smith, his stepfather's child by a previous marriage, was his blood brother. They were devoted to each other. It was not until 1921, when Eugene junior was eleven, that the dramatist and his son met.

CHAPTER

FOUR

ဢ

BEFORE THE MAST

Eugene decided to go "home"—back to his family. "Home," as usual, was somewhere on the theatrical circuit. Eugene journeyed to St. Louis, where *The White Sister* was playing. In the cast with James O'Neill were Viola Allen and William Farnum, of early cinema fame. Jamie, too, was a member of the cast, in a minor role.

Eugene's father decided that perhaps his ne'er-do-well son could be useful in the administrative end of the business. He appointed him assistant manager of the company. It was a courtesy title. Eugene sat by the gallery door and saw that the local ticket-taker didn't let in any of his friends. He despised the job.

Though the irregular hours left him a great deal of time for reading, he appeared more idle than ever. When the company arrived in Boston, Eugene and his father had a serious and violent discussion. His father accused him of wasting his opportunities, of filial ingratitude, of giving up his faith and of becoming a drunken bum. Eugene replied that he didn't like the stage and didn't want to be an actor. Dramatically, James O'Neill told his son there was only one thing left for him to do.

"Go before the mast!" he shouted, raising his arm and pointing presumably toward the sea.

Eugene had just finished reading Joseph Conrad's *The Nigger of the Narcissus* and the suggestion appealed to him. He went down to Boston's waterfront. "It happened quite naturally—'that voyage' —as a consequence of what was really inside me—what I really wanted," O'Neill later recalled. "I struck up at the Mystic Wharf in Boston with a bunch of sailors, mostly Norwegians and Swedes. I wanted to ship with somebody and they took me that afternoon to the captain. Signed up and the next thing we were off. . . ."

He had been signed on as a seaman aboard a Norwegian sailing vessel bound for Buenos Aires. It was a barque, or three-masted ship with foremast and mainmast square-rigged and the mizzenmast fore-and-aft-rigged. Ever after, O'Neill was most proud of his voyage; his ship was a real sailing vessel, and such craft were already fast disappearing from the seas.

"A man who hasn't made a trip on a windjammer," O'Neill said, "has never really been to sea."

He was pardonably proud of having been part of the great era of sail ships. When he finally came to ship aboard steam-powered vessels he loathed them. In his later years he collected prints of sailing ships, and a clipper ship's brass lantern adorned his study.

The trip to Buenos Aires took sixty-five days. O'Neill performed the usual chores of a seaman: He scrubbed decks, climbed the rigging, spliced ropes, and stood watch. He subsisted, like the others, on hardtack and dried codfish. At Buenos Aires he was paid off and loafed on the docks and in waterfront dives until his money ran out.

"I arrived a gentleman—so called," he has said, "and wound up a bum on the docks in fact."

O'Neill made friends with other sailors and down-and-outers on the waterfront and drank heavily. Frank Best has said that "O'Neill was never a bum nor a borrower. He frequented the haunts of bums and seamen seeking true facts." It is true that during this period O'Neill acquired the impressions which he later put to good use in his one-act plays of the sea, but it does not necessarily follow that he was then consciously looking for material, since he did not write his sea plays until he had been writing for at least two years on other subjects. O'Neill felt at home with drifters, bums, alcoholics—

or, more accurately, with failure—because he felt that he himself
was a failure.

After his money gave out in Buenos Aires, he got a job with
the local branch of the Westinghouse Electric Instrument Company
by saying that he was a draftsman. The manager soon knew that he
wasn't, when he put O'Neill to work tracing blueprints. In six weeks
Eugene was without a job again and he moved to La Plata, "the
Chicago of the Argentine." There he got a job with Swift & Company,
working in the warehouse where raw hides were sorted and stored. He
was to recall with vivid detail how "the smell got into his clothes, his
mouth, his eyes, his ears, his nose, and his hair." The job terminated
dramatically when the warehouse burned down.

Back in Buenos Aires, he got a job with the Singer Sewing
Machine Company. The manager of the local branch was soon to
retire, and he thought O'Neill could be trained to run the office. In
explaining the magnitude of the job, he asked O'Neill, "Do you
know how many different models Singer makes?"

"Fifty," O'Neill said, making a wild guess.

"Why," the manager said, "Singer makes five hundred and
fifty models!"

He explained that, as part of his training, O'Neill would have
to learn how to take all 550 models apart and put them back together again. After spending a few weeks with a sewing-machine re-
pairman, O'Neill had learned just one thing: He didn't like sewing
machines. In fact, he hated machinery and he was to say so over and
over in his plays.

Again he loafed, stranded "on the beach." One of his favorite
haunts in Buenos Aires was the Sailor's Opera, a huge café catering to
seamen. "There," he has said, "the seamen yarned of adventures in
strange seas, boasted of their exploits to officially pretty ladies, drank,
played cards, fought, and wallowed."

In a suburb of Buenos Aires called Barracas there was another
form of entertainment—moving pictures tailored for a strictly male
audience. "These moving pictures," he was to say of the Barracas
entertainment, "were mighty rough stuff. Nothing was left to the
imagination. Every form of perversity was enacted, and of course
sailors flocked to them. But, save for the usual exceptions, they were
not vicious men. They were in the main honest, good-natured, un-
heroically courageous men trying to pass the time pleasantly."

One of O'Neill's closest friends at this time was a young man whom he described as "an exquisite Englishman." O'Neill never revealed this man's identity but, in interviews, referred to him simply as "A." He and "A" took a room together for several months.

"When 'A' left a café," O'Neill was to say, "most of its liquor went along with him. He was very young, about twenty-five at the most, and extraordinarily handsome. Blond, almost too beautiful, he was, in appearance, very like Oscar Wilde's description of Dorian Gray, even his name was flowery. He was the younger son of a traditionally noble British family."

O'Neill took occasional jobs to get money for food and whisky. When he had no money, he slept in parks and in waterfront dives. Once he got a job on a cattle boat bound for Durban, South Africa. It was a long trip and he wanted to see Africa but, because he had no cash, he was not allowed to land. He returned to Buenos Aires and there followed what he was to describe as a "lengthy period of complete destitution—terminated by my signing as an ordinary seaman on a British tramp steamer bound home for New York."

On one of his voyages—there is some doubt as to just which one—O'Neill met a stoker named Driscoll. It happened on an American Line ship.

"He was a giant of a man, and absurdly strong," O'Neill said. "He thought a whole lot of himself, was a determined individualist. He was very proud of his strength, his capacity for grueling work. It seemed to give him mental poise to be able to dominate the stokehole, do more work than any of his mates.

"The voyage after I quit going to sea, Driscoll shipped on again as usual. I stayed behind at Jimmy the Priest's. When the ship returned to New York, Driscoll was the first to swing the saloon doors open and bellow for a drink. We could usually calculate the time of the ship's docking from the moment of Driscoll's appearance. Then I drifted away and later I heard that Driscoll had jumped overboard in mid-ocean. None of our mutual seamates knew why. I concluded something must have shaken his hard-boiled poise, for he wasn't the type who just give up, and he loved life. Anyway, it was his death that inspired the idea for the Yank of *The Hairy Ape*."

O'Neill's destitution once reached the point where he came close to becoming a criminal. In 1948 he told Hamilton Basso, during an interview for a *New York* profile, that he felt it was only an accident that he had not become one.

"I remember when I was on the beach in Buenos Aires," O'Neill said. "I was then twenty-two years old and a real down-and-outer—sleeping on park benches, hanging around waterfront dives, and absolutely alone. I knew a fellow who used to work on a railroad down there and who had given up his job. One day, he suggested that we hold up one of those places where foreign money is exchanged. Well, I have to admit I gave the matter serious consideration.

"I finally decided not to do it, but since you aren't given to taking a very moral view of things when you are sleeping on park benches and haven't a dime to your name, I decided what I did because I felt that we were almost certain to be caught. A few nights later, the fellow who had propositioned me stuck the place up with somebody he'd got to take my place, and he was caught. He was sent to prison and, for all I know, he died there. . . .

"There are times now when I feel sure I would have been a playwright no matter what happened, but when I remember Buenos Aires, and the fellow down there who wanted me to be a bandit, I'm not so sure."

When O'Neill returned in the United States in 1911, he was twenty-three. He was still wild, liked to drink in bars, recite poetry, and form warm friendships with "regular guys." He liked to read, but his concepts of life were not profound. His favorite authors were Jack London, Conrad, and Kipling, whom he was to quote in many of his plays. The dirty, broken-down tramp steamer aboard which O'Neill returned to the United States became, in his plays, the *S.S. Glencairn*. His early sea plays are known as the Glencairn cycle.

When the ship docked in the North River in New York, O'Neill again took a furnished room over Jimmy the Priest's waterfront saloon, where he did a great deal of talking, listening and drinking. O'Neill said in 1924 that this place was the original for Johnny the Priest's, the saloon locale in *Anna Christie*. Jimmy the Priest's was so nicknamed because Jimmy, the proprietor, with his pale, thin, clean-shaven face, mild blue eyes, and white hair, "seemed to be more suited for a cassock than the bartender's apron he wore."

"Above the saloon," according to O'Neill, "were a number of rooms rented out to seamen. . . . Jimmy the Priest's certainly was a hellhole. It was awful. The house was almost coming down and the principal house wreckers were vermin. I was absolutely down financially, those days, and you can get an idea of the kind of room I had when I tell you the rent was three dollars a month. One roommate of mine jumped out of the window. He was an Englishman and had been a star correspondent of an English newspaper syndicate. He covered the Boer War, for example. But all kinds of misfortune had got him; drink, too. When he'd get a job on a newspaper he'd last a few days and then get dead drunk on the first week's pay."

George Jean Nathan has identified him as Jimmy Beith. Beith was always just about to get shaved, have his suit pressed, and to-morrow he would get a job. He was the archetype of all the characters assembled in *The Iceman Cometh,* men and women who live on the pipe dream that everything will turn out all right tomorrow. His specific counterpart in the play was named James Cameron.

Once again, in 1912, O'Neill shipped out as an able-bodied seaman, aboard the *S.S. New York* of the American Line bound for Southampton, England. It was his last voyage. His pay was $27.50 a month. He returned on the *S.S. Philadelphia* of the North Atlantic Line. On leaving his ship in New York, he got his discharge paper, which designated him as Able Seaman E. G. O'Neill. He was to cherish that paper as if it were a diploma—which, in a sense, it was. When he showed it to friends he would sigh and say, "The last one I shipped on." It was the end of his education, the end of his life among people to whom he felt he belonged. Years later O'Neill was to tell a reporter, "They were the best friends I ever had."

By way of celebrating his home-coming, O'Neill gave a party at Jimmy the Priest's. He woke up two or three days later on a train near New Orleans, where *The Count of Monte Cristo* was currently on the boards.

James O'Neill refused to give Eugene any money, but he offered him a job. One of the cast had disappeared into the delightful under-world of the French Quarter. This actor had been playing two roles, a jailor and a gendarme. Young Eugene took over both parts. For the gendarme, his mustache was made to twist upward into two sharp points; for the jailor, it drooped *au naturel.* He learned his two short parts on the train going west with the troupe.

After his first performance, which was in Ogden, Utah, O'Neill said sternly to his son, "Sir, I am not satisfied with your per-formance."

"Sir," Eugene replied, "I am not satisfied with your play."

When James O'Neill complained once more that he was a ter-rible actor, Eugene answered, "It is a wonder that in a play like *Monte Cristo* I can do anything at all." He always admitted to his friends, however, that he had been a terrible actor and said that he hated acting. But he liked helping to ripple the green canvas waves through which Edmond Dantes swam to freedom.

James O'Neill actually played two shows a night on the road—one performance in the theater, and the other in a nearby barroom. He would greet the bartender, look slowly around, smiling, then say, "On Monte Cristo!" A little while after he had treated everybody present, he would again call out, "On Monte Cristo!" Everybody in the room would stand up, raise his glass, and drink to Monte Cristo's health. After a great many encores of this performance, James O'Neill sometimes had to be carried to his hotel room. Eugene was a witness on many of these occasions.

During this 1912 tour, Eugene and Jamie became so bored with the small towns to which *Monte Cristo* took them that they began to plot how to get back to New York. Jamie, particularly, was homesick for Broadway. One night they waited in the flies while their father did his great "the world is mine" scene. In it he slaps his pockets to indicate his wealth. As he came off stage, his sons told him what a beautiful performance he had put on, especially the part indicating how much money he had. Would he give them the price of railroad tickets to New York? Jamie and Eugene used to tell this story in bars. Eugene, when pressed, admitted it was their own invention. In one version of the tale, James O'Neill pulled his pockets inside out in order to prove to his sons he didn't have the wherewithal to grant their request.

At the end of a fifteen-week tour in the Far West, the *Monte Cristo* company closed for the season. In the summer of 1912 the family was together under one roof, in their New London summer home.

CHAPTER

FIVE

ƝƝ

NEW LONDON 1912:
THE "LONG DAY"

Eugene O'Neill chose an August day in the summer of 1912 for the time of *Long Day's Journey into Night,* his autobiographical play. All four members of his family were together that summer in their home at 325 Pequot Avenue facing the New London waterfront. An old resident has described the location as "on the fringe of the exclusive Pequot summer colony." The house itself, still standing, is a boxlike, white frame dwelling of cheap construction.

Most of the biographical details of his life at this time Eugene has told to his intimate friends. His life with his parents and brother preyed so insistently on his mind that, at times, he would even recount some of the most painful details to strangers in bars.

The mood of that summer of 1912 was created mainly by the drug addiction of Eugene's mother, who was then fifty-five.

Mrs. Samuel Green, who was a friend of Eugene's in New London, remembers Ella O'Neill as "a sweet-looking woman. Few of us got to know her. The O'Neills kept very much to themselves." But it was generally known that his mother took drugs, and it was very well known that her husband and her two sons drank heavily.

Ella O'Neill was pretty rather than beautiful, and in time inclined to be plump. Her nose was long and straight, her mouth wide, her forehead high and her hair, in 1912, white. Her eyes were dark brown and large, with dark eyebrows and curling lashes. Her voice was soft and she spoke with a slight Irish lilt. She had had no children since the birth of Eugene almost a quarter of a century before.

Ever since Betts Academy, Eugene had known that his mother was a drug addict and that she had acquired her habit as a result of the illness she suffered following his birth. There is some question as to how serious her addiction was. Addicts often overestimate the amount of drugs they think is required to sustain them. Most of the drugs to which they have access are heavily diluted. She may have depended on patent medicines, which in 1912 often contained morphine or cocaine. *Long Day's Journey* suggests that James O'Neill spent thousands of dollars sending his wife to sanatoriums to be cured.

Ella's drug addiction was not the only factor which isolated her from social groups in New London. She had never fully got over her feeling that she should have been a nun, and in consequence she had not adjusted well to the role of wife and mother; her picture of what she might have been contrasted sharply with what she was. She had never got over the cruel hurt she suffered when convent schoolmates from wealthy or socially ambitious Irish Catholic families would cut her for the sin of marrying an actor; and she had never got over her deep conviction that theater people were not her equals.

There is an echo of her regret at not belonging to the world of the "respectabilities" in what Mary Tyrone tells her sons in *Long Day's Journey:* "The Chatfields and people like them stand for something. I mean they have decent, presentable homes they don't have to be ashamed of. They have friends who entertain them and whom they entertain. They're not cut off from everyone."

Ella O'Neill knew that her actor husband and the reputation her sons had acquired for drinking and going around with "fast girls" were serious drawbacks to her being accepted socially.

There was in New London a theatrical colony, to which she probably would have been admitted had she been willing to make the effort. This group included Richard Mansfield, Edmund Breese,

Nance O'Neil (no relation), Tyrone Power, Mark Ellsworth and Frederick Develleville. The Mansfields held large soirees, to which the O'Neills were not invited. Some of the "respectabilities" who attended tittered about the social pretensions of the Mansfields. The actor had created his own family crest, a pair of clasped hands with the word *Maintenant* (Now) underneath. It adorned the mantelpiece in his living room.

Still another barrier between Ella and people like the "Chatfields" was the contempt with which so many native-born Anglo-Saxon Americans regarded the recently arrived Irish-Americans at that time.

Jamie and Eugene O'Neill were well aware of this. Jamie took a cynical, or typically bitter, view of what his mother called "nice people." Such people bored him to death, he said. Whores were infinitely superior to "nice girls." On the other hand, he often called his own father "an Irish bogtrotter."

James O'Neill was, in 1912, a big-chested, heavy-featured man who looked much younger than his actual age, sixty-seven. He walked erect, with an almost military carriage. He had a fine profile and light-brown, fairly deep-set eyes. His hair was iron gray. When he was not playing a role, there was a good deal of the Irish peasant about him.

His compulsion for trying to get things as cheaply as possible and not fritter his money away is understandable when one realizes that he was reared in the most incredible poverty. One of his intense preoccupations was dabbling in real estate, perhaps a reaction to his early poverty. He bought real estate in New London, an orange grove in California, tenement houses in New York and a farm in Maryland. He also invested in various businesses. In one, the Anchor Metal Novelty Company, he sank $30,000 "to help a friend." The firm went into bankruptcy. Another of his investments was in the "Uncle Sam" gold mine at Bodie, known as "the actors' mine" because so many actors invested in it.

One of his advisers on New London real estate was a friend who called himself Colonel Thomas Fortune D'Orsey. To D'Orsey, "James O'Neill was a softhearted man, always good for a touch. He was a great Irishman, a great Democrat and a good Catholic. He was one of the leading figures in the town."

Jamie was thirty-four that summer of 1912 and well on his way to becoming a hopeless alcoholic. Physically Jamie resembled his mother more than his father. He had what his brother called "irresponsible Irish charm." He was humorous, romantic, sentimentally poetic, and well liked by both men and women. His favorite poet was Ernest Dowson, and he liked especially to recite Dowson's famous line, "I have been faithful to thee, Cynara! in my fashion." He found perverse amusement in teaching his younger brother to drink and to be a "heller" with women. In moments of drunken confidence he told Eugene than he had done this because he realized how talented his brother was and that Eugene's success in the world would show him, Jamie, up for what he was—"a bum." Jamie was inordinately attached to his mother and never married.

A view of the two brothers that summer of 1912 is given by one of the "nice girls" whom Eugene courted. She said, "Eugene was a sweet boy, but I didn't like Jamie. Jamie was bitter and cynical, and drank terribly."

To judge by the recollections of those who knew Eugene in 1912, the impression emerges of a charming young man whose interests were all centered in literature. But he managed to find other interests, maintaining friendships with a number of girls, slightly younger than himself, from proper New London families. He had the capacity for geniune intellectual friendships with girls. "He was not a particularly sexy person," one of them has said. "He was loving, but not aggressive about making love."

The girl he saw the most of that summer he made the heroine of *Ah, Wilderness!*—the play of adolescence which he wrote in 1932. He called her Muriel McComber, a teen-age girl with whom Richard Miller (Eugene's characterization of himself) was in love. Because the real Muriel prefers not to have her name used, she will be called Muriel McComber here.

"Our engagement lasted about three years," she has said, "until about a year after he went into the sanatorium in the winter of 1912. I remember he read aloud a great deal to me—Oscar Wilde, Friedrich Nietzsche, Schopenhauer. I had just graduated from high school."

Eugene and Muriel saw each other almost every day for several years. He liked to recite to her from the Rubáiyát, especially the lines:

> *A Book of Verses underneath the Bough,*
> *A Jug of Wine, A Loaf of Bread—and Thou*
> *Beside me singing in the Wilderness.*

And the lines from Swinburne's "Anastasia," which he used in
Ah, Wilderness!:

> *Nay, let us walk from fire unto fire*
> *From passionate pain to deadlier delight—*
> *I am too young to live without desire,*
> *Too young art thou to waste this summer night . . .*

Muriel was regarded as one of the prettiest girls in New London. She was somewhat plump, but she had a graceful figure; she had light-brown hair and big, searching dark eyes and a roundish face with dimples, and she spoke with a slight drawl.

Although they lived only a few blocks apart, Eugene and Muriel wrote to each other almost every day, and he wrote to her when he was away from New London. Muriel has recalled that he was forever talking about the books and plays and short stories he was going to write. She said that their more or less platonic romance was fairly closely followed in the relationship between Richard and his girl in *Ah, Wilderness!*

The family of the real Muriel objected to Eugene first of all because he had been married and had a child. They felt that he was too old for her. They also objected to the O'Neills because they were a theatrical family and because of the generally poor reputation of its members. Muriel has recalled that she was not aware that Eugene drank. Furthermore, to her, he never seemed gloomy or depressing.

"He was delightful, lots of fun, and we had good times together," she said. "I didn't get to know his mother. Eugene never discussed his family with me. I had heard that his mother was a drug addict but naturally never discussed it with him. I remember James O'Neill, Gene's father, very well. He was a nice man. I liked him very much. He thought I was much too young for his son, much too sweet and simple."

For the family of the adolescent boy in *Ah, Wilderness!* Eugene chose that of one of his close friends, Arthur B. McGinley. That summer of 1912 both Eugene and Arthur were working for the New London *Telegraph*. Arthur McGinley's father, John McGinley, was editor of the rival New London *Day*. When the son saw *Ah, Wilderness!* he commented, "I can identify every character in the play, including myself and my brothers."

In the play, Nat Miller, father of the adolescent boy, is the editor and publisher of the town paper. (The part of Nat Miller was played by the late George M. Cohan.) Eugene endowed the character of Nat Miller with an attribute of his own father. James O'Neill had always said he could not eat bluefish because it contained a certain oil that poisoned him. After many years, his wife confessed that she had been serving him bluefish right along. She had called it whitefish, and he never knew the difference.

The elder McGinley was something like the father Eugene dreamed of having—he was wise, understanding, compassionate. Many people thought, when *Ah, Wilderness!* was produced, that Eugene had written about his own family when he was a youth. "The truth is," he said in reply, *"Ah, Wilderness!* was a nostalgia for a youth I never had." James O'Neill and John McGinley were good friends. McGinley, as a young reporter, had met James in New York. When James began to make money in *Monte Cristo* and wanted to buy a house, it was McGinley who persuaded him to settle in New London.

It was in May, 1912, that Eugene O'Neill went to work for the New London *Telegraph*. The publisher of the paper was Judge Frederick P. Latimer, who lived at Groton, Connecticut, across the river from New London. Eugene was the first reporter he hired after buying the paper.

Latimer was an interesting and versatile man. He had been graduated from Yale in 1898, had later studied at the Yale Law School, and was for a time a probate judge in Groton. He liked good conversation, good books, and fishing. He and Eugene became close friends. "I suspect my father and Eugene O'Neill were two of a kind," Latimer's daughter, Helen, has said. "My father was an unusual man and did many different things in his life." Latimer's son has said that his father and Eugene used to go off fishing together "when they felt like it, and my father had a way of liking it rather often all his life."

Of Judge Latimer, Eugene has said, "He was the first one who really thought I had something to say and believed I could say it." The judge told the elder O'Neill that he thought Eugene not only had talent but possessed a high order of genius. It was fortunate that Latimer regarded his protégé with such affection. Often in his excitement at the real-life drama he saw when he was sent to cover a story, Eugene would neglect to note down the names and addresses of the people involved.

"If I sent Eugene out to cover a fire," Frederick Latimer, Jr., has recalled his father saying, "he would come back with a lengthy and dramatic account of the fire, which was wonderful reading but might lack such prosaic but journalistically required details as who occupied the premises, when and how the fire started, and so forth."

His city editor, Malcolm Mollan, often had to upbraid the young reporter for failing to get all the facts. Once he sent him to cover a knife fight on Bradley Street, a tough section of New London. When Eugene returned Mollan read his copy. "This is a lovely story about the Bradley Street cutting!" he told his cub reporter. "The smell of the rooms is made convincing; the amount of blood on the floor is precisely measured; you have drawn a nice picture of the squalor and stupidity and degradation of that household. But would you mind finding out the name of the gentleman who carved the lady and whether the lady is his wife or daughter or who? And phone the hospital for a hint as to whether she is dead or discharged or what. Then put the facts into a hundred and fifty words and send this literary batik to the picture framer's!"

O'Neill never entertained any illusions about his abilities as a journalist. "I was a bum reporter," he has said, "but I gained a wonderful insight into small-town life."

Mollan later went to work for the Philadelphia *Public Ledger* and once interviewed O'Neill when the latter had become a famous playwright.

Latimer watched the sensitive cub reporter with great interest. He felt that the young man had "a literary style and that it gave evidence that this was no ordinary boy." In August he let Eugene try his hand at verse for an editorial-page column called "Laconics." He still helped cover the waterfront, fires, and the police beat, but twice a week Eugene wrote "Laconics." He signed twenty-four pieces of his newspaper verse, some as E. O'Neill or Eugene O'Neill and some as Tigean Te Oa'Neil. He liked this much better than writing routine newspaper stories. He wrote of the "sullen vessel straining at its chain" and the "bright green lawns that lean down to the bay." He also wrote parodies of Kipling, Robert Burns and Robert W. Service. The rhythms of Kipling rang loudest in his ears:

> *I have eaten my share of stock fish,*
> *On a steel Norwegian bark;*
> *With hands gripped hard to the royal yard*

I have swung through the rain and dark;
I have hauled upon the braces
And bawled the chantey song,
And the clutch of the wheel had a friendly feel
And the trade wind's kiss was strong.

So it's back to the sea, my brother
Back again to the sea;
I'm keen to land on a foreign strand;
Back again to the sea.

And these lines:

For it's grand to lie on the hatches
In the glowing tropic night,
When the sky is clear and stars seem near
And the wake is a trail of light.

He showed some humor about himself as a reporter when he wrote:

When my dreams come true all my comments wise and sage
   Will be featured double column on the editor's own page,
Personals will be no object, I won't have to go and hunt
   The history of the tugboats that infest the waterfront.
Fire alarms may go to blazes, suicides and murders too,
   I'll be editing Laconics when my dreams come true.

Getting into print in "Laconics" gave him confidence, and he began to send his verses to publications in New York. He was published in the *Masses,* the New York *Call,* and F.P.A.'s "Conning Tower," then in the New York *Tribune.* His first appearance in book form was in the Pleiades Club Year Book published in 1912, with a poem called "Free." In later years, he did not enjoy having his early verse resurrected. "I was trying," he explained, "to write popular humorous journalistic verse for a small-town paper and the stuff should be judged—nearly all of it—by that intent."

Some of his verse reflected his relationship with Muriel, and it is not without humor. In October he asked:

Is all off twixt I and you?
   Will you go and wed some other gent?

> *The things I done, I'd fain undo,*
> *Since thou hast went.*

At the end of November, he composed a long poem for "Laconics" called "The Lay of the Singer's Fall." In it he expressed his general disillusionment with life and with love:

> *And the singer was sad and he turned to Love*
> *And the arms of his ladye faire,*
> *He sang of her eyes as the stars above,*
> *He sang of—and kissed—her hair;*
> *Till the Devil whispered, 'I fondly trust*
> *This is folly and nought beside,*
> *For the greatest of loves is merely lust!'*
> *—And the soul of the sinner died.*

On December 9, 1912, Eugene published his last verse in the New London *Telegraph*. It was called "To Winter."

> *My eyes are red, my lips are blue,*
> *My ears frost bitt'n;*
> *Thy numbing kiss doth e'en extend*
> *Thro' my mitten.*
> *...O Winter, greater bards have* sung!
> *I loathe thee!*

Eight days after this verse was printed, a doctor told him he had tuberculosis and would have to go to a sanatorium.

It had started the previous October. About the middle of that month he began to suffer spells of nausea accompanied by loss of appetite. By the first of November he had a dry cough and at night cold sweats. A New London doctor diagnosed his ailment as pleurisy with effusion and treated it by tapping 1,000 cc. of fluid from his right lung. In *Long Day's Journey*, the son charges his father with calling on a quack instead of paying for a real doctor; O'Neill himself told a friend that his experience at the time of his illness had not been calculated to instill respect for his doctor's insight.

On November 1 he gave up his job on the *Telegraph*. He was now so ill that his family provided a nurse for him. Confined to his bed at home, he was unable to continue his secret meetings with

Muriel. Another friend, Mildred Culver, has recalled that O'Neill's nurse asked her to come and visit Eugene on Thanksgiving Day.

"He mainly wanted to talk about Muriel," Miss Culver has said. "I was one of her best friends, and also a friend of Gene's."

For some time, it would appear, there was confusion about the exact nature of his illness. After several weeks it was diagnosed as tuberculosis, and the question arose, where to send him to be cured? The painful and tragic conflict in the family as to whether he should go to the "state farm" for consumptives or to a private sanatorium became an important aspect of *Long Day's Journey.*

In 1912, poor people with tuberculosis were sent to the Connecticut "state farm" at Laurel Heights, where they usually died. In the play, Jamie says that his father is for sending Edmund there because he has the "bogtrotter idea that consumption is fatal" and therefore regards money spent on the boy as money wasted. James Tyrone justifies his position on the ground that he pays taxes and might as well get the benefit of the state institution. Later, he is shamed into admitting "there was another sanatorium the specialist recommended." This one was "endowed by a group of millionaire factory owners for their workers. But you're eligible. . . . It's only seven dollars a week," he added.

This description fits Gaylord Farm Sanatorium at Wallingford, Connecticut, located high on a wind-swept hill overlooking the Quinnipiac Valley. It cost a dollar a day, plus twenty-five cents a week for laundry. There were private sanatoriums at the time but they were much more expensive.

About the middle of December, 1912, Eugene was taken to New York and examined by an eminent lung specialist, who diagnosed O'Neill's ailment definitely as tuberculosis. It was he who recommended Gaylord, which preferred cases with good chances of recovery. The name of the specialist, later to become one of the leading tuberculosis authorities in the country, was Dr. James Alexander Miller. On December 17, 1912, Dr. Miller wrote his friend Dr. David Russell Lyman, founder of the ten-year-old Gaylord Farm Sanatorium:

"I have just seen a young man who I think is a good case for your sanatorium. His home is in New London. His name is O'Neil [sic] and he is stopping here in New York until I get him located permanently." He hoped that Lyman would take the patient "immediately."

It was a frightening prospect that faced Eugene O'Neill as the year 1912 drew to a close. There was more than the physical pain and discomfort of the disease itself, more than the uncertainties it raised in relation to his future. For O'Neill there was the hereditary terror of the "white plague." This dread was reinforced by the general belief that tuberculosis could be inherited—and Eugene had heard that both his grandfathers had died of it. Then, too, because the disease was considered so highly contagious, its victims were subjected to almost total ostracism.

It has been suggested that the picture was rendered still more hopeless by the special attitude of those Irish who were conscientious members of the Roman Catholic Church. "Treating an Irishman for t.b.," a specialist has said, "is extremely complicated. You are not only dealing with the disease and the fear of it, normal in any patient, but you have to deal with a patient who thinks he has the disease because God is punishing him for something he has done. Often the patient is ready to accept it as fatal and is ready to lie down and die, right then and there. You can't convince him he is not doomed."

O'Neill entered Gaylord on Christmas Eve, 1912.

CHAPTER

SIX

ΩΩ

"HILL FARM"

SANATORIUM

The only "heroic" thing about his entering Gaylord, O'Neill has said, was that it happened on Christmas Eve. And then he immediately minimized the importance of that circumstance. "To an actor's son, whose father had been on tour nearly every winter, Christmas meant less than nothing. As a boy, I never disbelieved in Santa Claus. I hardly heard there was one—we never had much chance for a winter home, and so Christmas was just a holiday without the usual associations."

It is possible that if he had not entered Gaylord immediately upon acceptance he would have missed his turn, for there was, as a rule, a waiting list there. But there were other reasons for getting him out of the house; a letter written by James O'Neill at this time indicates that the father was apprehensive that Eugene's mother would become infected if speedy action were not taken. This painful suggestion apparently was made to Eugene himself, for he remembered it when he was ready to return home.

The admitting doctor at Gaylord asked Eugene how he thought he had contracted tuberculosis. He replied that he "may have got infected while visiting dives and tenement houses as a reporter." Years later, in 1927, O'Neill told a friend that he had got "a dose of t.b. germs" in New York while living at Jimmy the Priest's with "lungers" who "were numerous among the lodgers of its airless rooms which were, in effect, cells." Later, he said, when he got run down after a long siege of "booze" and a theatrical tour with its "strain of free—not always—love and pretending to be an actor, the little bugs got me." He thought that he had only "contracted a very slight incipient case."

O'Neill gave his father's address as The Lambs club in New York and said his nearest friend was Charles Thompson of the New London *Telegraph*. He reported his earnings as twenty dollars a week.

The doctor noted that he was "nervous, gets to sleep easily but wakes up 6 or 7 times at night; no headache except on the 'morning after' . . . used to drink beer and whisky but has taken very little for past 8 months." He was only a few pounds underweight. His right lung had a dullness when thumped, but his left lung gave a "good note." There were rales (noises) heard in his right lung. A "good chance of arrest" was predicted.

The treatment of Gaylord was the best that science then had to offer, but its precautions against infection could not have been better calculated to deepen O'Neill's lifelong trait of "feeling alone, and above, and apart," of considering himself "a stranger who never feels at home," of assuming that he "is not really wanted." But in characteristic fashion he gave only oblique expression to his emotional reaction. Certainly he was voicing more than a humorous reflection on sanatorium routine when he wrote the parody:

> *A glass of milk and thou*
> *Coughing beside me in the wilderness—*
> *Ah, wilderness were Paradise enow!*

In his play *The Straw,* he dramatized the experiences of a tuberculosis patient. One scene focuses attention on the heroine's horror at being given her own cup, being cautioned about her coughing—in short, at learning that a consumptive is a pariah. The dreary routine of constant physical examination is emphasized, with specific concentration in one scene on the daily weighing ritual. In this part the action takes place in the recreation room, where a player piano is playing; suddenly the music stops and a platform scale is wheeled on stage.

The hero of *The Straw* is O'Neill himself, under the name of Stephen Murray, a newspaper reporter. His description of Murray is a description of himself at this time:

> A tall, slender, rather unusual-looking fellow with a pale face, sunken under high cheekbones, lined about the eyes and mouth, jaded and worn for one still so young. His intelligent eyes have a tired dispirited expression in repose but can quicken instantly with a concealment mechanism of mocking, careless humor whenever his inner privacy is threatened. His large mouth aids this process of protection by a quick change from its set apathy to a cheerful grin of cynical good nature. He gives the impression of being somehow dissatisfied with himself but not yet embittered enough by it to take it out on others.

One of the rules at Gaylord was so important it was called the "special" rule and it was stressed in the book of regulations given to Eugene when he entered. Dr. Lyman felt very strongly that his patients should resist the temptation of falling in love with each other. His special rule, which he defended on the ground of long experience with patients, held that "love affairs have no place in a sanatorium. Flirtations and love affairs do not go well with the cure." It was printed in bold type in the rule book: "SCATTER YOUR ATTENTION; DO NOT CONCENTRATE." O'Neill concentrated his attention on Mary Clark, the head nurse.

In *The Straw,* O'Neill has Eileen Carmody, the heroine, fall in love with Murray. Murray is attentive but not serious. The newspaperman starts to write the things he always wanted to, gets well, and leaves the "san." As soon as he leaves, Eileen's health declines. He returns for a visit and the head nurse tells him that Eileen is to be sent to the state farm, where she will die. Here, Eugene availed himself of one of the tragic aspects of Gaylord policy: The institution retained only those who responded to treatment; those who did not were sent to the state tuberculosis hospital at Laurel Heights. "It was known around Gaylord, by the patients' grapevine, that if a patient was transferred to Laurel Heights, it was curtains—he was on the way out," one of them has said.

There is no doubt that *The Straw* was based on reality. O'Neill had taken Mary Clark, Gaylord's head nurse, completely into his confidence. He showed her the short stories and poetry he was writing and she typed his manuscripts. His correspondence with Mary, to whom he inscribed a copy of *The Straw,* indicates they were very friendly. There is some suggestion that the young women patients wished he had turned his attention to them. One of them, who noted his interest in the head nurse, told another, "Perhaps I'm just as well off. My mother always tells me to beware of somber-eyed young men." Another young woman remembered him as "quiet, naturally aloof but generally admired." But Camilles never did seem to catch his fancy. He preferred strong women.

It is a tradition at Gaylord that Kitty McKay, of Waterbury, Connecticut, was the prototype for Eileen Carmody. The facts of her life and the circumstances surrounding her being at Gaylord certainly fit the heroine of *The Straw.* At the time she was at Gaylord, Kitty had four sisters and five brothers. Their mother had died, and Kitty, as the eldest sister, was looking after her father and the other children. She was stricken with tuberculosis and was sent to Gaylord, where she immediately won everyone's heart and Dr. Lyman found her "an exceptionally good girl, an excellent patient." Kitty's health improved and she returned home, where she resumed her back-breaking household chores. When she went back to Gaylord for a checkup, Dr. Lyman found she had "steadily, recently rather rapidly, lost ground and unless a quick change is made her life will be a short one."

Dr. Lyman wrote to Gaylord's visiting nurse in Waterbury, asking her to find some way to "give the girl a chance for her life." He didn't think her family realized that unless she was hospitalized "they will before long not only have to do without her services but [have] to nurse her besides." Kitty had told Dr. Lyman that she simply could not leave her family, that her father could not afford to let her go away. Dr. Lyman was so distressed about the situation that he offered "to look after her bills until we can see whether she has relapsed too far to respond to treatment." He was prepared to keep her a year "if necessary to get her on her feet."

In *The Straw,* Eugene dramatizes this tragic situation by having a scene take place in the patient's home, where the doctor confronts the father.

DR. GAYNOR. She'll have to go to a sanatorium at once. She ought to have been sent months ago. . . . She kept on doing her work, I suppose—taking care of her brothers and sisters, washing, cooking, sweeping, looking after your comfort—worn out—when she should have been in bed. . . . The damage is done.

BILL CARMODY. . . . It's all nonsense you're stuffin' me with, and lies, makin' things out to be worst in the world. She'll not move a step out of here, and I say so, and I'm her father!

The doctor finds it necessary to threaten the father with action by the Society for the Prevention of Tuberculosis. The father yields, and there is talk of money—the fee at the Hill Farm is seven dollars a week—"the price of a few rounds of drinks," the doctor bitingly adds. When the father balks still more at losing his daughter-housekeeper, the doctor says he will foot half the bill. The "bog-trotter" father finally yields to pressure, and Eileen goes to Hill Farm.

Kitty McKay died at her home in Waterbury just two years after O'Neill left Gaylord.

In *The Straw,* the head nurse asks Murray to tell Eileen that he loves her and wants to marry her. He can take her, she says, to some private sanatorium where "she'll be happy to the very last." Her father won't pay for her going anyplace. In a highly dramatic scene, Murray tells Eileen he loves her—and then discovers that he really does. He also lies and tells her he still has the disease himself. The play ends on the theme of what O'Neill called "the significance of human hope and the t.b. background." The head nurse, distressed at the situation she has brought about, wonders whether she has done a "great wrong by that lie" that has become a truth. The newspaperman replies," Come now, confess, damn it! There's always hope, isn't there? What do you *know?*"

Dr. Lyman did not care for *The Straw,* and he said so. He made it forbidden reading at Gaylord. He objected to it because it romanticized the very thing that he had continually cautioned his patients about—falling in love. It confirmed his belief in "the special rule for use in trying to avoid such complications, the heroine in *The Straw* having been one of the unfortunate cases for whom an apparently harmless flirtation developed into disastrous consequences."

O'Neill retorted, "I intend to use whatever I can make my own, to write about anything under the sun in any manner that fits or can be invented to fit the subject. And I shall never be influenced by any consideration but one: Is it the truth as I know it—or, better still, feel it?"

O'Neill did a great deal of reading at Gaylord. He told Hamilton Basso that he read Strindberg for the first time there and that after it he was not the same man. "It was reading his plays," he said, "that above all first gave me the vision of what modern drama could be and first inspired me with the urge to write for the theater myself. The influence of Strindberg runs clearly through more than a few of my plays and is plain for everyone to see."

George Jean Nathan and Barrett Clark both noted that O'Neill's hospitalization had had a profound effect on his development. He had matured, intellectually and psychologically, in his stay at Gaylord. He went in a youth and came out a man.

Although O'Neill suffered only "a very slight incipient case" of tuberculosis, he always felt the bond which ex-patients seem to have with one another. In 1930 he wrote an old friend, "I can really sympathize with your t.b. experience. I belong to the club, as you might say." To a writer for the *Journal of Outdoor Life* who asked him, in 1923, if he had any "message" for tuberculosis patients, he replied with both a message and a warning:

> Win out and God bless you! And here's my loudest cheers!
> Don't get snobbish! I remember I used to sort of despise the untutored ignorant folk who did not have or had not had t.b. I looked down upon such unfortunates as an unexperienced, inferior lot who, after all, couldn't know much about life or anything else. They simply didn't belong, thought I with a superior sniff—until one day a friend, an eminent t.b. specialist, sensing my attitude, maliciously told me the truth—that autopsies reveal the democratic fact that nearly everyone has had it! Which leaves us only one point of superiority to brag about: We know it and rest of them don't.

At the end of six months at Gaylord, on May 24, 1913, O'Neill was examined for the last time and found to be in "A-1 shape; no symptoms, moderate exercise, no fatigue, breathing much easier and stronger; looks and feels perfectly well." His left lung had suffered "some impairment of note at apex front and back and below scap." It was noted that he was going home to take a rest cure for the summer at his father's cottage at the seashore. He was advised against strenuous exercise of all kinds for the next year "but can resume work in Fall."

Four words ended the report: "Discharged arrested. Prognosis excellent."

When Eugene learned that he was going to be discharged as cured, he immediately wrote to his father at the Hotel Ascot on Madison Avenue in New York City to tell him the good news. He had "been declared absolutely free from contagion . . . so thoroughly cured that no one—not even [my] ailing mother can become infected with tuberculosis by living in the same house and eating at the same table with [me]."

James O'Neill, however, wrote to Dr. Lyman to ask "if this is true. I do not wish to jeopardize my wife's health; and our plans for the summer will depend on your reply which I hope will be as soon as possible."

Dr. Lyman answered that the son's case was known as "closed tuberculosis." There was "no sputum with bacilli, and in consequence no danger of contagion. I do not believe your son is absolutely cured, or that any case is in less than three or four years' time. But in his present condition he would not be a menace to anyone."

Although James O'Neill may have seemed unduly squeamish —and somewhat unsympathetic toward his son—in asking the doctor's reassurance before consenting to Eugene's return to the family, his attitude was not unwarranted. Tuberculosis in those days was a terrifying thing, and it was not unreasonable for a man to be concerned about the possible infection of his wife, even from their son. Eugene understood that, and, as it turned out, James did take his son back into their New London home. But Eugene never completely forgave his father for that qualified reception.

CHAPTER

SEVEN

ಬ

"SECOND BIRTH":

THE EARLIEST PLAYS

Eugene O'Neill returned to his family's summer home on June 3, 1913. He has described in several ways the effect that his five months' stay at Gaylord had had on him. "My mind," he said, "got the chance to establish itself, to digest and evaluate the impressions of many past years in which one experience had crowded on another with never a second's reflection. At Gaylord I really thought about my life for the first time, about past and future. Undoubtedly the inactivity forced upon me by the life at the san forced me to mental activity, especially as I had always been high-strung and nervous temperamentally."

A year after he left Gaylord he told Dr. Lyman that he would like to return for a visit, "because if it is sweet to visit the place where you were born, it would be doubly sweet to visit the place where one was reborn." His second birth, which he felt had taken place there, was the only one, he said, which had his full approval.

When he returned home it was to the old tensions. Formerly his

father had been disturbed by the fact that Gene didn't have any
definite idea what he wanted to do; now his son's intention to write
plays troubled him even more.

"My father was worried about me," Eugene has said of this
period. "He didn't know how to handle me, he didn't 'get' what I was
trying to do; he only wanted me to settle down and make a living.
He often used to think I was just crazy." A friend of the actor has
said that James O'Neill wanted his son to be a lawyer.

During his first three months at home, Eugene suffered a severe
case of hookworm. But he had returned with a determination not only
to work hard at writing plays but also to stay well, and he followed
a rigorous schedule of sunbathing and swimming every day. His appetite was good for the first time in many months.

James O'Neill talked about his problem son with Clayton
Hamilton, the dramatist, who often called at the O'Neill home. He told
Hamilton he didn't know what to do with Eugene—he was "a bad
boy." Could Hamilton find some good in him, perhaps devise some
method for developing the good? To this Hamilton replied, "I have
nothing to suggest."

Hamilton nevertheless was impressed by the fact that Eugene
had worked his way all over the world as a seaman. "I looked the
lad over," he wrote. "He had large and dreamy eyes, a slender, somewhat frail and yet athletic body, a habit of silence, and an evident
disease of shyness." Hamilton liked the young man, and Eugene liked
him. But Eugene did not mention his writing at this time. When
he did, later, he found a devoted ally.

As his health improved, he saw more of Judge Latimer, his old
editor on the *Telegraph*. They often rowed out on the Sound to fish
all day. Latimer read the poetry and the plays Eugene was writing
and told him he thought they were excellent. He was struck by
O'Neill's determination to produce "something worthwhile for the
sake of its own value and in utter scorn of its commercial value."
Latimer believed "there was something in Eugene, at that time, an
innate nobility which inspires and drives a man, against whatever
hindrance, to be himself, however heaven or hell conspires to rob him
of that birthright."

In many ways, the older man and Eugene were far apart. Latimer disapproved of what he called Eugene's "local acquaintances,
of a mildly Bohemian sort." He himself was a solid Republican
conformist, although in his own conservative circles he was regarded

as slightly eccentric. He became a perfect foil for Eugene's budding radical views and iconoclasm, and he listened sympathetically to the young man's tirades against religion. "As we used to talk together," Latimer has said, "and argue our different philosophies, I thought he was the most stubborn and irreconcilable social rebel I had ever met. We appreciated each other's sympathies, but to each, in the moralities and religious thought and political notions, the other was 'all wet.' Emphatically, he was 'different.' I thought it astonishing how keen was his wit, what a complete iconoclast he was, how richly he sympathized with the victims of man-made distress, how his imagination was running high as the festering skies above Ye Ancient Mariner."

Apparently Eugene's views made little impression on Latimer. Only a few years later, the former editor and judge went to work for United States Attorney General A. Mitchell Palmer and participated in the wholesale prosecution of radicals shortly after World War I.

But Latimer was genuinely devoted to Eugene. "He was adrift [that summer] in mind and spirit, and the body was threatened," he has said. "I was sorry for him. The four things about him that impressed me, at once, were his modesty, his native gentlemanliness, his wonderful eyes, and his literary style."

Though Latimer tried to serve as a literary ambassador from Eugene to his father, he did have one serious disagreement with Eugene. He thought Eugene should give up writing poetry and plays, and write novels. Eugene had had some luck with short stories, but not much. He found exposition extremely difficult and said the only way he seemed to be able to express himself was in dramatic dialogue and in descriptions of people and sets.

That summer Eugene continued to write poems—especially to girls. He had resumed his friendship with Muriel, but there were difficulties. It was apparent that he was a poor prospect as a provider; and, besides, she did not share, as Latimer put it, "his radical ways of looking at things." Muriel has recalled that "Judge Latimer was fond of both of us." And she remembers that that summer Eugene "used to say over and over again that he was going to be a great writer and that some day he would return to New London and show them. He was always bringing me short stories or plays to read. He opened up a whole new world to me—the world of literature."

In the fall the O'Neills closed their house and James agreed to pay for Eugene's keep at a Mrs. Rippin's, whose house overlooked Long Island Sound. It was one of the better boarding houses of the town. Among its frequent guests, when their own cottage was not open, were the Clayton Hamiltons. Mrs. Hamilton has recalled that "Mrs. Rippin was a 'homely' soul in the English sense of the word. She never found the aitches she had dropped in her native cockney environment." Mrs. Rippin read some of Eugene's early plays and didn't like them because the characters were " 'orrible." She liked Clayton Hamilton's plays because the people were "nice."

At Mrs. Rippin's, where he lived for sixteen months, Eugene had a real glimpse of a happy home life. Her daughters were devoted to him. They typed his manuscripts and took them to the post office —even providing the postage at times. He was writing one-act plays at the rate of one a month and was sending them off to Broadway producers. If Eugene overslept, Mrs. Rippin would rout him out of bed and threaten him with no breakfast if he failed to take his early-morning swim, which the doctor had ordered. Generally he prided himself on this self-torture, even when it was icy-cold. He mailed Dr. Lyman a photograph of himself in a bathing suit, noting on the snapshot that the temperature was 29 degrees and indicating the snow at his feet with an arrow. "Taken (cross my heart) January 1, 1914," he wrote; then he added from Kipling:

> *The uniform 'e wore*
> *Was nothin' much before,*
> *An' rather less than 'arf o' that be'ind.*

Although Eugene's long stay at Mrs. Rippin's boarding house sounds idyllic, Clayton Hamilton has written that, in putting him there, James O'Neill had "decided to adopt a punitive process that approached imprisonment. He let the lad alone throughout the winter." Mrs. Hamilton wrote that Eugene stayed at "the most hospitable and economical place he could choose with the $8 weekly allowance granted him by his father. James O'Neill considered even that much money badly spent, for he saw no future whatsoever for a son he then considered a wayward, worthless wanderer, unable to settle down to anything."

But Eugene was earning some money on the side. He wrote to Dr. Lyman in May, 1914, that he was at work playwriting and also "prostituting same" by doing movie scenarios for which he was earning thirty dollars a week. But he had high hopes. He expected Holbrook Blinn to produce two of his one-acters at the Princess Theatre. He was hard at work on a four-act play which he was sure would hit the footlights the next season.

By the fall he had written eleven one-act and two full-length plays. In between, he was reading Nietzsche and the plays of Wedekind. "I read everything I could lay my hands on," he has said, "the Greeks, the Elizabethans—practically all the classics—and, of course, all the moderns, like Ibsen and Strindberg, especially Strindberg."

Much of his reading was done in the apartment of Dr. Joseph M. Ganey, located above the doctor's office. The apartment was a hangout for a small group of intellectuals who called themselves the Second Story Club. Dr. Ganey was a short, heavy-set man with blue eyes and gray hair who didn't allow his books to be taken out of his apartment. His bookplate read: "I do not loan books, so please do not embarrass me by asking." Ganey said that Eugene read everything of Guy de Maupassant and believed the French writer had a tremendous influence on him.

The doctor also recalled a prophetic incident in the fall of 1912. Eugene, much the worse for wear after a drinking bout, walked into the city room of the *Telegraph*. The managing editor, when he noticed Eugene's condition, expressed his disapproval. "If you weren't James O'Neill's son," he said, "you'd be down in the gutter with all the rest of the bums."

Eugene was not abashed. "The day will come," he replied, "when James O'Neill will be remembered only as the father of Eugene O'Neill."

The members of the Second Story Club included a number of newspapermen; among them were Charles Thompson, Arthur Casey, Malcolm Mollan and Art McGinley. The principal activities of the club members were drinking, and playing penny ante, and swapping tales of amorous exploits. Eugene tried hard to be "one of the boys," but Ganey has recalled that when he occasionally joined in a game of penny ante his mind seemed to wander.

Years later, when he was chatting with Ganey in New York, O'Neill said, "I hate this town like poison. I always have and always will. I left New London because I wanted to make enough money to hire a four-in-hand, fill it up with obvious blond whores, and drive down Main Street scattering a bushel of dimes for the peasants to scramble after."

His first play—in any case, the first one he copyrighted—was a one-acter, *A Wife for a Life*. In this one, in a three-act play *Servitude,* and in a one-act play, *Abortion,* he clearly indicated his preoccupation with the problems of his first marriage, which had only recently ended in divorce.

The heroine of *Servitude* wants to "assert the freedom necessary for her individual development." She has been "awakened" by David Roylston, a playwright. As a "New Woman" she visits her "creator," Roylston, and notes that "the great emancipator" has turned his good wife into a virtual slave. She thereupon sets about to "rewaken" Roylston into recognition of the true worth of Mrs. Roylston. Reality, however, destroys her illusion. She returns to her husband, after learning from Mrs. Roylston that "love means servitude; and love is servitude." *Servitude* is short for a three-act play. The dialogue is inept, amateurish—a fault some think O'Neill never fully overcame.

In *A Wife for a Life,* O'Neill writes in a similar vein. A grizzled miner acts out a plot which says that "greater love hath no man . . . than that he giveth his wife for his friend." O'Neill said that he wrote this for the vaudeville stage. The idea for it had come to him when he was playing the Orpheum circuit with his father. It was, he said, the only play he ever wrote to make money. One cannot disagree too much with O'Neill that *A Wife for a Life,* which depends completely upon coincidence, was the worst play he ever wrote; but, like *Servitude* and all his early efforts it "plays" far better than it reads.

Abortion is the story of a college baseball hero who gets a girl into trouble. An abortion is arranged and the girl dies. Her brother learns what has happened and decides to go to the police. As a result, the baseball hero commits suicide.

O'Neill was apparently so intrigued by the theme of abortion that he wrote several versions of it. When talking about the play he varied the plot ingeniously. Nevertheless, *Abortion* is blatantly melodramatic and not one of his prouder efforts.

The Web, the earliest of O'Neill's plays which he later authorized for production, opens with the line, "Gawd! What a night!" It is straight melodrama concerning a prostitute and her protector. The scene is laid in a "squalid bedroom on the top floor of a rooming house on the lower East Side, New York." The woman has a baby, and the infant is a source of annoyance to her lover, Steve. The lover beats her and she falls to the floor. Another man rescues her in the nick of time. Steve warns her if she leaves or "holds out" on him, he will have her thrown in jail and will take the baby away from her. She is, obviously, caught in "the web." The good man, a fugitive from justice, gives the poor woman money to go away. Steve, who has been hiding nearby, comes on stage and kills the good man. He then plants the gun so that it will implicate the woman. When the police all too promptly arrive, they take the woman away. The baby cries, "Ma-a-a-a!" A detective takes the infant in his arms and says, "Mama's gone now. I'm your mama now."

This is generally believed to be the first play O'Neill ever wrote. Naturally it is crude, the plot is bad melodrama and the dialogue is poor. But as a first play, *The Web* is remarkable in that it includes many of O'Neill's characteristic elements: violent death, cruelty, tragedy and a good deal of theatrical action.

The Clayton Hamiltons stayed at Mrs. Rippin's for a winter vacation in January, 1914. Eugene did not immediately discuss his work with Hamilton, whom he saw daily at the breakfast table. Gladys Hamilton has recalled that he "seemed an unobtrusive young man who did not wish his silences interrupted." The couple respected his apparent desire to be let alone and it was Eugene who finally spoke about his work.

"I've been trying to write one-act plays," he said, "and I'd like to ask you how to do it."

"Never mind how plays are written," Hamilton replied. "Write down what you know about the sea, and about the men who sail before the mast. This has been done in the novel; it has been done in the short-story; it has not been done in the drama. Keep your eye on life—on life as you have seen it; and to hell with the rest."

The sea plays which Eugene began to write in the spring of 1914 were amateurish but powerful. In *Thirst,* he showed a West Indian mulatto sailor, a dancer and a gentleman on a raft, dying of thirst. The gentleman and the dancer think the mulatto has drinking water hidden somewhere on the raft. The dancer offers her necklace to the mulatto, and then her body, in exchange for water. He refuses both and she dies. The mulatto takes out his knife and indicates that he is going to satisfy his hunger and thirst. The gentleman pushes the woman's body into the sea. The mulatto thereupon plunges his knife into the gentleman. They wrestle and both men fall into the sea. The necklace remains on the raft glittering in the spotlight.

Thirst is incredibly melodramatic and probably derived from O'Neill's reading of Jack London. Eugene's difficulty with dialogue is apparent in the play's opening lines:

THE DANCER. My God! My God! This silence is driving me mad. Why do you not speak to me. Is there no ship in sight yet?

O'Neill's ear for actual spoken language was never too sharp, though he did pick up slang. However, it is neither necessary nor desirable for a playwright to reproduce contemporary speech; it is necessary to rise above it, to capture the rhythms of our lives and language, not just the words. And this O'Neill learned to do better than any American playwright before or since.

Fog is also laid on a life raft. The characters are a Poet, a Man of Business, a Peasant Woman, and a Dead Child. The life raft drifts close to an iceberg. They hear a steamer in the distance. The Man of Business wants to call out for help. The Poet will not let him because it may cause the ship to ram the iceberg. The fog lifts, the steamer looms. The sailors have been guided to the raft by the voice of the Child, they say. The Poet tells them the Child has been dead for twenty-four hours.

Fog is the best of the very early plays. It is not naturalistic, for the characters clearly symbolize the theme of greed versus idealism. There is a certain beauty in this drama that emerges in production and foreshadows the expressionism of such later plays as *The Hairy Ape*.

Warnings is about a wireless operator who, while on leave, learns that he may go stone-deaf at any time. He ships out on his transatlantic liner nonetheless. When the liner starts to sink, he sends a message asking for help, but he is unable to hear an answer because deafness has overtaken him. The play ends with his suicide. *Warnings* is a poor effort; the first scene, showing the man and his family, is too long, the entire plot seems contrived, and the wireless operator's character changes too suddenly and too inconsistently.

Late in the spring, Eugene wrote *Bound East for Cardiff*, which showed a tremendous advance in the quality of his work. The dialogue has an impressive honesty and the ring of truth about it. A sailor called Yank is dying from an accident aboard ship. Tough men of the sea reveal an awkward tenderness toward him. Driscoll, an Irishman, jokingly accuses Yank of wanting to die so that he will go to heaven. Yank says no, he is destined for hell; and he speaks with bitterness of the life of men at sea—one ship after another, hard work, small pay, bad food, no one to care if you're dead or alive. He recalls some of his adventures, many of them similar to Eugene's own. Yank remembers that he once killed a man with a knife in a fight at Cape Town. Will God hold it against him? God sees everything, God knows everything. Yank wonders if he will be buried at sea. In the end, he sees somebody standing in the cabin. Driscoll, seeing no one, asks who it is. Yank answers that is it a pretty lady dressed in black. He then dies. Driscoll sobs and kneels in prayer.

When the Hamiltons opened their cottage that summer of 1914, Eugene came down to call. Gladys Hamilton has recalled that he approached her husband with the utmost trepidation. He was halting and hesitant in his speech, "his eyes alone," she wrote, "supplying the eloquence his tongue denied." He gave Hamilton several of his one-act sea plays to read.

Hamilton read them but, he says, he decided not to tell Eugene how good he thought they were, or how promising. Actually, he was astounded at their power. Eugene had indicated he might like to study in Professor George Pierce Baker's 47 Workshop at Harvard. Hamilton knew Baker and thought he could get Eugene admitted. When he spoke to James O'Neill about sending Eugene to Harvard, James, according to Hamilton, was hesitant. He pointed out he had already sent his son to Princeton, where he had lasted only a year. Hamilton used all his eloquence in dealing with the old man, who respected the judgment of a drama critic and family friend. Eventually he was able to persuade the father that there was indeed hope for his wild, sea-roving son.

Although James O'Neill has been painted by Hamilton and others as something of a miser where his son was concerned, he did an extremely generous thing that summer. He put up a thousand dollars to subsidize a book of plays by Eugene. Richard Badger of the Gorham Press in Boston published the book under the title *Thirst*. It contained, besides the title play, *The Web, Recklessness, Fog,* and *Warnings*. There was little market for the work of an unknown playwright, and the publisher was able to sell only a few copies. After Eugene achieved recognition, *Thirst* became a collector's item. It is one of the scarcest of modern American first editions, and a copy has fetched as much as sixty-five dollars.

Hamilton eventually reviewed *Thirst* in the magazine *Vogue*.

It was the only review the book received, although copies were sent around to all the book and drama critics. He wrote:

> This writer's mood is one of horror. He deals with grim and ghastly situations that would become intolerable if they were protracted beyond the limits of a single sudden act. He seems to be familiar with the sea; for three of these plays deal with terrors that attend the tragedy of shipwrecks, revealing a keen sense of the reactions of character under stress of violent emotion; and his dialogue is almost brutal in its power. More than one of these plays should be available for such an institution as the Princess Theatre in New York.

Eugene O'Neill afterward wrote Hamilton: "You can't imagine what it meant coming from you. It held out a hope at a very hopeless time. It made me believe I was arriving with a bang; and at that period I very much needed someone whose authority I respected to admit I was getting somewhere."

Hamilton also gave O'Neill some good advice. Having learned that Eugene was sending his play manuscripts to managers as soon as he completed them, then living in hope that they would be quickly read and accepted, the successful dramatist told him, "When you send off a play, there is not one chance in a thousand it will ever be read, not one chance in a million of its ever being accepted; and if it is accepted it will probably never be produced. But if it is accepted and produced, say to yourself it's a miracle which can never happen again."

O'Neill thereupon decided, as he told Hamilton afterward, that his friend and mentor was "hardly a fit associate for budding aspirations. But finally I reflected that you knew whereof you spoke, that I was up against a hard game and might as well realize it and hew to the line without thought of commercial stage production. Your advice gradually bred in me a gloomy and soothing fatalism which kismeted many a rebuff and helped me to take my disappointments as all an inevitable part of the game. It was a bitter dose to swallow that day but it sure proved a vital shock-absorbing tonic in the long run. It taught me to 'take it'—and God knows that's the first thing most apprentice playwrights need to learn if they are not to turn into chronic whiners against fate or quitters before their good break comes."

Both Hamilton and Eugene wrote to Professor Baker at Harvard.

Eugene's first letter was a well-reasoned presentation of his candidacy for the 47 Workshop. He said that his father was the actor James O'Neill, and so he had been closely connected with the dramatic profession. He had been assistant manager in his father's company when Viola Allen played in *The White Sister,* and five of his own one-act plays were being brought out in book form.

In his second letter he sent along two of his plays. He also explained, apologetically, about leaving Princeton. He said he was "flunked out" for overcutting and had done very little work. He thanked Baker for his consideration and repeated that he hoped to become his student.

O'Neill was twenty-six that fall of 1914 when he journeyed to Cambridge, Massachusetts, to enter Baker's 47 Workshop. He was older than the other students. One of them, John V. A. Weaver, who married the actress Peggy Wood, was to gain fame as a poet. Some of the others, O'Neill recalled, appeared to be as uncomfortable at having "this dark-eyed Irishman" for a classmate as he was at having to be a college boy again. Eugene must have seemed strange indeed to those college boys, five or six years his junior.

His father gave him ten dollars a week for expenses, out of which he had to pay for his room, board, car fare, laundry and new clothes. He boarded with a Mennonite family and, he told friends, they were very kind to him. The food was good and plentiful, and he had a comfortable bed in a clean room.

One of the ways in which he revealed his annoyance at having to be a college boy again was to swear like a sailor when talking to his fellow students. He did this often in the presence of one particularly effete student, who decided that O'Neill was "foul-mouthed." The student also thought O'Neill's worst fault as a writer was "an ineptitude at dialogue, except when the speakers were raving drunk or profane." He recalled that *The Second Engineer,* one of the plays O'Neill wrote at Harvard was "labored and stiff." This play was also titled *The Personal Equation.* It is no longer in existence but, from all contemporary accounts, this is no great loss.

"He was good-looking," the student conceded, "very nervous, and extremely impatient with Forty-seven and anxious to get down to live in Greenwich Village. He was friendly, though rather uneasy and inarticulate at times. You got the impression that he trembled a little and seemed trying to keep from stuttering. But when he delivered himself of a remark, it was impressive."

Another of O'Neill's classmates summed up his impressions succinctly by describing him as "a sarcastic bastard."

Professor Baker, although sympathetic toward the idea of creating a new American theater, believed there were some useful things about playwriting to be learned from the past. But from the beginning O'Neill was bored by lectures on the theater. In one of his classes, the assignment consisted of diagramming the construction of a play by Augustus Thomas. O'Neill was so disgusted he got up and left the room. On another occasion Baker read *Bound East for Cardiff* and told O'Neill he didn't think it was a play at all. O'Neill himself thought the plays he wrote at Harvard were "rotten." One of them was a long, rambling affair about seamen and a strike of the ship's firemen. The other, *The Dear Doctor,* Baker thought slick enough for vaudeville; when O'Neill checked on the short story on which he had based his one-acter, he found that it had been stolen from an already successful vaudeville sketch.

Undoubtedly the best play O'Neill wrote during his year at Harvard was *The Sniper.* It concerns a Belgian peasant who has seen his family slain and his land taken by the Germans. He turns his gun on the Germans and is captured. This plot is sentimentally dramatized, but there is a professional air to it all the same, and "Bleeding Belgium" was on America's conscience in 1915. O'Neill wrote two other plays while at the workshop: *A Knock at the Door,* a comedy of little humor, and *Belshazzar,* a rather horrible Biblical play in six scenes on which Eugene and a fellow student, Colin Ford, collaborated.

The best description of O'Neill at Harvard was that of John V. A. Weaver, who said that O'Neill stood out "like an oyster in a lunchroom stew." The rest of the class, Weaver wrote,

> . . . listened with scared respect to the professorial admonitions, urgings, and objurgations. Not so the fierce-browed, sardonic young man at whose left I sat. These theoretical vaporings were to him simply so much asafoetida. While we sat open-mouthed and earnest, he would writhe and squirm in his chair, scowling and muttering in a *mezza voce* fearful imprecations and protests. Of him, too, we were frightened. He kept so much to himself. He did not invite approach. For some weeks, we let him alone. Then one day Dr. Baker read aloud a scenario by an aspirant. It was lugubrious, it was flamboyant, it was very, very

earnest. Several of us gave suggestions. It came O'Neill's turn. He waited some moments. Finally, he said, without a smile, 'Cut it to twenty minutes, give it a couple of tunes, and it's a sure-fire burly-cue.' We howled with laughter. Dr. Baker smiled. From that time until we all parted in June there was a new ease, a refreshing relaxation in the meetings."

On one occasion Weaver and a student named Elkins, who was something of a society man, joined O'Neill as he was leaving the classroom. The three went to a saloon frequented by Boston Irish and called, naturally, the Shamrock. They drank ale and nibbled at the free lunch until the early hours of the morning, told ribald tales and anecdotes of their experiences, and theorized about the drama. Then they took a decrepit horse-drawn hack to Cambridge and resumed their talk in O'Neill's room until about five in the morning. Weaver had a copy of Edgar Lee Masters' *Spoon River Anthology* he had bought that day. "When the dawn broke," Weaver wrote, "I was sitting on a trunk, Elkins sprawled across the bed, and O'Neill was reading, in his powerful melancholy bass, poem after poem from that disturbing collection."

Elkins, who was related to the Widener family of Philadelphia, had plenty of money and entree into the best social circles in Boston. A good conversationalist himself, he was delighted with O'Neill's description of his days with his father's *Monte Cristo* company. O'Neill embellished the story of his life somewhat. He described living in hobo camps, working as a stoker on ships, taking part in riots and street fights all over the world. Elkins sometimes took his two friends to formal dinners on Beacon Hill. But O'Neill refused to be impressed, as Weaver put it, "by flunkies and quiet elegance. He wore a dirty brown flannel shirt, and maintained an air of jocular insolence. He thrilled and appalled the Brahmins by his social views."

The three friends dined at Durgin's, where boiled beef and beer were in order, or at the Roma on salami and red wine. Once O'Neill outlined and acted out, in part, a comedy he proposed writing about upper-class Bostonians. But he never put it on paper. Now and then Elkins would take O'Neill and Weaver to the theater. He would buy an entire box, seating eight. After the three drama students were comfortably settled, Elkins would tear up the unused tickets with a grand air of "conspicuous waste." Despite his obvious enjoyment of the pleasures of the leisure class, O'Neill continued to startle his classmates with what Weaver called his "savage radicalism." Weaver was also impressed by O'Neill's compelling charm with women.

> Women were forever calling for Gene, [Weaver said]. There was something apparently irresistible in his strange combination of cruelty around his mouth, intelligence in his eyes, and sympathy in his voice and eyes. He was not good-looking. But one girl told me she could not get his face out of her thoughts. He was hard-boiled and whimsical. He was brutal and tender, so I was told. From shop girl to "sassiety queen," they all seemed to develop certain tendencies in his presence. What may have resulted, deponent sayeth not. About some things Gene was sphinxlike. All I can report is the phenomena.

The friendship of Elkins, Weaver and O'Neill ended with the course, a year later. On a stifling May morning they said good-by. Elkins went to the West Coast and Weaver found a job in Chicago.

What O'Neill got out of his year at Harvard was largely the result of his association with Baker, whose judgment he respected and whose interest he appreciated. Most of the plays he wrote there were poor and never were produced.

"I did get a great deal from Baker personally," O'Neill has said. "He encouraged me, made me feel it was worthwhile going ahead. My personal association with him meant a devil of a lot to me."

Baker noted that O'Neill "worked steadily and with increasing effectiveness. He seemed absorbedly interested in what he was trying to do. By the end of the year he already knew how to write well in the one-act form, but he could not as yet manage the longer forms." Baker wanted him to return for a second year, but he was given to understand that O'Neill could not afford to.

Professor Baker switched his drama workshop to Yale a few years later. When he died in 1935, O'Neill wrote a tribute in which he cited the "profound influence he exerted toward the encouragement and birth of the modern American drama. . . . He helped us to hope, and for that we owe him all the finest we have in memory of gratitude and friendship."

CHAPTER

EIGHT

ကာ

THE HELL HOLE

AND THE WHARF

After leaving Harvard at the end of the spring term of 1915, O'Neill went to live in Greenwich Village, where he took a room at 38 Washington Square West. His father continued to give him an allowance of ten dollars a week. His income aside from his allowance, according to a report he made to Dr. Lyman that year, was twenty-five dollars a week. For some months he drew this sum as drama critic on a magazine which was being planned, but the project was abandoned before the first issue was published. He continued his own writing at the rate of about seven hours a day.

He saw a good deal of his brother, Jamie, who was then frequenting a bar a few blocks away at Sixth Avenue and Christopher Street where John Masefield had once worked. Officially it was called the Columbian Saloon, but in popular parlance its name was the "Working Girls' Home." One of the regular patrons has recalled that Jamie looked, at this time, like a well-dressed official of Tammany Hall. He wore a derby at a sharp angle.

Jamie was by now a confirmed alcoholic. His favorite expression, especially when he had a hang-over, was "The Brooklyn boys are after me." He would look over his shoulder, run his hands through his hair, and roll his eyes. The "Brooklyn boys" were men a foot high who wore derbies and marched rapidly in step and in single file. They could walk through walls and closed doors and windows. A friend of Eugene's, Art McGinley, has recalled that Jamie was so sarcastic at times that his remarks "could cut through a steel bar." Jamie's taste in women ran to prostitutes with large bosoms. He still talked about getting a job on a newspaper.

While he has been described as a typical, waggish Irishman, Jamie's hail-fellow-well-met air was a cover for inner torment, for he was never able to overcome his feelings of insecurity. He had felt unwanted as a boy when his parents dropped him off in the kindergarten at Notre Dame. Devoted to his mother, Jamie was acutely conscious of her drug addiction. As he grew up, he wanted to become a newspaperman, but his father wanted him to be an actor. Jamie hated the stage and was not nearly the actor his father was. And finally, when he recognized the unmistakable signs of talent in his younger brother, he could not stop himself from feeling envy. He hated himself for it, but he could not prevent it, not even by trying to drown his consciousness in alcohol.

About the middle of 1915 Eugene found his own barroom headquarters, four blocks south of the Columbian Saloon, at the Golden Swan, more commonly known as the "Hell Hole." There he was to have his last long fling—a full year of it—at the kind of life he had led before his stay at the sanatorium. Thirty years later he was to re-create that establishment on the stage, as Harry Hope's saloon in *The Iceman Cometh.*

Just before settling down to his period of sustained drinking he paid a visit to his parents in New London. He also resumed his friendship with Muriel; but things had changed. She was interested in someone else and was planning marriage. It was clear that O'Neill was not, and they agreed it would be best if they stopped seeing each other. Their parting was friendly. Eugene returned all her letters; she kept his for a time and eventually burned them. As a parting gift he gave her a copy of *Thirst* in which he wrote: "To Muriel, in memory of all the seconds, minutes, hours and days we have spent together and which have now passed into eternity. Eugene."

Following his breakup with Muriel, O'Neill found consolation in a friendship with another New London girl, Beatrice Ashe. She sang in a church choir and is said to have been tall and beautiful. He addressed to her some sixty or seventy pieces of light verse, as well as numerous letters. In one of his verses he compared her to Dante's Beatrice. Although it appears patently amateurish, F.P.A. thought well enough of it to print it in his column, "The Conning Tower," in 1915. Its title was "Speaking to the Shades of Dante, of Beatrice."

> *Lo, even I am Beatrice!*
> *That line keeps singing in my bean*
> *As did the fluent Florentine*
> *Who heard the well-known hell-flame hiss.*
>
> *Dante, your damozel was tall*
> *And lean and sad—I've seen her face*
> *On many a best-parlor wall—*
> *I don't think she is such an ace.*
> *She doesn't class with mine at all.*
>
> *Her eyes were not so large or gray:*
> *She had no such heart-teasing smile,*
> *Or hair so beautiful; and say,*
> *I hate to state it, but her style*
> *Would never get her by today.*
>
> *I'm not denying that your queen*
> *In your eyes may have been a bear.*
> *You couldn't pull the stuff I've seen*
> *About her, if she wasn't there—*
> *The soft poetic bull I mean.*
>
> *But just to call your rhythmic bluff*
> *I'll say before I ring the bell*
> *And kill this roundelay of fluff,*
> *Like Dante, I'd go plumtoel*
> *For Beatrice—and that's enough!*

His friendships with Muriel and Beatrice are both examples of O'Neill's tendency to idealize "the nice girl." At the time he was seeing Beatrice, he was twenty-seven and she was some ten years younger. Although he had been married and had a son, he appeared to be as romantically and youthfully in love with her as if they were both in high school.

A New Londoner who knew him well has said of O'Neill at this period, "He was always the gloomy one, always the tragedian, always thinkin'. My God, when that young Eugene looked at you he seemed to be lookin' right through you, right into your soul. He never said much, and he spoke softly when he did speak. Brilliant he was too, always readin' books. We're all Irish around here and know the type. He was a real 'black' Irishman."

(A black Irishman has a slightly un-Irish look about his face. Some attribute this to a possible Spanish strain, the result of Spanish garrisons in Ireland and the wreck of some ships of the Spanish Armada on the Irish coast. The typical black Irishman has black hair, dark eyes, and a mystic nature.)

In later years, one of Eugene's friends said that the playwright reminded him of a story told about the poet Dante. The people of Ravenna would cross the street when they saw the poet approaching. They didn't want to look into his eyes, which they believed had looked upon the horrors of hell.

"That's the way I feel about O'Neill," the friend added. "We'll be talking and he'll go into one of those long, staring silences of his, and I'll half expect him to turn to me and say, 'You're not a bad fellow, as far as I know, but if your eyes had seen what *these* eyes have seen, you'd go on home to your wife and children and not expect me to be nice.' "

On the other hand, to at least one of his girls at this time he was "a delightful companion. He was certainly not the gloomy pessimistic fellow that so many people have painted."

O'Neill's friendship with his Beatrice ended some two years after they met. She eventually married an officer, who later became an admiral, in the United States Coast Guard.

In the fall of 1915 O'Neill returned to New York and began his sojourn at the Hell Hole. He had written nothing since the spring. And for the next eleven or twelve months his principal literary occupation was reciting, from memory, Francis Thompson's "The Hound of Heaven" for the benefit of truck drivers, members of the Hudson Dusters (a notorious gang of Manhattan gangsters), the usual saloon down-and-outers, and some Negroes from the Ninth Ward. Mary

Heaton Vorse, who sometimes joined O'Neill and an old-time anarchist named Terry Carlin in the Hell Hole, wrote that it reminded her of a scene from Hogarth.

The Hell Hole, the last of O'Neill's series of Mermaid Taverns, was located at the southeast corner of Sixth Avenue and West Fourth Street. Above the main entrance on Sixth Avenue hung a weather-beaten sign showing the faded-gold silhouette of a swan. Inside, the place was dimly lighted by flickering gas burners. A pot-bellied stove provided warmth in winter. Next to it was a windowlike opening in the wall; by knocking on the panel in the opening, a customer could get someone to take an order for food. The bill of fare was always the same—stewed tomatoes, spaghetti, sandwiches.

Entering by the side door, or Ladies' Entrance, a customer might see a moth-eaten, dusty stuffed swan floating on a pond of painted lily pads; he would also see an open sink, with a cracked mirror above it and usually a broken comb, a piece of soap, and a dirty towel nearby. In the back room there was generally only a couple or two, who seemed to prize their privacy; but sometimes there would be a big, noisy party.

The proprietor was John Wallace, who owned the saloon and the building above it. He was assisted by two bouncers, one known as John Bull, the other as Lefty Louis. Wallace also seemed to support a half-dozen bartenders who doubled as porters and lived in the building. The boss would join certain favored guests in drinking, talking and quarreling. They "roared at each other," according to Mary Heaton Vorse, "like aged aurochs in the spring." Long after the official closing time of 2 A.M., Wallace presented each staggering regular with a pint of whisky as he left. It was "the hair of the dog"—supplied by the owner of the kennel.

The Hell Hole opened at 6 A.M. There were always drinkers who hadn't gone to bed and wanted one for the road, and red-faced cab and carriage drivers who wanted a morning pick-me-up. Throughout the day it was generally quiet, but at five it came suddenly to life and stayed lively until John Bull and Lefty Louis began tumbling the drunks out on the pavement. Those who sat quietly sipping their beers at two in the morning could stay on.

Although the Hell Hole was in the heart of Greenwich Village, O'Neill had very little contact with struggling artists and writers. The self-conscious Bohemianism of the Village was too arty and too effete for him. He had no liking for the long-haired men and short-haired women, no patience with their candlelight readings of poetry, and no sympathy with their grimly casual practice of free love.

O'Neill now had a three-dollar-a-month room, which he referred to as the "garbage flat" because he and his friends kept it well stocked with raw onions and oysters—his hang-over food—and perhaps because the peelings and shells were not always promptly disposed of. His friends were what he has called the true native Villagers, the Negro and Italian inhabitants. They were older than the people in the artistic groups and, of course, tougher. He found sympathetic spirits among the alcoholics and down-and-outers, the Wobblies and anarchists who wandered into the Hell Hole to drink and talk; but he remained too much of an individualist to subscribe to their doctrinaire political philosophies.

The unself-conscious, often primitive, behavior and talk of his acquaintances in a low-class saloon were O'Neill's best source material for his writing. But that was not what drew him there. O'Neill felt that in a saloon he "belonged." In the eyes of his barroom companions, people were divided into two classes—those who belonged to their world, and those who didn't. O'Neill did, they agreed. He was not a literary man, nor a Princeton-Harvard man, nor the son of a famous actor. To them, he was Gene, a regular fellow. He came closer to feeling at home in the Hell Hole than he did anywhere else.

There was nothing self-conscious about the Hell Hole as an authentic part of the lower depths. The people who frequented it had their own kind of integrity, did not wear masks, and were proud of being outcasts. Thieves could mention their thievery and sense no disapproval. Truckers boasted of swiping a case of this or that from wagons. Once, on a cold winter evening, O'Neill absent-mindedly came into the Hell Hole without a coat. The Hudson Dusters had come to feel a deep affection for him and one of their members discreetly asked him what size overcoat he wore. So that O'Neill would not feel himself a recipient of charity, the man explained that the proper-size coat, with the color and fabric of O'Neill's own choosing, would be "boosted" from some rich man's store. O'Neill was touched by this solicitude but explained that he had an excellent coat in his room.

A good example of this kind of humanity was Wallace's treatment of a certain Mrs. McCarthy. Every night for twenty years Mrs.

McCarthy came to the Hell Hole to fetch her "pint." Her pitcher held almost a gallon. It was always filled. The price of the "pint" was always put on tick—"iver since, mind ya', McCarthy was killed."

According to the late Maxwell Bodenheim, poet, writer, and vagabond, O'Neill sometimes regarded his drinking companions at the Hell Hole with "mild contempt" and was, in a way, spiritually detached from them. Bodenheim has recalled an evening when he was drinking with O'Neill and some of the Hudson Dusters in the Hell Hole. The Dusters were discussing with O'Neill a man named Scotty who had cheated some of the Dusters in a furniture transaction. Bodenheim wrote that O'Neill "managed to smother their rage and induce them to forego their intended vengeance. He did this with a curious mixture of restrained profanity, mild contempt, and blunt camaraderie which showed that he shared the spirit of these roughnecks and yet failed to share it."

Bodenheim did not view the Hell Hole with the enthusiasm of Mary Vorse or Eugene O'Neill. He noted "its cheap prints of race horses and chromos of unadorned women, its round, spotty tables, and the instrument of brazen agonies that played tunes of the day when you dropped a nickel into it." He also looked with some disapproval at O'Neill, whose spirit, he thought, was made up of a mixture of "articulate proletarian" and "surface poet." To Bodenheim, O'Neill was not in any sense a "social radical"; the workers in his plays were always individuals, not working-class types.

But Bodenheim, whose Verlaine-like life was to end in drunken violence, was strongly impressed by O'Neill's drinking habits. In the Bodenheim profile of O'Neill which appeared in *The New Yorker* in 1926, he said that O'Neill "could imbibe from twilight to dawn without showing any effects save those of an occasional irascibility." Bodenheim watched as O'Neill's "sallowly brown face, with its small, black mustache, long nose, and black eyes crammed with humorous contempt, would seem to grow metallic beneath his words, in spite of endless drinks that he consumed."

It was almost twenty-five years before O'Neill got around to saying what he had to say about the inhabitants of the Hell Hole. *The Iceman Cometh,* which he wrote just before World War II, was the Hell Hole and its clients put on the stage. The title, of course, refers to death; for death—the sudden or the lingering—were never far from the Hell Hole.

"They manage to get drunk," O'Neill wrote of his saloon companions, "by hook or crook and keep their pipe dreams and that's all they ask of life. I've never known more contented men."

They were also, he said, the best friends he ever had.

The Hell Hole was torn down in 1930, when Sixth Avenue was widened. But the institution had died long before, when Prohibition blighted the country. Mary Vorse checked as best she could on Wallace and his bouncers. John Bull was said to have been killed in a fight. Lefty Louis opened up a speakeasy. Wallace died when the drys took over; the idea of operating a speakeasy was abhorrent to him.

It has been assumed that the year in which O'Neill spent most of his time in a saloon was a protracted bender. O'Neill's good friend George Jean Nathan has printed many colorful and perhaps exaggerated details regarding the dramatist's heavy drinking. He wrote that O'Neill went on benders that lasted an entire month, that he would sleep next to a whisky barrel and consume an eighth of its contents during the night.

While Barrett Clark was trying to get accurate facts about O'Neill's life, he asked Nathan what personal matters he should discuss with the dramatist. "Ask him what he used to drink," Nathan advised. "I know he used to take his whisky straight, but in South America he must have had strange and wonderful concoctions. Remember, if he hadn't drunk the way he did and mixed with so many kinds of people in those early days we probably should not have had his plays."

When Clark followed up the suggestion, he received a temperance lecture. "Altogether too much damn nonsense," O'Neill told him, "has been written since the beginning of time about the dissipation of artists. Why, there are fifty times more real drunkards among the Bohemians who only play at art, and probably more than that among the people who never think about art at all. The artist drinks, when he drinks at all, for relaxation, forgetfulness, excitement, for any purpose except his art. You've got to have all your critical and creative faculties about you when you're working. I never try to write a line when I'm not strictly on the wagon. I don't think anything worth reading was ever written by anyone who was drunk or even half drunk when he wrote it. This is not morality, it's plain physiology. Dope I know nothing about, but I suspect that even De Quincey was boasting what a devil he was!"

Nathan explained this unexpected turnabout on the grounds

that "like many another reformed bibber, he now views the wine cup
with superior dudgeon and is, on occasion, not adverse to delivering
himself of eloquent harangues against it and its evils."

That liquor had a serious hold on O'Neill is unlikely in the face
of his work record. His indulgence probably did not often exceed the
bounds of social drinking. He liked to drink with other men who
were drinking. He liked the comradeship that went with it. He knew
that men in their cups reveal themselves without their masks. Furthermore, in the world of seafaring men, of down-and-outers, not to
drink is antisocial. It is true that a few drinks tended to set him off
on a drinking spree that might last several days. But he always returned to his writing after he recovered from the physical devastation
of his hang-over and from the anguish of his guilt. His saloon friendships exerted at least as much pull on him as the actual drinking.
Giving up drinking meant giving up the one world in which he felt he
"belonged." Nevertheless, this is what he did when the time came to
protect his health and to get important work done.

One of his friends of the Hell Hole was to play a significant role
in his life. This was the convivial Terry Carlin, a tall, gaunt Irishman
whom the artist Peggy Beard has described as "a beautiful skeleton."
There was a whitish cast to his face and the skin appeared to be
drawn tightly over his skull. It was said that he had been a radical
syndicalist and later a philosophical anarchist. In his youth, he told
friends, he had taken a vow never to do a day's work in his life. According to an account he gave Malcolm Cowley, the one day he
worked was when the boss of a saloon let him tend bar on a Saturday
when the rush was on. He said he had looked forward to emptying
the till toward the end of the day and pocketing what he found. But
the proprietor emptied the till before Terry got to it. The experience
further embittered him and he lived to be eighty without ever working again.

Terry was a great talker, although some who remember him feel
that his talent lay in getting other people to talk. By listening, he
acquired the reputation of being understanding as well as charming.
O'Neill often bought him drinks during his year at the Hell Hole.
Art McGinley has recalled that Carlin was welcome everywhere he
went. Susan Jenkins (then Mrs. James Light) remembers that Carlin
was "a great one for agreeing with you. He would say, 'Now you take
time. What is time, really? Time is only relative. Today on this earth
may be yesterday or a thousand years from now on the planet Mars.'

You might make some banal observation about time and he would say, 'That's a wonderful idea, how brilliant of you.' Then on he would go about time. In many ways, he was an awful bore."

Carlin knew a number of writers and artists who spent their summers in the little fishing village of Provincetown, at the tip of Cape Cod. Mary Heaton Vorse had met him during her labor reporting days and had introduced him to the Provincetown group. As a result, Terry had somehow acquired possession of a shack at Truro, several miles below Provincetown. Some say it was the hull of a wrecked ship.

As the weather grew increasingly humid in New York in the summer of 1916, O'Neill told Carlin he would like to get out of town. He said he felt that if he were up on the Cape and living by the ocean he could begin writing again. Carlin invited him to share his Cape Cod shack. Soon after they were settled there, O'Neill began writing another play on his dilapidated portable typewriter. Marriage and its difficulties were still on his mind. The play was *Before Breakfast;* it is about a man who commits suicide under his wife's nagging.

While O'Neill worked, Terry Carlin spent his time sitting on the ridge of Truro hill, reading Greek classics in the original. Later in the summer, they were joined by another Hell Hole habitué named Hippolyte Havel, a sleek, mustached ex-radical of Greek descent who also read antique Greek. Both Carlin and Havel, like so many of O'Neill's drinking friends, were to turn up as characters in *The Iceman Cometh*. Carlin was said to be the original for Larry Slade and Havel the original for Hugo Kalmar.

As the days wore on, Carlin decided to take a walk up to Provincetown to see some of his friends. He didn't know it but he was about to forge another link in the chain of events which would fasten together O'Neill's past life with his future. For of all the places in the world O'Neill should have been that summer, of all the people in the world whom he should have got to know, the village of Provincetown and its little summer colony of artists and writers were exactly right for him and his career.

Before Mary Heaton Vorse discovered Provincetown in 1907, it was almost entirely occupied by Portuguese fisherfolk. Cape Cod thrusts out sixty miles into the sea "like an arm with a fist on the end," as Mary Vorse described it—after Thoreau—and Provincetown is on the tip. The town is three miles long and two streets wide. There, around Mary Vorse, grew up a summer colony of artists and writers. Hamilton Basso has written that she bore the same relation to early Provincetown as did Eliza Pinckney to early South Carolina.

The summer before, in 1915, a group of artists and writers in Provincetown had taken to writing plays and acting in them. The group included Susan Glaspell, the novelist, and her husband, George Cram Cook, a poet and playwright; Hutchins Hapgood, novelist and essayist, and his wife, Neith Boyce; Wilbur Daniel Steele, author, and his wife; William Zorach, the sculptor, and his wife; Robert Edmond Jones, a stage designer, and John Reed, the journalist and radical and future author of *Ten Days That Shook The World,* the story of the Russian Revolution. Jig Cook, as George Cram Cook was called, was the leader of the group. The first two plays produced by the group were staged in the home of Hutchins Hapgood. In one scene, the sea was the background and the audience watched the performance from the porch. One of the plays was called *Constancy* and was written by Neith Boyce Hapgood as a take-off on the violent love affair between Mabel Dodge (later to become Mable Dodge Luhan of Taos) and John Reed. The second play, *Suppressed Desires,* by Jig Cook and Susan Glaspell, was a satire on Freud, whose writings were then beginning to sweep the country.

Suppressed Desires has become a kind of classic. Theater groups all over the country have continued to produce it. Susan Glaspell and Jig Cook had previously submitted it to Broadway producers, who were sure that people would not pay to go to see it because it was "too special."

Later that summer the group decided to put on their plays in larger quarters. Mary Vorse and her husband, Joseph O'Brien, owned a fishing wharf at Provincetown which they had purchased in 1913 for fifty dollars. Like other wharves which had become obsolete as a result of the decline of Provincetown as a port, it had been converted into accommodations for summer people. On these wharves were barnlike structures which had once been used as fishhouses, storage places for coal or lumber, or as places to stow nets and other fishing and sailing gear.

The Vorse fishhouse was fifty feet wide and a hundred feet long. The planks in the flooring were so far apart that one could see the sea beneath. It was in this fishhouse, named the Wharf Theater by Jig Cook and Susan Glaspell, that the Provincetown Players flowered, writing and producing the plays that changed the character of the American stage.

The Provincetown group was driven by a creative philosophy which held that "true drama is born only of one feeling, animating all the members of a clan—a spirit shared by all and expressed by the few for all." Jig Cook kept on dreaming of a "whole community working together, developing unsuspected talents." He hated "the commercial thing imposed from without." At the end of that first summer, he began thinking what the group would do the next year. He went to the wharf, "stepped" the fishhouse, and sifted in his mind new ways of staging future plays. "If there is nothing," he and Neith Boyce agreed, "to take the place of the common religious purpose and passion of the primitive group out of which the Dionysian dance was born, no new vital drama can arise in any people."

The next summer—1916—new members joined the group: Harry Kemp, the poet, and his beautiful wife, Mary Pyne; Louise Bryant, afterward the wife of John Reed; Frederick Burt, a writer, and the B. J. O. Nordfeldts. Still another newcomer was Edna St. Vincent Millay.

Early that summer, while Terry Carlin was taking his walk to Provincetown, he met Susan Glaspell and Jig Cook and the trio stopped to chat. It was one of those chance meetings that O'Neill believed were designed by the gods in shaping man's destiny.

"Terry," Susan Glaspell said, "haven't you a play to read to us?"

"I don't write," Carlin said. "I just think and sometimes talk. But my young friend, Mr. O'Neill, has a trunkful of plays with him."

"Then tell Mr. O'Neill to come to our place tonight and bring one."

Carlin said he'd deliver the message.

The play O'Neill brought to the group was *Bound East for Cardiff*. It was the play which Professor Baker of Harvard had read and pronounced "not a play." Most of the writers present at the Cooks' home for this first reading of an O'Neill play have used the same adjectives in describing the playwright—"shy, dark and good-looking." He was dressed in cotton trousers and a sweater. Most writers are only too happy to read aloud, but O'Neill surprised the group by asking that someone else read his play. Frederick Burt read *Bound East* while O'Neill stayed in the dining room. Mary Vorse sensed instantly that his "tough, hard-boiled pose covered extreme sensitiveness." There was not one person in the group, Mary Vorse remembers, "who did not recognize the quality of this play." In it, he had followed the 1913 advice of Clayton Hamilton, "Write down what you know about the sea, and about the men who sail before the mast. . . ."

The reading finished, everyone in the group rushed into the dining room to cover O'Neill with their warm congratulations. He was embarrassed but pleased, and he was to show his gratitude in the years to come—he was always intensely loyal to his friends in the Provincetown group, and he saw them until circumstances and illness broke the bond.

Of that fateful evening, Susan Glaspell has written, "Then we knew what we were for." And Mary Vorse wrote, "From that moment he took his place as an important writer."

In one respect he disappointed the group. He didn't sit around and talk about art and literature. Endless talk has always been one of the occupational vices of writers living in proximity. Here again he was following the advice of Clayton Hamilton, "Keep your eye on life—on life as you have seen it; and to hell with the rest!"

Hamilton observed with satisfaction the behavior of the thirty-year-old playwright after the Provincetown group took him up. "He can think [at Provincetown] his thoughts and dream his dreams, in loneliness, beside the surging and suggestive sea; and he can write great dramas which the silly little world that is centered in Times Square can subsequently look upon with wonder. Eugene O'Neill has always written with eyes focused upon life, instead of writing with eyes focused on the theater."

During that summer, as well as subsequent ones, Mary Vorse and the others read O'Neill plays—or portions of them—aloud. Once O'Neill himself read. Harry Kemp, the self-styled "Vagabond Poet," who sometimes seemed truculent about O'Neill's recognition, wrote that the play was "frightfully bad, trite, and full of the most preposterous hokum. It was, as I remember, something about an American movie man who financed a Mexican revolution for the sake of filming its battles. One of the scenes depicted the hero's compelling the commanding generals on both sides—both being in his hire—to wage a battle all over again because it had not been fought the way he liked it!"

O'Neill wrote *The Movie Man* while at Harvard. He sent it to the Library of Congress to be registered for copyright. The copyright, which expired in 1941, was not renewed. It was Archibald MacLeish who learned of its existence and the existence of four other O'Neill plays when he became Librarian of Congress in 1939.

The Movie Man was a poor play. It was a contrived, but honest, attempt to make fun of Hollywood, a place which O'Neill never had seen and always resolutely avoided later on. O'Neill knew the play was not successful and later said it was not to be printed. His failure to renew its copyright, however, made it possible for a publisher, years later, to print it without paying royalties.

Bound East for Cardiff, the first Eugene O'Neill play ever to be produced, was given on the second bill of the Wharf Theatre in Provincetown that same summer.

"It has never been more authentically played," Mary Vorse has written, "than it was by our group of amateurs, on the old wharf, with the sound of the sea beneath it."

Susan Glaspell also wrote movingly of that night:

> "It seems to me I have never sat through a more moving production than our *Bound East for Cardiff,* when Eugene O'Neill was produced for the first time on any stage. The sea has been good to Eugene O'Neill. It was there for his opening. There was a fog, just as the script demanded, a fog bell in the harbor. The tide was in, and it washed under us and around, spraying through the holes in the floor, giving us the rhythm and flavor of the sea while the big dying sailor talked to his friend Driscoll of the life he had always wanted deep in the land, where you'd never see a ship or smell the sea."

The warm reception in Provincetown of *Bound East for Cardiff* served to bring O'Neill back into productivity. He wrote four more one-act plays: *In the Zone, Ile, The Long Voyage Home* and *The Moon of the Caribbees.* They were all plays of the sea and he wrote them beside the sea. He also completed *Before Breakfast,* which the group decided to produce in New York during the winter.

O'Neill had not planned to accompany them to New York. Provincetown suited him, and he had taken an apartment over a grocery store. There, on the rafters, he painted some lines written by a Hindu mystic in a book called *The Illuminated Way:*

Before the ear can hear it must have lost its sensitiveness!

Before the eyes can see they must be incapable of tears.

Before the voice can speak, it must have lost its power to wound!

Before the soul can fly, its wings must be washed in the blood of the heart.

John Francis, the storekeeper and landlord, did not object. Francis liked and respected the artists and writers who came, in increasing numbers, to spend their summers in Provincetown. Sometimes he accepted paintings from artists in lieu of rent, and he is said to have acquired over the years an excellent collection of contemporary American art.

In that apartment O'Neill wrote tirelessly. As often as possible, he went to the dunes to stare at the sea, as though to draw spiritual strength from the sounds of the wind, the waves, and the crying of gulls. As long as the weather permitted—and even when any reasonably cautious person might have stayed indoors—he went swimming. He also liked to lie naked on the sand, and to paddle his little Eskimo kayak seaward.

His Provincetown friends were deeply impressed by O'Neill's moods, particularly his periods of black despair. "There was no such darkness as Gene's," Mary Vorse has said, "He would sit silent and suffering and in darkness." Part of his suffering and his uncommunicativeness was due to terrible hang-overs.

O'Neill's feeling of isolation from his fellow man at times reached morbid depths. He once told a friend that he thought it was a mistake that he had been born a human being. He wondered if he should not have been born a fish or possibly a seagull. In his lowest moments he wondered if he should have been born at all. These thoughts persisted even on the threshold of success. For now, in addition to the triumph in Provincetown—for triumph it was, considering the men and women involved in that pioneer theatrical venture—other recognition followed. Besides completing the four sea plays in the winter of 1916–1917, O'Neill wrote the short story entitled "Tomorrow." It concerned the Englishman he had known in his Jimmy the Priest's days; he called him Jimmy Tomorrow. *The Seven Arts* bought the story for fifty dollars, and it was published in the June, 1917, issue.

A few weeks later, George Jean Nathan and Henry L. Mencken bought *The Long Voyage Home* for their *Smart Set* magazine and paid O'Neill seventy-five dollars. It was published in October, 1917.

The Provincetown group had rented a run-down brownstone-front house in Greenwich Village and had converted the parlor floor into a theater seating some 150 persons. The house was located at 139 Macdougal Street, about two and a half blocks from the Hell Hole. At the suggestion of O'Neill the theater was named the Playwrights' Theatre.

In the late fall of 1916 O'Neill journeyed to New York to be present at the rehearsals of *Before Breakfast*. He also assumed the role of the husband, whose part consists of a few lines spoken from the wings. Someone in the group, without telling Eugene, had invited James O'Neill to the theater. At one of the first rehearsals of the one-acter there was an unhappy confrontation.

Helen Deutsch and Stella Hanau wrote in their history of the theater, *The Provincetown:* "Father and son, in a perfect Freudian pattern, disagreed on every point. O'Neill senior tried to instill in Mary Pyne (Harry Kemp's wife) some of the histrionic technique of an era which the Players had no wish to revive, while O'Neill junior stalked up and down, muttering his displeasure."

Before Breakfast consists entirely of a querulous monologue addressed by a nagging wife to her husband, who is off stage throughout the play (at one point his hand is seen as it reaches out from behind a door for his shaving bowl). Just before the curtain falls, the husband is heard to moan and the wife discovers that he has committed suicide with his razor. In the premiere Mary Pyne, with her beautiful red hair done up in an untidy knot, gave a fine performance as the ugly ill-natured wife. O'Neill played the off-stage husband and later said of his bit that it was his favorite role and "my last appearance on *any* stage."

Although this play was one of O'Neill's earlier ones—it was written in Provincetown in 1916—it is considered quite good. The monologue succeeds in drawing two characters in sharp relief and presenting a dramatic conflict between them. The idea for this play may have been borrowed from Strindberg's *The Stronger*, but it is on the execution that O'Neill is to be judged.

Two more of his plays, *Fog* and *The Sniper*, both one-acters, were produced after Christmas. O'Neill had definitely arrived on the theatrical scene. Of course, he was at yet unknown, except to a very few, and his plays were not bringing him any money at all, but he was writing steadily now, he was learning his craft in the living theater, and he was imaginatively interpreting his past experiences. The following March, accompanied by a writer named Harold de Polo, O'Neill returned to Provincetown, where a bizarre experience awaited both.

CHAPTER

NINE

ຽຽ

O'NEILL AND

THE WAR

Provincetown, in March of 1917, was full of anxieties and was seething with rumors about the coming war. One of them was that German spies were flashing lights along the coast, signaling to waiting U-boats.

Because O'Neill's apartment above John Francis' store was being redecorated, he and De Polo stayed at the New Central Hotel. With time on their hands, they took long walks along the shore. O'Neill regarded with a loving and covetous eye the abandoned Coast Guard station which Mable Dodge Luhan had remodeled, at Peaked Hill Bars, three miles outside Provincetown, on the lonely "back" or ocean shore of the cape. Sometimes, when the weather permitted, he took his portable typewriter in its black case out among the dunes and wrote.

The overly patriotic town constable, Reuben O. Kelley, became convinced that O'Neill had a wireless set and was sending and receiving messages from German submarines. On March 19 Kelley went to the New Central Hotel at noon and arrested O'Neill and De Polo. The Provincetown *Advocate* said the constable had picked up the two writers at the request of the U.S. Coast Guard Station at North Truro, where they had been seen wandering along the shore. Kelley, who had sought legal advice on the danger of being sued for false arrest, booked them on a charge of vagrancy and locked them up in the town jail. The Boston office of the United States Secret Service was notified of the arrest and sent Agent Fred Weyand to Provincetown to examine the rooms and papers of O'Neill and De Polo. It was not until ten o'clock the next morning that he got around to questioning them. Meanwhile, it was rumored in Provincetown that the pair had produced drawn revolvers when arrested, were armed to the teeth, and possessed complete plans for the capture of all Cape Cod harbors and towns as well as all its radio stations.

O'Neill and De Polo were brought before Judge Welsh in the Second District Court, were found not guilty of being vagrants, and were discharged. According to Mary Vorse, the Secret Service left an agent on duty in Provincetown with instructions to read all O'Neill's mail. The agent and O'Neill became good friends, however, and had breakfast together regularly at the Atlantic House. During breakfast, the agent would let O'Neill know what he could expect in the morning's mail.

"Well, Gene," the agent would say, "you got a letter from your mother, but your girl forgot you today. Someone sent you a knitted tie just the same."

That spring, O'Neill dramatized the theme of an innocent man accused of being a spy, in a one-act play, *In the Zone*. He placed the scene in the bunk room of a ship which is making its way through submarine-infested waters. The crew suspects one of their number of being a German spy because he has been seen frequently with a small black box, which he zealously guards. Finally, the man's shipmates grab him, take his black box and open it. Inside the box are letters and some rose petals, the cherished relics of a tragic love affair. One of the men reads the letters aloud—the girl loves the man very much but has given him up because she has learned that he has failed to stop his drinking. The seaman who is hearing his personal letters read aloud moans in anguish, while his bunkmates sit in ashamed silence.

The play was theatrically effective. Its sharpest impact came not from the spoken lines but from the physical action—when the accuser opens the sinister-looking box and a dried rose petal flutters to the deck. O'Neill later turned against the play because he thought it too facile, too conventional, "too full of clever theatrical tricks," but his greatest objection to *In the Zone* was that it became "a headliner in vaudeville." In the movie *The Long Voyage Home,* based on O'Neill's sea plays, the opening of the black box was used as a dramatic—or melodramatic—climax.

When on April 4, 1917, in response to President Wilson's message, the Senate approved a declaration of war against Imperial Germany by a vote of eighty-two to six, Provincetown, like the rest of the country, enthusiastically supported the President's idealistic objective of making the world safe for democracy. Thirty-eight was Provincetown's quota for the draft, but three hundred men enlisted. Although O'Neill had said bitter and cynical things about the war aims, he tried to enlist in the Navy, concealing his tuberculosis record. However, he was turned down for what he afterward referred to as "minor defects." The rejection distressed him so much that it kept him from writing. Though O'Neill would have willingly served in the Navy, the prospect of becoming a foot soldier held no appeal for him.

In June he went to New London to visit his family. He found that his father had boasted in print that the O'Neills were fighters. Although he himself was too old to serve, his two sons would most assuredly do their duty, he declared.

Eugene and his father found in the war another fertile field of disagreement. The more James O'Neill declaimed the virtues of patriotism, the more Eugene expressed antiwar sentiments. When he visited the New London draft board, he told the members that he had tried to enlist in the Navy but had been turned down. They told him that he was taking orders from the board, not the Navy; he would have to go into the Army.

Having his destiny taken out of his hands by New London "peasants" on the draft board infuriated Eugene. He told his father that he had heard that conditions in the Army camps were intolerable; men were dying like flies; anyone who was at all susceptible to tuberculosis was sure to perish. Becoming more heated by the moment, he said he would be damned before he would go into the Army. He was willing to serve his country, but he was not willing to commit suicide for it. He shouted that he would tell the draft board what they could do with their war. After calming down, he claimed exemption from the draft on the ground that he was an arrested-tuberculosis case.

Eugene was drinking heavily that spring and summer, more than at any time since he had gone to the sanatorium. He quarreled not only with his father but with Beatrice, his New London girl at the time. Their divergent views about the war was one cause of their breakup. Art McGinley has recalled that he never heard anyone speak so bitterly about the war as Eugene that early summer. One night James O'Neill, obviously distressed, called McGinley and asked him to meet with him. Eugene had again been talking wildly about the war, claiming that big business interests were behind it all. Eugene's talk, his father said, was seditious. He couldn't understand how a son of his could feel this way when he, the father, was such a loyal and devoted American citizen. Of course, he added, Eugene had been drinking heavily. The night before, during an argument, he had even smashed a few things in the house. But the old actor had not entirely lost his sense of perspective.

"I think perhaps," James O'Neill said, "New London is getting on Eugene's nerves. He told me last night that I was the worst actor in America. That's a terrible thing for a father to have to hear from the lips of his own son. But I'll say this for him, he did amend that a little. He said I was the second worst actor in the country. Corse Peyton, he said, was the worst."

McGinley agreed to get Eugene out of town. Eugene, who thought McGinley was a great wit and had often urged him to do some humorous writing, had invited him to Provincetown; now was the time to go.

They left New London at an early hour on a summer morning in 1917, and at Boston they boarded a boat bound for Provincetown. En route, Eugene handed his flask of whisky to members of the crew. Everybody was having a fine time, when the captain appeared and told Eugene and McGinley that he would put them in irons if they didn't behave themselves and stop giving the crew liquor.

When they arrived at Provincetown, they were greeted by a reception committee from the Provincetown Players—Jig Cook, Susan Glaspell, Mary Vorse, Wilbur Daniel Steele and Harry Kemp. The group proceeded to a saloon and a party began. McGinley was amazed at the devotion shown to his friend.

"These men and women," he said, "who had made their mark

in literature, in art, in music and the allied fields, had a profound respect for his opinions. I never knew anyone who had such an all-encompassing knowledge. Eugene was equally well-fortified if the talk happened to be of history, science, or government. It was all the more remarkable to me because he had virtually no formal education."

As McGinley got to know the Provincetown group, he became overawed by their high-sounding intellectual talk. He told Eugene that he felt mentally inferior to most of them.

"You don't have to feel inferior at all," O'Neill said to him. "What they talk about is all theory. It is not based on experience in life. You have had more experience in life and know more than they do."

Housekeeping at O'Neill's was somewhat informal. Once O'Neill put a potful of oatmeal on the stove for supper. Plans were changed and he went out to dinner. At the end of the summer the same oatmeal was still sitting on the stove.

O'Neill stopped drinking suddenly and went to work. He wrote all day and sometimes into the night. On especially hot days he took his battered portable typewriter off to the dunes, remaining out there until dark.

In getting down to work after a drinking spree, he was following a pattern he had established when he first came to Provincetown, the year before. He was to continue following it for a decade. After his sessions of drinking in New York or New London, he would return to Provincetown to fight his remorse and guilt and go to work.

Most of that summer of 1917, O'Neill struggled with another short story. This story, which contained the germ of the idea for *The Hairy Ape,* was never published. It dealt with a man's desire to belong. Wanting to belong and not belonging, not wanting to be alone and always being alone were themes O'Neill treated often in his work. That summer he felt particularly unwanted. The Navy had rejected him, his father was angry with him for his reluctance to go into the Army. His New London girl disapproved of him. Later, in letters, O'Neill compared his loneliness to his character's yearning "to belong."

Later in the summer, while he was sitting on the beach one day, he noticed a little boy playing near him. The child kept asking O'Neill the sort of simple but monumentally difficult questions that children ask. O'Neill was gentle and patient.

"What's beyond the ocean?" the boy asked.

"Europe," O'Neill said.

"What's beyond Europe?"

"The horizon."

"What's beyond the horizon?"

Beyond the horizon! The phrase stayed with him. It seemed the perfect title for a play he had been planning. In the months ahead he was to write that play and to test the ideas that had inspired it.

It has been said that to grasp the importance of the part played by the Provincetown Players (who, at O'Neill's insistence, called their theater in New York City the Playwrights' Theatre) one should try to visualize what the American theater would be today without their having existed.

The group's purpose, in the words of the constitution, was "to establish a stage where playwrights of sincere, poetic, literary and dramatic purpose could see their plays in action and superintend their production without submitting to the commercial manager's interpretation of public taste."

In less than ten years the Players produced ninety-three new plays and forty-seven playwrights. They erased the stigma attached to the word "amateur," for both Broadway producers and the theater-going public learned that these writers and actors who cultivated the theater for personal gratification were people of exceptional talent and ability.

By 1925 there were nineteen hundred "little" theaters throughout the country. The Provincetown Players had created such enthusiasm for drama that the decline of the touring companies was offset by community and college drama groups. The theater became less dependent upon the whims and decisions of the New York drama critics. The Washington Square Players, the Neighborhood Playhouse and the Theatre Guild all benefited from the Provincetown Players.

All this suggests that the Players' biggest achievement in relation to the American theater was that it introduced new ways of producing, staging and acting and, most important, new types of plays, plays with some depth, plays that had some relation to American life and thought, plays that formed the nucleus of American dramatic literature. Early in its existence, the group adopted the principle, strongly advocated by O'Neill, of producing only plays by American playwrights.

Perhaps the Provincetown Players' most signal contribution was Eugene O'Neill himself, but there were many others, among them e.e. cummings, Edmund Wilson, Edna St. Vincent Millay, Susan Glaspell, Edna Ferber, Virgil Geddes, Wilbur Daniel Steele, Mary Heaton Vorse, Harry Kemp, Paul Green, James Light, William Zorach, Alfred Kreymborg, Louis Wolheim, Walter Abel, Charles Gilpin, Aline MacMahon, Ann Harding. And the American theater owes an incalculable debt of gratitude to Eleanor Fitzgerald, who not only was one of the founders of the Provincetown Players but also held the many and diverse elements together and in working order.

Despite the war, the Provincetown Players carried on at 139 Macdougal Street in the fall of 1917. Their Playwrights' Theatre was attracting national attention. O'Neill came down from Provincetown to take part in rehearsals and, as a board member, to help shape plans for the new season. On one of his visits, he nearly lost his life in a scene of comic-opera violence.

An interesting character associated with the PP's, as they were called, was Christine Ell, a large woman with abundant red hair, a big mouth, and green eyes. She was neither writer nor actress but had a concession on the second floor of the theater to provide meals for the group at sixty cents a head. Her husband, Louis Ell, did some stage carpentry for productions.

Christine lodged her aged mother in a hall bedroom. Her mother regarded the entire group as not only godless but agents of the devil. One evening she learned that O'Neill had been encouraging Christine to read Nietzsche. Furious at this new attempt to corrupt her daughter, she rushed into a room where the group was gathered, wielding a meat cleaver and wearing only a suit of long woolen underwear. O'Neill tried to calm her but finally retreated.

"For a moment," according to the Misses Deutsch and Hanau, "the future of the American theater was at stake."

Later the group moved into a stable at 133 Macdougal Street, three doors away from the brownstone. While Louis Ell was helping to remodel it into a playhouse, he became annoyed at people leaving the door open. He posted a sign which read, "Cloze the door was you born in a stabel." A hitching ring had been left on one of the walls, and one of the group polished it, then posted a sign underneath reading "Here Pegasus was hitched."

The Players produced three of O'Neill's one-act plays that winter.

They were *In the Zone, The Long Voyage Home,* and *Ile,* all sea plays.

In *The Long Voyage Home,* Olson a sailor, yearns for the farm in Sweden where his mother and brother are living. (Every sailor means to go back to the land, but when he comes ashore with his pay he gets drunk, and back to the ship he goes.) Olson takes only a nonalcoholic drink and talks to a girl, Freda, of his farm and of his mother, who is old and might soon die. The girl slips a drug into his drink and Olson is shanghaied—back to the sea from which he was trying to escape—on a ship noted as the most wretched on the sea.

This play shows one half of what O'Neill has said about man's yearning for something "beyond"—the good life. The seaman yearns for the good life on the land, on the farm; the farmer yearns for something beyond the horizon, perhaps the sea or faraway places. Technically, the play is not well constructed, because, like so many of O'Neill's early plays, it relies on coincidence; Olson's tragedy is not the outgrowth of forces within himself. The dialogue is excellent, however, the characters come alive immediately, and the play is marvelously theatrical, accomplishing a great deal in relatively few lines.

When the movie *The Long Voyage Home* was made, this play gave the film its feeling—the sadness of the men who go to sea and hate it, always returning for one reason or another. O'Neill created a mood in this play that carried through *Anna Christie, The Hairy Ape* and several other of his more successful works. The play's ending can be justified if one considers O'Neill's later statement that retribution takes place in all his plays. Perhaps Olson's sin was that he tarried, talking to Freda, when he knew he should be returning to his mother. Freda is corrupted by greed for money. O'Neill was crystallizing a concept of life's tragedy, one which he would make ample use of in the future.

Ile, a one-acter written in the winter of 1917, is in a class with *The Moon of the Caribbees, Bound East for Cardiff,* and *The Long Voyage Home,* probably the best American one-act plays written up to that time. In the play a captain has taken his wife on the voyage. They have been at sea two years and are now waiting for an ice jam to break, and she is going mad, playing odd sounds on a hand organ. At first the captain refuses to head back for land, even suppressing a mutiny of sailors desperate for the sight of land, but when it becomes apparent that his wife is quite far gone, he relents. Then, suddenly, the ice breaks and whales are sighted five miles away. "I can't turn back now, you see don't ye?" he tells his wife, who is now quite insane, sounding wildly discordant notes on the organ. I've got to get the ile [whale oil]. Answer me! You ain't mad, be you?"

This is a play of sheer defeat. The captain's character is completely corrupted by pride and greed, and the sea wins. Again evil is punished (although it is not clear just what the wife's sin really is—perhaps her original romantic imaginings about the sea). *Ile* plays very well, for it is extraordinarily exciting, and the organ music is a surprisingly successful device.

Despite his position of pre-eminence with the Provincetown group, O'Neill had no enthusiasm for the art-for-art's-sake talk of its members after working hours; he still felt himself to be an outsider among them and preferred to spend his leisure hours among people with whom he felt more at home—usually at the "Hell Hole," which was nearby. Now and then, however, he would form a casual association with one or another of the many attractive women in the group. Only one such relationship was generally regarded as an "affair"— the one with Louise Bryant.

Miss Bryant had been married to a small-town dentist in the Midwest. She joined the Provincetown group early in 1916, and in the fall of that year the Players produced *The Game,* a play that she had written. She was tall and has been described as "pretty, with soft black hair and very blue eyes"; she also is said to have had an Irish beauty—which may have been one of her chief charms for O'Neill—and a volatile disposition. She was vigorously unconventional; according to Mabel Dodge Luhan, Miss Bryant contended that a woman could love two men at the same time and that she put that precept into practice in her relations with O'Neill and John Reed, the Harvard-educated radical and author of *Ten Days That Shook the World.* She had lived with Reed before the time of her reported romance with O'Neill, and as Reed's wife she later went to Moscow when Reed took a post with the Soviet government; she also remained with him there until his death in 1920.

Whatever the nature of O'Neill's association with Louise Bryant, it is known that he had more than a casual affection for her. Several women who knew O'Neill during this period have said he was not a ladies' man in the usual sense of the term, but "lovable," not exactly sensual, and capable of treating women as friends. "When you'd meet him," one of them has said, "he was like a loving brother. He would put his arms around you, maybe kiss you, but it only meant he wanted to be loving and affectionate. The women who ended up in bed with him were generally ones who had set their cap for him."

However that may be, it was in the fall of 1917 that O'Neill met the woman who was to become his second wife. He met her not in the Provincetown Playhouse but in the Hell Hole.

CHAPTER

TEN

৯৫

THE SECOND

MARRIAGE

Agnes Boulton Burton was a twenty-four-year-old widow with a year-and-a-half-old daughter when O'Neill met her in the fall of 1917. Of a Philadelphia family, she had been born in London on September 19, 1893, while her parents were abroad on a trip. Both her parents were of English descent. She was the great-niece of Margery Williams Bianco, the author of several classic children's books, whose husband, Francesco Bianco, wrote poetry in Italian. Agnes' father, Edward W. Boulton, was an artist of some distinction who had exhibited in both Philadelphia and New York. He had been a protégé of Frederick Eakins, whom he assisted in taking Walt Whitman's death mask. He helped found the Philadelphia Art Students League and was elected its first president.

Agnes was brought up by governesses in her very early years. Later she attended the Convent of the Holy Child at Sharon Hill near Philadelphia. Her mother, a Catholic, had dedicated Agnes to the Virgin Mary for the first seven years of her life. Her father, not a

Catholic, did not share his wife's deep faith. Agnes eventually drifted away from the Church.

She studied art at the Philadelphia School of Industrial Arts but changed her mind about being an artist and decided to become a writer. When she was sixteen she sold her first short story, and in a few years she was making a reasonably good living writing stories for the pulp magazines published by Frank A. Munsey. She also wrote literary short stories for *Smart Set* and other magazines. Two of her stories were included in the annual *Best Short Stories* collections of Edward J. O'Brien.

In 1917, Agnes was living on a 350-acre farm at Cornwall Bridge, Connecticut, near her father and mother, who had a farm in nearby Woodville. Now and then she would leave her baby daughter with her mother and go into New York to see magazine editors and look up old friends.

At the end of October, 1917, Agnes came to New York and took a room at the Hotel Brevoort. When she telephoned her friend Christine Ell, Christine suggested that Agnes meet her at the Hell Hole, describing it as "one of the new amusing Village hangouts." A lot of writers were congregating there, she said. Christine gave Agnes specific instructions on how to gain admission to "the back room."

Agnes arrived at the Hell Hole before Christine. The strange-looking clients and the sinister atmosphere of the place interested her. She particularly noticed a thin, dark-complexioned, mustached man who was casting glances in her direction. It is not surprising that Eugene O'Neill noticed this unfamiliar figure in the Hell Hole. Agnes was a strikingly handsome woman with a well-formed figure, dark-blond, wavy hair, clear blue eyes, and an interesting angular face with high cheekbones.

When Christine arrived, O'Neill walked over to their table. Christine introduced him to Agnes and he sat down with them. It was clear that he had been drinking, but he was not objectionable. One of his ways of entertaining his friends in the Hell Hole was to recite poetry. He particularly liked to recite the rolling, rhythmic lines of Francis Thompson's "The Hound of Heaven," which he had first read at Gaylord Sanatorium five years before:

> *I fled Him, down the nights and down the days;*
> *I fled Him, down the arches of the years;*
> *I fled Him, down the labyrinthine ways*

Of my own mind; and in the midst of tears
I hid from Him, and under running laughter. . . .

O'Neill must have recited it with more than ordinary barroom eloquence. One of his listeners about this time, a writer named Dorothy Day, was so stirred by his recitation in the Hell Hole that she says she took stock of her whole life and eventually embraced the Catholic faith. She founded and became editor of *The Catholic Worker,* and she established a settlement house for homeless men on New York's Bowery.

O'Neill later took Agnes to her hotel. When he said good night to her in front of the Brevoort he told her, "I want to spend every night of my life, from now on, with you. I mean this. Every night of my life."

The next night he met her at a party given by Christine Ell. Many of the Provincetown Players group were there—George Cram Cook, Lawrence Vail (who later married Kay Boyle), Mary Pyne, Susan Glaspell, Saxe Commins (who became O'Neill's lifetime friend and editor, and whose play, *The Obituary,* was produced by the Players in 1916), among others. O'Neill arrived late and drunk. In those days he carried a flask or a pint of whisky around New York to help him face people. Apparently, whisky helped him foster the illusion that he was a different person.

Many at the party immediately noted the resemblance between Agnes and Eugene's old love, Louise Bryant (who had gone off to Russia with John Reed). At one point during the evening, with a theatrical flourish he turned back the hands of a big clock and cried, "Turn back the universe and give me yesterday." He offered no explanation, but those who were present assumed that it was the time of his association with Louise Bryant that he wished to return to.

It seemed to Agnes that he wore "the mask or echo of a sardonic laughter, at times ribald and again becoming painful, etched on his restless face." She walked up to him and said, "Remember me?"

"It's a cold night—good night for a party!" he answered. "The iceman cometh." That was all they said to each other that evening, but already she loved him.

During the next weeks and months, Eugene continued to recite poetry to Agnes, making love to her with the words of Ernest Dowson, Byron and Shelley. She was struck by his painful shyness and his need for protection. Agnes saw in O'Neill a sensitive poet and also a revolutionary. Although he appealed somewhat to her maternal instincts, he was also a man—forceful and slightly rough. But what interested her more than anything, she has said, "is the creative thing in people, in artists and writers, the creative drive." She would cope with the world for him, for she believed that art was the ultimate reason for living. Agnes listened gravely, with a reassuring smile, as O'Neill talked. She exuded faith and hope and affirmation of life.

O'Neill spoke to Agnes of the terrors that stalked him. "He saw life as a tragedy and had neither the desire nor the curiosity to go beyond the limits of his own vision. He loved his own tragic conception of life and would not have given it up for the world." She greeted his fears and his searing depressions with friendly laughter. As he wrote to her, "With a laughing breath you blew my 'cursed hill' away and here we are!" Courting Agnes that winter, O'Neill appears to have been happier than he ever had been before, and yet he was an erratic lover. Once, after an all-night drinking session, he directed "a tirade against [her] in language that he had learned at sea" for no apparent reason at all. "He was full of spite (at times), even of hatred . . . and made ironic and unkind comments about supposed friends—people to whom he was charming face to face."

On the other hand, Eugene told Agnes shortly after he met her, "You are the only one who can make me sure of myself—sure about everything. . . . I want you alone—in an aloneness broken by nothing. Not even by children. I don't understand children, they make me uneasy and I don't know how to act with them." Like so many of Eugene O'Neill's words, these proved prophetic.

In that fall of 1917 O'Neill did very little writing, and toward the end of the season he grew uneasy. He wanted very much to return to Provincetown, and he wanted Agnes to go with him. He was in no financial position to marry, for the Provincetown Players paid no royalties; in fact, he still required the dollar-a-day allowance from his father. Nevertheless, Agnes agreed to go.

Before they could leave, however, Eugene had to keep a promise made earlier to spend an evening with a friend, Louis Holliday. He had been out of town and wanted now to celebrate the happy resolution of a romantic problem. On the day of Holliday's return Eugene saw him briefly and the two men arranged to meet again in the evening. But that date was never kept. Holliday's bright expectations were suddenly crushed by the woman he loved, and a few hours later he committed suicide in a Village restaurant. A friend who was with him then immediately rushed to O'Neill and asked him to hurry over to the restaurant. But O'Neill was so shaken—as he always was, in any association with death—that he refused. Instead, he went to the Hell Hole and got horribly drunk. It was several days later when Eugene and Agnes left for Provincetown.

They spent that winter of 1917–1918 in a stove-heated studio rented to them by John Francis, and they were very happy. In the spring they received word that the vaudeville rights to *In the Zone* had been sold. It was to play for forty weeks on the Keith-Orpheum circuit and royalties would be fifty dollars a week. Eugene at once asked Agnes to marry him. The details were arranged by Alice Woods Ullman, a writer whom Agnes remembers as a "charming woman with blond-gray hair and a gay, kind face . . . , pretty and bright-looking." On the evening of April 12, 1918, in the home of a Presbyterian minister Eugene and Agnes were married.

O'Neill had been writing steadily since his return to Provincetown, and early in 1918 he had completed two one-act plays, *Where the Cross Is Made* and *The Dreamy Kid*. In the former, the son of a retired sea captain is arranging with a doctor to have the old man committed to an insane asylum. We learn that the father had once been marooned on an island, where he found a great treasure and buried it, and that he had brought home a map showing where it lay. The captain later sent out a crew to unearth the treasure, but their ship was lost and all hands perished; after that, he gave his son a copy of the map and shut himself in an attic room, which is a replica of his ship's cabin. Now the old man has lost his mind, and the son is troubled by his own involvement in his father's dream—and greed. To free himself, he burns his map and resolves to devote himself to his own dream, the completion of a book which he has been writing.

Just as the asylum attendants arrive to take him away, the father dies. In his hand is another copy of the treasure map. The son sees it, his greed is reawakened, and he cries, "It isn't lost for me after all. There's still a chance—my chance. . . . I'll go and find it."

This is a far too obvious statement of the O'Neill theme that man is corrupted by the lust for gold. The characters announce their intentions to the audience before undertaking any action, and what with insanity, buried treasure and three maps, the long arm of coincidence suffers multiple fractures.

The Dreamy Kid is a melodramatic story, set in Greenwich Village, of a Negro murderer who returns home to see his dying grandmother. He is being pursued by the police, and his girl comes to warn him. He refuses to leave because, as he says, if he goes before his grandmother dies, her dying curse will bring him bad luck the rest of his life. The police come. His grandmother begs him to pray for her. She tells him he got the nickname Dreamy when he was a baby because of his "big eyes jest adreamin' and adreamin'." (The dialogue is in awkward Negro dialect—probably better spoken than read.) As the police make a noise outside the door, the grandmother dies. Dreamy holds his pistol in one hand and his grandmother's hand in the other. "Dey don't git de Dreamy! Not while he's 'live! Lawd Jesus, no suh!"

O'Neill thought well enough of the play to include it in the 1934 three-volume collection of his plays. It is not very profound and too obviously melodramatic.

O'Neill was working on *Beyond the Horizon,* Agnes was turning out pulp stories, and their lives were proceeding placidly enough when one day a letter arrived from Louise Bryant. She wanted Eugene back and wrote that she had come "three thousand miles across the steppes of Russia" to see him; he must meet her in New York right away. O'Neill was considerably disturbed. He let Agnes know that Louise had told him that although she was married to John Reed, he was ill and unable to have sexual relations. Understandably Agnes refused to let Eugene go to New York, but agreed to a meeting in Fall River. Louise was furious and soon returned to Russia. John Reed died in 1920, and in 1923 Louise married William C. Bullitt, later United States Ambassador to Russia. Years later they were divorced and she ended her days in the *bistros* of Paris.

It was not long after this that O'Neill completed a draft of *Beyond the Horizon.* He had got the idea for it from a Norwegian shipmate on the voyage from Buenos Aires to New York. The sailor habitually cursed the day when he left his farm and went to sea twenty years before. This was a familiar lament among seamen, and O'Neill realized that this man was too much "a creature of the God of Things as They Are" to have stayed at home. But the playwright began to speculate about "a more intellectual, civilized type" in a comparable situation. In such a man, the "inborn craving for the sea's unrest" would be "intellectually diluted into a vague, intangible wanderlust. His powers of resistance, both moral and physical, would also be correspondingly watered."

Out of this speculation grew the story of two brothers and a girl—Andrew Mayo, practical man and promising farmer; Robert Mayo, dreamer and poet; and Ruth, the girl who is expected to become Andrew's wife. Robert has signed up for a berth on his uncle's ship; he is about to begin his search for "the secret which is hidden . . . beyond the horizon." On the eve of his departure, however, he tells Ruth that he loves her, and she decides that she really loves him. She agrees to marry him, and Robert puts aside his dream of wandering. Andrew, when he is told about this, gives up his place on the farm and goes to sea in Robert's stead. A few years later Andrew, who has grown wealthy, pays a visit to the farm. Robert, who has inherited the farm, has ruined it by his mismanagement and has fallen ill of tuberculosis. Ruth has become embittered; she has come to hate her husband, and she now realizes that she should have married Andrew; but Andrew has long since recovered from the "silly nonsense" of love. In the final scene Robert drags himself to the crest of a hill, to look once more at his beloved horizon. Ruth and Andrew find him there. The dreamer tells his brother to be kind to Ruth because she has suffered; as for himself, he welcomes his approaching death as a release. Robert dies, and Ruth looks at Andrew "dully with the sad humility of exhaustion. . . ."

Beyond the Horizon, although it eventually won O'Neill his first Pulitzer Prize, cannot be numbered among his better plays. When he prepared it for publication, he cut one fifth of it. In addition to its prolixity (a weakness O'Neill was never able to overcome completely), the drama sinks beneath the weight of its allegorical intentions; the poet husband and the materialist brother become obvious representations instead of dramatically satisfying characters. However, as the sixth full-length play O'Neill wrote, it represents an important advance in his ability to deal with his own inner material.

One may speculate on the significance of this play in relation to O'Neill's own life at this time. He had just recently undertaken to settle down and stay put for a while. Perhaps he was again feeling that "inborn craving for the sea's unrest." And perhaps he imagined himself in the position of the character he visualized when he first thought of the play: a man who "would throw away his instinctive dream and accept the thralldom of the farm for—why, for almost any nice little poetical craving—the romance of sex, say." He certainly gave no indication of any dissatisfaction with married life in his inscription on the flyleaf of the book when *Beyond the Horizon* was published two years later. It read:

> To Agnes— This our play in memory of the old mad studio days when it was written—but much more in memory of the wonderful moment when first in your eyes I saw the promise of a land more beautiful than any I had ever known, a land of which I had dreamed only hopelessly, a land beyond my horizon.

O'Neill sent the manuscript of *Beyond the Horizon* to producer John D. Williams, who quickly took a six-month option on it, whereupon Eugene and Agnes left immediately for New York. They had planned to stay for two weeks, but Gene and his brother, Jamie, went on a week's bender at the Garden Hotel. At the end of their third week in New York, Agnes got Eugene back to Provincetown, and Jamie went with them. The three of them moved into Gene's old apartment above Francis' store, the brothers "dried out," and Gene went back to work. That summer he wrote much of *The Straw* and conceived *Chris Christopherson*. Jamie soon moved to an apartment next door, remained quite sober and spent the days pottering about the beach. He did not return to New York until the end of the summer, and the three lived in close amiability.

Jamie had been in love with Pauline Frederick, the actress, and they had been engaged. She told him he would have to choose between the bottle and herself, and Jamie chose the bottle. "Pauline is just an image that you fool around with in your sentimental moments," Gene told Jamie. "You convince yourself that if she married you, you wouldn't be hanging on to Mama and letting her secretly hand you out a quarter a day." Jamie's devotion to his mother was perhaps unnatural.

Eugene and Agnes often took long walks along the Provincetown dunes, and occasionally they walked out to the Peaked Hill Bars Coast Guard station, which was buried up to the windows in sand drifts. It had been completely redecorated and they both thought it would make an ideal home, as it would afford O'Neill the complete seclusion he needed for his work. In order to get to it, one had to walk or ride horseback. If they ever got hold of enough money, they would buy the place.

They returned to New York in November when Jim Cook urgently requested O'Neill's presence at rehearsals of *Where the Cross Is Made*. There was something about the city that invariably brought out the worst in O'Neill. The Provincetown group held a party to welcome back their playwright, and sometime during the evening Eugene took violent exception to Agnes' supposed attentions to Teddy Ballantine, an actor and painter. He swung his arm "as hard as possible" and hit her across the face with the back of his hand. Later, after Agnes had returned to the hotel, Eugene turned up full of whisky and remorse. "I saw a sick man standing in front of me," she says. She had seen him tortured and bitter, but she had never expected to see his bitterness turn against her. It was only the beginning.

The next day Eugene was in no condition to visit his parents at the Prince George Hotel, as had previously been planned. Agnes phoned them and made the excuses—something she was to do very often during their ten years of marriage. They went the following day, though. Agnes found the O'Neills a sweet, attractive, charming elderly couple, and James and Ella were delighted with their daughter-in-law. "There was certainly no indication," Agnes has said, "when I saw Ella then, or later, of any drug addiction. I recall that Gene had talked vaguely about his mother having had some trouble with drugs many, many years before. She was in fine shape when I saw her. Nothing in her behavior seemed unusual. . . . She was a beautiful person." The visit was somewhat marred when Jamie turned up drunk.

Several days later, Eugene and Agnes went to Old House, the Boultons' summer home at West Point Pleasant near Barnegat Bay in New Jersey. It is an old farmhouse with big rooms heated by fireplaces and stoves and a large studio with a skylight. Point Pleasant is less than two hours by train from New York, and O'Neill was able to get into the city, when necessary, and return the same day. At the end of November he was traveling into New York to attend rehearsals for *Where the Cross Is Made* and hurrying back to Agnes in Point Pleasant, where he continued to work on the first draft of *The Straw*. A full-length play based on his experiences at Gaylord Farm Sanatorium, it was the first play in which he expressed a strong affirmation of life. *The Straw* and *Ah, Wilderness!*, which he wrote much later, are often coupled together as the only plays in which O'Neill did not project the theme of defeatism which dominates his work, although *Lazarus Laughed* is suffused with a fatalistic optimism about Life with a capital "L." Agnes was at least partly responsible for the strain of hope in *The Straw*.

Life wasn't as grim as he made it in his plays, she often told him. O'Neill agreed that the way things were going for Agnes and himself, life was good. In his plays, he said, it was a matter of "Life is a tragedy. Hurrah!" This became a private joke between them and was called upon during rough times.

Unquestionably O'Neill's plays reflected his state of mind when he was working on them, and a good index to his marital happiness that winter when he was writing *The Straw* is the last line of the play. The heroine tells Stephen (a thinly disguised Eugene O'Neill of the sanatorium days), "I'll have to look out for you, Stephen, won't I? From now on."

Things were looking up for O'Neill. Boni and Liveright scheduled a book containing six of his one-act plays—*The Moon of the Caribbees, In the Zone, Where the Cross Is Made, The Rope, The Long Voyage Home,* and *Ile.*

The Moon of the Caribbees opens with an odd singing effect, keening (an effect very much like the organ in *The Long Voyage Home* and the drumbeats in *The Emperor Jones*). A ship is docked in the Caribbees and a native funeral is in progress on shore. Some native women come aboard offering rum and their bodies for sale, and there is a knife fight and a riot. One sailor, incidentally, calls another a "hairy ape." Smitty, "the exquisite Englishman" O'Neill had met in Buenos Aires, is an alcoholic, pining away for the love of a good woman in London. His memories haunt and torture him (in much the same way as Jamie O'Neill was tortured). After the riot, Smitty staggers back to his bunk, and in the stage directions O'Neill wrote that on the boat deck there was silence, broken only by the brooding music. It is far off now, getting fainter "like the mood of the moonlight made audible."

This is a successful play. The seamen immediately characterize themselves vividly, the violent action seems plausible enough, and the over-all mood is intense and real. O'Neill himself attached great importance to *The Moon* because it was his "first real break with theatrical traditions. Once [I] had taken this initial step, other plays followed logically." How rapidly O'Neill was improving is evident if one compares his first sea plays (*Warnings, Thirst, Fog*) with the plays of the Glencairn cycle.

The Rope is particularly interesting because it anticipates one of O'Neill's best plays, *Desire under the Elms*. Here, too, is one of his favorite themes—the corruption of character by greed. This is the story of Abraham Bentley, a miser and Scripture-quoting New England hypocrite, who owns a farm bordering on the sea. He has been married twice and has a daughter by his first wife and a son by the second. The son steals money from his father and runs away, and Bentley puts a rope, fashioned into a noose, in the barn. He tells his daughter that the son must use the rope to hang himself. When the prodigal son returns he makes a pact with his sister and her husband to torture the old man into revealing where he has hidden some new money obtained from mortgaging the farm. Meanwhile, an eight-year-old grandchild wanders into the barn and plays with the rope, which "seems to part where it is fixed to the beam. A dirty gray bag tied to the end of the rope falls to the floor with a muffled, metallic thud." Mary, the child, is delighted because she discovers the gold pieces are better than skipping-stones. One by one, she skips them into the ocean, and the play ends.

The Rope, written in the winter of 1917–18, was the last of *The Moon of the Caribbees* cycle of plays. Despite its easy ironies, the play is impressive, not only as a prelude but in its own right.

There was another sign that winter that O'Neill's literary fortunes were on the rise. John D. Williams gave him a contract, which called for the production of *Beyond the Horizon* and gave Williams an option on all O'Neill's future plays.

Meanwhile, O'Neill was writing one of his great and enduring successes, drawn from his experiences at Jimmy the Priest's. He titled this play *Chris Christophersen*. Later he learned from the American-Scandinavian Foundation that the last syllable should be spelled *son*. This play was rewritten and produced as *Anna Christie* in 1921. (In 1957 it was made into a musical comedy called *New Girl in Town*.)

Chris was an actual person, with the same name, whom O'Neill had once known. "He had followed the sea so long," O'Neill said of the real Chris, "that he got sick at the thought of it. When I knew him, he was on the beach, a real down-and-outer. He wouldn't ship out, although it was the only work he knew, and he spent his time getting drunk and cursing the sea. 'Dat old devil,' he called it. He got terribly drunk down at Jimmy's one Christmas Eve and reeled off at about two o'clock in the morning for his barge. On Christmas morning he was found in the river, frozen to death. He must have fallen in."

Eventually, Anna Christie, whom O'Neill created as a fictional daughter of Chris Christopherson, came to dominate the play. Her father had deserted Anna and her mother in Sweden and had gone off to sea. After the death of Anna's mother, Chris brought the child to America, to live with relatives on a Minnesota farm. There she was debauched by her cousins and fled to the city, where she got a job as a nurse in a family home. There, too, she was violated by the men of the family. Again she fled and she eventually turned to prostitution. Finally she seeks out her father and, when the two meet, Chris tries to explain why he deserted her when she was a baby, and why he did not keep in touch with her after her mother's death. The best explanation he can give is "dat ole davil sea make dem crazy fools with her dirty tricks." In the barge home of her father, Anna meets the stoker Matt Burke, and the two fall in love. She is purified by her love and by her wholesome contact with the sea, and the two lovers are betrothed as the story ends.

Despite its Hollywood ending, *Anna Christie* is a fine play. The dialogue is immensely improved, becoming lyrical and dramatic at the same time; the characters are simply themselves and yet representative of all that O'Neill thought was inherent and inescapable in human nature. To a vast public, Anna has become well known in the likeness of Greta Garbo, who portrayed her so effectively in the motion picture. Like Tennessee Williams' Blanche DuBois, Anna is an instantly memorable person, one of O'Neill's truly great creations. The direct force of her characterization in the development of the play overcomes the premise of a somewhat gaudy background. She is what she is, and there is no denying Anna as an unforgettable personality in dramatic literature.

O'Neill felt that he had lost face, especially with his literary friends, because of what the critics called the play's "happy ending." Couldn't people understand that ultimately the Furies would get Anna and her sailor friend? "The decision," he wrote, "still rests with the sea, which has achieved the conquest of Anna." He explained to

George Jean Nathan, "The happy ending is merely the comma at the end of a gaudy introductory clause with the body of the sentence still unwritten."

There was still a very much unwritten sentence in O'Neill's own life. Like Chris, O'Neill had deserted his wife and baby and gone off to sea, and had seen his baby just once. Eugene junior was living with a man he thought his real father. Years later, when the sentence was finally completed, there was no happy ending. There have been no happy endings for any of the O'Neills.

CHAPTER

ELEVEN

ॐ

DEATH OF THE

COUNT

Eugene O'Neill said that he wanted to show in his plays the impelling, inscrutable forces behind the things that happen in life. He was always acutely conscious of what he called the Force. He was not sure whether this Force was Fate or our biological past creating the present, but he believed strongly in a central mystery that often revealed itself through accident.

It may have been that on December 6, 1918, some such compelling, inscrutable force caused James O'Neill to be struck by an automobile. He and Ella were getting off a streetcar at Broadway and Twenty-seventh Street. They had been on their way to their hotel, the Prince George at Twenty-eighth Street just east of Fifth Avenue. Helped by passersby, James and Ella took a taxi to the hotel, where a doctor found lacerations of the hands, knees, and right foot. Although the doctor said that the injuries were not as serious as was at first expected and that the seventy-three-year-old actor would be out of bed in a day or two, James O'Neill never fully recovered.

Eugene and Jamie hastened to their father's bedside. So that he might get to New York more frequently—partly on his father's account—Eugene stayed at West Point Pleasant well into the spring, instead of proceeding to Provincetown. During that winter he had been working steadily on his play about Chris, and in April he completed it. He had it typed and he arranged for a copy to be sent to Nathan. He noted in his letter to Nathan that Williams' dilatory tactics had driven him to using an agent—the American Play Company. Meanwhile, he was sending along two copies of the newly published book of his plays, *The Moon of the Caribbees,* for Nathan and Henry L. Mencken. Eugene wanted to show his gratitude to the two editors for their encouragement and constructive criticism. He had not yet met either of them in person, and he told Nathan that he would drop around at his office in the hope of meeting him. He also wrote Barrett Clark and George Tyler, his father's old producer, that he would like to see them while he was in New York.

In March, 1919, Agnes learned that she was pregnant. The doctor told her the baby was due about the first of October. Unlike most expectant mothers, Agnes did not rush home to tell her husband the good news. But then, the O'Neills were not only unlike most people; they were unlike everyone else. They lived in a world of their own making. Eugene had just received a most encouraging letter from Barrett Clark and he was finishing the last scene of *The Straw.* Agnes did not want to disturb him, and she remembered that he wanted her alone, without children. She told him the next day. "His first reaction was that the doctor had made a mistake; his second reaction was silence."

The elder O'Neills, however, were made very happy by the news. Perhaps, at last, their strange, wayward, wandering son was going to settle down with this nice woman and have babies and live like a proper Irish Catholic.

Eugene and Agnes went to New York for several days during the middle of May, 1919. O'Neill dropped around to the *Smart Set's* "editorial chambers," as Nathan called his offices, at Eighth Avenue and Thirty-fourth Street.

"I found O'Neill to be an extremely shy fellow," Nathan has said, "but one who nevertheless appeared to have a vast confidence in himself."

Nathan was a man who appeared to have a vast confidence in himself, too. He was dark and handsome, and he probably was the most urbane man in American letters; he had a patrician manner, a quiet but mordant wit, and a long black cigarette holder. Nathan, an acquaintance has remarked, was a connoisseur, a gentleman and a scholar.

O'Neill and Nathan liked each other immediately and chatted for almost an hour. They had in common a strong desire to get serious drama onto the American stage. Before O'Neill, the American theater had been cheap, sentimental and tawdry. It was "afraid of its own emotions," as Eugene said, and Nathan could not have agreed with him more. It would not be too great an exaggeration to say that the emergence of an important American theater is due in very great measure to the efforts of these two men—O'Neill with his honest and moving dramas, Nathan with his pointed criticism and his belief in O'Neill as the first fine American playwright.

O'Neill promised Nathan that he would show him everything he wrote. "This he did," said Nathan. "O'Neill is a deep-running personality—the most ambitious mind I have encountered among American dramatists—an uncommon talent." Eugene found the critic "warm and friendly and human," and he admitted that he had been "three-quarters blotto" at the encounter. Later, Nathan wrote O'Neill to say that he was glad to know that Eugene was as proficient at drinking cocktails as he was at concocting dramas. The suspicion remains that, despite the cordial correspondence between the two men, O'Neill had been very nervous about meeting the formidable Nathan.

Before O'Neill and Agnes left for Provincetown, Eugene arranged to have *The Straw* typed. It began to go the rounds of the producers. Williams had turned down *Chris,* but he had liked *The Straw.* He did not take an option on it, however.

It was James O'Neill's old friend, Tyler, who showed interest in *Chris.* Tyler, a veteran Broadway producer since the 1880s, had been the producer of some of the elder O'Neill's plays, and he had been on tour with James and Ella when Eugene, then a year-old baby, turned almost black in a Chicago hotel room. Tyler went out in search of a doctor at four o'clock in the morning. Ella was frantic; she thought Eugene was dying, but the doctor said it was only colic. In later years Tyler enjoyed kidding Eugene about saving his life.

Tyler also had some criticisms of *Chris,* and all through the summer and into the fall O'Neill rewrote the play to accord with Tyler's views. The trouble lay in the ending, which Tyler felt should be strengthened. He also objected to the fact that Chris was left in the last scene with very little to do or say. In one version, O'Neill made the climax of the play what one director called a "rather theatric and ultimately futile attack with a knife." William Farnum was asked to play Chris but, although he liked the play, he was unable to fit it into his schedule. Later, Emmet Corrigan was hired. It was O'Neill's opinion that, from an artistic standpoint, Corrigan was better than Farnum, who had spent too many years in Hollywood.

In May, Eugene and Agnes went to Provincetown again and were met at the station by John Francis. Gene had asked him to find a house for rent on the dunes. Francis told them they didn't have to rent a house, and he handed them the deed to the Peaked Hill cottage that Gene had mentioned to his parents as a place he longed for. He had also let it be known that it was for sale. Ella had convinced James that Eugene needed a home for Agnes, and James had sent Francis a check in full payment for the house and had had the deed made out in the name of Eugene Gladstone O'Neill.

The description of the property lines in the deed used words which, in a very real sense, also describe the boundaries of the murky, lost world of Eugene O'Neill and his plays: "Bounded on the East by land unknown . . . on the South by land unknown . . . on the West by lands unknown . . . bounded on the North by the Atlantic ocean. . . ."

The place had been owned by a wealthy New York financier and art patron named Sam Lewisohn. Mabel Dodge had lived there for a short time with her painter husband, Maurice Sterne. It was she who had first found the place, in 1914. Then, it was half covered with sand, "lonely and aloof on the high sand above the beach, wild enough to suit anyone." Sam Lewisohn, a friend of Sterne's, told her to buy and do over the station and they would take turns using it as a summer place. He would pay the bills.

It turned out that the building was in excellent condition, tight and shiplike. Mabel Dodge had had the interior walls painted white and blue and the hardwood floors cleaned and waxed. From Boston she had sent down a complete set of Italian dishes decorated with fish. At the end of the living room she had built a great brick fireplace. She had furnished the room with low couches and cushions in blue and white; two of the couches were from the "Ark," the home of Isadora Duncan. There were also huge majolica platters hung here and there. She had even had books on the sea placed on the bookshelves.

Eugene and Agnes settled at Peaked Hill. Once a week they walked to town and then, laden with groceries, hired a wagon to take them back. O'Neill was delighted with his new home—his first home, actually—and told friends that it was a strange toy which Sam Lewisohn, "the millionaire," had fixed up and had grown tired of. He boasted of having the Atlantic as his front lawn and miles of sand dunes as his back yard. He didn't have to wear clothes, as there were no houses within sight and there were none of "the unrefined refinements of civilization." He described the three-mile walk to town, up and down over sand dunes, as the penalty one paid for communication with the world of people.

At the end of September, John D. Williams, the producer, who still held an option on *Beyond the Horizon,* told O'Neill he was about to begin casting the play. Then he procrastinated. Tyler, meanwhile, was still holding back on the production of *Chris.* O'Neill with two proposed Broadway productions, was just on the edge of the big time, but he couldn't seem to get over the edge.

He and Agnes moved into Provincetown, where they rented a heated house from a Portuguese fisherman. He wrote Tyler he could not go to New York for the rehearsals of *Chris.* Hadn't the Governor, as he called his father, told him he was going to have a grandchild? O'Neill was saying, at the end of September, that he expected the child any day and that he wanted more than anything to remain with Agnes during her confinement. Really, Agnes has said, he wanted more than anything to get his work done. He used her pregnancy as an excuse. The Provincetown Players produced *The Dreamy Kid* in New York on October 31, but O'Neill did not attend those rehearsals either.

At this point, Williams offered him a small advance on *The Straw* but Eugene turned the offer down. He asked Richard Madden, his play agent, to send the script to Tyler. Tyler wrote that he had the script and was praying for Agnes and her unborn child. In thanking him, O'Neill made a special plea that he read *The Straw.* In many of his letters, O'Neill has indicated that he believed few producers or actors read the plays that were sent to them. He said *The Straw* was ten times better than *Chris.*

All during September, O'Neill worried not only about the coming birth of his child but about money. *In the Zone* was no longer bringing him royalties. The flu epidemic had cut audiences down, and with the ending of the war the play had become outdated. Tyler offered to let him have some money, but O'Neill refused. If he did reach such dire straits where an SOS was necessary, he wrote, he would apply to Tyler, not as to a theatrical manager but as to a friend.

Early on the morning of October 30, 1919, Agnes gave birth to their long-awaited baby. Being overdue, he weighed about ten pounds. His voice carried, O'Neill told a friend, farther than his old man's. O'Neill had asked James Stephens, the Irish poet and novelist, with whom he had corresponded, for some good Irish names. Stephens had sent him a list of first names for both sexes, among them the one O'Neill chose for his new son, Shane Rudraighe O'Neill. He was a dark-haired, delicate-featured little baby with black eyelashes. He was, in fact, a black Irishman like his father; even as a baby he had what O'Neill often referred to, in descriptions of the characters in his plays, as an "Irish look." He sent word to Tyler that the great event had taken place, and that now he knew that "a theatrical manager's prayers are given the big time on High." If O'Neill thought of his first son, Eugene junior, at this time, he never mentioned it to anyone.

In November Tyler read *The Straw,* liked it, and said he would produce it. He thought, and O'Neill agreed, that it should come into New York in the wake of *Chris.* On November 13, Tyler gave O'Neill a check and a contract for the production of *Straw.* O'Neill, in thanking Tyler, said he was glad he had not had to borrow money from anyone during this trying period. He knew that if he had appealed to his father he could have had money, but he would never allow himself to need money that much. Meanwhile, although O'Neill now had three plays under contract, none seemed to be going into production. Williams had still not cast *Beyond,* which he had been sure he was going to open that fall. Tyler was still having trouble with the script of *Chris.* In the last scene of the latest rewrite, Chris was to call out "Dat ole davil sea, she ain't God." O'Neill was for having a steamer's whistle answer just before the collision. There would be an impressive pause that would give suspense before the curtain. But the actors objected; they wanted, not silences, but something to say. Tyler confessed it was extremely difficult trying to get the play into shape without having O'Neill on hand.

It is scarcely any wonder that O'Neill spent the winter working

on a play he called *Gold*. The last act of the play is a rewrite of
Where the Cross Is Made. The old sea captain confesses that he
murdered two men where the treasure is buried. He has saved a bit
of the treasure and, dying, he shows it to his son, who tells him that
his "gold" is worthless junk. The old man dies, the son is saved,
sobbing, "What a damn fool I've been." The corruption of character
by greed is a theme underlying many of O'Neill's plays and *Gold* is a
blatant example. Nathan thought *Gold* showed an advance in O'Neill's
work but Barrett Clark disagrees, saying that in none of his previous
plays were O'Neill's "basic shortcomings as a playmaker more strikingly evident."

Gold is a very poor play indeed, awkward and unconvincing
in every aspect. Naturally, it possesses the same faults as *Where the
Cross Is Made*. The plot is so contrived that the characters could
not be made convincing or sympathetic even if their dialogue were
good, which it is not.

O'Neill well knew the power for evil and the cancerous corruption
that can lie in both the possession of money and the striving for it.
If anything was successful, if it made money, O'Neill was suspicious.
Even when some of his own work was commercially successful, he
was troubled. "When everybody likes something," he often told
friends, "watch out!"

Williams eventually put *Beyond the Horizon* into rehearsal in
January, 1920. He began the O'Neill invasion of Broadway by
stealth. His plan was to offer the play in a series of matinees. If it
looked as if it were going to be successful, he would put it on at night.

O'Neill, leaving Agnes and Shane in Provincetown, in the care
of a nurse, went to New York. He managed to attend rehearsals and
also to see a good deal of his mother and father at the Prince George.
For the first time in his life he was beginning to come to terms with
his father. The old actor's respect for Eugene had been mounting
steadily in proportion to the attention that professional producers
were giving to his son's plays. James O'Neill was far more interested
in a play's commercial success than in its artistic merits. Furthermore, it looked as if his son had finally settled down. Certainly he
was working hard.

James O'Neill's pride in his son reached a climax when *Beyond
the Horizon* opened at a matinee performance on Saturday, February
2, 1920, at the Morosco Theatre. Richard Bennett, who had helped
persuade Williams to produce the play, was the lead. James not only

attended the opening but took an entire box. Seated with the happy, smiling old actor were his wife, Jamie, George Tyler and other friends.

James O'Neill was probably not aware of it, but he was seeing the passing of his kind of American theater with its old-fashioned, flamboyant acting. Melodrama, pathos, blood and thunder, hearts and flowers were already a little passé. They were yielding to the neo-realism—to the interpretation of contemporary experience—that constitutes the serious aspect of Broadway today, and which his son was inaugurating. Naturally, *Beyond the Horizon* puzzled James O'Neill with its sadness, its frustrations, its tragic ending. It was easy for him to sense that the audience responded well, but his reaction was unfavorable according to Eugene's report of their conversation after the performance. "It's all right," the old man said, "if that's what you want to write, but people come to the theater to forget their troubles, not to be reminded of them. What are you trying to do—send them home to commit suicide?"

"I didn't try to answer my father," O'Neill later commented. "He and I hadn't got along so well. We had had a running battle for a good many years, and I know there were times when he's just about given me up. Not that I can blame him. If anything, he was too patient with me. What I wonder now is why he didn't kick me out. I gave him every chance to. And yet, as sometimes happens, we were close to each other—we were a very close family. My father, somehow or other, managed to believe in me.

"When he read the plays in *Thirst,* which he hadn't seen before they were published, he threw up his hands. 'My God!' he said. 'Where did you get such thoughts?' But he encouraged me to go ahead. I didn't expect him to like *Beyond the Horizon,* which wasn't the sort of thing he *could* like, so I wasn't surprised by what he said. All the same, I think he was pleased."

At The Players, the actors' club on Gramercy Park, where James occasionally dropped in for a drink, he reveled in the role of the proud father. He was particularly pleased when it was announced that *Beyond the Horizon* had been awarded the Pulitzer Prize for Drama. Clayton Hamilton was one of those who congratulated James on his son's success, as they stood at the bar in The Players. Hamilton, too, felt pride in the young playwright, whom he rightfully regarded as a protégé. James O'Neill became expansive with fatherly pride.

"My boy Eugene—I always knew he had it in him!" the old man

said. "I remember, Clayton, how I always used to say that he would do something big some day. People told me he was wild and good for nothing, but I always knew he had it in him, didn't I?"

Hamilton did not remind him that he could remember a day when the father was convinced that Eugene would never amount to anything.

Soon after the opening of *Beyond,* Williams put it on the boards six nights a week. It ran for 111 performances. The box-office gross was $117,071. Eugene's share, including out-of-town performances, was $7,600.

Although this was one of the happiest periods in Eugene's life, his finely attuned ears heard the distinct roll of thunder. You always paid for success—hadn't he said so himself? For one thing, he was having misgivings about whether *Beyond* was really a good play, despite the fact that it had been hailed enthusiastically. Some of Eugene's friends had reservations. Barrett Clark thought *Beyond* was "overpraised and too long," and Richard Dana Skinner said it was the first fully rounded, "if somewhat vague, statement of the poet's problem." True, George Jean Nathan and Clayton Hamilton praised the play without reservation.

"The people of this play," Hamilton wrote, "are absolutely real and utterly alive. The action is absorbing from the outset. The dialogue is masterly in its simplicity and in its strict fidelity to character. Here is a play which Americans may well be proud of. It is the first great tragedy that has been contributed to the drama of the world by a native American playwright." But Nathan and Hamilton had been on his side from the first and, like so many artists, good and bad, Eugene continued to have self-doubts. Perhaps if no one had liked *Beyond the Horizon,* he would have thought it a good play.

O'Neill was in Provincetown when he received the news that he was getting the Pulitzer Prize. He said that he thought it was simply "some wooden medal or something." When he heard that five hundred dollars came with it, he "nearly fell in the ocean." The money came in "damn handy," he said, for he had a lot of bills to pay off.

If Eugene really feared that success brought its own form of retribution, his fears were soon enough realized. Shortly after the opening of *Beyond,* his mother fell ill of the flu. Eugene, who had been staying at the Prince George, caught it from her. Bedridden in New York, he worried about his wife and child in Provincetown. At the same time, George Tyler, who had decided to produce *Chris Christopherson,* wanted Eugene to make changes in the script.

Just as Ella and Eugene began to recover, James O'Neill, who had never completely regained his health since his accident the previous spring, suffered a stroke. Eugene had begun to attend rehearsals of *Chris.* Agnes, meanwhile, wrote from Provincetown that life without her husband was increasingly difficult.

Eugene talked at length to his father, now bed-bound, about what he was trying to do in his plays. He said he wanted to follow the dream, to live for the dream alone. In time, after long hard work, he might be able to conquer the problem of expressing his own real, possibly significant, bit of truth. He knew it would be a long struggle. Meanwhile, he said, he would try and have the guts to ignore what he called "the magaphone men" and all that they stood for.

James, who like his son was a romanticist, said he understood perfectly. He, too, had wanted to follow the dream. There had been a time when it was thought that he would become the finest Shakespearean actor of his time. Had he not listened to the "megaphone men," he might have stood alongside Edwin Booth as one of the theater's greats. As it was, James said, he had fallen for the mirage of easy popularity and easy money by going on playing, season after season, *The Count of Monte Cristo.* This play, which he knew in his heart was tripe, had been, he said, his curse. By playing in it, he had supported a group of actor-yokels in his old age. And what made it all the harder to face was the fact that he had benefited little from the riches the play had yielded. Much of the money had been thrown away, lost in ridiculous speculations. He had never found time to find out how to invest wisely. He had trusted incompetents.

His father's bitterness made a deep impression on Eugene. He told himself that he would never sell out, and that he would never stay put at any one successful stage of his career.

Early in March, Agnes fell ill in Provincetown and Eugene left New York to be with her and Shane. He knew it was important to stay in New York for the rehearsals of *Chris.* Agnes, however, was bedridden and there were no trained nurses available anywhere near Provincetown. When he was chided for not being on hand for the final rehearsals of *Chris,* he said that Agnes' call on him was stronger than all the plays he could ever write. Agnes later remarked that "O'Neill returned to Provincetown because he was ill from the flu and too much booze." Again, she feels, he used her as an excuse.

Chris Christopherson opened at Atlantic City on March 8, 1920, to an audience of what one producer called gum-chewing sweethearts and tango lovers, and moved on to Philadelphia. O'Neill didn't see the performances; he sent Richard Madden, his play agent to view it for him. The notices were fair but the play never came into New York. O'Neill charged that Tyler had cut it injudiciously and thus had spoiled the characterizations. The producer, he said, had taken all the "quality and guts out of the play." Eugene also said that *Chris's* failure was largely a matter of bad luck. He was obsessed, as he was always to be, by the idea that doom was haunting him. The truth was that Tyler should probably not have been working with O'Neill as a producer. The two men stood for different kinds of theater, different values, even different ages.

The Provincetown Players produced his *Exorcism* at the end of March. Although O'Neill was receiving no royalties from the Provincetown productions of his plays, he insisted on working with his old group. *Exorcism* is the story of a young man who, unable to abide living in the slums, takes poison in his tenement flat. Two friends find him unconscious and call a doctor, who gets there just in time to save his life. This was a play that O'Neill thought less and less of, with considerable justification.

As the spring wore on, O'Neill became convinced that ill fortune was hounding him. He was deeply depressed. Agnes remained bedridden, although she was somewhat better toward the end of March. He was unable to get any writing done. The failure of *Chris* disheartened him. *The Straw* which Williams and several other producers talked about producing, appeared to be a lost cause.

From New York came word that a number of specialists had conferred regarding his father's illness and were considering the question of surgery. Eugene was torn by remorse over all the years that he and his father had lived in misunderstanding. Now, just when he and his father were finding some kind of common ground, the gods were threatening to take him away.

At about this time Tyler decided he would produce *The Straw*, perhaps try it out with a few matinees in Boston. O'Neill objected vigorously; obviously, Tyler was showing lack of confidence in the play. "Wouldn't it be unfair to have to give up a month's hard work at creative writing for one experimental-acting matinee?" O'Neill wanted the rehearsals held in New York. His parents were there and he felt more at home in New York than in Boston. He insisted that he was "the only one who can tell the cast what, how and why they ought to behave." Referring to the fact that he was ill when rehearsals for *The Straw* were scheduled, Eugene wrote, "I'll come into town, hell and high water—if I have to be carried in on a stretcher."

He also objected to the idea of Helen Hayes playing Eileen, the lead. The role, he said, was so tremendous and its requirements were so many that only one of the best dramatic actresses in America should be cast in this part. Using Helen Hayes would be "in the nature of a hunch bet, a radical experiment, a gambling on the unknown."

He was convinced that his bad luck would doom *The Straw,* and his letters to Tyler were full of complaints. Some were even hostile. At times he would grow remorseful over his treatment of his father's old friend, who was, after all, only trying to produce his plays. He explained his behavior on the grounds that his nerves had been so frayed and frazzled ever since the previous fall that he could not even get along with himself. Now that he was beside the sea again and breathing salt air, he felt he was returning to sanity. He even went so far as to write Tyler that he didn't blame anyone but himself for the failure of Chris.

By the end of April doctors decided nothing good could come of an operation on James O'Neill. This was the old actor's death warrant and he knew it. Jamie gave Eugene the news in a letter and Agnes decided to go down to New York, taking Shane with her, since James had never seen his grandchild. Perhaps the sight of what Eugene called the lusty heir to this branch of the clan would "cheer up the Governor." Ella was also extremely anxious to see Shane. It had been a long time since she had held an O'Neill baby in her arms.

James O'Neill made a great to-do over Shane. The old actor recited to the infant all the "glorious deeds of Shane the Proud and all the other O'Neills." The part of the ancient and dying patriarch was a great role for James. He was the chief clansman seeing the last of his line that he would ever lay eyes on. "Remember, lad," he said to Shane, "you are a descendant of Irish kings. In your veins flows the blood of John the Proud, Lord of the Red Hand. You'll carry the line on and on into the future."

It was an odd but happy family group. Ella and James agreed to visit Agnes and Eugene at Peaked Hill the next summer. When they left, Agnes took Shane to New Jersey on a visit to her mother and father at Point Pleasant before going back to Provincetown.

George Tyler visited the elder O'Neill's while Eugene was in

Provincetown. He had a long talk with Jamie about *The Straw*. He described it as a Romeo-and-Juliet-type play with a lot of "coughing and spitting" in it. Of course, he said, the weighing scene in the first act would have to be cut out.

Jamie, who often teased his younger brother about his pretensions as a serious playwright, reported the conversation to Eugene, who was, naturally enough, furious. He swore that there were only a few coughs and not one spit. He wrote Tyler an intemperate letter in which he proposed to pay back his advance to Tyler and withdraw the play. Furthermore, this time there would be no tryout before the gum-chewing sweethearts of Atlantic City. There would not be any rewriting. *The Straw* was his play and he would fight for it, line by line. He could get it published in book form and that was the way he would have the play judged. At the end of the letter, he insisted he was writing with no "bitterness or any animus whatsoever."

Tyler thought otherwise. It may have been that, besides the letter, he had heard some of the tirades Eugene had launched against him and all other money-grubbing producers. He replied that all the worry about what he (Tyler) thought of *The Straw* was the result of Eugene's imaginings. He was sorry that Eugene thought him an idiot manager blind to the artistic side of the theater and caring only for financial success. He felt that Eugene had reached a "perfectly stupid conclusion" about what he (Tyler) thought of *The Straw*. Eugene replied that no play was worth all this unpleasantness. Tyler could keep the play until his option ran out but he never wanted to hear about it again except as a book.

In June, James O'Neill took a turn for the worse and was taken to St. Vincent's Hospital in Greenwich Village. But he rallied quickly, and later that month he and Ella were able to go to New London. James's old friend and real-estate manager, Thomas Fortune D'Orsey, has said that James O'Neill "came back to New London to die." Perhaps a less dramatic reason was that New London was cooler than New York. James had hardly settled in New London when he took ill again and was taken to the Lawrence Memorial Hospital.

Jamie and Eugene came at once. Art McGinley has recalled that both of them did a good deal of drinking at local bars during June and July. It was about then that Eugene received a check for $1,500, part of his proceeds from *Beyond*. He showed it to his barroom friends as proof that he could amount to something, and he offered to share it with his old friend McGinley.

James O'Neill was bitter at being ill. From his bedside, he

continued to pour out his lifelong regrets to Eugene. He felt his illness was retribution for the sins of his past life, for having had an illegitimate child, for having betrayed his talents as an actor and sold out for money. He cursed the money he had made, for it had done him no good. He had gold mines that yielded prairie dogs, oil wells that gave water and coal lands that produced rock. He seemed, to Eugene, a broken, unhappy man. He talked on and on about how life was "a damned hard billet to chew." Eugene reflected at length on the spectacle of this man, whom all the world regarded as a rich, famous, and respected actor, dying so miserably. As the hot days of July wore on, James slipped into unconsciousness. Agnes came down from Provincetown.

James lived another month. It was a harrowing summer for those close to him. Eugene has recalled to friends that toward the end his father's speech began to fail him; his voice, often called a gift of God, was growing faint. His last words to his younger son were: "Eugene, I am going to a better sort of life. This sort of life—here—all froth—no good—rottenness." Later, Eugene told friends that these words were written indelibly on his brain. He vowed that he would never end his days bitter and unhappy. He would always be true to himself, faithful to the truth that was in him.

Shortly after midnight on August 10, 1920, James O'Neill died, with Ella, Jamie, Eugene and Agnes at his bedside. A priest gave him extreme unction. The funeral was held on the fourth day following his death; and there was a requiem mass at St. Mary's Catholic Church. He was laid to rest in St. Mary's Cemetery beside his infant son, Edmund Dantes O'Neill. Also beside James, on the high, flat ground at New London, was his mother-in-law, Bridget Quinlan, who had died in New London in 1887, a year before the birth of Eugene.

His death received good notices. *The New York Times* gave his age as seventy. He had lived exactly seventy-four years, nine months and twenty-seven days. The *Times* did not stress his perennial playing of *Monte Cristo* but spoke of his having played in "repertory" during the last twenty years of his career, listed *Fontanelle, Virginius, Richelieu, Hamlet, The Three Musketeers,* the *Manxman,* and *Monte Cristo,* and referred to his "being compelled by contract to play in the last-named piece more often than the others because of its never-ending popularity with the masses."

The obituary also touched on the fact that James O'Neill's death had helped close an era in the American theater: "O'Neill was one of the last of the old school of actors well grounded in their profession, always effective and a lover of all that is true and good in dramatic art, always holding up with authority the best traditions of the American stage."

Both Eugene and Jamie took their father's death very hard. They went on one of the most protracted benders that ever have been seen in New London. It was in the tradition of an Irish wake—a celebration of a fine man's entering into the kingdom of God—but, tradition or not, it was some drunk!

Eugene later revealed something of what he felt about his father in *The Great God Brown:* "What aliens we were to each other! When he lay dead, his face looked so familiar that I wondered where I had met that man before. Only at the second of my conception. After that, we grew hostile with concealed shame."

CHAPTER

TWELVE

ཙཙ

PORTRAIT IN

MID-CAREER

On a foggy day in Provincetown, about a week after the death of James O'Neill, Olin Downes, music critic on the New York *Call,* accompanied by a friend, walked the three miles to Peaked Hill. Surprised to see two strangers approaching the house, Eugene stepped outside. Downes quickly explained that he was a newspaperman and asked the playwright if he would talk.

"I'll try anything once," O'Neill said, and he invited Downes and his friend in. Downes asked, "Any wrecks hereabouts?" and O'Neill replied, "Not lately, or I might have a bottle with a label on it to offer you." Agnes greeted the two men and went to make tea.

Downes had come to listen and observe. He observed that the living room was like a Washington Square studio. There was a fire in the big open fireplace. The wind "hummed in the timbers" and he would not have been surprised, he wrote afterward, to see the bowsprit of the *Flying Dutchman* coming through the fog. O'Neill reminded him of another Eugene—Eugene Marchbanks, the hero

of Shaw's *Candida*—because of his "almost feminine sensibilities
and his physical tremors and fears." At the same time, Downes wrote
"this O'Neill is a man's man, an adventurer born, reasonably close-
cropped, spare, fit-looking and very brown, loathing soiled shirts
and regretting passage of the Eighteenth Amendment."

O'Neill quickly reviewed his early life for Downes. Then he told,
with a trace of pride, how he had sailed from Mystic Wharf in
Boston on a Norwegian barque.

"You're musical," he remarked suddenly to Downes. "Well,
let me ask you, did you ever hear chanting sung on the sea? You
never did? It's not surprising. There are even fewer sailing vessels
now than there were ten short years ago when I pulled out for the
open. They don't have to sing as they haul the ropes. They don't
humor a privileged devil who has a fine voice and hell inside of him
as he chants that wonderful stuff and they pull to the rhythm of the
song and the waves. Ah, but I wish you might hear that and feel the
roll of the ship and I wish you might listen to an accordion going in
the forecastle, through the sighing of winds and the wash of the sea."

As O'Neill warmed to his subject, Downes noted that a "fey"
look came into his eyes.

"They [the seamen] were fine fellows. I've never forgotten them,
nor, I hope, they me. Indeed, I look on a sailor man as my particular
brother and next to the passing of the Eighteenth Amendment perhaps
you can put down my regret that the hangout of many of my old
pals, Jimmy the Priest's down by Fulton Street in New York, has
gone the way of many good things, nevermore to be seen. "

He talked of his gold prospecting trip to Spanish Honduras. He
said he never knew there could be such a variety of insects, of "creep-
ing, crawling, flying, stinging things—some of them rank poison—in
the world." Contrary to what people said, however, few died of the
bite of the tarantula. The hunting and fishing were great, and now
and then there was "a jaguar up on the hillside yowling you to sleep."

On his last voyage, O'Neill said proudly, he was an able seaman.
"That means you can box the compass and do several other things
which the ordinary seaman cannot. I sailed on a line which ran from
South America to Cherbourg. It was an ugly tedious job and no
place for a man who wanted to call his soul his own. I did not love
it. This was a steamer, you know, and what we did mainly was to
swab decks and shift baggage and mail. Those South American Germans—they used to send the folks home souvenirs and Christmas

presents which included stuffed beasts, ore, anything in the world, provided, as it seemed to me, that it would break your back for you."

He told how, when at last he came home, his father had given him a job as an actor in a *Monte Cristo* troupe that was touring the Orpheum circuit in the West. "In four days," he said, "on the train from New Orleans to a place in Utah, I memorized the part of Albert, son of Marcades. I was scared stiff on the stage and was a very poor actor. I'd never have been able to keep the job as long as I did if it had not been for my father. The audiences were great fun, though, and I suppose the experience of the stage was some help to me later on."

The talk turned to writing plays and O'Neill said he didn't think "any real dramatic stuff is created off the top of your head. That is, the roots of a drama have to be in life, however fine and delicate or symbolic or fanciful the development. . . . My real start as a dramatist was when I got out of an academy and among men on the sea."

Not only the sea but other experiences, O'Neill continued, served him. "As I've said," he went on, "I have never written anything which did not come directly or indirectly from some event or impression of my own, but these things often develop very differently from what you expect. For example, I intended at first, in *Beyond the Horizon,* to portray, in a series of disconnected scenes, the life of a dreamer who pursues his vision over the world, apparently without success, or a completed deed in his life. At the same time, it was my intention to show at least a real accretion from his wandering and dreaming, a thing intangible but real and precious beyond compare, which he had successfully made his own. But the technical difficulty of the task proved enormous, and I was led to a grimmer thing: the tragedy of the man who looks over the horizon, who longs with his whole soul to depart on the quest but whom destiny confines to a place and a task that are not his."

Listening intently, Downes became convinced that O'Neill might have been the hero of *Beyond* if he had stayed on in commonplace security and if he had not met "a kindred spirit in his wife." When Agnes brought Shane into the living room, O'Neill remarked that they planned to take a trip up the Amazon the following year, if Agnes' mother could be induced to take care of the baby.

Downes questioned O'Neill about his reading. Had it affected his work very much?

"Oh, yes, very much indeed, from the beginning," O'Neill said. "And with reading, as with my college studies, it was not until I had to shift, mentally as well as physically, for myself, that my awakenings came. Thus, in college, a work which made an indelible impression on me was Wilde's *Dorian Gray*.

"Meanwhile, I was studying Shakespeare in class and this study made me afraid of him. I've only recently explored Shakespeare with profit and pleasure untold. Then there were the Russians; certain novels of Dostoievsky and Tolstoi's *War and Peace* have become parts of my life.

"In college, Oscar Wilde, Jack London and Joseph Conrad were much nearer to me than Shakespeare. And so, later, was Ibsen."

When Downes expressed surprise at his interest in Ibsen, O'Neill said that people are too apt to think of Ibsen as merely dreadful and deep. "He's deep all right," O'Neill continued, "and sometimes dreadful, like life itself, but he's also intensely human and understandable. I needed no professor to tell me that Ibsen as dramatist knew whereof he spoke. I found him for myself outside college grounds and hours. If I had met him inside I might still be a stranger to Ibsen."

Suddenly he asked, "Why can't our education respond logically to our needs? If it did, we'd grab for these things and hold on to them at the right time—when we've grown used to them and know we need them."

Olin Downes was most impressed that August day in 1920 by the complete integration of O'Neill's life and work. Downes wrote that he "never saw a man whose life, personality and work seemed more of a piece. I suppose I may see him some night, all dolled up, in a theater, bowing to applause, but I shall always remember him in his old duds, in the fog. Why is it, anyhow, that we read Irish plays of Yeats or Synge, marveling at their seascapes, and the sense of nature, brooding and strange and wild, which permeates every line of the stuff, and then leave it to a wandering poet to discover the same wonderful thing—*inexplorada*—in odd corners of places lying ready to hand, such as, for instance, Cape Cod?

"There are men, you know—witness O'Neill—whose home is, as regards the particular, nowhere," Downes concluded. "For them, home is where it is most free. His adventures will never come to an end, not while he lives nor, if he has his way, after he dies. On him is the stamp—the curse, if you like—of the beauty of the far-off and unknown—the secret which is hidden just over there, beyond the horizon—and now I'm quoting from his play."

The Downes' interview reveals clearly Eugene O'Neill's attitude toward his past. In a way he was stuffy about it, and sentimental, too. Certainly, he romanticized his seafaring days for Downes and Downes went right along with him. But, like so many writers, O'Neill had a proprietary feeling about his past that is simultaneously personal and impersonal. As Hemingway talks about big-game hunting and bull-fighting, so O'Neill talked about the sea and his shipmates. He was saying, "This is my territory. I lived through it and I know how it is. I've been there, and I'm the one to show you what it was like."

CHAPTER

THIRTEEN

ॐ

O'NEILL AS A

FAMILY MAN

In the early twenties, domesticity descended on the house of Eugene O'Neill, and he made a brief appearance as a father and family man. It was a role to which he was not altogether suited and it proved a short engagement. But happily for his mother, who came to Province-town in the fall of 1920, this was the role she saw him in—for the first and, as it turned out, the last time in her life. Jamie accompanied her.

Jamie was charming that fall, Agnes has recalled, and he made a great hit with Gene's friends. For the first time in his life he was on the wagon. The death of his father had had—literally—a sober-ing effect on him. He had vowed that he would henceforth devote his life to taking care of his mother. So far he had kept his pledge not to take another drink. He told this to a number of people, and Art McGinley said that Jamie even spoke of his pledge in front of his mother at a dinner in New York. There was obviously a deep bond between them. "They looked at each other with deep feeling and understanding," McGinley said. "Mrs. O'Neill wore a dress made of some stiff black material. She looked very regal. There were strings of pearls around her neck and she wore all the beautiful diamonds that her husband had bought for her. James O'Neill was a great one for diamonds, he liked to shower them on his wife."

James O'Neill had left all his earthly goods to his wife, including the prairie-dog gold mines, assorted pieces of real estate, stocks or interests in oil enterprises. His estate, as his famous son phrased it, was "a tangled, chaotic affair." But Eugene noticed that his mother had suddenly developed a business instinct. It was a merciful thing, he told friends, because it had given her no time to brood. She quickly turned from being a helpless, well-bred old lady into a "keenly interested business man." Jamie—perhaps before Eugene—realized that she might bring to the surface the long buried treasure of Monte Cristo.

But there was no great treasure to be discovered. It seems incredible that James O'Neill could have ended up with so little to show for the countless seasons of acting the lead in a successful play of which he was the owner. Season after season he had earned $40,000, but even with Ella's good management his estate amounted to only $165,000.

The entire family had Thanksgiving Day dinner together in Provincetown. Shane was just a year old. The grownups, especially Grandmother O'Neill, made a great fuss over him. Eugene was carefree and for once not weighed down by his real or imagined responsibilities. He told his mother and brother, and friends as well, that he was going to stay on at Peaked Hill. But as his fame grew, the place became less and less isolated from the world.

"Peaked Hill became a shrine," Mary Vorse has said. "Writers, students, tourists, everybody trekked out to the dunes to see what Gene looked like, to pay their respect as if they were pilgrims. Gene didn't like it. Eventually, this sort of thing caused him to leave Provincetown."

Only a few of the visitors who came to Peaked Hill ever noticed Shane, who was taken care of by his nurse, Madame Fifine Foucher Clark, whom Shane called Gaga. Madame Clark had been born in France and when Agnes found her was working as housekeeper for a Provincetown antique and junk dealer. Madame Clark's employer had a circular sign which read "Antiques" for the benefit of the

Eugene O'Neill with his second wife, Agnes Boulton,
and their son, Shane

summer people. After Labor Day he turned the sign around and it read "Old Junk."

There were many potential playmates for Shane those summers at Provincetown—the Hutchins Hapgoods had children, so did Edith and Frank Shay, and the Wilbur Daniel Steeles, and Susan Glaspell and Jig Cook, and the Lucian Careys. But these families lived in town. It took them an hour or so to get out to the O'Neills'; furthermore, knowing Gene O'Neill, they understood they could not casually drop in.

One of the visitors who came to Peaked Hill wrote: "It is a desolation of sand and sea, but very beautiful—also very remote! Few persons could plow through the soft sand to reach it; fewer still would do so. From it, not another house is to be seen. The only human habitations are the new Coast Guard station, a quarter of a mile away, and a small shack. But these are hidden by the hills of sand."

In late fall, when the cold and the storms drove them out, the O'Neills rented a winter house in Provincetown. O'Neill had to go to New York now and then for rehearsals of his plays, and at these times Shane missed him terribly. He used to point at his father's photograph and smile and say, "Daddee, Daddee."

Whenever the O'Neill family settled down, the primary requirement was a workshop for the father. Shane, and later Oona, had to learn that they must never disturb their father while he was at work. Eugene was erratic in his behavior with Shane. At times he would get very interested and play with the baby, but then he "quickly tired" of it. The one world in which Shane and his father did meet freely was the world at the edge of the sea. O'Neill's writing schedule included daily interruptions for his swimming. The children waited at the edge of the sea for their father to emerge like some half-human, half-sea creature come ashore. Then they ran toward him, shrieking with delight.

The O'Neills had a dog called Matt Burke, after the character in *Anna Christie*. One day, while Shane was holding a piece of meat in his hand and making Matt jump for it, higher and higher, Matt snapped and missed, and sank his teeth into Shane's cheek. Agnes and Gene realized that the quickest way to get the wound treated would be to start walking immediately to Provincetown. Carrying the child, they went straight to Mary Vorse's house and called the doctor. Shane stayed on for several days at Mary Vorse's, where it was easier for the doctor to change his dressings. His face still bears the marks of Matt Burke's teeth.

O'Neill wrote two plays that fall of 1920. The first was the two-act drama, *Diff'rent,* which presents two episodes, thirty years apart, in the tragically unfulfilled love life of a New England girl. In the first act, set in 1890, Emma Crosby breaks her engagement with sea captain Caleb Williams when she learns that he once succumbed to the enticements of a seductive and enterprising South Sea Islands girl. Caleb vows to wait for thirty years, if necessary, for Emma to change her mind. The second act, set in 1920, shows Emma as a lonely, repressed old maid in love with Benny, the twenty-year-old World War veteran, ne'er-do-well nephew of her old suitor. When Caleb tries to warn her of the folly of her attachment, she quarrels with him. Benny, who has been interested only in the occasional gifts of money that he has been receiving from her, now heartlessly reveals his plan to extort "real money" from the uncle by offering to let the old captain buy him off. But Caleb has gone to the barn and hanged himself. Benny is called to the barn, and grief-stricken Emma is on her way to end her own life when the curtain falls.

Diff'rent was presented at the Playwrights' Theater on December 27, 1920, and was not well received; among the critics, only George Jean Nathan said he liked it. Although the action of the play in general proceeds logically from the characterization, the resolution seems spurious; it would take a rather humorless man and woman to feel that suicide was the only way out of the situation depicted in the play. But O'Neill himself was often humorless, and perhaps the hundred and one alternatives that would have been more dramatically satisfying never even occurred to him.

Meanwhile, *Gold* remained unproduced, as did *The Straw.* Eugene told friends he was convinced there was a curse on him. Despite having a hit in *Beyond the Horizon* and winning a Pulitzer Prize, he still felt that he was being dogged by misfortune.

The other play he wrote that fall was based on an idea he had had for some time. It had come to him some years before in a bar at the old Garden Hotel at Madison Avenue and Twenty-seventh Street. Among the habitués of the bar was an old circus man who talked entertainingly. One night he talked about a man named Vilbrun Guillaume Sam who had seized control of the island of

Haiti. As President Sam, he lasted about six months, and then the natives went after him. This strong, arrogant, superstitious, bold ruler had taken refuge finally in the French legation at Port au Prince.

"They'll never get me with a lead bullet. I'll kill myself with a silver bullet first. Only a silver bullet can kill me," he told his followers.

O'Neill was fascinated by the man's belief that only a silver bullet could kill him. Had he known that the silver-bullet idea appears in folk cultures the world over, he might have been less struck by it. Then O'Neill got another idea. "One day I was reading," he has said, "of the religious feasts in the Congo and the uses to which the drum is put there—how it starts at a normal pulse and is slowly accelerated until the heartbeat of everyone present corresponds to the frenzied beat of the drum. Here was an idea for an experiment. How could this sort of thing work on an audience in a theater?"

Again, O'Neill's lack of erudition stood him well. In 1906, fourteen years before, Austin Strong had written a melodrama, *The Drums of Oude,* which employed slow, stepped-up drumbeats to excite an audience. James Light, O'Neill's friend and colleague in the Provincetown Players, who was to direct several productions of this new O'Neill play, has said that O'Neill did not get the drumbeat idea exactly right. The trick, according to Light, was to begin the tempo of the drums below the level of the normal pulse beat of seventy-eight per minute—to, say, about thirty-five—then increase the beat imperceptibly.

The third idea that went into O'Neill's creation of *The Emperor Jones* was having a dense forest "close in" the stage. He had carried back from Honduras the effect of "tropical forest on the imagination."

O'Neill read *The Emperor Jones* to Susan Glaspell and her husband, Jig Cook, early in the fall of 1920. The Provincetown Players, with Cook directing, went immediately into rehearsal. The production cost $502.38, most of it going into a plaster-and-lathe dome which the Provincetown Players, with the help of Louis Ell, built on the stage of The Playwrights' Theater on Macdougal Street, where *The Emperor Jones* opened on November 3, 1920. Its impact on the critics and the public thrust the Provincetown Players and O'Neill into world prominence.

O'Neill fused the various elements into the story of Brutus Jones, deposed as head of the Negroes on an island kingdom, hunted, obsessed by fear. He is trying to make his way through the thick, dark jungle, and the drums of his former subjects beat out the message that he must die. Although not the best play that Eugene O'Neill ever wrote, it is in many ways the most theatrical—the most theatrical play by the most theatrical playwright of his time.

The usually caustic Alexander Woollcott wrote in the *Times* that the Provincetown Players had launched their new season "with the impetus of a new play by the as yet unbridled Eugene O'Neill, an extraordinarily striking and dramatic study of panic fear. It reinforces the impression that for strength and originality he has no rival among the American writers for the stage."

The lead was played by Charles Gilpin, who had played the slave in John Drinkwater's *Abraham Lincoln*. He received a salary of fifty dollars a week. His success in *The Emperor* ruined him. He began to think he was an emperor, an illusion not difficult to sustain on bootleg whisky, which he consumed in enormous quantities even when he was acting the part on the stage.

On the morning after the opening, there was a line about a block long leading to the box office. One had to be a subscriber to the Provincetown Players to see *The Emperor,* and a thousand new ones were enrolled in one week. The play was scheduled to run a fortnight but this was extended to eight weeks, after which it was taken uptown for a series of matinees. After five weeks of matinees it began a regular engagement and played 490 performances in New York before going out on the road.

Soon productions of *The Emperor Jones* were offered on the stages of Buenos Aires, Paris, London, Berlin, even Tokyo. Some reports of the foreign productions annoyed O'Neill. In the Berlin production, natives ran back and forth across the stage—which was, of course, entirely contrary to the sense of the play. Brutus Jones's panic was translated into many languages, his actions were understandable in many cultures.

Though the play laid the foundation for O'Neill's world-wide reputation, nevertheless he was still so hard up that he told a friend that if he didn't get a commercial production soon he was going to have to give up writing. For the first time he asked the Provincetown Players to give him some royalties on *The Emperor Jones*. They gave him "fifty dollars a week to keep going."

O'Neill was proud in the face of needing money. Speaking of his lack of means to George Tyler, the producer, he said he wasn't making a veiled hint for financial assistance; he didn't want anything from anyone and wouldn't accept it if offered. Tyler wanted to put a new production of *The Count of Monte Cristo* on Broadway and asked O'Neill to write a new version. Eugene said he would do it only if he could make *Monte Cristo* into something entirely new, discarding everything he thought was cheap and dishonest. He wanted to make the characters human beings and he wanted a new staging; he would make the play better than the novel, something far surpassing any of the old melodramas of his father's era. Nothing ever came of this scheme, however. What O'Neill really wanted was to get *The Straw* and the new *Chris* into production.

O'Neill grew more and more bitter about his lack of money in 1921. As a family man with Agnes and Shane to care for, he was increasingly weighed down by his responsibilities. He might just as well be the scurviest typewriter puncher among playwrights, he said, for the condition he was in. Being known in the drama columns as the great hope of the theater made him laugh. It would be more practical to play roulette for a living. It would certainly be more amusing. He also complained that uncertainty about production made it difficult for him to get his writing done.

Despite his despondency, he spent the early months of 1921 writing *The First Man*, and the spring writing *The Fountain. The First Man*, which was produced in March, 1922, at the Neighborhood Playhouse, was a failure. In it, a scientist is about to set forth on an expedition in search of the earliest traces of man. He intends to take his wife with him but she gets pregnant. The scientist thinks his career is ruined because he cannot go. His wife dies giving birth, and his relatives try to prove the child is not his. They try to prevent him from going on the expedition, saying it will "look bad," but he leaves, shouting that he will return to teach his son "to know a big, free life." *The First Man* has been called an ambitious failure; it certainly is a failure, ambitious or otherwise. The talk is seemingly endless and action does not grow out of character. Fortunately, this play was a departure for O'Neill. Every so often he decided that he was an intellectual and wrote what might be called "think plays." The results added little to his stature.

O'Neill was in New York for a ten-day stay in March. He wanted to talk to Tyler, who planned to cast Margalo Gillmore in *The Straw*. O'Neill thought her "too inexperienced," but when the play was produced Miss Gillmore played the lead. Tyler urged

O'Neill to see Miss Gillmore perform in the Boston opening, but O'Neill was reluctant to meet the actresses in any of his plays. When Tyler charged him with being shy with young ladies, O'Neill was quick to reply that he was now a family man. Before his marriage, he boasted, he was not so particular. His new virtue, he said, was keenly appreciated by his wife, and Tyler should not scoff.

It was true that O'Neill refused to mingle with actors and actresses. It was almost as if he had contempt for them, in spite of, or perhaps because of, the fact that it had been his father's profession. In one way this was an advantage, for in the casting of his plays O'Neill was never subject to pressure through personal friendships.

John D. Williams produced *Gold* in June, but it was not a success. Tyler wrote O'Neill not to worry. O'Neill replied that he wouldn't, but that the tax collectors, the landlords, the grocers, the butchers and "other canaille" were going to have to worry if he didn't.

Tyler lost his option on the new *Chris,* now called *Anna Christie.* The Theatre Guild had planned, for a time, to take over his option but later dropped the idea. Finally, Nathan prodded Arthur Hopkins into producing *Anna.* O'Neill now had two shows moving into commercial production for the fall, but his heart seemed to be in *Anna* and he did not attend rehearsals for *The Straw.* Also, Jimmy Light was directing the cast for the London production of *Emperor,* and O'Neill hoped to go there. The new lead was a young unknown Negro baritone named Paul Robeson.

In the fall of 1921, Agnes and Eugene took an apartment on the upper East Side, in the house in which Robert Edmond Jones had a bachelor apartment. "Bobby" Jones was one of the Provincetown group and without question was the most talented stage designer of his time. He and O'Neill were constantly experimenting with different and imaginative ways of staging productions. Jones was very close to O'Neill and stayed with Agnes and Gene for long periods. Agnes didn't like staying in Provincetown when Gene was in New York on theatrical business. For one thing, she knew he did a good deal of drinking in New York. When he was missing he could generally be found at the Hell Hole, sitting with his old down-and-out friends at one of the tables in the back room, or "sleeping it off" upstairs in one of the furnished rooms.

Anna Christie opened November 2, 1921, at the Vanderbilt Theatre. "The Old Davil," as O'Neill had been calling the play that had caused him so much trouble, was well received by both reviewers and audiences. But even though O'Neill was awarded his second Pulitzer Prize, there was some critical kidding about *Anna*'s "happy ending," and O'Neill, a man who took himself and his art very seriously, was not at all amused. He was hurt that people could think him capable of writing anything so dishonest as a happy ending to please the public. "The play has no ending," he said. "The curtain falls. Behind it their lives go on."

Agnes arranged a party at their apartment after the opening. O'Neill was terrified. Pauline Lord, the actress, who played the lead, found him in the bathroom sitting unsteadily on the edge of the tub; beads of perspiration stood out on his forehead, and he was sick to his stomach.

Meanwhile, Tyler had been working on *The Straw*. One of the places he tried it out was New London. Some of the O'Neill relatives in the town were furious because they felt that he had made fun of them in his portrayal of low-class Irish. *The Straw* opened in New York November 10, was panned, and closed in a few nights. Tyler blamed the subject matter, which was depressing and, to some, distasteful. O'Neill, who never saw it played, ascribed its failure to the fact that he had not attended rehearsals.

Late in 1921, O'Neill went back to Provincetown and set to work on *The Hairy Ape,* finishing it up in three weeks. He interrupted his work only to go to New York to see his mother and Jamie before they left for California. They were going to sell an orange grove, one of the interesting parcels of real estate bequeathed by James O'Neill.

That winter, Eugene met his first-born son for the first time in eleven years. Kathleen had married Pitt-Smith when Eugene junior was only a few years old, and the boy had been brought up as Richard Pitt-Smith. Early in 1922, as *Anna Christie* became more and more talked about, a friend of Kathleen's, a lawyer who had helped her get her divorce from O'Neill, called her attention to the fact that the play was a hit. He reasoned that O'Neill was probably making a lot of money. (Actually, he made only $9,360 out of *Anna*'s 177 New York performances.) The lawyer felt that now might be a good time to suggest that the playwright pay for their son's education. Kathleen agreed to let the lawyer make the suggestion to O'Neill. It was a hard decision for her to make. It would mean telling Eugene junior who his real father was.

Young Eugene, approaching his twelfth birthday, was not a happy boy. He had not adjusted well to school. A few years before, his mother, acting in accordance with a then honored notion about difficult boys, packed him off to a military school in the Hudson Valley. He ran away twice. The first time, when he arrived at home his mother told him not to take his coat off—he was going straight back. The second time he anticipated that the agent at the local railroad station had been asked to detain him, so he walked farther down the river, to the next station. He kept this up, and the school authorities eventually alerted all the stations down the line toward New York. Obviously, he was not the type of boy who would benefit from military school.

O'Neill was friendly to the lawyer's overture. He said that not only would he undertake his son's education but he also would like to meet his son. Kathleen took Eugene by subway as far as the entrance of the building in which O'Neill lived. She told him that he was not Richard Pitt-Smith, that his real father was a very famous man. He should ask for Eugene O'Neill's apartment and he would meet his father. Then she left.

O'Neill was shy and embarrassed, Agnes has recalled, but the meeting went off well. Though surprised to learn that Gene had been married and had another child, Agnes was delighted at the prospect of welcoming a second son into the group. She herself had had a daughter by a previous marriage. She told Eugene junior that he must come often and must visit them at Peaked Hill.

For his part, Eugene junior was delighted with his new father. He found him easy to talk with and interested in the same things he was interested in. When he returned home to his mother he told her that he was luckier, he felt, than most boys. "I had one father and now I have two."

Kathleen was glad things had gone well but, as she told a friend, "I feel peculiar. They hit it off so well that I feel that I'm losing my son."

Later, Eugene junior visited his father and Agnes in Provincetown. When he returned home to his mother he carried a letter from O'Neill to Kathleen. The letter has been destroyed, but a friend of Kathleen's who read it has said, "The letter gave Kathleen full credit for the fine boy she'd raised. O'Neill was full of praise for the way he had been brought up, said he was such a brilliant boy."

O'Neill decided that young Eugene had an excellent mind and

should go to a first-rate college. He paid the boy's way at the Horace Mann School for Boys, a preparatory school in the Bronx, and Eugene junior turned, almost overnight, into a serious and hard-working student. His best subjects were English and music, in which he received grades of ninety, and he began writing for the school literary magazine. At least one of his masters early noted, however, that the boy was insecure and highly sensitive.

"He was very touchy," the master has said, "about anyone making reference to his father. He acted as if he felt very much unwanted. Often I had the feeling that he was convinced that he was illegitimate. But he was brilliant and made a fine scholastic record here."

The Hairy Ape, a play in eight scenes, opened at the Playwrights' Theater on March 9, 1922, with Louis Wolheim and Mary Blair in the principal roles. James Light directed, and Robert Edmond Jones and Cleon Throckmorton designed the sets. In this play, more clearly than in any other, O'Neill revealed one of the anxieties that haunted him throughout his life—the fear of rejection, or of not "belonging."

The story derives from the unexplained suicide of Driscoll, a one-time shipmate of O'Neill's, and a fellow customer at Jimmy the Priest's. O'Neill, along with others who knew the man, tried to imagine the explanation. Drawing upon his own experience with the impulse toward self-destruction, O'Neill envisioned Driscoll as having suffered the loss of his feeling of belonging. In the manner of subjective thinkers, he also jumped to the generalization that the actuality of not belonging was a condition that threatened all mankind.

In writing the play, then, O'Neill set out to express in dramatic form the concept that man "has lost his old harmony with nature, the harmony which he used to have as an animal and has not acquired in a spiritual way." The result was dramatized philosophy rather than a persuasive drama involving credible, individual human characters.

The play tells the story of a powerful stoker, Yank, who "Belongs" wherever brute strength is the measure of a man, and for whom no other standards exist. He is at work in the boiler room of his ship when a bored society girl drops in on a sightseeing visit. She is overcome with revulsion at the sight of the coal-blackened Yank and exclaims, "Oh, the filthy beast!" Fainting, she is led from the

room, and Yank is restrained when he goes after her. His feeling
of belonging has been shaken, and he swears he will "get even." In a
succession of short scenes he is shown in search of revenge against
the girl and the society she represents. He is arrested for jostling
well-dressed Fifth Avenue promenaders and is thrown into jail. There
he learns something about the I.W.W. After his release he goes to an
I.W.W. meeting and is thrown out because his direct-action proposals
are too violent for the group. In the final scene, in the zoo, he sets
free a gorilla, which crushes him in its arms and tosses him into the
empty cage. There Yank dies. In his stage direction in the very last
line of the script, O'Neill suggests that "perhaps the Hairy Ape at
last belongs."

A few days before the opening, O'Neill learned that his mother
had died of a brain tumor on the last day of February, 1922, in Los
Angeles. The orange grove had been sold and the money was in
Jamie's name. He sent word that he was bringing her body back
to New York by train. When Agnes and Eugene met the train and
located Jamie, he was roaring drunk. He told his brother that while
their mother was ill in the hospital, he had gone off the wagon. His
mother had fallen into unconsciousness and he was beside himself
with grief. After getting drunk, he returned to the hospital and stood
at the foot of her bed. She opened her eyes, he said, just long enough
to see that he was drunk again. Then, Jamie said, she closed her eyes
and died—"glad to die," Jamie was sure.

He repeated this harrowing tale over and over again as long as
he lived. He told strangers that when he brought his dead mother
back from the Coast, he took a drawing room on the transcontinental
train and stocked it with a case of whisky. As the train made its way
on its eastward journey, he got drunker and drunker. He did not stay
in his stateroom but wandered, or rather reeled, up and down the
cars, searching for drinking companions. He became so objectionable
that the conductor threatened to put him off the train if he didn't
behave.

Then, he said, he devised another method of passing the time
and trying to forget that his mother was up ahead, lying dead in her
coffin. In *A Moon for the Misbegotten*, O'Neill has James Tyrone,
the character representing his brother, explain the details of this
horror-ridden journey.

"But I'd spotted," James Tyrone tells Josie, the big Connecticut
farm girl, "one passenger who was used to drunks and could pretend
to like them, if there was enough dough in it. She had parlor house

written all over her—a blond pig who looked more like a whore than twenty-five whores, with a face like an overgrown doll's and a come-on smile as cold as a polar bear's feet. I bribed the porter to take a message to her and that night she sneaked into my drawing room. She was bound for New York. So every night—for fifty bucks a night . . ." But "I didn't even forget in that pig's arms."

This was substantially the same story that Jamie told over and over again, sometimes lasping into an old tear-jerker ballad of the 1890's:

> *And baby's cries can't waken her*
> *In the baggage coach ahead.*

In *Moon for the Misbegotten*, Eugene went into even greater detail about Jamie and the death of his mother. James Tyrone, Jr., tells Josie: "When Mama died, I'd been on the wagon for nearly two years. Not even a glass of beer. Honestly. And I know I would have stayed on. For her sake. She had no one but me. The old man was dead. My brother had married—had a kid—had his own life to live. She'd lost him. She had only me to attend to things for her and take care of her."

He adds, however, "But there are things I can never forget— the undertakers, and her body in a coffin with her face made up. I couldn't hardly recognize her. She looked young and pretty like someone I remembered meeting long ago. Practically a stranger. To whom I was a stranger. Cold and indifferent. Not worried about me any more. Free at last. Free from worry. From pain. From me. I stood looking down on her, and something happened to me. I found I couldn't feel anything."

In a number of the plays he wrote, Eugene put a coffin on the stage. Seeing the dead bodies of his father and mother had had a deep effect on him.

After the requiem Mass in New York, Ella's body was taken to New London, the town she had never particularly liked, and where she had never made many friends. She was laid to rest in St. Mary's Cemetery, in the plot her husband had purchased almost forty years before.

Eugene received a half share in his mother's estate, amounting to approximately $56,000.

Meanwhile, the success scored by *The Hairy Ape* brought it to the attention of Arthur Hopkins, who contracted to produce it up-

town at the Plymouth Theatre. An immediate casualty of this move
was Mary Blair. It was now thought that her part called for an actress
who looked more like a society woman. The actress finally chosen
was Carlotta Monterey, an extremely beautiful woman who was just
about to marry the artist Ralph Barton. O'Neill did not have anything
to do with the casting. James Light has recalled that Carlotta kept
after him to introduce her to the author.

"We all liked Carlotta backstage," Light said. "She was great
fun. I told her I'd introduce her to Gene but it was not easy. You
know how he made himself scarce at rehearsals. One afternoon, Gene
and I were standing after a rehearsal at the back of the audience room
Carlotta came up to me and asked to be introduced to 'Mr. O'Neill.'
I introduced her. Gene was embarrassed and Carlotta departed
through the lobby.

" 'What was that for?' Gene asked.

" 'You come to the theater,' I told him. 'All the gals go for you.
There's only a single gal in this play.' "

O'Neill believed that chance sometimes played a decisive role
in the lives of men. The development of his story of *The Hairy Ape*
turned on such fortuitousness. In his own life, the apparently in-
significant incident of his meeting with Carlotta Monterey was to be
repeated in a similarly accidental way; but on the second occurrence
it was to bring about a complete break with his previous way of
living and with the family that had been a part of it.

CHAPTER

FOURTEEN

೧೧

THE COUNTRY

SQUIRE

In the summer of 1922 Agnes and Gene decided to buy a house. It was to be a place in which they could settle down during the fall, winter, and spring—or, as some of his friends put it, where O'Neill could become a country squire. It was an aspect of the playwright which so intrigued *The American Magazine* that it assigned Mary B. Mullett to write "The Extraordinary Story of Eugene O'Neill."

Miss Mullett went to Peaked Hill for the interview and was much impressed with the solid citizen she found. Under the heading "They All Have to Come to It—Even Geniuses!" the story said:

> O'Neill has a regular habit of work. The craving for freedom, for the indulgence of his own desires, which controlled his early manhood, is subordinated now to the good of his work. He, who used to be a rebel against routine, voluntarily follows a routine now in this direction. Like the rest of us, he has found that he must follow a regular habit of work if he is to accomplish anything.

An excellent description of O'Neill at this time is provided by Miss Mullett:

> He is tall and dark and thin. Everything about him (except his hair and eyes!) seems to be long and thin. I believe his hands, for instance, are the longest and the most slender I ever have seen. They are the type of hands that go with the dreamer temperament.
>
> His eyes are very dark, very intense. His hair is dark; but, young as he is, it is already showing a little gray at the temples. He is quiet and slow of speech with strangers. When it comes to ordinary "small talk" he is a good imitation of a sphinx. Even when he is interested, there are long pauses in which, unless you know his ways, you think he isn't going to say anything more. Then, unexpectedly, he begins again; and he is likely to say something so interesting that you soon learn not to break in on these pauses.

O'Neill always worried that people did not "get" what he was trying to say in his plays, and during that interview he commented that everyone seemed to have misunderstood what he was trying to say about Yank in *The Hairy Ape*. No, he was not trying to get sympathy for sailors. In fact, he said:

> "Labor leaders have organized the seamen and have got them to thinking more about what is due them than what is due from them to the vessel. The new type of sailor wants his contract, all down in black and white; such and such work, so many hours, for so many dollars. But, under it, there has been lost the old spirit.
>
> "Yank is really yourself, and myself. He is every human being. But, apparently, very few people get this. They have written, picking out one thing or another in the play and saying 'how true' it is. But no one has said, 'I am Yank! Yank is my own self!'
>
> "Yet that was what I meant him to be. His struggle to 'belong,' to find the thread that will make him a part of the fabric of Life—we are all struggling to do just that. One idea I had in writing the play was to show that the missing thread, literally 'the tie that binds,' is our understanding of one another."

In answer to a question about his methods of work, O'Neill said that he first wrote a play out in longhand. "Then, I go over it, and rewrite it in longhand. Then I type it, making a good many changes as I go along." After that, he put it away for a time.

Asked if he thought his success was a danger to him, O'Neill replied that if a writer finds the one best formula for doing something and then thinks all he has to do is to go on repeating himself, then he is in trouble. And he added, "So long as a person is searching for better ways of doing his work he is fairly safe."

Pressed to state his "fundamental scheme of life; a creed, a philosophy," he replied:

> "People talk of the 'tragedy' in [my plays], and call it 'sordid,' 'depressing,' 'pessimistic'—the words usually applied to anything of a tragic nature. But tragedy, I think, has the meaning the Greeks gave it. To them it brought exaltation, an urge toward life and ever more life. It roused them to deeper spiritual understandings and released them from the petty greeds of everyday existence. When they saw a tragedy on the stage they felt their own hopeless hopes ennobled in art."

They are hopeless hopes, O'Neill went on to explain,

> "because any victory we may win is never the one we dreamed of winning. The point is that life in itself is nothing. It is the dream that keeps us fighting, willing—living! Achievement, in the narrow sense of possession, is a stale finale. The dreams that can be completely realized are not worth dreaming. The higher the dream, the more impossible it is to realize it fully. But you would not say, since this is true, that we should dream only of the easily attained. A man wills his own defeat when he pursues the unattainable. But his struggle is his success! He is an example of the spiritual significance which life attains when it aims high enough, when the individual fights all the hostile forces within and without himself to achieve a future of nobler values.

> "Such a figure is necessarily tragic. But to me he is not depressing; he is exhilarating! He may be a failure in our materialistic sense. His treasures are in other kingdoms. Yet, isn't he the most inspiring of all successes?

> "If a person is to get the meaning of life he must 'learn to like' the facts about himself—ugly as they seem to his senti-

mental vanity—before he can lay hold on the truth *behind* the facts; and the truth is never ugly!"

For the first time, O'Neill found himself financially well-off. Not only did he have money coming from his mother's estate, but he figured his own weekly earnings from royalties at approximately $850 a week. Late in 1922 he bought Brook Farm at Ridgefield, Connecticut. About thirty-two acres went with the big, rambling white colonial house perched high on a hill overlooking the Ridgefield–New Canaan road. There were some outbuildings, a formal garden, and a large apple orchard.

His settling at Brook Farm realized an ambition never really achieved by his father—to own and live in a gracious homestead in which one's children, and perhaps one's children's children, would grow up. This would be a place, unlike the Pequot Avenue place in New London, where an O'Neill family could acquire happy memories. Agnes would have preferred a smaller place, but O'Neill always insisted he must have a big house. He felt that at Brook Farm he could at last "belong."

The O'Neills engaged a local couple of Italian descent, Vincent and Maria Bedini, to help out on the place. Maria worked in the house, and Vincent did the gardening and occasionally chauffeured the O'Neill touring car. A Japanese butler cooked and served the meals. There was also a second maid and a laundress. Gaga was there to look after Shane. Finn, an Irish wolfhound, the royal dog of Irish kings, completed the ménage.

A fleeting gloomy glimpse of O'Neill at Ridgefield comes from Stark Young. One night Eugene was working on outlines and sketches for his plays. "He was sunk in some nervous mood," Young wrote, "and heard footsteps outside during the night going round the house, and during the day when he was writing he would feel someone looking over his shoulder."

Agnes and O'Neill were encountering some difficulties in their marriage that first year at Ridgefield. There were many pressures. Both were strong-minded and temperamental. Both were writers. And both were very much in love. But Agnes could not share O'Neill's passionate devotion to the theater. A good deal of what went on in order to get a play into production, she thought, was silly and nonsensical. There were quarrels, and at times he went at her with his fists, but afterward he would suffer terrible remorse.

The old Provincetown group was breaking up. With Robert Edmond Jones and Kenneth Macgowan, O'Neill formed his own organization, the Greenwich Village Theatre. He had finished *Welded* by the end of the winter of 1923 and decided to let the new group put it on. For a time he did no more writing as he worked on plans for the new theater and read scripts.

It was not until he was back at Peaked Hill for the summer that O'Neill got down to work. There he outlined *Marco Millions,* but he wrote only one scene. As fall approached he set to work on *All God's Chillun Got Wings.* He wrote Nathan that he was working eight to ten hours a day and that his plays seemed to be crowding themselves right out of the one-act form. He found writing long plays great sport. He wanted Nathan's approval more than anyone's, and he sent his plays on to the critic as fast as he could get them typed.

Jamie had retired to Riverlawn Sanitarium at Paterson, New Jersey, a confirmed alcoholic and now seriously ill from arteriosclerosis. Early in November he suffered a cerebral hemorrhage, and on November 8, at the age of forty-five, he died.

O'Neill was more than ever convinced that some terrible force was at work in his life. Was he paying for his success? "Just think," he told friends, "my entire family was wiped out in three years— three out of the four of us." Now, more than ever, he felt that he was really alone.

He told Agnes he could not face going to Paterson to arrange the details and escort the body to New London. Agnes, as usual, did the chores that the sensitive O'Neill could not manage. Eugene got frightfully drunk and stayed that way. Emotionally and physically, he was unable to cope with Jamie's death.

The sanitarium shipped the body to a New York funeral home, where Agnes was horrified to discover that Jamie was clothed only in underwear; his tremendous wardrobe had been stolen or had disappeared at Riverlawn. Agnes remembers that the suit which the undertaker provided was backless. She and her sister Marjory boarded a train in New York City with Jamie's body. At New London they were met by the O'Neill relatives, the Sheridans. After a Catholic Mass, Jamie was buried in the family plot in St. Mary's Cemetery.

Jamie had died without making a will, and Eugene, being the sole surviving heir, inherited the estate, which amounted to $73,593.68. This sum represented Jamie's half of his mother's estate, which had risen in value because of the sale of the orange grove.

Eugene, now a man of comfortable means, remarked, "Booze got Jamie in the end." He was convinced that Jamie had wanted to die, that after his mother's death he had had nothing to live for.

By the end of November, 1923, the O'Neills were back at Ridgefield. Agnes was pregnant again and Eugene had plunged into the writing of *Desire under the Elms*. Today, in Ridgefield, the townspeople still call the house "the O'Neill place."

O'Neill was living in a New England of his own creation. Agnes thinks that his knowledge of Puritan decadence came from his acquaintance with families in New London and with those she had told him about in New Preston, where her mother had a farm.

Shane had reached his fourth birthday that fall and those who visited Brook Farm remember him as a lonely child wandering around the big house. O'Neill worked in his bedroom. Mrs. Bedini has recalled that in his room was a metal crucifix which had once belonged to his mother. He often worked in bed all morning and always demanded that the house be quiet. Gaga and Mrs. Bedini were responsible for keeping Shane out of mischief.

In some ways, Mrs. Bedini has recalled, O'Neill was something of a figure of terror in the household. If Shane cut up, just O'Neill's appearance at the stair landing was enough to quiet him. She well remembers the face of the tall, dark, silent, brooding figure in a dressing gown scowling down at his son, his eyes luminous in the gloom.

The Bedinis own son, Silvio, remembers that Shane had many toys, more toys than he, Silvio, had ever dreamed of—an extraordinary electric train completely equipped with yards of tracks, automatic signals, a miniature passenger station and all the rest. Shane gave Silvio one of the engines but his parents made him return it for fear it wasn't a bona fide gift. In some respects, Shane was the poor little rich boy. To the Bedinis, he was "spoiled" and was "given his way too much."

What was a fairly typical weekend at Brook Farm has been described by Malcolm Cowley, who with his wife, Peggy Baird, took the poet Hart Crane to visit the O'Neills early one fall. They were met at the train station by Vincent Bedini in the Packard and taken to Brook Farm, where O'Neill greeted them. Cowley was surprised to be ushered immediately in to dinner. He had expected and rather hoped for cocktails, but none was forthcoming. The dinner was excellent, but what really impressed the visitors was Finn; it was the first time Cowley had ever encountered a dog that was taller than he, and the first time he had ever met a representative of what the *Encyclopaedia Britannica* listed as "an extinct breed."

Cowley, like O'Neill, was somewhat shy. He was younger than O'Neill and one of the rising postwar literary figures. After lunch on Saturday of that weekend the two talked in a window nook just off the big living room. O'Neill picked up a green textbook-type volume from the table and explained that it was William Stekel's treatises on sexual aberrations, *The Disguises of Love,* recently translated from the German. He said there were enough case histories in the book to furnish plots to all the playwrights who ever lived. He turned to a case history of a mother who seduced her only son and drove him insane.

He said that he had been reading the plays of the German expressionists Toller and Kaiser and Hasenclever, because he had been told that their work resembled his own. He thought their work was "bold, interesting but much too easy." Then he said a few illuminating words about *Anna Christie,* which he no longer cared to defend.

"I never liked it so well," he told Cowley, "as some of my other plays. In telling the story I deliberately employed all the Broadway tricks I had learned in my stage training. Using the same technique and, with my early experience as a background, I could turn out dozens of plays like *Anna Christie,* but I won't ever try. It would be too easy."

O'Neill took Cowley upstairs and showed him the bedroom where he worked. There were no books or pictures, and Cowley thought it "looked like an abbot's cell." He has written about that visit:

> Between the two north windows is a dark mahogany secretary, with drawers at the bottom, a cabinet at the top, and drop-leaf table for writing. There are no papers on the writing surface. Gene opens the doors of the cabinet and takes out two or three medium-sized bound ledgers. "I write in these," he says. Each ledger contains several plays. Opening one of them, he shows me the the text of *The Emperor Jones,* written with a very fine pen, in characters so small that they are illegible without a reading glass. There are no blank lines and the text of the whole play fills only three pages of the ledger—or is it five? I think of the Lord's Prayer engraved on the head of a pin.

O'Neill mentioned briefly that he was working on a play about New England, but he didn't pursue the matter. He was always reticent about work in progress except to say, as he generally did, that it was "the greatest" or "the finest thing" he had ever done.

Late that evening, O'Neill took Crane and Cowley down into the cellar. Vincent Bedini had gathered the apples from the orchard and had filled three 53-gallon casks with cider.

"Let's broach a cask," suggested Hart Crane, who liked alcohol even more than poetry. O'Neill, knowing his own weakness, hesitated, saying that Vincent might not approve; the cider was only three weeks old. But his qualms were quickly overcome. While Cowley tapped a barrel, O'Neill went upstairs to the kitchen and got a white ironstone pitcher and three glasses. Cowley spilled quite a little cider before he filled the pitcher. The three men held aloft their glasses.

"I can see the beaded bubbles winking at the brim," Crane said, quoting Keats. Then, Cowley wrote, "Gene takes a sip of cider, holds it in his mouth apprehensively, gives his glass a gloomy look, then empties the glass in two deep, nervous swallows. After a while we fill the pitcher again. When I go upstairs to bed, long after midnight, Gene is on his knees drawing another pitcher of cider, and Hart stands over him gesturing with a dead cigar as he declaims some lines composed that afternoon." O'Neill responded by singing some of his sea chanties. His favorite was "Blow the Man Down." When O'Neill said the line, "Way-o, blow the man down," it was like the movement of a ship breasting a big wave, and he illustrated his meaning with a wavelike gesture of his right hand. O'Neill and Crane had sealed their friendship, and Crane stayed at Brook Farm until after Christmas.

Following the cider barrel weekend, O'Neill was consumed by wanderlust. He took a train to New York and headed straight for the Hell Hole, where he got really drunk. Agnes later went there to look for him. He was "sleeping it off" in one of the furnished rooms upstairs. He told her the upstairs of the Hell Hole was a wonderful place. An aged crone, a witchlike creature, he said, wandered about there, opening and closing doors and muttering incantations. Agnes lost no time in getting him back to Brook Farm.

Recovered from his celebration, O'Neill made a start on the writing of an introduction to a book of verse by Hart Crane. Horace Liveright had agreed to publish the volume on the condition that the poet get O'Neill to write the introductory piece. But O'Neill was unable to do it; writing simple exposition was, for him, virtually impossible. In the end, Allen Tate wrote the introduction and Liveright settled for a jacket blurb from O'Neill.

In March, 1924, Agnes and Gene went to New York for rehearsals of *Welded* which Macgowan, Jones and O'Neill were producing in association with the Selwyns. *Welded* is the story of a married couple whose principal link, besides a marriage certificate, is desire. They are jealous of each other, the husband goes to a prostitute and the wife offers herself to a friend who is in love with her. But at the final moment neither is able to consummate the attempted infidelity, and the couple return to each other, forced to admit that they are, for better or worse, welded. The play is not realized dramatically. It is not felt but intellectualized, and the characters never emerge fully developed.

Doris Keane, the lead, thought the speeches the wife made in the play were too stilted. Stark Young has said that, although Miss Keane had wanted to withdraw, "she was too fine an artist to disdain a script from a sincere creator, no matter what she thought of the quality displayed. And I knew that in her tender heart, she discerned the torment that underlay the lines themselves, and sensed that the words were a misplaced travesty of some genuine feeling, the results of an uncertain taste and an uncertain sense of the banal, along with a semiadolescent ambition toward the literary."

Young watched Agnes and Gene at the rehearsals of *Welded*. "I knew that Gene's personal life in the period that *Welded* came out of had not been all smoothness—not between two such vivid temperaments as he and Agnes, his wife, for all the love between them—and I felt that this play was in the nature of a confession and a benediction. I can see them now at some of the rehearsals sitting side by side there in the third row and listening to every speech, good or bad, and taking it all as bona fide and their own. At least for the love of them I could wish that the mild success the play had when it was produced had been greater."

Welded opened on March 17, 1924, at the Thirty-ninth Street Theatre. In April the Provincetown Playhouse produced an O'Neill adaptation of *The Ancient Mariner,* and in May they produced *All God's Chillun Got Wings.* The latter immediately ran into censorship trouble because in it a white actress kisses a Negro actor's hand; O'Neill himself received threats from the Ku Klux Klan.

All God's Chillun is about the marriage of a Negro to a white

girl and the troubles they encounter. It opens with Negro and white
children playing together happily. In New York, in order to make
things difficult for the play, the authorities refused to let child actors
play the parts. As a result, the play was presented without the children appearing. Their parts were read by adult actors from behind
the wings. The audience understood the problem and applauded enthusiastically.

Although the play is warm and poignant, it is also obvious and
dated. The girl simply cannot adjust to being married to a Negro (at
one point she attacks him with a knife). He keeps failing his bar
exams, saying that the mere thought of white men watching him
defeats him at the last moment. These things tend to tax the credulity
of American audiences, who find the play melodramatic and over-
written. *All God's Chillun* has become mildly popular in the Soviet
Union, because it portrays the tragedy of the Negro in America as the
Russians want to believe it.

To a Princeton classmate who praised the play, O'Neill wrote:

Any appreciation of the worth of that play is doubly appreciated by me because of all the prejudiced and unjust knocks
it received when it was enjoying such a storm of unwelcome
notoriety. It seemed for a time, there, as if all the feeble-witted
both in and out of the K.K.K. were hurling newspaper bricks in
my direction—not to speak of the anonymous letters which
ranged from those of infuriated Irish Catholics who threatened
to pull my ears off as a disgrace to their race and religion to
those of equally infuriated Nordic Kluxers who 'knew' that I
had Negro blood, or else was a Jewish pervert masquerading
under a Christian name in order to do subversive propaganda
for the Pope! This sounds like a burlesque, but the letters were
more so.

And then when the play opened, nothing at all happened,
not even a senile egg. It was a dreadful anticlimax for all concerned, particularly the critics who seemed to feel cheated that
there hadn't been at least one murder that first night. And so on,
ever since. The whole affair was really a most ludicrous episode
—not so ludicrous for me, however, since it put the whole
theme of the play on a false basis and thereby threw my whole
intent in the production into the discard.

During the summer of 1924, the O'Neill ménage moved again to Peaked Hill. Bee, Agnes' daughter by her first marriage, and Eugene junior came to visit. Both were in their teens and proved very congenial. Shane was going on five but was still being looked after by Gaga.

O'Neill had resumed work on *Marco Millions.* "This play," he wrote, "is an attempt to render poetic justice to one long famous as a traveler, unjustly world-renowned as a liar, but sadly unrecognized by posterity in his true eminence as a man and a citizen—Marco Polo of Venice."

He got the idea of writing the play, which made fun of businessmen, as a result of a conversation with Otto Kahn, the fabulous millionaire patron of the arts. Kahn wanted O'Neill to write something that he (Kahn) might be proud to endorse.

"And what would you suggest, Mr. Kahn?" O'Neill asked.

"A play apotheosizing American big business and the American businessman," Kahn said. "I could take you down to Wall Street and let you attend a private directors' meeting."

O'Neill did not accept the offer, but later, in telling about the conversation, he said, "A lot I'd have learned there! Can you imagine those fellows exposing their big schemes in the presence of a suspicious-looking outsider?"

The title was O'Neill's attempt to translate the nickname which the Venetians gave to Marco Polo—*il Milione,* "the millionaire." It infuriated him that people insisted on calling the play "Marco's Millions." He was now so interested in writing plays longer than the one-act form that he projected *Marco* so that it would run for two nights. Just before sending it on to Nathan, however, he rewrote and condensed it.

Meanwhile, *Desire under the Elms,* produced by the Provincetown Playhouse, Inc., opened at the Greenwich Village Theatre on November 11, 1924. It ran a year in New York and there were two road companies. Brooks Atkinson, drama critic of *The New York Times,* called the play "an ode to greed and lust and murder without remorse" and said that it "may turn out to be the greatest play written by an American. [It] has the grand design of a masterpiece."

In *Desire under the Elms* O'Neill again deals with his favorite theme—greed. The locale of the play is rural New England in the year 1850. Seventy-five-year-old Ephraim Cabot, who has outlived two wives, has just married a third, Abbie Putnam, half his age. She is resented by the old farmer's three sons, two of whom leave the farm. The youngest son, Eben, stays on to fight for his inheritance. To obtain an ascendancy with the old man, Abbie promises him a child. She then seduces Eben and, in time, bears a son, to whom Cabot wills all his property. Meanwhile the relationship between Abbie and Eben has turned to ardent love until Eben discovers that he has been tricked into siring an heir who will pre-empt his heritage. To prove her love and placate Eben, Abbie murders her child. Eben, horrified, calls the sheriff and then assumes part of the guilt in order to share Abbie's fate. The play ends as they are led away to jail.

In one sense, this is the great American domestic horror story. Everyone is awful and everyone loses. O'Neill fulfilled his stated theorem: "There is beauty to me even in ugliness—I don't love life because it's pretty; prettiness is only clothes-deep. I am a truer lover than that. I love it naked." In *Desire under the Elms* the characters are gradually stripped naked and they are not pretty. As in so many of O'Neill's really good plays, the characters are not simply true to life, they are larger than life. They are what they are, and something more. They are all of us. The last line beautifully illustrates O'Neill's central theme—the corruption of character (even the law's character)—when the sheriff looks covetously over the Cabot farm and says, "It's a jim-dandy farm, no denyin'. Wished I owned it!"

In the moment of triumph O'Neill received word that Eugene junior had fallen off his bicycle near his home in Douglaston and was in the hospital, unconscious. O'Neill sent word to the boy's mother to spare no expense, that he would pay all the medical and hospital bills. "That boy is brilliant," he told Kathleen, "and I want everything in the world done to save his life." But he did not go to the hospital.

CHAPTER

FIFTEEN

ಬಿಜ

FLIGHT FROM

HIMSELF

Although Eugene O'Neill felt that his life was controlled by mysterious external forces, it is by no means certain that he was ever able
to identify these personal Furies. And in a very real sense, he gazed
unblinkingly at his life sliding impersonally by before him.

Now he had reached a new phase of urgent restlessness. The
life of a "country squire" had palled completely. He was going more
and more often to New York; and whenever he did so he found himself, at journey's end, brooding in the gloomy depths of the Hell
Hole. The stage was now set for the long flight from himself, an
ordeal from which his family was to suffer even more savagely than
himself. For it was at this juncture that he received a letter from his
old Greenwich Village companion, Harold de Polo, who wrote from
Bermuda that the island was a great place for writers. Why not come
down?

O'Neill went, taking his family with him. It was December,
1924. The O'Neills took a cottage called Campsea, on the South
Shore, Paget West. It suited O'Neill, who wrote Nathan and others

that they should come down for a winter vacation. The climate was "grand," and he highly recommended the German bottled beer and the English bottled ale. He spent the winter working on *The Great God Brown.*

Gaga was looking after Shane then, for Agnes was carrying her second child by O'Neill. Shane's life was showing a startling parallel to that of his father at the same age. His parents had been continually on the move. Now he was in school in Bermuda and, like his father before him, he was being taught by convent nuns.

Late in the evening of May 13, 1925, Oona was born. Shane recalls that he was awakened by his mother and told that he would have to spend the rest of the night in his father's bedroom. Although Shane was five and a half, the events of that night vividly impressed themselves on his mind.

"It was very dark, I remember," Shane has said. "Mother woke me up and said, 'You must go in and sleep with your father.' Then, I recall being in the bedroom with my father and talking with him. He was terribly worried. He didn't like the waiting. There was a lot of activity going on in Mother's room. We could hear it. My father got very confidential with me, told me how worried he was.

"We talked the rest of the night. Finally, somebody called my father and told him the baby was born. It was a girl. The arrival of the baby was kind of a letdown after all the excitement of the night. I remember when they took me into Mother's bedroom and showed me the baby; she had dark hair and dark eyelashes. Then they took me right out again."

By the end of May O'Neill was sure he wanted to live permanently in Bermuda, and he looked around for a bigger house. He told friends that he was not going to keep Agnes in any boxy little house like the New London home that his father had provided for *his* wife. Wherever he lived the houses he bought were always big, as if their very size would insure stability and permanence. They never did.

That spring he was disturbed because *The Fountain,* had been rejected by most of the producers, including the Theatre Guild. He told Nathan he thought there was a jinx attached to the play. *The Fountain* is a dramatization of Ponce de Leon's search for the fountain of youth. In the O'Neill version of the story, Ponce de Leon learns that, although he does not find what he was searching for, the effort was worthwhile; he also discovers that "there is no gold but love." O'Neill filled the play with poetry, but not first-rate poetry. In general, he seemed to be writing of the poet's eternal aspirations and exultations—something he seems not to have felt himself, but to have thought he should feel. As a result, the play is emotionally and imaginatively unsatisfying.

By letter and cable, he carried on a petty dispute with Horace Liveright, the publisher, over the number of sheets O'Neill had signed for the limited edition of the *Complete Works of Eugene O'Neill*. Liveright afterward said he had sent 1,250 sheets to Bermuda for O'Neill to sign. But O'Neill claimed he got suspicious at the size of the package and, as a result, he and Agnes counted them. They figured there were at least 1,700 sheets, and perhaps 1,800. As a result, O'Neill told his agent, Richard Madden, that he thought there was something "on the queer" with all these so-called limited editions and he didn't want to be a party to them. He also thought he had been short-changed by Liveright on the matter of royalties. Furthermore he told Madden not to deposit any more of his royalties in the bank at Ridgefield because it was a small bank and for all he, O'Neill, knew, the teller might be playing the horses! If so, using O'Neill money would be sure to put the "hoodoo" on him and the teller would lose his shirt "on the bangtails."

Although Oona was only a little more than a month old, the O'Neills left for the States at the end of June, 1925. In New York Eugene told reporters that he had completed *The Great God Brown* and was going to produce it in partnership with Robert Edmond Jones and Kenneth Macgowan. Agnes and the children went to a rented house at Nantucket (the O'Neills had decided not to return to Provincetown), and Eugene stayed in New York, where he was treated by a doctor for his "nerves." Family life made O'Neill nervous, he was an extremely uneasy father, and relations between him and Agnes were not uniformly peaceful. He went to Nantucket after a short time and there resumed his writing.

In the fall of 1925, O'Neill wrote half of the first draft of *Lazarus Laughed*. As always, he was "searching for better ways of doing his work," and he had decided to write a play of ideas. *Lazarus* attempts to come to grips with the question of living for the present or living in anticipation of future judgment. Lazarus rises from his tomb with this doctrine (as stated by the chorus):

> Laugh! Laugh! There is only life!
> There is only laughter! Fear is no more!
> Death is dead!

This philosophic concept is not the most original in the world, nor is affirmation (of life) by exclamation point necessarily the most effective way of stating it. *Lazarus Laughed* is, as O'Neill said, a play for the imaginative theater. It is perhaps best read, best left in the theater of the mind, despite the many old and interesting stage devices (chorus, masks, etc.) employed. Even Barrett Clark, O'Neill's devoted admirer, was forced to admit that the playwright's "ideas as contributions to contemporary thought are negligible" and that he should be content to portray "life with truth and passion." *Lazarus Laughed* was never produced on Broadway. O'Neill always insisted, however, that it was one of his great plays and that it had a great message.

It was at Nantucket that O'Neill received a letter from Clark asking if he could do a biography of him. O'Neill replied that he thought he didn't deserve a book—as yet. He thought there was too much of "this premature sort of thing being done in America," but he said that he would meet Clark at Ridgefield at the end of September and talk over the project. He spent part of the fall in New York at rehearsals of *The Fountain,* while Agnes, Shane and Oona were ensconced in Ridgefield with Gaga and the Bedinis. Both in New York and at Ridgefield much of his time was taken up with being a celebrity. At Ridgefield, he sat for a sculptor who was doing a bust of him. The star of his fame was still in the ascendent. Brooks Atkinson wrote a long article in the *Times* about O'Neill's development. In England, John Galsworthy praised his work, but Arnold Bennett said that, as a playwright, O'Neill was inferior to George M. Cohan.

In a Provincetown Playhouse playbill, O'Neill blasted the commercial theater—the eternal showshop, as he called it. This was an "era when the theater is primarily a realtor's medium for expression. One mistake and then comes the landlord with a notice of eviction. He is usually not an artist in the theater, this landlord! He could see Shakespeare boiled alive in Socony gasoline and have qualms only as to our diminishing national Standard Oil reserves." The answer to the difficulty, O'Neill felt, would be the inauguration of a repertory theater. Then he went on to voice one of his lifelong complaints about the American theater: the quality of acting. "Great acting has frequently made bad plays seem good," he said, "but a good play cannot penetrate bad acting without emerging distorted."

The magazine *New Masses* was launched that fall of 1925 with a million and a half dollars provided by a young Bostonian, Charles

Garland, who had refused to accept an inheritance from his father and had donated the money to a fund to be used "for the benefit of all." O'Neill was featured as a contributing editor along with Sherwood Anderson, Van Wyck Brooks, Carl Sandburg, Boardman Robinson and Max Eastman. Besides containing criticism of the arts, the magazine announced it would carry "first hand reports of big strikes and other national events." Although O'Neill was friendly with the leading liberals and radicals of his day, he was not a doctrinaire left-winger. If his heart was with members of the lower classes, it was with those who didn't work because they didn't want to.

In December, of 1925 O'Neill, Kenneth Macgowan and Robert Edmond Jones, in association with A. L. Jones and Morris Green, produced *The Fountain* at the Greenwich Village Theatre. In a program note, O'Neill tried to explain what the play meant. His explanation was not very successful, except when it was about what the play was not. "I wish to take solemn oath," he said, "right here and now that *The Fountain* is not morbid realism." Even Brooks Atkinson wrote that the austere self-criticism that prompted Mr. O'Neill to destroy sixteen of his dramas as unworthy of production has in this instance indulged him too freely."

As for *The Great God Brown,* not only the commercial producers but the leading New York patron of the arts, Otto Kahn, refused to back it. With Jones and Macgowan assisting, O'Neill produced it himself, defraying much of the cost of the production out of his own pocket. Clark told O'Neill he figured the play would run about two weeks, long enough for O'Neill fans to take a look at it.

The Great God Brown is a strange play which O'Neill never quite succeeded in explaining. Its principal innovation was the introduction of masks, which, according to Kenneth Macgowan, were used for the first time "to dramatize changes and conflicts in character. O'Neill uses them as a means of dramatizing a transfer of personality from one man to another." O'Neill himself wrote that "the use of masks will be discovered to be the freest solution of the modern dramatist's problem as to how he can express those profound hidden conflicts of mind which the probings of psychology continue to disclose to us. What, at bottom, is the new psychological insight into human cause and effect but a study in masks, an exercise in unmasking?" He said he wanted to reveal "the mystical pattern which manifests itself as an overtone in *The Great God Brown,* dimly behind and beyond the words and action of the characters."

The Great God Brown was written in 1925. Certainly one must read and reread the play to grasp not only its meaning but even its plot. The play presents the families of two partners in an architectural firm. Their sons are opposites: an idealist and a materialist. The girl, Margaret, is in love with Dion Anthony. Billy Brown is in love with Margaret. Dion wears the mask of a wastrel but beneath it he is terribly sensitive. Margaret, it seems, loves the Dion who wears the mask of Pan. (There is little doubt that O'Neill was thinking of himself when he wrote the part of Dion. Perhaps he was trying to explain the curious combination of drunken saloon habitué and shy, retiring man too sensitive to function in the rough-and-tumble everyday world).

Dion Anthony wastes his life in dissipation. Only with a prostitute, Cybel, is he able to discard his Pan mask. Margaret has destroyed him by loving only his mask. At the end of the play, Dion dies and gives his Dion mask to Billy Brown so that he can live with Margaret, who loves Brown-Dion much more than she ever loved Dion Anthony. Brown dies—killed by the police for allegedly murdering Dion. Margaret kisses the mask of Dion (which is all she has ever seen) and says, "You will sleep under my heart."

Needless to say, the play is taxing to an audience. It is certainly one of O'Neill's most challenging plays, breaking new frontiers in the drama. *The Great God Brown* represented the best lyrical writing he had done, the style well fitted to the theme and the action. But still the play is often awkward, tedious and always self-conscious. Actors and audience spent too much time wondering what O'Neill was trying to say ever to get emotionally involved in the lives of the characters. O'Neill himself appears to have had difficulty in explaining the play. "It is a mystery—the mystery any one man or woman can feel but not understand as the meaning of any event—or accident—in any life on earth." Whatever that means it does not do much to clear up *The Great God Brown.* At another time he said that the play was a mystery but, instead of dealing with crooks and police, "it's about the mystery of personality and life." One thing is sure: The play is mysterious.

O'Neill had the last laugh on Barrett Clark as to how much of *The Great God Brown* the public would take. The play moved uptown and ran nearly a year. Clark himself liked to tell the story of the two shopgirls who went to see it. After the third act, one of them said, "Gee, it's awful artistic, ain't it?" To which her friend answered, "Yes, but it's good all the same."

For their second winter in Bermuda, the O'Neills rented a house called Bellevue, a big Victorian mansion with Greek columns and a wide porch and set off by a spacious lawn. While living there, O'Neill negotiated the purchase of a larger place which he planned to make his permanent home. His choice was a big stone palace on thirteen and a half acres of land overlooking Hamilton harbor. Spithead, as it was called, had been built early in the nineteenth century by a Captain Hezekiah Frith, who was reported to have made a fortune from privateering. The main house, containing several dozen rooms, is at the very edge of the water. There was also a small house next to it and a gardener's cottage on the side of a hill. The estate had been abandoned for some years and was in need of extensive repairs. O'Neill was soon conferring with architects and builders about plans for restoring Spithead to its old grandeur. Always the romanticist, he was excited by the history that went with the old place. He told Agnes that he thought he would be at home in a pirate's house. Perhaps, he said, Spithead would turn out to be one place where he at last belonged.

He was now at work on *Strange Interlude,* for which he had made notes in the fall of 1923. "It was in the previous summer," he said, "in Provincetown, that I heard from an aviator, formerly of the Lafayette Escadrille, the story of a girl whose aviator fiancé had been shot down just before the armistice. The girl went to pieces from the shock. She later married, not because she loved the man but because she wanted to have a child. She hoped through motherhood to win back a measure of contentment from life."

Strange Interlude was the most ambitious play O'Neill had undertaken up to this point in his career. It carries four characters through searing emotional crises in their lives over a period of twenty-eight years. Like the girl O'Neill had heard about, Nina Leeds, the beautiful daughter of a college professor, had been engaged to an aviator who was killed in World War I. Her stern and Puritanical father had not permitted her to marry her fiancé and had prevented them from making love. She leaves home, becomes a nurse, and turns rebel and promiscuous. She eventually marries a man she doesn't love, in order to settle down and have children, but after the marriage the husband's mother tells Nina that she must not have children because there is insanity in the husband's family. Nina has a child by her lover and lets her husband think it is his. Toward the end of the play, the child has become a man and he slaps his real father without knowing him to be his father. The play ends with the boy flying away in a plane with his fiancée. Nina has been defeated by time and by the spirit of youth in her son—the same spirit which caused her to rebel in her own youth. The characters all speak their thoughts aloud, a development of the old-fashioned asides used in the theater of James O'Neill's day. It is also notably an outgrowth of the stream-of-consciousness writing that James Joyce had begun to employ so effectively, as had Arthur Schnitzler, the Viennese novelists, dramatist, and friend and admirer of Freud.

"My people," O'Neill said in discussing the device, "speak aloud what they think and what others aren't supposed to hear. They talk in prose, realistic or otherwise, blank verse or hexameter or rhymed couplets." The dialogue in *Strange Interlude* is occasionally powerful enough to make one gasp. As Arthur Hobson Quinn has said, "You always apprehend that a soul is speaking who has something important to say."

Strange Interlude will probably always stand out, with *Mourning Becomes Electra* and *Long Day's Journey into Night,* as one of O'Neill's three great plays. All three are Gargantuan; they center upon large families and deal with at least two generations. Perhaps *Strange Interlude* will again become popular when it is at last permitted to be cut. It will become a better play, at any rate. If it is dated, it is dated in the peculiarly memorable way of Scott Fitzgerald's *The Great Gatsby.* In both, one finds real clues to the temperament of the 1920s and upper-class society.

O'Neill's biography by Barrett Clark was now in page proofs. Clark, a painstaking researcher, had been most judicious in quoting from pieces written by critics and journalists who had interviewed O'Neill. Yet O'Neill proved difficult to please. He began by praising the job Clark had done—the writing had a fine intelligent quality, the main part of the biography was excellent in every way. Then he proceeded to tear to shreds much of what Clark had written, especially where competent interviewers had quoted O'Neill directly. Most accounts of his early life were legend, he said; the truth would be more interesting, more incredible, and he (O'Neill) should really write his own biography and shame the devil.

On the other hand, maybe he should not write about himself. When his memory brought back this or that episode in his life, he could not, or would not, as he said, recognize the person as himself or understand the acts as his. Reason told him he had done this or

O'Neill with his son, Eugene, Jr., at Belgrade Lakes, Maine

that, said this or that, but the feeling that it was another person remained. Although some of those who had quoted him were the best reporters in the country, O'Neill wanted to edit the quotes they had attributed to him. He kept wanting to change what he had said so that it "better expressed the truth."

He wanted Clark's biography to be more concise, and to be a more "interest-catching piece of writing." Though he thought a photograph of himself ought to go into the book, he wanted to "O.K. it, as some of the photos of me are very poor." He strongly recommended an enlargement of a snapshot which Nicholas Muray had taken at Peaked Hill. It was the best of all, O'Neill thought, and "really represents me."

Clark wrote O'Neill that he was most discouraged. He said it was difficult, in a biography, "to get anyone" unless the biographer had lived alongside his subject from childhood up. O'Neill replied that he didn't see any reason for Clark to be discouraged. With a flash of insight, he observed that a man reading his own biography resembles a man looking into a mirror while he has on a new hat. He inevitably looks "a bit queer and ridiculous to himself" and wonders who the stranger is. Clark went ahead with publication, but the volume he published in the fall was pitifully thin, because of the deletions which O'Neill had demanded.

Something of O'Neill's state of mind at this time may be seen in some paragraphs, full of sour notes as they are, by John V. A. Weaver in the New York *World*. "Something has happened to O'Neill," he wrote. He had seen him only twice since he had studied with him at Harvard, and he found him "a stranger."

"Gone is the old swaggering zest, vanished is the charming swashbuckling. He looks tired and tortured. Probably it is my fault but he finds little beyond monosyllables to say to me. Even his infuriated sense of humor seems to have lost all its edge." Weaver explained all this on the ground that O'Neill was surrounded by "sycophants, his Village yes men. No human could withstand, I suppose, the frightful adulation which has been his lot. His work looks bad, too, these days."

Weaver said he had not seen *The Great God Brown*. Nevertheless, he felt free to pass judgment on it. "From what I hear," he said, "there is too much in it of this artificial, manufactured Great God O'Neill. As for *Welded, All God's Chillun, Desire under the Elms* and

The Fountain—well, they all have the appearance, to me, of rungs down a ladder into sterility." This was harsh, and Weaver knew it. "I'm sorry," he wrote. "One cannot help a little sadness over the spectacle of a high, exuberant spirit becoming lacquered. I would like to hear that he had vanished, full of hooch and hellishness, for parts unknown, beyond some new horizon, to touch the earth again and return plain Gene and not the deity of Washington Square."

Weaver had written, that year, an unsuccessful musical comedy called *Love 'Em and Leave 'Em*. He had written it cynically, he said, to prove to his friends that he could write a hit musical comedy. It was the only play he was ever to have on the boards. He suggested that O'Neill go to see this play and then sit with him over "a flock of beers and tear hell out of it. But I guess he will not. We aren't high-brow enough, I'm sure, for this strange, literary O'Neill. We wouldn't be worth bothering about. Things change."

As O'Neill pushed through the first half of *Strange Interlude* in the spring of 1926, he also completed all the details of his purchase of Spithead. The big house in Bermuda would take some months before it could be made ready for occupancy. Meanwhile he moved Agnes and the children into the small house next to it. Brook Farm had not been sold, but he proceeded with Spithead nevertheless.

"He really loved Bermuda," Agnes has said. "He told me he was convinced that Spithead was where he wanted to spend the rest of his life. Conferring with workmen and architects on doing over Spithead gave him a great deal of pleasure."

On June 15, 1926, O'Neill and Agnes sailed for New York. Shane was six, Oona a year old. The family went directly to Ridgefield. O'Neill had a day in New York and conferred with Clark. On June 23, he and Agnes drove in a rented limousine to New Haven, where he received an honorary degree from Yale. As usual, the prospect of appearing in public, to be "on view" before a large audience, distressed O'Neill and he worried and fretted all the way to New Haven. It would be awful. What would he do? Would he not make a fool of himself? Agnes tried to reassure him.

They were the house guests of Professor Baker. Also receiving an honorary degree was Andrew Mellon, Secretary of the Treasury under President Hoover. James Rowland Angell, president of Yale, gave a luncheon for his distinguished guests, among them the Crown Prince of Sweden. Later, at the commencement exercises, the degree of Doctor of Literature was conferred upon O'Neill with the words (probably written by William Lyon Phelps):

"As a creative contributor of new and moving forms to one of the oldest of arts, as the first American playwright to receive both wide and serious recognition upon the stage of Europe ..." As the citation was being read, O'Neill looked desperately from side to side, then bowed his head in terror. But when he mounted the platform to receive the parchment and heard the applause, a smile spread over his face. He even took a little bow.

He and Agnes stayed on in Baker's house for several days. After dinner one night, and after Agnes had gone to bed, O'Neill took a walk around the Yale campus. According to George Jean Nathan, O'Neill noticed a number of old Yale grads "having a hot reunion with themselves." Three of them, in particular, drew O'Neill's attention because they were "so grandly stewed." One was the president of a big bank, another was a vice-president of one of the big railroads, and a third was a United States senator. Nathan did not make it clear how O'Neill knew their names and exact titles.

"After playing leapfrog for about ten minutes," Nathan wrote, "during which one of them fell down and rolled halfway into a sewer, the three, singing barber-shop songs at the top of their lungs, wobbled across the street to the opposite corner, where there was a mailbox. Whereupon the senator proceeded to use the mailbox for a purpose generally reserved for telegraph poles and the sides of barns."

According to Nathan, O'Neill delighted in telling this story. After finishing it, he would always break into boisterous laughter —the only occasions Nathan ever saw him do so. O'Neill's delight in presenting and exaggerating three ultra "respectabilities" as vulgarians is characteristic of him.

The summer of 1926 O'Neill and his family spent at Belgrade Lakes, near the heart of the pine region in Maine. The period should be labeled, Agnes has said, with the name of the cabin they lived in— "Lune Lodge."

Supposedly, O'Neill was hard at work finishing the second half of *Strange Interlude*. Elizabeth Shepley Sergeant, the biographer, visited Lune Lodge that summer and found him sitting by the Maine lake "with Shane, pulling perch off shore, and a well-ordered domestic life in full swing up the hill."

All the children were in the house that summer. Gaga, too, was there. During most of the day, the children were required to stay away from the lodge. There was to be absolute quiet while O'Neill worked.

Propped up in bed with pillows, he spent the morning writing in longhand. While Agnes took care of Oona, Gaga took the other children for walks through the woods or down to the lake to swim.

Besides his daily writing stints, O'Neill was also carrying on a steady correspondence with the architects and builders who were doing over Spithead. On some afternoons he received writers and journalists who came up to Maine to interview him.

There was some social life at Belgrade Lakes. One of O'Neill's neighbors was Elizabeth Marbury, a wealthy and fashionable New York spinster who was a theatrical producer and author of the recently published book *My Crystal Ball*. Her house guests included Florence Reed, star of the Broadway hit *Shangai Gesture,* and Lady Mendl. Also included in the Marbury household that summer was the recently divorced wife of the *New Yorker* caricaturist Ralph Barton —Carlotta Monterey.

This second meeting of O'Neill and the actress who had starred in *The Hairy Ape* took place in the living room of Lune Lodge. Miss Marbury and her house guests came to call, Carlotta among them. She was the same age as O'Neill, thirty-eight; she was a successful actress of stage and screen; and she was spectacularly good-looking.

Carlotta Monterey has given the date of her birth as December, 1888, and the place as San Francisco, whose records were destroyed in the Great Fire. She made her debut on the stage in London when she was only sixteen and proceeded to study acting, voice culture and pantomine in London and Paris. Her first New York stage appearance was with Lou Tellegen in *Taking Chances,* which opened at the Thirty-ninth Street Theatre in June, 1915. She played Lucy Gallon, and her role was described as that of "a picturesque, petulant and pouting adventuress." She then succeeded Lenore Ulric in the leading role of *The Bird of Paradise*. After playing several vampire parts, she retired from the stage for two years, during which her name was linked with that of a well-known millionaire philanthropist of the period. About 1920 she returned to the Broadway stage in *Mr. Barnum,* and subsequently she played in *Be Calm, Camilla, A Sleepless Night, Bavu,* and *Voltaire*.

In her book *Past Imperfect*, Ilka Chase states that Carlotta was born Hazel Tauzig, but in an interview he gave the Kansas City *Star* Ralph Barton said her maiden name was Neilson Tassinge. Carlotta

Monterey is most probably a stage name although it has already been chiseled on her tombstone in a Boston cemetery alongside the name of Eugene O'Neill. Her first husband is reported to have been named Chapman; by him, she had a daughter named Cynthia. Her second husband is said to have been an Englishman named Coates.

During the two years Carlotta and Barton were married she met most of the members of the group around Harold Ross, editor of *The New Yorker,* and his wife, Jane Grant, but the group took an unsympathetic view of her seemingly violent jealousy. Carlotta didn't fit in.

During the year preceding her visit to Belgrade Lakes, she had played in several motion pictures. She had parts in *Soul Fire* with Richard Barthelmess and in *The King on Main Street* with Adolphe Menjou. In a Broadway play, *The Red Falcon* by Stark Young, she was in the same cast with Ilka Chase. Miss Chase, who had two minor parts—a nun and a serving maid—found Carlotta "kind and funny, remarkably ribald . . . she dressed like a Dutch burgher's wife . . . had strong capable hands and feet and superb dark eyes."

Carlotta liked to dress in immaculate white linen and had her shoes made to order of a special leather. Her neck, Ilka said, was the neck of a Javanese or a Russian, whereas "her body was Dutch or Danish." Carlotta often told friends that her mother was of Dutch descent and her father was Danish. Miss Chase noted that Carlotta's apartment always "shone like a minted coin." One of the most interesting observations Miss Chase made about Carlotta was that "she hated the theater."

O'Neill himself was getting fed up with the theater that summer —at least that's what he told Nathan. The eternal showshop, he termed it, from which nothing ever emerged but more showshop. Agnes could write her short stories and send them off, to be published or not. Fiction writers had the best of it all, he said. It was humiliating for an artist to have to put up with what he was going through. The Theatre Guild was dallying over when and whether to produce *Marco Millions.* The Actors Theatre was trying to raise money to do *Lazarus Laughed* but was having a hard time getting it from "the ranks of million-talking jitney-giving Lorenzos."

Agnes has recalled that when Carlotta came to their house that summer afternoon with Elizabeth Marbury and the others, they all seemed a rather strident, mannish group. She was unaware that Carlotta had made any particular impression on her husband.

The children, however, were more observant. They buzzed among themselves about the beautiful woman who wore a bathing suit the likes of which they had never seen before; it was one piece and there was "so little of it." They had noticed her when she came to call with the fashionable ladies. Down at the lake, they had seen her talking to Father and he had seemed quite taken. But if O'Neill's children were instinctively aware of something unusual, there is no suggestion in the pieces written about O'Neill that summer that he was preoccupied with anything but his work and his family.

"When O'Neill steps lightly along some pagan shore with Shane," Elizabeth Shepley Sergeant wrote of her visit with him, "he walks a little behind, a tall figure in a bathing suit, with limbs burnt to a pagan blackness; and on his face the look, not of a 'father' but of some trusting child who has grown up into a strange world." Miss Sergeant worried about Shane during her visit to Lune Lodge that summer. He seemed a lonely little boy, lost among the older children and the celebrities trekking to O'Neill's doorstep.

When David Karsner came to do a long magazine piece on O'Neill for the *New York Herald Tribune,* he talked first with Agnes on the wide porch of Lune Lodge. Karsner found her "a girlish woman with a manner as straightforward and unassuming and unaffected as I have ever encountered." They heard footsteps, and Agnes quickly disappeared.

Karsner saw O'Neill step "briskly forward, attired in loose-fitting trousers, white sneakers and a sweater. His greeting was cordial and unaffected, and yet, I had the feeling that it was quite detached and aloof, albeit unconsciously so." Karsner was more disturbed by O'Neill than by any of the celebrated people he had ever interviewed. "I cannot recall a single person whose burning eyes, intense, almost nervous exterior had the same effect upon me. . . . It was what gave those eyes of his their burning luster and what contributed to his intense, almost jerky exterior that mattered. You felt the deep tone of his nature, like the mid-regions of the sea that are solid and tranquil."

"Every person," O'Neill told him, "has within him his own kind of truth, and that truth has little if any application outside its possessor." He added that no longer did he have any fixed opinions about anything. There were always too many things to consider from which opinions are derived.

In general, Karsner decided at the end of their talk, "the theme which furnishes the basis of nearly all of O'Neill's plays is man's rebellion against his environment."

Darkness descended as the two men talked. O'Neill was silent for what seemed like an hour to Karsner, who likewise remained silent. It was an effect that other writers had experienced on meeting O'Neill. Stark Young has said, "As was usual in his case I felt vaguely an emotion of pity and defense. Though there was nothing particularly to defend him against, I wanted to defend him, to take his part."

Lawrence Langner, head of the Theatre Guild, had a similar feeling of admiration and protection for O'Neill. "The kindness of his smile," Langner said, "the gentleness of his spirit, the philosophical detachment of his mind, his Olympian view of human destiny, were not only inspiring but so endeared him to you that you wanted to lay down your life in his service."

"Night had come," Karsner wrote, "and laid a dark hand over the lake among the pines in the Maine woods. He sat gazing at the still water and listening to it splash upon the shore and run back again to its own. In that unforgettable hour there seemed to hang over us like a blanket the balanced pain of the world.

" 'There can be no such thing,' O'Neill suddenly said, 'as an ivory tower for a playwright. He either lives in the theater of his time or he never lives at all.' "

O'Neill and Agnes stayed on at Belgrade Lakes until the end of September. He accomplished little besides catching up on his correspondence. *Lazarus* still had not been sold, although O'Neill had hopes that S. Hurok might put it on with Chaliapin in the lead. He heard that Max Reinhardt was interested in doing it—the German impresario was coming to New York to put on a revival of *The Miracle*. But nothing of O'Neill's was to be put on the boards for two years.

Something was troubling him. Jimmy Light wrote to cheer him up. What especially pleased the playwright was that Light said there was so much of the real O'Neill in *Lazarus*. O'Neill told his old friend Fitzie—Eleanor Fitzgerald of the Provincetown—that Light's words had cheered him no end and were worth "a gallon of licker" in overcoming self-pity and self-indulgence. He resumed working.

Although he put all his creative energies into finishing the second half of *Strange Interlude,* O'Neill was already conceiving *Mourning Becomes Electra.* The previous spring in Bermuda, when he began

Interlude, he wrote in his work diary that he might write a "modern psychological drama using one of the old legend plots of Greek tragedy." He asked himself if it would be possible to "get a modern psychological approximation of [the] Greek sense of fate" into this sort of play. The problem was that a modern audience possessed no belief in gods or in supernatural retribution. For the Greek sense of fate, the concept of the Furies and the avenging gods, he would substitute "the Puritan conviction of man born to sin and punishment." He would also throw in some of the tenets of the enemy of Puritanism, Dr. Sigmund Freud. He would have his characters trapped psychologically, using the Freudian concept that a man's adult relationship with a woman is in part predetermined by the development of his unconscious sexual strivings for his mother, and that a woman's relationship with a man is predetermined in complementary fashion.

One might assume that, if O'Neill was thinking in such Freudian terms when he was writing *Strange Interlude,* that play, too, would have a Freudian orientation. In fact, the critic and teacher Joseph Wood Krutch believed that it did, and he wrote that "the intellectual framework [of *Strange Interlude*] is supplied by Freudian psychology." But Doris Alexander, an O'Neill scholar, has written that *Interlude* is based squarely on the philosophy of Schopenhauer, who believed that "all love, however ethereally it may bear itself, is rooted in the sexual impulse alone." In O'Neill's *Interlude,* the characters are not motivated, according to the Freudian rationale. Rather, as Doris Alexander points out, they "are at the mercy of irrational forces." Darrell, the psychiatrist, fled his affair with Nina, the heroine, and supposedly went to Europe to study. He returns years later and confesses to Nina, "I didn't study! I didn't live. I longed for you—and suffered." The ending of *Strange Interlude,* an ending of sheer exhaustion, as John Gassner has said, is the perfect expression of the pessimistic philosophy of Schopenhauer.

There is no doubt that O'Neill was steeped in the writings of Schopenhauer along with those of Nietzsche. He discussed their work in an introduction he wrote to Benjamin De Casseres' *Anathema! Litanies of Negation.* They mixed, he said, despair and rhapsody. He told De Casseres that Nietzsche's *Thus Spake Zarathustra* had had more influence on him than any other book he had read up to 1927. He had found it on the shelf of a Greenwich Village bookshop run by Benjamin Tucker. Sometimes, O'Neill confessed, he thought his work—and his life—a pitiful contradiction of the *Zarathustra* influence. Nonetheless, he read his copy every year or so and was "never disappointed," which was more than he could say for any other book.

During the writing of *Interlude,* O'Neill was also reading Freud. He read *Beyond the Pleasure Principle* and probably *A General Introduction to Psychoanalysis.* Through Kenneth Macgowan, he became friends with a practicing analyst, Dr. Gilbert van Tassle Hamilton, who was doing a study called *A Research in Marriage,* a psychological investigation of the love and sex behavior of two hundred married men and women. Agnes and O'Neill allowed themselves to be questioned. In return, Dr. Hamilton said that any of those who helped in the study could have, at its conclusion, a free analysis. O'Neill not only took him up on the offer, but also consulted Dr. Hamilton on certain psychological aspects of *Strange Interlude.*

In October, O'Neill and his family moved to Ridgefield. Despite the fact that it was a time of prosperity, Brook Farm had found no buyers. At the end of November, the O'Neills boarded the Furness-Bermuda liner *Fort St. George* bound for Bermuda. At the sailing, O'Neill talked to the ship-news reporters about Spithead. He described it as a house that was old "when Admiral Paul Jones was flying his flag in West Indian waters," and he spoke of its having been occupied by "a man named Frith who made a fortune out of the prizes he took when he commanded a privateer." For all his shyness, O'Neill was never at a loss in providing good copy for the press.

After settling in Spithead, O'Neill fitted out a study in the big house at the water's edge. His windows looked out over the docks where the boats were tied up and where his guests went swimming. That winter and into the spring of 1927, he worked on his final draft of *Strange Interlude.*

There were many visitors in the spring. James Light came down with his bride, a Philadelphia-born society girl and artist, dark-haired and pretty. Bessie Breuer, novelist and editor, came with her husband, Henry Varnum Poor, the painter. She loved both O'Neill and Agnes, but she saw, as Stark Young had seen, that some terrible tension, a disturbing jealousy, existed between them.

"Gene could get jealous of Agnes," Miss Breuer has said, "just watching her smoke a cigarette. They would fall to arguing and be late for a dinner party. Then Gene would want her to hurry and she would lose her shoe and there would be more arguing. Then she would find the shoe under the bed. By then it would be almost midnight.

"Agnes was as much his sister as a woman could be. They were like two children. Both were delicate, beautiful creatures. Agnes was so beautiful. She had long tapering fingers, a lithe, thin body. As for Gene, when I think of him I always see his eyes. They were always turned inward. They were bottomless. He spoke with his eyes. He received you into his face with his eyes. As you talked with him, you entered into another life. That was the kind of profundity he had.

"Gene was a person of love, not just personal love. Nobody he ever knew did he leave untouched. He always left on them the imprint of his purity. There was always a tentative distance between himself and others, however. He had, of course, great, great reserve.

"Gene starts in a world of pain. He created a world of love and pain everywhere he went. He had in him the poetry of life, the poetry of passion. Of course, he was destroyed in the end. This kind of poetry cannot be translated into ordinary life. As for what happened to his children, he couldn't help them because he couldn't help himself."

One of the O'Neills' guests has recalled that Eugene junior, then seventeen, used to break out into recitations of poetry loud enough for his father to hear. "It was as if the boy," the guest has observed, "was making love to his father with poetry. O'Neill would stop work and come down to the dock to listen to his son. He was delighted and would declaim a few lines of poetry himself."

Some of the poetry Eugene junior recited was his own:

> *They did not recognize me,*
> *Me, son of God!*
> *Born of a Virgin*
> *I told them who I was.*
> *They gave me a brain examination.*
> *They did not phase me,*
> *No! Not me!*
>
> *Jesus Christ come again to Earth.*
> *I preached my simple teaching.*
> *The world would not listen.*
> *They sent me to the electric chair,*
> *Crucified me again!*

> But on the chair I laughed at them.
> They made me a Cynic! So I laughed.

> "Did you have a funny dream, Eugene,
> that you laughed so in your sleep?
> Why are you still laughing?"

> Did I not see something down there?
> In that Infinite Hole?
> Was it God?
> Or nothing?
> Maybe God if The Nothing.

Young Eugene's deification of his father was well developed by that summer. In Douglaston, where he lived with his mother, step-brother and stepfather, he was introduced at a party at a neighbor's house as "the son of Eugene O'Neill, one of our best dramatists."

"What do you mean," young Eugene quickly interjected, *"one* of our best? My father is *the* greatest dramatist in the entire world."

For Shane, who was not quite eight, that summer was one of the happiest in his life. Like his father, he had taken the sea as his own. He swam almost as well as an adult. He fished off the dock for "yeller grunts," though they were not big and not good to eat, and his chief ambition was to catch a shark. He had a bulldog named Bowser, who wandered off now and then for a few days but always came back. He also had a girl friend, Peggy Ann, the daughter of a neighboring family named Hulburt, with whom he played a great deal. The grownups smiled, and they told each other that it was a "match." Shane missed Gaga, who was in Provincetown, and Gaga missed him even more. Agnes reported details of Shane's life to Gaga by letter.

Shane was only vaguely aware of the shadow that was beginning to fall over his mother and father that year. He recalls there was a good deal of talk about "that woman," but there were other interesting things going on that made greater impressions. A famous actress was thinking of doing one of Daddy's plays called *Strange Interlude.* Then, all of a sudden, a man named Lawrence Langner of the Theatre Guild in New York came to Bermuda and held long conferences with Daddy. Mr. Langner refused to go into the ocean although Daddy urged him to join the family in their afternoon swim. One evening he took *Strange Interlude* back to his hotel. That night there was a terrible storm, and in the morning when it had cleared, Daddy and Mother were in good spirits. Mr. Langner said he was going to put *Strange Interlude* on Broadway.

Before Mr. Langner left Bermuda to return to New York, he came down to the beach and took moving pictures of Daddy swimming. Daddy swam extra well that afternoon. There always seemed to be a lot of picture-taking in Bermuda. Everybody who came down brought a camera, and soon Daddy and Mother, Shane and Oona, were being asked to stand here and sit there. Some of the pictures turned up in newspapers and magazines.

Jimmy Light, unlike so many of the important people who came to Bermuda to see Daddy, paid a lot of attention to Shane. He was sympathetic to Shane's idea of catching a shark but, like Shane, he settled for catching "yeller grunts." Daddy seemed more cheerful with Jimmy Light, and so did Mother. The Lights stayed two months. Shane, especially, was sorry to see them go.

When summer came to Bermuda, the heat drove many of the inhabitants off the island—but not the O'Neills. Shane noticed his father getting restless and bored. "Here in Bermuda," O'Neill told a friend, "one rarely gets the chance, especially now in the slack season, to say a word to a human being above the intellectual and spiritual level of a land crab and this solitude gets damned oppressive at times."

In August, Shane had no guests with whom to swim or fish. Daddy was sick in bed for ten days. "I've had a rather rotten time of it," O'Neill told a friend, "generally bunged up and no pep. Summer flu, particularly in this climate, is not what I would wish on anyone seeking the well-known joy of living."

Shane was used to being alone; he seemed most at home between the sea and the shore. His father noticed it, too. "One of these days," he said to Shane, "I expect you'll turn into one of 'them yeller grunts' yourself and swim out and leave us, and then we'll have to set the fish font to catch you and bring you home again!" At times like these, father and son laughed easily together. It was not difficult for O'Neill to communicate with his son when he thought to do it.

Late in the summer of 1927, O'Neill read an article about himself by Ben De Casseres. In general he liked it, but he objected to De Casseres' saying that "nerves" had landed him in a sanatorium; it was "T.B. bugs," O'Neill answered, which he had picked up at Jimmy the Priest's. He also wanted to take issue with De Casseres for having said that O'Neill had shoved off the vultures which were ready to feed off his fame and corrupt him. The O'Neill vultures were still flapping around and thank God! They were still hungry and undaunted but, O'Neill insisted, he was proud of them because they were a test—they justified his existence. Should they desert him, he would feel he was a success and "a complete loss." As yet, they had not been able to gorge themselves "fat and comfortable" on what the reporters called fame. O'Neill said his birds luckily fly from the "great dark behind and inside and not from the bright lights without." He anticipated one last visit of these vultures when their wings would blot out the sky and they would tear loose the last of the O'Neill liver.

O'Neill postponed his departure from Bermuda several times that summer because he was ill. But he had to get to New York because the Guild was preparing to cast *Marco Millions* and *Strange Interlude*. School opened before he left, and Shane brought his copybook home and showed it to his father. O'Neill only glanced at it. If only he did not have to leave Spithead, he said, and go to that terrible city . . .

The day of departure came. He kissed Agnes and Oona and Shane and boarded the ship for New York. He was off on a journey that would take him around the world, a long day's journey that would plunge him and his family into night.

CHAPTER

SIXTEEN

ಞ

INTERLUDE

IN MANHATTAN

When O'Neill arrived in New York in the fall of 1927, he stayed for two weeks with the Lawrence Langners on Eleventh Street. The purpose of the visit was "to go into all phases of" *Marco Millions* and *Strange Interlude,* which were about to be produced by the Theatre Guild. Langner has said that O'Neill, contrary to popular belief, was often willing to cut his plays. For example, he told Langner that he was "always on the lookout for helpful cuts right up to the last week of rehearsals."

The Langners had wanted to entertain O'Neill, but he was a reluctant guest. "I avoid parties," he told Langner, "because I'm extremely bashful. In my younger days I used to drink in order to get up the nerve to meet people. Since I've quit drinking, it's become worse. When I once started [drinking] I was like a sailor on shore leave—a holdover from my seafaring days."

He said he had been thinking a lot about the matter of drinking. A doctor had told him that the effect of alcohol was "just like turning the albumin in your brain into the white of a poached egg." He was so convincing about the evils of alcohol that Langner was never able, thereafter, to take a drink without feeling uneasy.

O'Neill was unhappy about his reputation as a drunkard. He told Langner that once, in the Provincetown Playhouse, he had heard a woman say to her escort, "Do you know that Eugene O'Neill, the author of this play, is a terrible drunkard?" The young man said, "No!" "Yes," the woman said, "and not only does he drink to excess but he takes drugs, too."

"Excuse me, Miss," O'Neill had interrupted, "you are wrong there. I do *not* take drugs."

There are a number of explanations for O'Neill's giving up drinking—which he did at about this time. He told Elizabeth Shepley Sergeant that the fact that his mother had been able to overcome her addiction to drugs was a big factor. There is also reason to suppose that his psychoanalytic sessions with Dr. Hamilton were a factor, although the sessions were not extensive and there is no direct word from O'Neill himself on the effects of his experience with analysis.

After leaving the home of the Langners, O'Neill moved into the Hotel Wentworth, an inexpensive hotel just off the Broadway district, on Forty-sixth Street. Shane wrote him there about the usual activities: He had caught eight yellow grunts; Bowser had wandered off again but had come home on his own; but most important, Shane reported, he had been diving off the springboard!

"Your Daddy," O'Neill replied to Shane, "meaning myself, was certainly tickled to death to get your nice letter!

"It is lonely for me, living in this hotel where I don't know anyone, and I often think of you and Oona—and I miss you both like the devil! You mustn't tell Oona this, though—at least, when you tell her you must say 'like the deuce' instead of 'like the devil' to ladies, and Oona, let us hope, is a perfect lady!"

In unconsciously prophetic words, O'Neill bestowed on his son the mantle of the household: "You take good care of Mother and Oona while I'm away. You're the only O'Neill man down there now and I'm relying on you to see that none of those fool women get into trouble! However, they can't help being that way because it isn't their fault they are born girls—so I guess you better kiss all three of them for me because they really are nice to have around! Even if they are crazy! And you realize that when you're far away from them and all alone in a big city and exposed to temptations like I am now!"

Although this part of the letter was not clear to Shane at the time, later he realized that there was more to his father's secret than was revealed in this letter. O'Neill must have been aware that Agnes would take a dim view of his "temptations" and he added: "But maybe you better not read Mother this part of my letter. She might get mad and raise hell with me when I get back. Remember, us men has got to stick together!"

Shane had no inkling that Daddy might never come back. In fact, it sounded as if he were very, very anxious to come back home as soon as possible. "I'm terribly homesick," O'Neill told his son, "and I hope it won't be long before I can get back to Spithead again. Write to me again." At that time, O'Neill was also writing Agnes how much he loved Spithead and how anxious he was to return. "Like the hairy ape," he said, "at last I can belong."

Shane wanted his own boat, but O'Neill took the view that Shane must earn his right to it. "Keep on with your lessons," O'Neill wrote him. "What I saw in your copybook was fine. If you keep on that way it won't be long before you can learn to typewrite and be my secretary and write down all my plays and I'll pay you a big salary and you'll be able to buy a big boat of your own or anything you like."

There was a long time in the fall months when Shane did not hear from his father. His mother bought him some chickens to raise, helped him set them up in a hen house and showed him how to feed and care for them. Shane asked Peggy Ann to come over to Spithead to admire them. He did not know that that fall Daddy was writing to Agnes that she was not to take seriously any rumor she might have heard about his having an "affair." "It is as innocent," he told Agnes, "as Shane kissing Peggy Ann."

There are several explanations of exactly how it happened that O'Neill resumed his acquaintance with Carlotta Monterey that fall. One is that they were both scheduled to have their photographs taken at the studio of Nicholas Muray, a leading magazine photographer, and some mix-up developed about the exact times of the sittings. After both of them had been photographed, O'Neill, Muray and Carlotta went out to lunch. At the restaurant it was obvious to those who saw them together that O'Neill was much taken with Carlotta.

Carlotta had known little about O'Neill, she has said, except that he was a successful dramatist. "He asked me if he could come to tea. I hardly knew the man. He came up on three afternoons. And he never said to me, 'I love you, I think you are wonderful.' He kept saying, 'I need you. I need you.' And he did need me, I discovered. He was never in good health. He talked about his early life—that he had had no real home, no mother in the real sense, or father, no one to treat him as a child should be treated—and his face became sadder and sadder."

O'Neill's courtship of Carlotta—if it is rightly considered a courtship—was certainly unique. Evidently he saw in her (among other things) a protecting mother, a woman who could understand and requite his desperate need for maternal affection. And so, as Carlotta listened in amazement and compassion, O'Neill talked the afternoons away, telling about his life, his work, and his dreams. Then, as evening fell, he would suddenly leave off, ask what time it was, and rush away. The next day he would return and continue his pensive self-revelation.

To Carlotta's credit, she understood what he was trying to tell her. Although she herself was an actress, she respected the poet of the theater far more than the player. She believed that a man like O'Neill had a rightful claim to special protection from the world, and she soon was prepared to afford him that protection. As she frequently told her intimate friends, O'Neill at that time appealed primarily to her maternal instinct. She also added half seriously that that was how it had all started.

In a rather metaphorical but nevertheless real sense, Carlotta was knowingly flinging herself upon the burning fires of O'Neill's genius. She was also throwing away an already well-established career as a dramatic actress.

Late one chill evening that fall, the doorbell rang in the Greenwich Village apartment of a couple who had been close friends of O'Neill's from the old Provincetown Playhouse days. The couple opened their front door and saw a tall figure dressed in a black fur-lined greatcoat with a mink collar and a black Homburg hat. On his face was a wide little-boy grin. He wanted to know how they thought he looked in his fancy coat. It had been given to him, he said, by Carlotta Monterey, the rich and beautiful actress.

It was not long before most of O'Neill's friends knew all about his seeing Carlotta. Soon all of New York knew it. It was said he had fallen desperately in love, that he was torn between his love for Agnes and the children and his love for the actress.

"Everybody was worried about Gene," Susan Jenkins Brown, one of his old group, remembers. "The idea was that the great man could do no wrong." Whatever was decided, everyone seemed to agree, nothing should interfere with his genius.

By December, O'Neill was busy attending rehearsals for both *Marco Millions* and *Strange Interlude.* He said he was "so crowded" that he didn't know where he was at. He was still being sought after for interviews and photographs, but he put off all such requests. He was so tired at night, he told friends, that he went straight back to his hotel room and went to bed.

Marco Millions, with Alfred Lunt in the lead, opened at the Guild Theatre on January 9, 1928. The play makes fun of a big businessman. Marco is a Babbitt, and in his travels in the Orient all the beauty and excitement of the East are lost on him. The trip is merely an opportunity to amass a fortune. George Jean Nathan called the play "the sourest and most magnificent poke in the jaw that American big business and the American big businessman have ever got." Nevertheless, the comedy is thin and the satire is almost belligerently obvious, relying heavily upon costumes and stage trickery for its effect.

The Theatre Guild gave *Marco* a most ambitious and elaborate production. Like so many O'Neill plays, *Marco Millions* contained a most unusual bit of stage direction. After the last act, a man rises from his seat in the first row of the audience. He is dressed in the robes of a thirteenth-century Venetian merchant. He takes his hat, walks to the lobby, looks around, bored, and then hails his limousine and is driven away by his chauffeur. The man emits "a satisfied sigh at the sheer comfort of it all." It is Marco. In a program note, O'Neill said his purpose in writing the play was to show that Polo was "really a man of brass tacks [who] became celebrated as an extravagant romancer."

The critics were somewhat enthusiastic, but when the subscribers had used up their tickets the play closed. *Strange Interlude,* featuring Lynn Fontanne, Earle Larimore, Glenn Anders and Tom Powers, opened three weeks after *Marco,* at the John Golden Theatre. It was a fabulous success; seats were sold out all spring. Road companies were soon formed; the play was duly banned in Boston, and arrangements had to be made to have it performed in nearby Quincy. Seeing *Strange Interlude* became the thing to do in New York, but it achieved only a mild success in London. In May *Strange Interlude* won O'Neill his third Pulitzer Prize. Although it was widely reported to have made O'Neill a million dollars, he actually netted, according to his own figures, only $275,000.

During the opening performance, Langner went to the telephone and reported to O'Neill in his hotel room how things were going. Later, he told O'Neill that all the reviews were raves. A single untoward incident had to do with Alexander Woollcott, the caustic and petulant drama critic for the *World*. Woollcott had obtained a copy of the script from a member of the cast and wrote an advance review of the play for *Vanity Fair* in which he made fun of the asides O'Neill had used, as well as of the play in general. *Vanity Fair* came out several days before *Interlude* opened. The late Herbert Bayard Swope, editor of the *World,* was furious. He assigned Dudley Nichols, one of his best reporters, to review the play. Nichols was delighted with the play and said so in print. Woollcott resigned from the *World* in anger.

Strange Interlude was one of the longest plays ever produced. It lasted from five-thirty in the afternoon until eleven at night, with eighty minutes' intermission for supper. Restaurants in the neighborhood of the theater did a thriving business. One of them named a multilayered sandwich "Strange Interlude."

With both his plays launched, O'Neill took time to see something of Eugene junior and to write to Shane in Bermuda.

"I saw Eugene the other night," he wrote Shane. "He had dinner with me here at the hotel and then I took him and Jimmy Light to see a prize fight—or I ought to say prize fights because there were four of them and they were all very exciting although none got knocked out.

"Eugene is even bigger than when he was down this summer. He weighs 165 now. He told me to give you and Oona his love when I wrote to you."

On February 7 the Guild announced that O'Neill was going to California for rehearsals of *Lazarus Laughed* at the Pasadena Community Playhouse. Just before he was scheduled to leave, he realized that he hadn't written to Shane "for a long, long time."

I have been meaning to write you [O'Neill told his son], but I have been so busy going to daily rehearsals of my two new plays that have just opened that I honestly haven't had a chance. Or when I did have a few minutes to spare I was always so tired out that all I could do was to lie down and rest. So I know that you will forgive me. And now, just when I get through with those two plays, I have to travel way across America to California to watch them putting on another play of mine called "Lazarus Laughed" in the city of Pasadena.

I will go in swimming out there in an ocean I have never been in before—the Pacific. I hope it is as beautiful water as the water in Bermuda.

Do you go in swimming every day now? Or is it too cold for you? But you are such a big boy now that you shouldn't mind water that is 60 degrees and you really ought to get Mother to let you swim every day because that's the only way you can get good practice and be able to swim the crawl as well as Eugene does. It may be too cold for Oona to go in now but it shouldn't be for you.

In February, 1928, O'Neill went to London. He had made his decision to leave his wife and children. Agnes received the news in Bermuda in a wire from the New York *World* which asked her about reports of a divorce between herself and O'Neill.

In his farewell words to Shane, who was asked to pass them on to Oona, then only four, O'Neill asked him to

write me a long letter sometime soon and tell me everything that you and Oona are doing because it will probably be a long, long time before I will be able to see you both again. But I will often think of you and I will miss you both very much. I often lie in bed before I go to sleep—or when I can't go to sleep— and I picture to myself all about Spithead and what you both have been doing all day and I wonder how you are—and then I feel very sad and life seems to me a silly, stupid thing, even at best, when one lives it according to the truth that is in one.

But you are not old enough to know what that feeling is— and I hope to God you never will know, but that your life will always be simple and contented!

But always remember that I love you and Oona an awful lot—and please don't ever forget your Daddy.

I am enclosing a check for fifteen dollars. Ten of it is to buy you a present with and five is to buy Oona a present. You must both go to town with Mother and pick out whatever you want most.

Don't forget your Daddy!
All my love to you, dear son!

FATHER

To Shane, this letter was a shattering experience, perhaps as cruel a letter, for all its expressions of affection, as any child has ever received from a father fleeing from his responsibilities. To adult eyes its self-pity is somewhat transparent. And yet, when all this has been said, it is perhaps necessary to add that O'Neill, like any lesser man in a similar situation, was not only a husband and a father, but also himself, an individual fulfilling, somewhat painfully, his own destiny.

O'Neill tarried in London a while and then fled to France. He kept his whereabouts a secret. Naturally, the newspapers wanted to know why he had left his wife. And for whom.

"The scent after me here in France," he told Benjamin De Casseres, "has been getting pretty hot and I'm afraid every day of being smoked out—which would be fatal, under the circumstances, and playing right into my wife's hands, to say nothing of the scandal which would injure the last person in the world I want to hurt."

O'Neill asked De Casseres to "give my old group the report that you've heard from me in Prague and that I was planning to go to Russia for 'Laz' and then back to Italy to finish 'Dynamo.' I want the boys thrown as completely off the scent as possible." The false report was duly spread and printed in the papers. Actually, O'Neill was spending the summer in France and was to make a trip to the Far East in the fall.

CHAPTER

SEVENTEEN

༄

THE EXILE

Two decades had passed since Eugene O'Neill had shipped out to foreign ports. That February of 1928, when he boarded a vessel for England, he was within a few months of his fortieth birthday. To Carlotta he played the role of "a rather tough Irishman," as she put it. He chuckled at the idea of the old able-bodied seaman sailing first class, and he looked longingly at the roustabouts on the docks and at the sailors on deck performing their chores.

He refused to eat in the ship's dining room; he said it made him nervous. This was painfully true, as Carlotta soon found out.

O'Neill "didn't care anything for being with people," she said years later. "He had this terrible nervous disease. In a public dining room his hands would begin to shake and his face would sink, and he would get circles under his eyes and begin to sweat. We could never go to the theater here. We never saw one of his plays open. We saw the dress rehearsal, and when the dress rehearsal was over, the car would be outside, and we would hop in and go. He always used to say to me, 'If only I could just write and never bother to go to New York.' "

It was certainly true that there were few uptown people—the "respectabilities"—with whom O'Neill could feel at home. As for his distress in going into public dining rooms, there was good reason for this. He was a fastidious man and he was also extremely self-conscious, almost to the degree of psychosis. The trembling of his hands, noticeable even then, made eating and drinking difficult. Nathan said that when he lifted a highball glass to his lips, his hand shook the ice in it so hard that he sounded "like a Swiss bell ringer." Naturally, the thought of people watching him drop food from his fork was abhorrent to him.

When O'Neill arrived in London, he later told Nathan, Carlotta urged him to go out and buy the things that he had never permitted himself to have. She believed it was especially important for him to be well dressed; she thought it would give him greater poise and self-confidence. At first he resisted her suggestions, but Carlotta eventually persuaded him to have his suits made by a tailor of whom she approved. O'Neill complained to Nathan that she was making a "gigolo" out of him, and when she suggested that he have his shoes made to order he put his foot down. But the foot was soon up again and being fitted for the first of the seventy-five pairs of shoes that were to be made for him during his stay abroad.

O'Neill never acquired a taste for elegance in dress, but he did learn that one can be well dressed without being affected; in fact, good grooming, at least in public, became a habit of his.

One of the things O'Neill had wanted all his life was a carriage dog, a spotted Dalmatian such as he had seen running alongside the carriages of the rich when he was a boy in New London. That year he bought Blemie, just such a dog, who was to remain with O'Neill and Carlotta for the next two decades.

O'Neill did his banking with the Guaranty Trust Company and arranged for its London branch at 50 Pall Mall to forward all his mail but to keep his exact whereabouts secret. At the end of April he was staying at Guéthary, in the Basque country of southwest France, where he set to work writing *Dynamo*. The play is about a young man who loses his faith in God and places it in science, as symbolized by a dynamo. He falls in love with the daughter of an atheist family. His love for his mother and for the dynamo fuse into the same sort of all-embracing emotion. He kills the girl, after denouncing her as a harlot (as his mother has done), and then flings himself into the dynamo. His cries are swallowed in the hum of the dynamo. Many meanings can be read into this play—altogether too many, in fact. But, as one of the playwright's friends said, "At least you grant that O'Neill was not afraid to come to grips with great themes." In this instance, his grip was not too firm.

Although it was one of his poorest plays, when he sent it to Langner O'Neill said it was "the real stuff." The idea for it had come to him near Ridgefield, where he saw a dynamo powered by a river. He heard its eerie hum and had the feeling of looking at some modern god. *Dynamo,* O'Neill wrote, was a

> . . . symbolical and factual biography of what is happening in a large section of the American soul right now. It is really the first play of a trilogy that will dig at the roots of the sickness of to-day as I feel it—the death of an old god and the failure of science and materialism to give any satisfying new one for the surviving, primitive, religious instinct to find a meaning for life in, and to comfort its fears of death with. It seems to me that anyone trying to do big work nowadays must have this big subject behind all the little subjects of his plays or novels, or he is simply scribbling around on the surface of things and has no more real status than a parlor entertainer. The other two plays will be *Without Ending of Days* [O'Neill later changed this to *Days Without End*] and *It Cannot Be Mad.*

As Clark noted, "There was an ominous note in all this. O'Neill seemed to be worrying too much about God and his own soul. I believe he was doing too much of his own private thinking aloud, playing an autobiographical *Strange Interlude* with long asides." Clark suggested that O'Neill simply could not let his philosophy mature but "must out with it incontinently."

It is ironic that, at the precise time that O'Neill was running away from his wife and two children, he should have been so deeply concerned with immorality and the "sickness of today." To a friend he said that he was writing about "the spiritual uneasiness and degeneration into which the sterile failure of science and materialism to give birth to a new God that can satisfy our primitive religious cravings has thrown us."

Did O'Neill relate any of his deep concerns about morality to his own personal situation? At the end of April, 1928, while he was at Guéthary, he had to apologize to his friend De Casseres for having failed to keep his promise to write the introduction to De Casseres' book. He couldn't get settled down or get his mind on an even keel. He was all shot to pieces over his "gathering domestic troubles" and the unceasing barrage of the "hounding yellow press." They were constantly on his tail—so much so that at times his brain was unable to concentrate. Hate appeared to be suffocating him.

From what he told many of his friends, he felt that Agnes was his enemy, the "agent" of his vultures. Some of the people who knew him then have remarked that it was almost as if he were furious with Agnes and the children because he had deserted them. He quoted Agnes as having said she was going "to take him for all he's got." (Agnes has denied she ever said anything of the sort.) He said that she was "evidently" going to take advantage of his present situation in spite of the pledge on which their marriage had been made—that when love ended they would break clear. He wanted things to be arranged without friction and "the inevitable publicity." He was being "forced to stand up for his economic rights." Otherwise his entire economic future would be mortgaged, he complained.

To some of the people to whom he wrote letters he said he was in Prague, although he was in Guéthary. To others he confided his real whereabouts, but he cautioned them against ever telling anyone. He felt like a rabbit in an open field being sniped at and unable to run. This internal strife and frustration had been going on, he said, a half year before he left New York. As he used to say, over and over again, "it was raining boxing gloves."

By July, he was able to finish his introduction to De Casseres' book, *Anathema of Litanies*. In sending it off, he told De Casseres to change it any way he liked. Things seemed to be going better for him, O'Neill said, although he had to be constantly moving about Europe.

In the middle of September he reported that he had finished *Dynamo* and that it was "one of my ones." He seemed to take delight in the idea that he would catch it "down his neck" for what he had written. The fundamentalist brethren already thought of him, he said, as some sort of Antichrist. He had thought up an over-all title for the trilogy of which *Dynamo* was a part: *God is Dead! Long Live— What?*

The irony of O'Neill's putting himself in a position to judge the American soul at this juncture of his life may never have occurred to him. He perhaps explained the magic formula of the lenses through which he looked at life by a rhetorical question he asked a friend at this time— "And what is truth but a point of view after all?" Eugene O'Neill played by different rules, and it is perhaps irrelevant to judge him by our conventions, for he danced to a different music, his own music.

At times he felt that the gods of happiness were about to smile on him. He thought that he had found exactly what he was looking for—love and peace to support him and give him strength in his weak moments. No longer would he have to live and dream just by his own effort.

But just the thought of Agnes was like a rock splashing the serenity of a garden pool. When he had managed to put her out of his mind and had re-established some degree of equanimity, something always occurred to change his mood—a letter, a talk with a friend, a cable from his lawyer in New York. O'Neill complained that he had been double-crossed and annoyed by Agnes in every conceivable way. The manner in which she had treated him had hurt his pride and had upset his faith in human nature. Until now, nobody had ever taken him for a ride—that is, in anything but inconsequential matters. In dealing with whores and bums, he said, he had always got an even break when he had had occasion to lay himself open to "the works." He was sure that back in New York tall tales were being circulated about his "cruelty and parsimony." His friends, or anyone who knew his family life, would know such talk was all the bunk. But women were like that—always had to get sympathy for themselves— that is, some women. And the most fantastic thing of all was that he, O'Neill, had not wanted to fight but had been forced to; the whole thing was Agnes' fault.

Actually, the only real indictment O'Neill could make against Agnes was that she existed. If anything, she tended to be too submissive in dealing with O'Neill's lawyers. For some time, at O'Neill's insistence, Harry Weinberger acted for both of them. He was supposed to be a go-between arranging a "friendly divorce." Agnes did feel she should protect the economic futures of her children. As for herself, she wanted only enough money to keep her until she could start writing again. Many of O'Neill's friends told Agnes that he should and must properly provide for her and the children. There was some gossip about what was going on, but mostly, one suspects, O'Neill's conscience was producing his own hellish fantasies of Agnes as a woman scorned. For, after all, no matter how much he told himself that he needed another love, Eugene O'Neill was still a man who had deserted his wife and children and had run off to seek his own separate happiness.

On October 4, Langner cabled O'Neill that *Dynamo* had been accepted by the Theatre Guild "with enthusiasm." O'Neill received the message as he was boarding ship in Marseilles to sail around the world. As he told Langner, he planned to settle down in Hong Kong and do some writing. It was going to be a romantic adventure, something he had wanted to do all his life—travel in style to the far-off and unknown. He was going to see the East of Kipling, the seas of Conrad. Already he was quoting from the "Road to Mandalay." To Carlotta he said that he longed to watch "the dawn come up like thunder out of China 'cross the bay." He wrote a card to Langner on "a balmy Mediterranean day" and mailed it in Egypt. His plan, he said, was to visit India and China and perhaps South Africa.

Postcards from all the strange faraway places fluttered from his pen like autumn leaves. Some went to Shane and Oona, some to Bio and Ben De Casseres. From Singapore he wrote Oona that he hoped she had thought of him a few days before, on his birthday, October 16. From Saigon in Indochina he sent De Casseres a card showing a native smoking opium. He said the man looked as if his "brand of Nirvana was not altogether wrong." He liked Saigon better than any place he had seen.

The romantic idyll of this trip to the Far East began to fade as O'Neill's ship made its way through the Suez Canal, down the Red Sea and into the vast Indian Ocean. His mind was not entirely on Kipling's mysterious East nor on his own great love. His mind was on himself and his guilt. Also he really didn't much like being a tourist. He was not free—free to get drunk, free to forget who he was and what he was doing in all these strange places. Probably out of boredom, perhaps partly in self-loathing, O'Neill turned to his notebook. If he could not abide the reality of his trip, of his situation, of his life, then he could create his own reality within his mind. And yet, like typical tourists, he and Carlotta bought native costumes, tribal masks and drums, and all sorts of junky oddities. O'Neill went around the world not unlike one of his characters, Marco Millions.

In his notebook, he datelined his entries according to the sea he was crossing. Late in October, in the "Arabian Sea en route for

China," he wrote: "Greek tragedy plot idea—story of Electra and family psychologically most interesting—most comprehensive, intense basic human interrelationships—can be easily widened in scope to include still others."

In November, under "China Sea" he wrote: "Greek plot idea—give modern Electra figure in play tragic ending worthy of character In Greek story she peters out to undramatic married banality. Such a character contained too much tragic fate within her soul to permit this—why should the Furies have let Electra escape unpunished? Why did the chain of fated crime and retribution ignore her mother's murderess?—weakness in what remains to us of Greek tragedy that there is no play about Electra's life after murder of Clytemnestra Surely it possesses as imaginative tragic possibilities as any of their plots!"

Not until six months later did O'Neill do any extensive thinking about his magnificent American version of a Greek tragedy. The Furies in his own unmanageable universe began to buzz around him In Saigon he was ill, he didn't like Singapore, and he liked Hong Kong less. He had entertained the idea of stopping in Hong Kong and writing, but when he got there he found it not very interesting and the climate "hot now and damp and enervating"; this was not the place to work. He sent Langner a postcard saying he was off to Kobe and Yokohama and would probably settle in Japan.

At Saigon, reporters tried to interview the world-famous dramatist who had deserted his wife and children. O'Neill seemed outraged that anyone should pay the slightest heed to his whereabouts or to the identity of his companion.

He arrived in Shanghai about the middle of November and registered at the Astor House, where a Mr. Wasser, the manager, took him under his wing. O'Neill's ability to inspire friends to protect him from the world and to look after him was still working for him.

Something serious happened to O'Neill in Shanghai soon after he arrived there. The record shows only that he fell off the wagon. He went into a local bar and filled up. One report held that he announced to his fellow drinkers that he was Eugene O'Neill, the playwright, and by God he didn't care who knew it. He was sick and tired of traveling under assumed names in weird disguises and ducking newspaper reporters. Several of the habitués of this Shanghai equivalent of the Hell Hole told O'Neill that he was "a bloody faker." If he was Eugene O'Neill they were the King of England and the

Archbishop of Canterbury, he afterward related. But the whole experience was not funny; he was missing for about two weeks, and Carlotta was at a complete loss as to what to do.

When, at length, he was found, he was deathly ill from alcohol and a bad case of bronchitis. Doctors said he was in the process of a slight nervous breakdown. O'Neill said his brains were "woolly with hatred." He was placed in the hands of Dr. Alexander Renner, an Austrian nerve specialist (as a psychiatrist was then called), and was treated "for alcoholism." Later, O'Neill described his stay in the hospital in China as being of five weeks' duration. Whatever the illness which struck him—physical, mental, or both—it was devastating.

When insight came to him, he was to describe his state of mind as "a continual inward state of bitter fury and resentment. . . . I was blind." His accounts of what had happened to put him in a hospital varied according to the person to whom he was writing. He told his agent, Richard Madden, that he got a sunstroke from swimming in the sun; "wasn't it a damn-fool thing for a man approaching forty to have done?" He made many allusions to his age at this time; the idea of having reached forty plagued him.

Art McGinley cabled him that the newspapers had reported him dead in China. He replied that he would have to say with Mark Twain that "reports of my death were greatly exaggerated."

His mental state was not helped by the fact that on December 10, 1928, news of his illness was flashed around the world. The next day *The New York Times* reported that he was "improved." Two days later it was reported that he was leaving for Hawaii. Dr. Renner was issuing statements that O'Neill was "rapidly recovering." By this time, O'Neill was undergoing treatment in his hotel room in the Astor House.

According to the Associated Press correspondent, O'Neill sent word by messenger that he was leaving Shanghai immediately. He was furious because so many persons were seeking to interview him, so many people were inquiring into his personal affairs. Because of what he called Shanghai's "wholesome virtues," he felt that that city was no place in which to accomplish his work, even though he was "well physically." He was sorry to leave without saying good-by to Dr. Renner but he was sailing that day for Honolulu in quest of "peace and solitude which, if I do not find them there, I will find if I have to proceed to the South Pole."

He had come to China "seeking peace and quiet and hoping that, here at least, people would mind their business and allow me to mind mine. But I have found more snoops and gossips per square inch than there is in any New England town of one thousand inhabitants. This does not apply to American newspaper correspondents who have been most decent, carrying out their duties in a most gentlemanly manner." Later he changed this slightly to read that he was "deadly ill of being a public personage" and being written about by "the murderous reporters."

The manager of the Astor said O'Neill had sailed for Hong Kong on the *President Monroe*. At the Dollar Steamship Line's local office, it was said that O'Neill had *not* sailed aboard the *President Monroe*. Then it was reported that the American dramatist and his secretary, Mrs. Drew, who had described herself "as a Swedish masseuse and a graduate physician serving Mr. O'Neill as secretary," had left the Astor on December 12. Four days later the *President Monroe* docked in Hong Kong, but there was no O'Neill aboard.

In New York, Lawrence Langner was worried about his missing or dead dramatist. He cabled a business associate, A. Krisel, in Shanghai, to find O'Neill and see that he got good medical care. But it was the vigilant Associated Press that finally located O'Neill on a German steamer, the *Koblenz,* in Manila Harbor. He was traveling as "the Reverend William O'Brien." He stayed aboard ship in Manila, and by Christmas Eve he had disembarked at Singapore. Langner's cable was rerouted to him at Singapore. Obviously, O'Neill was embarrassed by the world-wide publicity he was getting. He complained in a cable to Langner about the "idiotic publicity of my discovery disappearance kidnaped bandits death etc." Anyway, he added, "Merry Christmas to Langner and his family!"

O'Neill dropped the idea of going on to South Africa. He would return to France instead. Carlotta was sure she could find peace and happiness for him there. The China experience was over and he felt that it had done many things for him, "done a lot for my soul." It had matured him as an artist. He could live now, and living would collaborate with writing instead of always being an obstacle to be overcome and beaten under by writing. Forty, he now said, was the "right age to begin to learn." And he added, "I've regained my sanity again."

Perhaps a significant indication of the effects of O'Neill's illness in China lies in something he wrote to Shane, at that time nine years old. He told Shane to tell his mother that "when I was very sick in the hospital in Shanghai all the bitterness got burned out of me and the future years will prove this."

By the end of January O'Neill was back in France at the Villa Mimosa on the Boulevard de la Mer in Cap d'Ail. Among the people to whom he sent this "confidential address" was Horace Liveright, his publisher. Carlotta wrote in longhand for O'Neill a letter asking Liveright to send a complete set of O'Neill plays to two people who had been extremely kind to him in the East and to whom he owed much gratitude. O'Neill added a postscript to the letter saying that he had had a wonderful trip and had got a lot out of it "in spite of snooping reporters and severe illness on way out."

The villa he lived in at Cap d'Ail faced the sea but, O'Neill wrote Shane, it was too cold to go in swimming. In back of his house were high mountains and he could walk all the way to the top of them on some days. He told Shane there were all kinds of boats off the shore, "big steamers and sailboats and speedy motorboats—like Bermuda only more of them."

From New York, O'Neill received word that *Dynamo* had opened at the Martin Beck Theatre on February 11, 1929, with Claudette Colbert in the lead. O'Neill resented the fact that some critics paid more attention to Miss Colbert's legs than they did to the real meaning of *Dynamo*. The Theatre Guild, which had produced *Dynamo*, closed it "reluctantly" after fifty performances. It was not popular with audiences, and O'Neill's artistic friends didn't like it, either. That spring of 1929 he was writing letters furiously, defending *Dynamo*. Although he did admit to Langner that he had written it "in a distraught state of mind," he ascribed its failure to his not having been present at rehearsals.

In discussing *Dynamo* with De Casseres, O'Neill complained that a play was written as a *living* thing but on the stage it was *acting*, no matter what. He cited the fact that in his sea plays he had written sailors, real sailors, into them. But were the actors who played in those plays sailors? Absolutely not! Maybe they seemed like sailors to audiences who didn't know sailors. In all the various productions of *The Hairy Ape*, O'Neill said, he had never seen a "Yank" who even remotely resembled the real-life Driscoll. At another time, however, he listed Louis Wolheim, who starred in the first production of the play, as one of the "only three actors who managed to realize the characters they played as I originally saw them"; the other two were

Charles Gilpin, in *The Emperor Jones,* and Walter Huston, in *Desire under the Elms.*

One of the interesting comments O'Neill made in defense of *Dynamo* was that his hero's psychological struggle began when he was betrayed by his mother. He cast her off along with his father's God. In the end the boy was forced to sacrifice his girl, whom his mother hated, "to a maternal deity whom he loves sexually." What makes it more interesting is that in a few months O'Neill was to marry a woman whom he was to hail as his mother in an inscription to his new play.

Along with his heavy correspondence, O'Neill was filling his notebook, that spring of 1929, with final ideas for the theme and structure of *Mourning Becomes Electra.* In April he noted again that it would be a "Greek tragedy plot idea." It would be, primarily, a drama of hidden life forces—fate—behind the lives of the characters. The background would be the "drama of murderous family love and hate." Later in the month he decided he would lay the scene in a New England shipbuilding town. He seems to have had New London in mind. The family would be the best in town and their money derived from shipbuilding. The house would be the Greek-temple front which was part of the Greek Revival period, circa 1840, in American architecture. He then outlined how he would translate or adapt the "Greek plot of crime and retribution, chain of fate—Puritan conviction of man born to sin and punishment—Orestes, Furies within him, his conscience—etc."

He also drew on the Freudian ideas communicated to him by his friend Dr. Hamilton, the psychoanalyst. In Dr. Hamilton's scholarly paper on marriage he had said that "the examiner recalls a family in his birthplace that was cursed in this way through five generations. Perhaps it led even farther back, but at any rate, the great-grandmother had not loved her husband and had held him up to ridicule before her daughter. That daughter and her daughter's daughter went through the same experience. A happy marriage was impossible for these women. Here, indeed, were the sins of the mother visited upon the children even unto the fourth and fifth generations."

Life had merged with plot, for O'Neill was passing along, unconsciously, to his own children a heritage of insecurity similar to that which his own parents had given him.

CHAPTER

EIGHTEEN

ฌฌ

THE REJECTED

FAMILY

On June 22, 1928, *The New York Times* reported that O'Neill's wife would seek a divorce. Though terribly hurt and disillusioned, she had remained the idealist; if O'Neill no longer needed or wanted her, he had the right to go, and she would not stand in his way. She remembered something that Mary Pyne had observed when Gene was courting her. "I sometimes think that Gene enjoys being tortured," Mary had said. "What you give him is something else, but he may someday want to go back to the pleasure of being tortured."

Well, Agnes would let him go but, for her, there remained a responsibility for her children, a responsibility that Eugene did not seem to share. What would she do about the support of her family? Where would they live? She simply did not know what to do. Gaga, too, was wondering; she wrote to Shane, "I have been watching to get some news from you and Mother but seems that I am disappointed each time to ask Mother to write to Gaga and tell Gaga when she is coming back to the States."

As hot summer descended on Bermuda, Agnes decided to take her brood—and her problems—back to the mainland. Shane put away his fishing gear, walked along the shore around Spithead, and went to say good-by to Peggy Ann. Agnes closed up the house and said good-by to a part of her life, and the rejected family sailed for New York, where Gaga joined them. All together, then, they proceeded to Old House, at West Point Pleasant, where Agnes might plan her future course, and do what must be done.

Harry Weinberger, O'Neill's friend and lawyer, had assured her that he would gladly represent her as well as her husband, and Agnes went into New York frequently to get his advice on her problems. She also discussed her affairs with a few friends, and they strongly urged her to find her own lawyer, who would be able to concern himself more exclusively with the interests of herself and her children. Apparently they made their point well, for she retained Charles Driscoll, of New York, to represent her.

At West Point Pleasant, Gaga tried to make up to Shane for his mother's frequent absences and for the loss of his father. Gaga was important to Shane, and he loved her very much, especially when she took him to nearby Frog's Neck, where there was a wonderful merry-go-round, imported from Germany. He always rode a horse on the rim so he could reach for the brass ring. Since his father's departure he had felt very lonely. Now, with Gaga, he was happier. He has ever since associated happiness with the music and the lights and the marvelously carved heads of the horses.

After two weeks at Old House, Gaga took Shane and Oona to Agnes' mother's farm at Upper Merryall, in Connecticut. Except for visits from her daughters, Mrs. Boulton was now alone, her husband having died two years before. Gaga stayed on at the Boulton place to look after Oona. Shane quickly found a stream, and sat quietly all day long on the bank waiting for a fish to bite.

"Shane caught more fish that summer," one of the people who knew him then has said, "than all the rest of us combined. I remember him as a beautiful child with golden ringlets and beautiful eyes and extraordinary long eyelashes which brought forth 'oohs' and 'ahs' from grownups. He was extraordinarily generous. It was not a thought-out or learned kind of generosity. Whatever was his belonged also to those around him. He was such a beautiful human being."

At the end of the summer, Gaga took Oona and Shane back to

Point Pleasant, and Agnes' sister Cecil, a painter, came along. Agnes still had to go to New York frequently for conferences with lawyers. Not until the following February did the lawyers finally reach a separation agreement. O'Neill was still complaining in letters to his friends that Agnes was "trying to take me for all I've got" and that he was going to have his "whole future mortgaged to the ears." That summer he was still in Guéthary, France, not yet embarked on his trip to the Orient. His whereabouts were kept secret from the world, and especially from Agnes.

There were endless matters yet to be decided between them. There were piles of house furnishings from the Ridgefield house stored in Manhattan, and all of O'Neill's personal belongings, including manuscripts, letters and papers, were still at Spithead; but the main concern, at least for Agnes, was about the children. O'Neill was for putting them in boarding schools. Agnes remembered that several years earlier O'Neill had held the view that children should be sent to boarding schools as early as possible. "The English send their children away when they're very young and they turn out all right," he had said; he also had reminded her that he had been sent off to school when he was five. When he had proposed sending Shane away at seven, Agnes refused and said that the boy was much too young.

Now Agnes found herself in a situation that left her little choice. Oona, too young to be sent away, could stay at Old House with Cecil and Gaga, but Shane would have to go to a small progressive boarding school at Lenox, Massachusetts. In the fall Shane, feeling that lots of things were happening awfully fast, said good-by to his mother and Oona and Gaga and the rest. He was a shy little boy who would be reaching his ninth birthday in a few weeks.

The long, rasping letters between Agnes and Gene had increased in bitterness and misunderstanding; then all communication had to be channeled through Weinberger—an arrangement that continued through the years. But the separation agreement was eventually settled. It had taken more than a year. Agnes suggested a Connecticut divorce, but Weinberger persuaded her that by going to Reno she would attract less attention and the grounds could be simple incompatibility. The separation agreement and details of the divorce were to be kept secret, and Agnes agreed to leave for Reno at the end of March, 1929.

That March, Shane recalls, he heard the grownups at his school

whispering that his mother was getting a divorce. Details of the
negotiation had leaked out and were published in the New York
World, March 25. A reporter had somehow obtained copies of some
of O'Neill's letters to Agnes. The story purported to have been based
on the letters, but the reporter's interpretation of them set in motion
another O'Neill legend. The headline read: TILL LOVE DO US PART/
O'NEILL'S WEDDING PACT. A subhead said: "And when husband
wrote of another woman, wife kept agreement, started for Reno."

The story stated flatly that the phrase, "until love do us part"
was "a codicil to the marriage ceremony privately agreed upon by
Eugene O'Neill, playwright, and his wife, Agnes Boulton O'Neill."
According to the *World,* O'Neill had sent word to Agnes from London that "I love someone else deeply. There is no possible doubt of
this. And the someone loves me. Of that I am as deeply certain. We
have often promised each other that if one ever came to the other and
said they loved someone else that we would understand—that we
would know that love is something which cannot be denied or argued
with." He also urged Agnes to go back to work. "You are never" he
said, "going to amount to a damn so long as you depend on me for
everything . . . my happiness cannot be complete until I know that
you have gone back to work."

It was a far cry from the sentiments of a husband who had written at Peaked Hill in the flyleaf of the first edition of his play, *Gold:*
"To the Treasure who is Real Gold this bit of my gold which glittered
not on Broadway. GENE."

The story went on to suggest that O'Neill no longer cared about
Spithead. He gave Agnes a lifetime interest in the Bermuda estate
because, he said, he "never intended to live there again anyhow," and
he justified not giving it to her outright on the grounds that "You can
scarcely expect me to furnish a beautiful home for any possibly broke
and grafting husband." If and when Agnes remarried, the agreement
stipulated, she would lose Spithead.

As for Shane and Oona, their destinies had been spelled out in
a document of some three dozen pages to be incorporated into Agnes'
divorce papers. "The husband and wife," the agreement stated, "shall
have equal control of the said children and equal rights of visitation
and right to sole custody at various times, to be arranged; but said
arrangement shall not interfere with the health, welfare, or schooling
of said children. When said children are attending school, the husband may have custody one-half of their vacation time." Should

O'Neill or Agnes die, the survivor would have sole custody of the children. As to their schooling, it stated that "at the age of 13 years, Shane and Oona shall enter a first-class American preparatory boarding school, these schools to be chosen by mutual agreement." O'Neill had insisted on this clause.

Agnes was to receive $6,000 a year plus certain amounts varying in accordance with O'Neill's income. But the top figure she could receive was $10,000 a year, and she could receive this only if O'Neill's income reached $30,000 a year. "All school or college fees of the children" were to be paid by Agnes as long as she received $8,000 a year. If her alimony payments went under that, O'Neill would pay the tuition. In the event of O'Neill's death, payments would continue from his estate but they were not to exceed half of the entire income from the estate.

These divorce terms could hardly be construed as excessive. If anything, Agnes settled for too little. O'Neill lost many friends who felt that he was treating Agnes and the children very shabbily indeed.

Shane wrote to his father all during the fall of 1928. The letters went to Shanghai, where they arrived after O'Neill had sailed, then chased him, as O'Neill put it, all the way back to London. In his letters to Shane, he went into some detail about his wonderful trip through the East. Sumatra impressed him very much. He said it was a wild tropic colony owned by the Dutch and one of the most interesting places he'd ever been to. "There are lots of wild animals there," he wrote, "and it is one of the places where the people go who catch them and sell them to the zoos." He said he had been sick the last part of the voyage to the East and most of the time he was in Shanghai, but he wouldn't have missed the trip for a million dollars.

"I saw all kinds of strange places and met so many different kinds of people on the boats I was on, and ashore in the towns, that I feel as if I'd added a whole new world to my experience," O'Neill wrote to his son. He would have stayed away longer, but he had had trouble working in the Far East. The heat had taken away all his strength and ambition. He was back in Europe to get on with the job of writing a new play. He had already started it, although he had been back only ten days.

Shane wrote to his father about what Oona was doing, and Oona wrote about Shane. O'Neill was delighted to hear all the news. In his letters, he speculated on how much they had grown in the year and a half since he had last seen them. He was thinking about them a lot, he wrote, and wanted to see them so much that he often thought of taking the first boat back to America. But, he added, he had such important business to attend to in Europe that he had to stay for a while longer.

Harry Weinberger had written O'Neill that Gaga was quite ill and O'Neill had cabled money for her. He asked Shane if Gaga got the money, a question Shane could hardly have answered since he was not at Point Pleasant with Gaga. Apparently Weinberger had told O'Neill that Agnes was sick, for O'Neill asked Shane to tell Agnes he was sincerely sorry to learn about it. O'Neill seemed to live in terror that his children would forget him—even forget what he looked like. Don't forget me, he said over and over again, in his letters to his son.

While Shane was still away at boarding school in Massachusetts, he received word that Gaga had died at Point Pleasant. His whole world seemed to be collapsing. When he left school for his summer vacation and returned home—which was now at Old House—his mother was still in Reno awaiting her divorce, for which she was suing on the grounds of desertion. Agnes' sister and Oona's nurse were there when Shane arrived. He didn't talk at all about Gaga's death, but they noticed that he wouldn't go into the room where Gaga had died.

O'Neill knew in March, while he was at Cap d'Ail, that Agnes had agreed to go to Reno to get a divorce. He was not particularly gracious in talking to his friends about it. He said he couldn't come home until Agnes "deigns to grant me my liberty and I can marry again." Then, he would return and live in California, he said, and make the West his "stamping ground for the future." He said his "release" had been postponed until July.

His curiosity as to what the future held for him kept mounting all spring. He asked Bio De Casseres to conduct a long-distance reading of his palm. She was to imagine looking at his palm at 11:30 P.M. on April 1, which was 6:30 P.M., New York time. When, he mainly wanted to know, was he going to have the peace for which he craved with all his heart and mind? In May Bio told him that everything would be all right. She repeated what she had told him in New York —that when he reached the age of forty-one he would have a new life. O'Neill seemed to set great store by this. He was going to have his inner self freed from the dead at forty-one and be consciously alive in his new self. He would be, as he had once told Dr. Lyman, "liberated and reborn."

Agnes was granted her divorce on the afternoon of July 2. Three weeks later, on July 22, 1929, Eugene O'Neill and Carlotta Monterey Barton were married in a civil ceremony in Paris. "Grand news!" he cabled Lawrence Langner of the Theatre Guild. Later, he told him that the "French civil ceremony proved to be quite impressive—we like it, felt it meant something—not like our buy-a-dog-license variety in U.S." He wrote Benjamin De Casseres on July 26 that the peace that De Casseres' wife, Bio, had promised him was now due to set in. He wrote Horace Liveright that now that the excitement was over he'd be getting down to hard work again.

For the next two years, Shane and Oona lived in Point Pleasant. The elder Boultons had bought Old House in 1892 and had used it off and on over the years. They had never made any effort to have a social life with what they called "the natives." The natives, in turn, regarded the Boultons as not only city people but, worse, eccentric artists. This fact tended to set Shane apart from the children of the town.

Late in August, 1929, an incident occurred which entailed unpleasant repercussions for the O'Neill family in Point Pleasant. Agnes was giving a party for some of her out-of-town friends, one of whom was James J. Delaney, an Albany newspaperman. After the party had begun Agnes discovered there was not enough ginger ale. She asked Delaney to go to the store for some, suggesting that he use her car, not realizing that he was somewhat under the weather. Driving into the town of Toms River, Delaney struck three cars in succession and was immediately arrested for reckless driving and for driving while intoxicated. He was arraigned before a justice of the peace, who gave him his choice of jail or paying a fine of $451. Since he was unable to pay the fine, Agnes had to put up the money to keep him from going to jail.

The incident caused a stir in Point Pleasant. Because she was known as the "divorced wife of Eugene O'Neill," details of the story were carried on the wires of the Associated Press and printed in papers throughout the country. Shane became known in the community not only as "the son of that fellow who writes plays and deserted his family for an actress" but also as the son of "that writer who was involved in a drunken automobile accident."

Shane continued to write to his father, but the answers became less and less frequent. O'Neill urged his son to write to his half brother, who had just completed his freshman year at Yale. He told Shane that Eugene junior was rowing a lot and was on the freshman crew. Although O'Neill was only trying to keep some kind of family feeling among his children, these constant reminders of how well his older brother was doing in sports and in his studies tended further to destroy Shane's already shattered view of his own importance.

Shane's loss of his father and of Gaga was somewhat assuaged by his proximity to the ocean. The big waves lapping the beach, the fishing boats anchored at the quays, brought back memories of Provincetown and Spithead. Sometimes, at dusk, he looked at the beautiful carousel on which Gaga had given him rides, the organ that played the German waltzes, the bright lights, the prancing colored horses. Sometimes he fished in the creeks that emptied into the ocean near Point Pleasant. He stayed alone a great deal, just sitting on the banks of the melancholy marshes, identifying the different species of ducks and geese that swooped down from the skies on their way south.

CHAPTER

NINETEEN

იი

THE MANDARIN IN
THE FRENCH CHÂTEAU

In May, 1929, Saxe and Dorothy Commins visited O'Neill at Cap d'Ail. O'Neill told Bio De Casseres how devoted he was to Saxe. "A fine person, Saxe! And his wife is too." Commins remarked that O'Neill seemed to be preparing himself for still another role, the very antithesis of that of his seafaring and Hell Hole days.

As early as May 10 O'Neill and Carlotta were planning to move into a château in Touraine where they hoped to live, he wrote Bio, "for three years." Later it was reported that he and Carlotta had leased it for thirteen years. The place was the Château de Plessis at St. Antoine du Rocher, twenty-five miles from Tours. There was a six-hundred-acre game preserve with it, one of the finest in France. In the château were several towers, a number of rooms with marble floors, and forty-five bedrooms, but no electric lighting, no heat, and no bathroom. Carlotta's first improvement, after they moved in, was to convert one of the bedrooms into a bath.

O'Neill had been reluctant to rent such an imposing residence.

"He had never lived in a château," Carlotta has explained, "and the idea of a château he thought was chichi and putting on airs." But, as Carlotta has put it, "though he was a rather tough Irishman, he saw that you could really be polite and live in a charming place, and you didn't have to be ridiculous, and he loved it."

Arrangements for renting the château were made when O'Neill and Carlotta signed a contract before they were married. At Carlotta's insistence, the Countess de Bonville (the owner of the château) reluctantly agreed to the installation of a swimming pool, a roof garden and a garden and a gymnasium. Carlotta had "insisted" on a thirteen-year lease, but the Countess "didn't want to grant it" and apparently didn't yield on that.

O'Neill quickly became enthusiastic about the château idea and began to endow it with his own brand of romanticism. He told friends he would be living in the real French countryside, in the beautiful valley of the Loire, the land of Rabelais and Balzac. He spoke glowingly of the woods, the streams, and the farm run by the Countess de Bonville. It was a lovely country house with "grand furniture." The annual rental would be insanely low for a comparable place in United States. He seemed to be enjoying his bargain.

He was hardly unpacked when the wings of his vultures began to flap about his ears. A woman writer in New York sued him for $1,750,000, alleging that he had plagiarized *Strange Interlude* from a novel she had paid to have printed. "Blackmail!" cried O'Neill. He cabled Harry Weinberger that the woman was crazy. What especially infuriated him, he said, was that she was getting a million dollars' worth of publicity for nothing.

A revised edition of Barrett Clark's biography reached O'Neill on May 29, 1929. Most of the material in it O'Neill had seen, checked, discussed, revised and re-revised, but he wrote a long letter to Clark about it. One of his deletions was a favorable reference to Agnes. But what especially annoyed O'Neill was that Clark had written, "That such fame has already done him some harm cannot be doubted, but I hardly think it can seriously alter his determination to pursue his own course in his own way." O'Neill said it "got his goat." Why, he had spent a great part of his time ducking fame so he could get on with his work. All fame had ever done for him was to subject him to petty bothers, irritating nuisances and dirty, low-down publicity. He well knew the danger of being influenced by fame and assiduously avoided it. He also wrote that it was too bad that Clark had not written a chapter in the book telling all the details of how the production of O'Neill plays in so many countries had resulted in "around-the-world recognition of an American playwright for the first time in history." O'Neill insisted Clark could put in what the critics from foreign lands had said against his plays as well as criticism favorable to his plays.

In June, O'Neill continued to write his friends in the United States that he was expecting them to visit him at his beautiful place. It had an atmosphere, he said, of calm and peace, of life, centuries-rooted in the soil. He asked Clark to come over, Horace Liveright, Stark Young, Eleanor Fitzgerald, and others.

In his letter to Young he expressed some of his old contempt for the "respectabilities." The ladies of the Countess de Bonville's family, had not been in the château's kitchen for three years, and it had taken no end of water, scrubbing, and whitewash, to get it in shape. The sewage tank was inside the house, over the great salon. The only way you could tell when it needed emptying was by the stains which began to spread down the ancient tapestries.

Only a few days after O'Neill moved into the château, he told a friend, he felt perfectly at home. It was precisely what his spirit had been longing for for years. George Jean Nathan came to visit in June, as did Lillian Gish. Dr. Alexander Renner, the Austrian psychiatrist who had treated him for alcoholism in Shanghai, and Renner's wife, also were visitors. When Liveright cabled him congratulations on his divorce, O'Neill thanked him and added that he was working on "something big and new—the most ambitious stuff I've ever tackled." He asked Liveright how much he thought he could get for all his play manuscripts. A dealer had already offered him "fifty grand." Couldn't he maybe get one hundred? He needed the money.

Every morning at Le Plessis O'Neill was at work by nine, and he remained at work until half past one, when he knocked off for lunch, which was very formal, the food beautifully prepared and served. A menu, written on a little marble tablet, was set before each person. He finished the scenario of the first of the *Electra* trilogy on June 20 and called it *Homecoming*. On July 11, he finished the second part and called it *The Hunted*. In August, he finished the third part, *The Haunted,* noting that he had given his Yankee Electra "a tragic end worthy of her—and Orestes, too."

He was still worried about "the blackmailing plagiarist ladies"

especially the "barefaced publicity hound" who was suing him for
$1,750,000. To add insult to injury, he complained, the litigating
lady had announced to the press that he had "made a travesty of my
work."

She claimed to be a poet and cited that in one month she had
written to one man seventy-five love sonnets and that all were "in
the Elizabethan style." She told of her "shock and amazement when
I went to see *Strange Interlude,* for the first time, three months ago.
Eugene O'Neill had used my material but used it all wrong. He took
a beautiful ideal and brought it so low that I was shocked and
scandalized. He has pandered to the licentious. He made a travesty
of my work and turned pure English into the argot of the day."

She claimed that she had sent her novel, *The Temple of Pallas
Athenae,* to Lawrence Langner of the Theatre Guild and that he had
given it to O'Neill to dramatize. Fortunately, Langner looked in his
library and found he had not returned the volume to her. The pages
were still uncut. But despite the absurdity of the woman's allegation,
the case eventually went to trial in March of 1931.

O'Neill noted that he finished the first draft of "M.B.E.," as he
called *Mourning Becomes Electra* in his work diary, on February 21,
1930. He was dead tired, he told a friend, and had never worked
so hard for a continuous stretch on any of his plays before. He had
lived night and day with the writing of it for four months steady,
seven days a week. He put in seven hours each day. This, he said,
was grueling for most any kind of writing, let alone "intense stuff,"
as O'Neill called what he had put in "M.B.E." When he finally inscribed the finished manuscript to Carlotta, he gave some indication
of what it had been like while he was working on the play. The inscription read:

> In memory of the interminable days of rain in which you
> bravely suffered in silence that this trilogy might be born—days
> when I had my work but you had nothing but household frets,
> and a black vista through the salon windows of Le Plessis with
> the black trees still and dripping, and the mist wraiths mourning
> over the drowned fields or days when you had self-forgetting
> love to greet my lunchtime, depressing such preoccupations with
> a courageous, charming banter on days which for you were
> bitterly lonely, when I seemed far away and lost to you in a grim

savage gloomy country of my own, days which were for you like hateful, boring, inseparable enemies, nagging at nerves and spirit with an intolerable ennui and life sickness which poisoned your spirit!

For a vacation, they motored through parts of France that the playwright had never seen before. Carlotta had lived in France when she was a girl and she loved taking him on guided tours of the country. They also made a short visit to Spain and then returned to spend two weeks in Paris.

Carlotta often wondered whether O'Neill really enjoyed the trips she took him on during these years in Europe. "I said to him once—half jokingly— 'I have dragged you about Europe, I have worked like anything to show you all [the] beautiful spots, and I have never heard you say once that you like this or that or the other.' 'Well,' he said, 'I liked them, but they weren't very exciting.' So that was that."

It never ceased to amaze Carlotta that O'Neill liked to tell friends stories of his seafaring days, his being penniless on the beach at Buenos Aires, his being a down-and-out drunkard at Jimmy the Priest's, and his living in the "garbage flat." "Gene's pride seemed to be in those years," she said wistfully, four years after he died.

O'Neill and Carlotta returned to Le Plessis at the end of February. His spirit was refreshed, he told a friend, and he had a bit of perspective with which he could look at his first draft.

On February 27, 1930, he noted that he had read over the first draft of "M.B.E." and found it "scrawny stuff" but thought it served the purpose as a first try. Parts of it were "thrilling" but "lots more [were] lousy." It needed meat. Aegisthus' counterpart was "hackneyed and thin."

O'Neill finished the second draft of *Mourning Becomes Electra* on July 11, after three months of concentrated writing in which he worked morning, afternoon and night without letup. He noted that he had never worked so intensively over such a long period. He wished he hadn't attempted "the damn thing."

He was also having trouble with his teeth and went to a Paris dentist for treatment. This was the best antidote for pernicious brooding over one's inadequacies, he related. His suffering of recent months would seem a positive delight compared with his agony when the dentist's drill bore down on the O'Neill teeth.

From many of the reports about the O'Neills at the ancient Château de Plessis, one gets the feeling that they were playing roles against an Old World theatrical set, not only for each other but with visitors as audience. O'Neill wore the robes of a Chinese mandarin when receiving guests. Sometimes Carlotta wore the dress of a Chinese princess; at others, according to one visitor, she wore big floppy hats along with "simple dresses for gardening."

Theresea Helburn and her husband, John B. Opdycke, visited the O'Neills at this time. Miss Helburn, an executive of the Theatre Guild, took back to New York an outline of *Mourning Becomes Electra*. O'Neill told her he was getting homesick and would probably stay in France only long enough to see one more spring at Le Plessis and in Paris.

Another visitor was the New York drama critic Richard Watts, Jr., who wrote:

> Of all the genuinely distinguished writing men of our time it is probable that only Eugene O'Neill and William Butler Yeats live up to what one hopes for their physical appearance. The bronzed, handsome, graying Mr. O'Neill is pretty much the ideal of what a great melancholy and brooding playwright should look like, just as the fine, ecstatic brow of Yeats gives, to its possessor, the ideal manner and appearance of an Olympian poet.

Not all callers were so complimentary in their reports. Some of the actresses who visited Le Plessis came back to America with accounts of the theatricality of the O'Neill ménage. They told of sitting in the beautiful garden with Gene and Carlotta dressed in their startling royal Chinese robes and drinking what was apparently the only nonalcoholic beverage available in France at the time, an American importation known as Moxie. O'Neill was very much on the wagon.

O'Neill's old friend, James Light, in France on a Guggenheim Fellowship, came with his wife. He told the O'Neill's that one of his projects was the establishment of a French equivalent of the Provincetown Playhouse near the Café du Dôme in the Montparnasse section of Paris. Eugène Jolas, he said, was contemplating financing the project.

Carlotta was immediately hostile to the idea. "Don't try and start a Provincetown Playhouse in Europe, the Provincetown is dead and gone," she said.

Light, somewhat taken aback, started to protest, "But Carlotta—"

"From now on, Mr. Light," Carlotta said stiffly, "I am Mrs. O'Neill to you."

Eugene junior came that summer of 1930 to stay at Le Plessis. A news photographer took his picture beside the swimming pool with his father. Young Gene looked like his father and was almost as tall. He had just completed his sophomore year at Yale, where some verse he had written for *The Helicon,* an undergraduate publication, was given considerable publicity. Like the verse he had written at Horace Mann, it was not cheerful. Titled "The Song of the Freight," some of its lines, in the light of future events, are revealing:

Two short howls of mournful hopelessness,
A long rattling crescendo of protesting crashes,
And a great voice shrieking like a lunatic with the Christ bug.

The song of the freight is the moan and the broken cry
   of a woman dying in a train wreck,
The clear sharp challenge hurled at the moon by a
   lonely defiant farm-dog,
A nocturne in an unknown key torn by the wind from the
   throat of a steam whistle in a nightmare.

Singing of all the places and people that he has seen
   with his one great eye.
And the roaring Cyclops passes on still singing to a
   world where no one listens.

Gene junior was learning to live with the famous name he bore. That spring, during the nights when the junior fraternity delegations called at the dormitory quarters of the sophomores, he had been visited by virtually all of them. But when the bids were sent out, Eugene did not receive a single invitation to join. Later, some of the fraternity men admitted that they had called on him "just to see what the son of Eugene O'Neill looked like."

Far more serious than this, however, were the difficulties that young Gene had recently encountered at home. For several years, his stepfather had been an invalid, unable to work, and his mother had taken a job on a newspaper on Long Island. His stepbrother,

George Pitt-Smith, Jr., who also had become ill, had jumped or fallen to his death one day from a window in the anteroom of a Manhattan doctor's office. Eugene had been devoted to his stepbrother, and he took his death very hard. However, he told friends, his stepbrother's death had served to bring him closer to his Uncle George, as he had called his stepfather ever since he had learned the identity of his real father. "I felt like his son after that," he said.

O'Neill, who paid for Eugene junior's trip to France, always seemed partial to his first-born child. For one thing, there had been no apparent bitterness between him and his first wife. Then, too, the father and son shared a strong mutual interest in literature, especially drama and poetry. O'Neill urged the fledgling scholar to steep himself in the Greek writers and philosophers. Eugene junior took this advice literally and made the study of the Greek classics his life's work. The son's visit with his father that summer of 1930 was a happy one. They took walks in the countryside, swam in the Château's pool, and visited Paris together.

Meanwhile Shane had entered St. Peter's Parochial School at Point Pleasant, run by the Sisters of Charity. Agnes' decision to send him there was based on a number of considerations: She understood it was a better school than the Point Pleasant public school; there was closer supervision, and the students were kept occupied longer in the afternoon; and Agnes had been a practicing Catholic for much of her life. As for Shane, he adjusted easily to St. Peter's. His already fertile Irish imagination, his natural love of color and music and pageantry, found satisfaction in the ancient rituals of the Church. He made his first Communion and was confirmed.

Shane wrote his father often in 1930. He told him jokes that he heard in the school and said he was going to submit them in a joke contest. Oona had cut the whiskers off the cat. O'Neill replied that he thought Shane's jokes were very funny, and said he wished he had a snapshot not only of Shane and Oona, but also of the cat "with his close shave."

"Do you think," he asked, "you could get the cat to pose for a picture without whiskers? I imagine she (or is it a he?) would not want to, because she'd feel naked and ashamed as if she had lost her clothes. Poor Pussy! Oona should not do that. Cats are very sensitive and delicate when it comes to their whiskers."

O'Neill waxed enthusiastic about his racing automobile. He spoke of it almost as if he were one teen-ager talking to another. Soon, he said, he would send a snapshot of it so that Shane could see what it looked like. "It is a beauty and very fast," O'Neill wrote, "and I have a lot of fun driving it. It isn't dangerous to drive fast here because the roads are fine and straight and there is very little traffic and they have no speed limits except going through towns."

In that letter he did not say exactly how fast he drove the car, and he must have understated the danger involved; on the other hand, he did not mention the benefit he derived from his fast driving. Carlotta has recalled that "when he was very nervous and tired, he would go out in this racer and drive ninety-five, ninety-eight miles an hour, looking nineteen years old and perfectly relaxed." However, when she went with him she was terrified. O'Neill had a marvelous time, speeding over the open roads; but after he left France he never drove again, because he hated driving in traffic.

In the spring Shane got odd jobs, weekday afternoons and on Saturdays, on the waterfront, getting the charter boats conditioned, carrying things for the workmen on the docks and doing a little painting. He wrote his father with pride that he was making money. He had become more aware of how his father earned his living, and he asked when he was going to have another play produced in New York.

Shane didn't hear from his father again until school was almost out. At the end of May, O'Neill answered Shane's inquiry about his work in considerable detail. He said the play he was working on, *Mourning Becomes Electra,* would not be ready for production by the next season so he would not have anything on Broadway unless someone produced *Lazarus Laughed.* He said there was some talk of *Lazarus* being done but he doubted that anyone would really have the nerve to put it on.

About *Electra,* he told Shane, "The thing I am writing is the biggest and hardest I have ever tackled and, after working on it almost a year now I am only one-third through the second draft. As I intend to do a third draft, too, you will see I still have a lot to do.

"I know I am a bum," he said, "for not having written you in so long. I am getting to be a lazier and lazier letter writer as time goes on, I guess. But I really have this excuse that I have been working harder on my new plays than I ever worked before and usually when I get through for the day my head and eyes are so tired I don't want to write anything else that day. And so it goes on day after day, and the letters I ought to write don't get written."

Once again, O'Neill reminded Shane how well Eugene junior was doing. He asked Shane how *he* was doing in school. Was it a good school? Eugene, he said, was studying very hard at Yale and was eighth in a class of five hundred. Didn't Shane think that was awfully good? Of course, Shane would work as hard as Eugene when he went to college. Incidentally, what college did he like best?

Looking at O'Neill's letters in 1930, one is struck by the fact that, in writing about his work to Shane, he spoke almost on the same level as to his literary friends, Barrett Clark and Ben De Casseres. He told Shane about Europe's not having much use for American plays —"except cheap or bad ones." But, he said with pride, the Kamerny Theater of Moscow was touring Europe and on the morrow (May 28, 1930), he was going up to Paris to see them do *All God's Children* and *Desire under the Elms*. The Kamerny, he said, was one of the most famous theaters in the world and of the three serious plays they were doing, two of them were his. "And so this," he wrote, "is an unusual honor to me."

He suggested that Shane send snapshots of himself and Oona, and he asked Shane to tell Oona he had received a letter from her quite sometime ago. He had not answered it, but he wanted Shane to tell her, "I know it would be a good letter if I could read the language she writes in." Oona was then going on five. Also Shane was to ask her if she got the birthday present he sent her on the fourteenth of May; two weeks had gone by and she had not written to thank him. In any case, Shane should kiss Oona for him, and he enclosed a check for Shane.

O'Neill's demands on himself in writing *Mourning Becomes Electra* were rigorous in the extreme. He wanted the words used in dialogue to be simple words in a monotonous driving insistence "in thought repetition," similar to the tom-tom in *The Emperor Jones*. In an early version of *Electra*, he had had the characters speak in asides as they had done in *Strange Interlude*. Now he decided to cut out all the asides. He began rewriting the entire play and continued at it all summer. He told a friend he was engaged in the most ambitious piece of work he had ever undertaken and would remain in Europe until it was completed.

On September 16, he finished this rewrite, and four days later he was staying in Paris at the Hôtel du Rhin. While Carlotta shopped, he visited with George Jean Nathan in the latter's rooms on the Avenue Maréchal-Foch. Nathan asked him what he would like, more than anything else, out of life. The Nobel Prize, perhaps?

"On careful consideration, and no sour grapes about it because I have no hopes," O'Neill replied, sipping his tea,. "I think the Nobel Prize, until you become very old and childlike, costs more than it's worth. It's an anchor around one's neck that one would never be able to shake off."

The talk turned to theatrical criticism. Would O'Neill perhaps wish for more intelligent criticism of his plays?

"When they knock me," O'Neill said, "what the devil! They're really boosting me with their wholesale condemnations, for the reaction against such nonsense will come soon enough."

(O'Neill once told Nathan that he was neither much disturbed by adverse criticism nor unduly elated by favorable reviews, prizes, or other honors. Like George Bernard Shaw, he believed that he was his own most reliable critic. Praise was pleasant and disapproval was superfluous, when they coincided with his own estimate; both were fatuous when they didn't.)

That afternoon, O'Neill talked at great length about how happy he was, how he had, for the first time, got what he wanted in life —existence "as a living being quite outside of the life in my work." At this point, Nathan wrote, Carlotta came in, put her arm around him, and kissed him. "Where've you been?" O'Neill asked. Nathan noticed that his face suddenly lapsed into "that perverse little-boy expression." Carlotta let him have another little kiss. "I've been shopping for dresses, Genie dear," she said, "blue ones."

After a week in Paris, O'Neill returned to Le Plessis and on September 23 began still another rewrite of *Mourning Becomes Electra,* which he finished on October 15. Soon after that, he and Carlotta left for a month's trip through Spain and Morocco. Spain— particularly Andalusia—delighted him, and he decided that Spain was the most interesting country in Europe.

On November 19, he again read the play and was only "fairly well" satisfied; he wanted more quality in it. He began his fifth writing. In December of 1930, when the writing was in its last stage, he told a friend it was an exhausting job. He had lost all perspective on it; in fact, he had about as much perspective on what he had written as a fly had on a sheet of flypaper to which he had become stuck; all effort must be made to get unstuck. He worked straight through the Christmas holidays, but he made one concession as always when working on his plays—he didn't work on Christmas Eve.

In January, 1931, the weather matched the gloom of *Mourning Becomes Electra.* It had been raining for what seemed like months and O'Neill remarked that the sunny land of Touraine looked very much like a bog. In the midst of this gloom, word came from the United States that a fifty-mile gale accompanied by a heavy tide had swept the New England coast. Great waves had washed over Peaked Hill at the tip of Cape Cod and a portion of his house there had been washed out to sea. Then some visitors from England brought with them, O'Neill was convinced, "a simon-pure London species of grippe," and both O'Neill and Carlotta were struck down by it as if they had "both been hit over the head with a croquet mallet." Their illnesses were so severe that they went to Paris, Carlotta to enter the American Hospital and Eugene to stay at the Hôtel du Rhin.

Although he was still suffering from the after effects of his grippe, O'Neill worked steadily through the latter part of January. Page by page he passed his manuscript to a typist, till the job was completed early in February.

By February 7, 1931, O'Neill and Carlotta were home, seeing the "black vista through the salon windows." Although he was generally run-down, O'Neill continued to study the manuscript of his new play. Perhaps his depression colored his outlook on his work, but he decided that most of the "new stuff" he had written into the play added too many complications, too many new values; some of the effects were blurred; he would revert to the former version entirely.

On February 20, he and Carlotta set out for a visit to the Canary Islands. They stayed at Las Palmas, and there he worked on the typed script of *Mourning Becomes Electra*. The typed play looked different, somehow, from the longhand version—it seemed more dynamic; but it needed condensing. He noted that he was getting no vacation because of the work he was doing.

By March 26 he had finished this final revision, and Eugene and Carlotta returned to France, with stopovers at Tangier and Casablanca. They went by ship to Marseilles and by train to Paris, where they arrived on April 4. There he made one last change—Scenes One and Two of Act One of *The Hunted* became Acts One and Two. He had the entire script retyped once more, and on April 9 he sent copies to the Theatre Guild. Reporters in Paris tried to get him to say what the title of his new play was but he said only, "It is really three separate plays which will require three consecutive nights for presentation." By April 14, 1931, O'Neill and Carlotta were back at Le Plessis.

Suddenly, the sun was shining and the vultures were scattered. Word came that the $1,750,000 plagiarism suit which Gladys Adelena Selma Lewys had launched against him had been dismissed as "preposterous," and that she had been ordered by Judge John M. Woolsey (later to become famous for his *Ulysses* decision) to pay $17,500 in counsel fees to O'Neill's lawyers. Naturally, O'Neill and Carlotta were delighted. Lawrence Langner had taken the stand and had offered in evidence his copy of the novel with the pages uncut. He said a circular came with the book describing its contents in somewhat suggestive language. "I read the circular," Langner testified, "and had an idea that it was one of those privately printed naughty books, but after reading one or two pages, I found it wasn't naughty and I didn't finish it."

A few days after winning the suit, O'Neill received word from Langner, as head of the Theatre Guild, that once he had started to read *Mourning Becomes Electra,* he had not been able to put it down. He read all three of the plays one after the other. "The effect," he said, "was to knock me silly for the rest of the day." The Guild wished to go into casting and production immediately. O'Neill sent word that he would come on to New York and "assist in the production." He had had enough of France and Europe. He would sail for America, where the sun was shining. "I have been able to get a good perspective on America," he told an interviewer, "by staying in France, and I have been able to see it more clearly. But, also, I can appreciate it a devil of a lot more now." As for plans, he said that he might settle in Virginia or in California, where Carlotta's mother lived. In any case, he would be going home.

Once again O'Neill enthusiasm had collapsed, again his dream of settling down was shattered. Although he was at the height of his creative powers and he had made what now seemed a most successful marriage, after all the unpleasantness and despair that surrounded his divorce from Agnes, O'Neill still felt essentially "alone and above and apart . . . a stranger . . . who did not really want and [was] not really wanted, who can never belong. . . ." And yet O'Neill, at this time, was almost joyful and serene, for he looked forward hopefully to starting all over with Carlotta in America.

CHAPTER

TWENTY

ଧ୍ୟ

FATHER AND SONS

When Eugene O'Neill and Carlotta arrived in the United States on the *Statendam*, Sunday, May 17, 1931, he was in an extraordinarily happy mood. He and Carlotta intended to tarry in New York City only a few days. Their plan was to go immediately to San Francisco to visit Carlotta's mother. They had even left instructions in France for all their mail to be forwarded directly to the West Coast. The Ralph Barton suicide that week wrecked their plans as well as their new found serenity.

That week he told a press conference at the Guild Theatre that Federal Judge Woolsey had delivered "the best possible elegy over plagiarism and *Strange Interlude*." He also said that he would not return to Europe at all if it weren't for the fact that his lease at Château de Plessis still had a year to run. Although he had been most enthusiastic about the original manner in which his plays had been produced by the Swedes and the Russians, O'Neill said, it was his opinion that the American theater was superior to the European theater, and that "Europe looks with hope to America's dynamic quality." He predicted that this idea would soon win wide acceptance.

"The ordinary tourists," O'Neill continued, "go over, stay only a short time and get the idea that culture is there. I have talked with a number of people in the theatrical world and they all have the feeling that the American stage has a freshness theirs lacks. This may sound like patriotic ballyhoo of the worst kind but it isn't. Before long they will be coming over here to learn from us. And the intelligent ones among them know it."

O'Neill said he didn't care where he lived in the United States as long as it was "where there is sun." He spoke of having worked on *Mourning Becomes Electra* "like a Trappist monk" and said he regarded it as "my pet of them all." In the play he had tried to get into it "the idea of fate."

At about that time O'Neill became involved in a lengthy, defensive discussion of his work with Barrett Clark, who had written him that *Mourning Becomes Electra* was rather heavily Freudian. Suppose, O'Neill replied, Stendhal and Balzac and Strindberg and Dostoievsky were writing their novels now. Think what Freudian stuff the critics would read into their work. He, O'Neill, knew enough about the behavior of men and women to have written *Mourning Becomes Electra* without ever having heard of Freud or Jung or any of the others. Most good authors were psychologists before the so-called science of psychology was discovered. He had read only four books by such people as Freud and Jung. Jung was the only one who interested him. He would admit, however, that a psychological writer of the past, like Dostoievsky, had had great influence on him. The interpretations in *Mourning Becomes Electra* were such as might occur to almost any writer "with a deep curiosity about the underlying motives that actuate interrelationships in the family."

As Manhattan grew uncomfortably hot that June, O'Neill decided to spend the summer on Long Island. Carlotta leased a white clapboard house by the sea at Northport, The location was more in keeping with his new role as a "respectability." He even bought a twelve-cylinder Cadillac limousine. When Brooks Atkinson teased him about it, O'Neill quickly explained that it was a bargain. It had been driven only two thousand miles, had an ironclad guarantee, looked brand-new, and was sold to him at a thousand dollars off the list price. He said he could not resist "this splendid gift of world depression." After all, he said, he had always been an "A-one snob" as far as cars and boats were concerned. O'Neill then painted a picture of the late James O'Neill, Sr., as a loving father who gave his sons "only the classiest cars and boats." The Count of Monte Cristo, as Eugene referred to him, "sported the first Packard in New London." He and Jamie had taken her out on the open road and got her up to forty miles per hour. The Packard, he said, had never fully recovered.

Twenty years later, in *Long Day's Journey into Night,* O'Neill touched on snobbery in connection with the make of automobile one owned, when Ella Tyrone, the play's counterpart of Eugene's mother, calls attention to the Chatfields driving by in their beautiful new Mercedes. The Chatfields are the town's "swells," and Ella makes it clear to her husband and two sons that, compared to the Chatfield's, the Tyrones are social outcasts. She says that the Mercedes is far superior to the second-hand Packard that her husband has bought for her, and she chides him for hiring an incompetent helper in the garage as their chauffeur. (James O'Neill bought a Packard for his wife after she was discharged from the sanatorium to which she had been sent for treatment as a drug addict.)

That summer of 1931, O'Neill invited Brooks Atkinson out to Northport to discuss the author's basic aims in writing *Mourning Becomes Electra,* which was about to go into production. Most of that summer, the O'Neills sat on the beach in the sun, trying to make up for the gloomy darkness and chill of their winters at Le Plessis. They were photographed for the rotogravure sections of the Sunday papers, sitting together in bathing suits on the beach.

O'Neill's work diary shows that he put aside for a while work on *Mourning Becomes Electra,* his "trilogy of the damned," as he called it. When, in August, Liveright sent him the galley proofs of the play, O'Neill noted that he had not looked at it for four months. Reading the play in type made him feel that his main purpose had been achieved. There was the feeling of fate in it, "a psychological modern approximation of the fate in the Greek tragedies on this theme—attained without benefit of the supernatural." However, some cutting was needed, especially in the first and third plays of his trilogy.

Nathan came out to stay and found O'Neill having a "devil of a time trying to solve a problem in one act." Then, one night, after a particularly trying day "and mopish gloom it had imposed on him, O'Neill burst into my bedroom at 3 A.M., gleefully shouting that he had at last seen what was wrong with the play; what it had needed was simply the transposition of a first-act scene into the third act."

"Maybe," O'Neill told Nathan, "if I were a drinking man I would have seen it more clearly at the start. There are times in the writing of drama when a bit of cloudiness can bring a sudden gleam of light more effectively than too-long studious analysis."

O'Neill saw little or nothing of his children that summer. Young Gene had just completed his junior year at Yale and was becoming something of a person in his own right. He had been awarded the Winthrop Prize for his knowledge of Greek and Latin poetry, and he had been tapped for Skull and Bones, Yale's most exclusive senior-class society, which enrolls only fifteen members out of six hundred fourth-year men. Among those tapped with him were Frederick B. Adams, today head of the Morgan Library, and Tex McCrary, the television commentator and public relations man.

Gene junior had also become engaged. Because Yale under-graduates were then forbidden to be married while in college, he sought and obtained permission from the school authorities. His fiancée was Elizabeth Green of Forest Hills, the daughter of a wealthy paint manufacturer. Gene and Miss Green were married in Long Island City, New York, on June 15. Announcement of the wedding was made by the groom's mother, Mrs. Kathleen Pitt-Smith, who said there was no parental objection to the marriage from either side of the family. She and Miss Green's father were the only witnesses to the ceremony.

O'Neill was staying at the Madison and spending weekends at Northport, but reporters were unable to reach him and ask why he had not attended the wedding. One reporter talked to Harry Wein-berger, O'Neill's attorney, who expressed surprise and, after checking presumably with O'Neill, refused to confirm or deny that the wedding had taken place.

Arranging for O'Neill to see his children had become especially difficult in the case of Oona and Shane. All communication between Agnes and O'Neill had to filter through Harry Weinberger. That sum-mer of 1931, Oona had just passed her sixth birthday and Shane was going on eleven. After some weeks, a meeting was arranged. With his chauffeur-driven Cadillac, O'Neill and Carlotta took the two children for a ride. Shane was painfully shy, as was his father, and Oona became carsick. Carlotta tried to make them all feel comfortable, but the reunion was not a success.

Early in the summer, Agnes began looking for "a first-class American preparatory boarding school" to which she might send

Shane, in compliance with the terms of her separation agreement with O'Neill. Shane remembers his mother driving with him to look over various schools. She included Lawrenceville because it was nearby and she thought Shane might be less homesick if he were not too far from Point Pleasant.

Shane seemed to like the Lawrenceville campus and buildings but he was extremely shy when he met the masters. She noticed, as she had before, that he seemed to be developing a shyness, like his father's, about going out in public. After a long talk with W. A. Jameson, the school's registrar, Agnes agreed to have Shane tutored in English and mathematics. Jameson was to be Shane's housemaster. It was decided that Agnes would have Shane come to Lawrenceville a week before school started so that Jameson could tutor him "in an effort to put him in the best possible condition to carry on our work." Shane began his career at Lawrenceville on September 21, 1931.

Lawrenceville is one of the oldest and most patrician of American preparatory schools. Had Shane been merely the son of a wealthy father, the faculty and students would easily have taken him in stride. But he was the son of a man whom most of the civilized world had already acclaimed as a great genius. Shane was conscious of this. He was also troubled that he didn't know more about his father and his work, and he was embarrassed when people questioned him about his father, or asked him which of his father's plays he liked best. He didn't know the answers.

The first month he was there, Shane's masters at Lawrenceville knew they had an extremely difficult problem on their hands. He did fairly well in his studies at first, but his worst subject was English, in which he was expected to excel. His conduct record was satisfactory, but Jameson observed Shane's insecurity and asked Agnes to come over to Lawrenceville for a conference. The gist of what he said was that Shane "must develop far greater powers of self-reliance and responsibility." But matters did not improve. In the first quarterly report, the middle of November, all of Shane's marks dropped. He failed in English and ranked thirty-second in a class of forty-three.

A distinguished Lawrenceville master writes: "I remember Shane very well. He is one of the few boys out of 1,000 I'll never forget. I used to see him in school and in chapel. As a very small boy, he was one of the most attractive kids I'd ever seen: handsome, dark hair and eyes, appealing face, always quiet, friendly, pleasant

nd a nice smile. I'll never forget him as a small boy because he
eemed to be just what a child that age should be."

O'Neill did so much rewriting on the proofs of *Mourning Be-
omes Electra* that his publishers decided it might be cheaper to reset
he entire play. Liveright sent the new set of galleys to O'Neill in
September. Even then, O'Neill judged that Act Two of *The Haunted*
needed some more work, but he decided to postpone any more
ewriting until he had heard the cast read it; then it would "hit my
ar," he told a friend. After the reading and his subsequent reworking
f the "muzzy spots," he believed that he had made the trilogy clearer,
nore compact, and smoother running.

Plans for the production of the trilogy were announced by the
Theatre Guild on September 9, 1931. Alice Brady accepted the part
f Lavinia. She had always regretted turning down the part of Nina
n *Strange Interlude.* Her father, William A. Brady, the theatrical
producer and a friend of James O'Neill, had urged her to take the
part. Alla Nazimova was cast as Christine, and Earle Larimore as
Orin. Philip Moeller was engaged to direct and Robert Edmond Jones
o do the sets.

O'Neill and Carlotta attended seven weeks of rehearsals of
Mourning Becomes Electra. Though they both were familiar with
he long, confusing, and often agonizing process of producing a play
rom manuscript to première, they were fascinated by what they saw
nd heard. O'Neill was particularly interested in the characterizations
f Nazimova and Alice Brady, for their respective interpretations
vere at the same time more and less than what O'Neill had imagined.
As always, he found that as soon as actors spoke his lines, the lines
hemselves seemed changed.

The three parts of O'Neill's trilogy are called *Homecoming,*
The Hunted, and *The Haunted.* All of the action takes place within the
ear following the end of the Civil War. Ezra Mannon, wealthy ship-
wner, judge, mayor and now a general in the Union Army, is about
o return from the war. His wife, Christine, is having an affair with
a sea captain, Adam Brant, the son of a disgraced uncle of Ezra.
Lavinia, the Mannons' twenty-three-year-old daughter, who hates her
mother and is abnormally devoted to her father, learns about the
iaison and threatens Christine with exposure if the affair is not immediately ended. The mother pretends to submit to the ultimatum,
but with the aid of her lover she plots the murder of her husband.

On the night of his return, Ezra Mannon dies, and Lavinia finds the box which held the poison that Christine has administered. The doctor, however, attributes the death to heart failure.

Orin, the Mannons' twenty-year-old son, who loves his mother with more than filial affection, returns from the Army two days later. Lavinia plays upon his jealousy of his mother and enlists his aid in her plan to avenge their father's death. Together they follow Christine to a shipboard tryst with Brant and they listen to the incriminating conversation of the lovers. When Christine leaves, Orin kills Brant, and Lavinia helps him to leave evidence that causes the police to ascribe the slaying to an attack by waterfront thieves. Later, Lavinia and Orin tell their mother of the death of her lover. Christine shoots herself and her death is publicly laid to grief over her husband's death.

Lavinia takes Orin away on a year's journey in the South Seas. When they return Lavinia has become a beautiful woman very much resembling her mother, and Orin has acquired the looks of his father. Lavinia has hopes that now she and Orin will be able to build their separate futures away from the Mannon curse, but Orin, maddened by his feeling of guilt, threatens to publish the whole Mannon story unless Lavinia gives up all intentions of marrying, and he vows that he himself will not marry. He makes incestuous advances to her, and then he shoots himself. Lavinia, knowing that the dark story of the Mannon deaths will prevent her ever achieving happiness, decides to immure herself in the family mansion and never emerge from it until her death. The window shutters are being sealed and she closes the front door as the curtain falls.

Mourning Becomes Electra is a modern counterpart of the *Oresteia* trilogy in which Aeschylus narrated the revenge of Orestes and his sister, Electra, for the murder of their father, Agamemnon, by their mother, Clytemnestra, and her lover, Aegisthus. As in the Greek drama, the O'Neill characters are shown struggling against a code, of myth—in this case, the New England "best family" code. But the development of the new *Electra* is based on sound modern concepts of psychological and biological cause and effect, not upon the inspiration of the Furies. Nevertheless, he succeeded in creating an overriding impression of inevitability more powerful than the strivings of all the Mannons, and in this he caught some of the essence of classic Greek tragedy.

After a tryout in Boston, *Mourning Becomes Electra* was presented in New York at the Guild Theatre on October 26, 1931. The enthusiasm with which the critics received it surpassed that accorded any other new play in the history of the modern theater. Brooks Atkinson of *The New York Times* called it O'Neill's masterpiece and said it was "heroically thought out and magnificently wrought in style and structure." John Mason Brown called it "an achievement which restores the theater to its high estate." Joseph Wood Krutch wrote in *The Nation* that "it may turn out to be the only permanent contribution yet made by the twentieth century to dramatic literature." *Time* magazine had O'Neill's picture on its cover and called him "a mature genius at 43."

The play began at five o'clock in the afternoon and, including an hour's intermission for dinner, lasted five hours. Robert Benchley of *The New Yorker* said he liked the play all right but, at its end, he was "cushion conscious." Another published witticism said you had to stay in the theater until Mourning Became Electra. Alexander Woollcott reported that he overheard the conversation of two ladies lunching at the Colony restaurant. "Just tell me this, my dear," one said, "has there ever been any incest in your family?"

The play ran for 250 performances. It was so difficult to get seats that O'Neill had to buy some for the opening to give to friends. He himself left for Northport the day the play opened. When Art McGinley wrote for tickets, O'Neill replied that it was tough even for a playwright to *buy* seats for a Guild play when it was a hit. Guild subscribers filled the house every night for six weeks before seats were sold to the public. O'Neill said he felt pretty ragged and wished he could go on a "booze bust . . . a good antidote—but I haven't used that way out in so many years it makes me feel old to think of them." These were his standard remarks to his old drinking friends, reflecting nostalgia more than actual intention.

Shane was extremely anxious to see the play. His fellow students jokingly asked him to get them passes. Finally he wrote his father and asked him directly whether he could come to New York to see the play. His father did not reply, but Shane received a typewritten letter from Carlotta. She began by saying that his father, as well as herself, was delighted to have received his letters and to hear that his days at Lawrenceville were proving happy as well as busy.

No, dear child, Carlotta told Shane, you cannot see *Mourning Becomes Electra*. She listed her reasons. First and foremost, Shane would not enjoy it. Anyone taking him would look conspicuous and ridiculous in the audience and would call down well-deserved and unpleasant criticism upon his own head. She pointed out that Shane's father was never conspicuous or ostentatious and those who loved him must follow his example. His father's next play, she assured him, would be one that Shane would enjoy. Then they could all make a family party and turn out in great style.

Early in November, O'Neill and Carlotta decided to live in Manhattan. He reasoned that "after two years in dismal Touraine there might be something in New York that might be good" for his work, and some things "to be done and seen," which he ought not to miss. They leased a duplex apartment at 1095 Park Avenue and spent some $25,000 in alterations.

Fred Pasley made a number of visits there to get material for a series of six articles for the Sunday *News*. O'Neill met him at the door of the apartment. Pasley found him "the most approachable and understanding person" he had ever encountered and described O'Neill as "six feet of sinewy physique, not fat, very slender; a finely molded head; thick black hair, tipped with gray; a heavy lock falling over the right temple, accentuating the massive brow; its height and breadth overhanging the sensitive features like a crag. Luminous black eyes, unusually large and round; unusually tense and brooding; of compelling, searching intelligence which shines through them; and they have the faculty of eloquent speech when the lips are mute." O'Neill introduced him to Blemie, his pet Dalmation. Carlotta had luncheon ready for the two men. Because Pasley had had a good deal of experience as a police reporter, the O'Neills asked him many questions about "gangsters, prohibition, and bootleg wars."

Afterward, O'Neill took his guest upstairs to his study. On the way Pasley noticed some of the furnishings—a grotesque mask, a grinning little wooden idol suspended from the wall, a drum cylindrical in shape and about six feet long, which the player beats while sitting astride it. In O'Neill's study were a ship's brass lantern and many pictures of clipper ships. There was also a wooden model of a clipper ship. During their talk O'Neill took his ship's discharge papers out of his top desk drawer and showed them to Pasley with pride and obvious nostalgia.

Pasley stayed the rest of the afternoon, taking notes as O'Neill talked. Carlotta brought them tea. O'Neill talked in "measured tones, whose cadences somehow reminds you of the ebbs and flow of the tides. His humor is precious and enhanced by the solemnity of his face. He has a slow-motion, whimsical grin which is always accompanied by a lifting of his bushy eyebrows. These are uncannily expressive. They actually seem to shrug themselves at times."

O'Neill poured tea and talked about the seaman who had given him the idea for *The Hairy Ape*. He would see a woman on the street and call out, "Hello, Kiddo. How's ev'ry little t'ing? Got anything on for tonight? I know an old boiler down by the docks we kin crawl into." Obviously, O'Neill wanted so much to be accepted by rough-and-tumble guys, dese-and-dose guys, regular guys. Suddenly, he saw himself sipping tea with one of them and sensed that the man was impressed with the luxurious apartment. Then, as if reading the reporter's thoughts, he said, "They said I went high-hat because I moved uptown. I moved here simply because I found the sort of apartment I wanted."

In the middle of November, although scarcely settled at 1095 Park Avenue, O'Neill decided he needed a change. Ilka Chase suggested that fashionable Sea Island, Georgia, would please O'Neill. He could live by the sea and go swimming as much as he wanted. O'Neill said he needed a change of scene and climate to "snap me out of this slough and start me off on my new work." He couldn't "think serious" because of his "present dumb state of gray matter."

The O'Neills stopped at a few places en route. Carlotta wrote letters to Shane and Oona because O'Neill did not feel up to it. She told Shane that they had arrived at Sea Island and found the sun warm and lovely; that the water was warmer than on Long Island during the past summer—at least, that was what his father reported —she did not like swimming very much. She said that Sea Island was charming, with all kinds of sports—riding, swimming, golf, tennis, shooting, fishing, and boating—and that there was even an airport nearby.

In New York again during the winter of 1931–32, O'Neill was unable to get any writing done. In March, he was lionized, along with Gerhart Hauptmann, the German dramatist, at a sumptuous luncheon at the home of Otto Kahn. When Hauptmann sailed, he told reporters that "the two outstanding things in my visit were meeting O'Neill and attending *Mourning Becomes Electra*." But to Carlotta's continued puzzlement, O'Neill seemed to prefer his old friends. One of them was Walter "Ice" Casey. According to Nathan, "Ice" was the son of the iceman in New London and "remained one of Gene's favorite friends in later years, despite his wife's protestations that the fellow was scarcely of social status worthy of the O'Neill eminence." Carlotta has said that O'Neill didn't like to see people except that "sometimes what he would call his business associates would turn up from odd points of the globe and they would talk [with her husband] and then he would go back to work again."

Sometimes, O'Neill would encounter an old friend from his Jimmy the Priest's or seafaring days, and they would slip into a speakeasy to talk over old times. Most of them had not heard about his success as a playwright. One, a barker on a sightseeing bus in New York, after learning his old pal had a play on Broadway, made it a point to have the bus pass the Guild Theatre. *"The greatest play in the world by the greatest playwright in the world—Eugene O'Neill,"* he would bellow through his megaphone. Many of his friends put "the touch" on O'Neill and he generally responded. Carlotta took an extremely dim view of this.

In talking about those "wonderful" days, O'Neill often spoke to Carlotta of the nickelodeons they had in the New Orleans bagnios and other low dives he had frequented. He could hum or sing many of the old tunes. In an attempt to console O'Neill in his nostalgia, Carlotta went to a music store and asked if they could provide her with a player piano of this kind. In the storage room he found the very thing. A madame in a bagnio had failed to keep up her payments and her player piano had been repossessed. It was painted green and was adorned with roses and cupids; and colored lights flashed as it played. With it came old rolls of music, including "All Alone," "Springtime Rag," "That Mysterious Rag," "Waiting At the Church," "Alexander's Ragtime Band," and "The Robert E. Lee." Carlotta gave it to O'Neill for his birthday, saying that she wanted him to have all the things his heart desired.

O'Neill named the piano Rosie and kept a derby hat on top of it half filled with nickels. Many years later, he told Hamilton Basso that he was not sure playing Rosie so much was a good idea. "I try to remember," he said, "a beautiful verse from Verlaine and come up with a line of 'Everybody's Doing It' or 'Oh, You Great Big Beautiful Doll.' "

O'Neill had not lived at 1095 Park Avenue for six months before he was saying that he had had a "bellyful" of New York and was "yawning himself to death with boredom." They would have to move to a more satisfactory place. The alterations on the apartment had been made at great expense, but he consoled himself with the thought that if he and Carlotta hadn't tried out living in the town of his birth, they would always have regretted it. Never again would he try and live in a city! He gave expression to his disenchantment with New York in one of his infrequent little jokes: "The only time the Indians ever swindled the white man was when they sold the island of Manhattan for twenty-four dollars."

So, once again, the O'Neills were looking for a new home. Carlotta has suggested, as an explanation for this constant moving from place to place, that like many other invalids O'Neill chose to ascribe his discomfort to the nature of his environment rather than to the infirmity of his own body. No doubt there was much wisdom in her observation. But O'Neill's restlessness was lifelong, and in this case there was another, more immediate cause.

At this time O'Neill was not writing, but he was thinking, he told the Guild, about a cycle of three plays, one at the time of the Revolution, another in 1840 and a third "at the present." This ambitious trilogy of plays would one day grow to eleven and dominate his life. He had already given some thought to it in France. But, there was no sea to look out upon on Park Avenue and he could not get his creative drive into motion. These plays, he said sadly, "were not yet ripe enough in my mind for doing." He continued to be ill and bedridden at frequent intervals. He complained to a friend that he was "stale and seedy." He was sick of "blind alleys."

O'Neill bought a piece of land in a secluded spot on the beach at Sea Island and, under Carlotta's supervision, an architect began building a twenty-two room house facing the sea and surrounded by a wall. Because Carlotta was deathly afraid of fire, the house was built of brick and stucco, with a roof of slate. *House & Garden* described it as "a combination of the early Majorcan peasant house of the sixteenth century tinctured with a flavor of the fifteenth-century monastery. . . ."

O'Neill planned to go down to Sea Island at the end of March, 1932, but he was stricken with influenza, and it was April before he and Carlotta sublet their apartment and left New York—seemingly for good. For a time they stayed at the Cloisters, Sea Island, until their house was ready for occupancy; then, in June, they moved in. Invitations to his friends once more fluttered from O'Neill's pen. He wrote how proud he was of his new home and how anxious he was to show it off and "delight the beholder." It was the first time he or Carlotta had ever lived in a place they had themselves designed and built. His previous homes, he related, were always "other folks' houses" which he had bought. They never satisfy—"no matter what good luck is in the house."

They named their new home Casa Genotta, a blending of their pet names for each other—Gene and Lotta. It was Carlotta's idea.

After a good deal of arranging of dates through O'Neill's lawyer, Shane was invited down to Sea Island for a visit at Casa Genotta during the summer of 1932. When he got off the train at Brunswick, the nearest railroad town to Sea Island, Herbert Freeman, the O'Neills' new chauffeur, met him in the big, brown Cadillac limousine and they drove the twelve miles to Casa Genotta. Shane found his father's house beautiful and immaculate, its schedule as precise as a well-run hospital.

When O'Neill finished his morning's stint of writing, he took Shane up to see his study. It was designed to simulate the captain's quarters of an old-time sailing vessel. The ceiling and walls were supported by hand-adzed timbers. A bank of windows facing the sea formed a bay that bulged like the stern of a Spanish galleon. The study was furnished with an Early American table to which was drawn a Windsor chair. Below a lookout window was a high desk at which O'Neill would occasionally write standing up. Many things in it could not have been better selected to please the heart of an imaginative, father-starved, thirteen-year-old boy. There were ship models, clocks that chimed the ship's watches, a mast running up inside the room with marlinespikes on one side, and a variety of nautical gadgets. There was even an iron spiral staircase leading up to a secret lookout where O'Neill could sun-bathe in privacy.

After lunch at Casa Genotta, a formal affair with servants, Carlotta and O'Neill took Shane for a drive around Sea Island. Shane remembers that he did not get a chance to talk alone with his father but that his concept of him as a romantic figure, to be admired and loved, grew and grew. Both were shy with each other.

Shane had been there only a short time when Eugene O'Neill, Jr., arrived with his bride of a year. He had just been graduated from Yale with the highest honors. Following his father's advice to study the Greek classics, he had won the Noyes Cutter prize "for the highest degree of excellency in interpreting the Greek of the New Testament into modern English." He also won the Soldiers Memorial Foote Fellowship in Classics and the Jacob Cooper prize in Greek. He was going to teach at Yale and take his doctorate there. In a month he would be off, with his wife, to study at the University of Freiburg in Germany.

Shane could easily see how proud his father was of his elder son and namesake, whose wife, Betty, was vivacious, beautiful, and an heiress. Eugene junior had none of the shyness that seemed to afflict Shane and their father. Eugene was extremely articulate, his voice resonant and melodious. He could quote extensively from the classics and was able to discuss literature with his father, virtually as an equal. Eugene junior seemed an overwhelming figure, indeed, for the thirteen-year-old Shane to compete with for his father's affection and attention.

Shane and the younger Eugene O'Neills ended their visit at the same time and made the trip north together. "I'll always remember that visit to Sea Island," Shane said recently, "because it was then that I first got to know my brother." Shane had had only a dim recollection of young Eugene in Provincetown and in Bermuda. As for getting to know his father, Shane felt that he had failed. He seemed unable to reach his father, to make him understand how much he loved him, how much he admired him, how much he wanted to do as well as Eugene junior in order to please him. And somehow he felt that it was all his fault.

In the fall, soon after Shane returned to the Second Form at Lawrenceville, it was evident that he was not doing well. His conduct record was poor and he failed in English and in Latin. "I think Shane was sent away from home too young," William Wyman, one of Shane's housemasters has said. "A small, shy boy has a rough time in a boarding school."

By the end of November, Shane was still doing badly. The masters at Lawrenceville take the problem of a boy who is failing as a challenge. They especially wanted to succeed with Shane. Both the faculty and Dr. Abbott, the headmaster, felt that Shane's main problem was a need for approval from his father—to have his father notice him, pay attention to him, show him he cared. Dr. Abbott was less inclined than some of the other faculty members to take the view that Shane could pull himself out of his own difficulties. He wrote to

O'Neill, saying quite frankly that Shane needed his approval very much and that, in his experience, a father's taking special pains to show concern about the scholastic progress of his son generally worked wonders.

The reply he received told him that, under no circumstances, was there to be any direct communication between Lawrenceville and Mr. O'Neill. All communications were to be sent through the offices of Harry Weinberger, Mr. O'Neill's attorney. Dr. Abbott told Agnes of the letter. Yes, she said, O'Neill was completely cut off, not only from herself—the mother of Shane—but from his children.

"We have tried everything to make Shane study," Dr. Abbott wrote to Agnes. "Shane just worships his father. I did not know I was doing anything wrong in the letter I wrote to Mr. O'Neill. . . . I am sorry if I should not have done this. We cannot make Shane study. He has a brilliant mind, but he will not study. One word from his father would have made him study—he worships his father so. I suppose that is all wrong, but he does. Hereafter I shall write to no one but you."

CHAPTER

TWENTY-ONE

ನಿಐ

THE "BLESSED ISLE"

O'Neill was so pleased with Sea Island and so grateful to Ilka Chase for having urged him to settle there that he gave her a copy of *Mourning Becomes Electra* with the following inscription:

> To Ilka—who found our Blessed Isle for us—with profoundest gratitude.

EUGENE O'NEILL

He and Carlotta were "installed and all set" on the first of July, 1932. From that date, he told friends, they became "adopted Georgia crackers" and were going to remain so "for the rest of our days, we hope." He said he had taken a great liking to "the folks down here. . . . The depression seems to leave them quite unhysterical, even entirely calm. They've lived in one ever since the Civil War and 'what of it?' seems to be the slogan." After the "perpetual whine" of people in New York complaining about the depression, he found this attitude distinctly refreshing. But, best of all, his writing was going well, had the right feel. The play was *Days Without End* and he told a friend that, in it, there was "a fresh vision, a new understanding, an inner yea-saying" that intrigued and stimulated him no end. He was going to have "a grand time" writing this one.

Days Without End presents the story of a conflict within the soul of John Loving, who is torn between religious faith and atheistic rationalism. The two tendencies are personified on the stage as individual characters. As John he is dealt with by the other persons in the play; as Loving he is seen only by John (and the audience); Loving's utterances are heard by the other characters as emanating from John. The question to which John Loving is seeking an answer is crystallized in a dilemma arising from an instance of marital infidelity on his part: Should he tell his wife about it and thus lose her love and respect; or should he conceal it and thus be false to his ideal of truthfulness?

He has almost completed the writing of a novel which tells the story of his life and sets forth the questions which he has not yet been able to answer. Loving is taunting John about his indecision when John Loving's uncle, Father Baird, calls upon him at his office. The priest is quite familiar with his nephew's atheistic thinking from his close association with him in earlier years. He also is ready to discuss the questions which perplex the younger man.

John takes his uncle home with him to meet his wife, and the three spend the evening together. Mrs. Loving prevails upon John to read what he has written and in the reading she is able to discern the fact of John's infidelity. Mrs. Loving was married once before, and she divorced her husband who had been repeatedly unfaithf' to her. Her unhappy memories of the previous marriage serve to i tensify her shock on learning of John's infidelity. As a result, she suffers the relapse of an illness and is about to die, partly because she doesn't care to live. Eventually John, gaining the ascendancy over Loving, makes his decision and Mrs. Loving finds it possible to forgive her husband and at the same moment begins to recover.

In a final scene, John prostrates himself before a crucifix at the altar of a church, while a weakened Loving falls down beside him. "Thou hast conquered, Lord. . . . Forgive the damned soul of John Loving," he says. John then rises to become once more the whole person, John Loving.

The play is both tedious and cumbersome, and though there are some moving scenes *Days Without End* was not so much imagined dramatically as it was conceived in intellectual ferment. Thus the play fails on three counts: The story is uninteresting, the characters are undeveloped, and the construction is uncertain. Even O'Neill admitted to George Jean Nathan, who disliked the play, that the "hero's final gesture calls for alteration." Obviously, he was agreeing with the Great Skeptic that Loving's prostration before the cross was taking the easy way out. Ironically enough, just before Nathan died in 1958 he became a Catholic.

Days Without End proved to be the most unfortunate play O'Neill ever wrote—both for his writing career and in terms of his own state of mind. In a sense, it was part of the *Dynamo* cycle of three plays which dealt with "the sickness of today." O'Neill, of course, was seeking an answer to man's quest for spiritual certainty, but closer examination of the play in relation to O'Neill's personal life indicates that he may have been seeking a solution to his own spiritual doubts. In many ways the plot and its characters suggest himself and Carlotta—just as *Welded* reflected himself and Agnes.

Throughout the spring, summer and early fall of 1932, O'Neill worked on *Days Without End*. One of the characters in the play, the clergyman who shows John Loving the way to salvation through Christ, O'Neill first made a Protestant minister, because he felt that a Protestant clergyman of an unspecified denomination would cause less controversy. Later, he decided that it would be more effective if the clergyman was a Catholic priest with the distinctive attire of his calling. In New York he talked with Father John Ford, a cultured and sophisticated priest with a patrician background. Father Ford said that many priests wore the black cassock and biretta (a square hat with three or four arched projections radiating from the center of the crown), rather than the more usual black suit and turned-around white collar.

There is some evidence that O'Neill may have been contemplating a return to the Catholic Church at the time he was writing *Days Without End*. Richard Dana Skinner, the drama critic for the Catholic *Commonweal* magazine thought so. "In *Days Without End*," he wrote, "O'Neill sought directly, in surrender to the Christ crucified, a truth that would set him free. But it must have been a difficult play to write."

Father Ford had several talks with O'Neill, but he has recalled that there was little discussion on the subject of Catholic faith and morals. Often O'Neill would make an urgent telephone call to Father

Ford and arrange for the priest to come up to his apartment. Generally, just before the time for the appointment, Father Ford has recalled, Carlotta would telephone and say that O'Neill was not well and was unable to keep the appointment.

"It is my opinion," Father Ford has said, "that O'Neill was a long way from returning to the Church. We discussed certain matters. But you didn't tell Eugene O'Neill anything about philosophy or theology."

Skinner, who appears to have been closer to O'Neill's spiritual struggles than Father Ford, wrote a book about O'Neill's inner conflict—*Eugene O'Neill: A Poet's Quest*. Skinner felt that Catholics should recognize and support "what O'Neill's change of heart means in the literary world."

"I can assure you," Skinner wrote Father Michael Earls, a Jesuit priest in Boston, "that the play [*Days Without End*] was written not only with the utmost sincerity but only as a result of a terrific interior and personal struggle on O'Neill's part. It may interest you to know that his wife is working very hard to bring about his definite return to the Catholic Church, as she feels that that is his one salvation. As you know, he was born a Catholic but lost his faith rather early in life."

Skinner explained to Father Earls that O'Neill's marriages to Kathleen and to Agnes had taken place "outside the Church." As both these marriages were "subsequent to the regulations of 1908, [they] would be invalid from the Catholic point of view, and therefore, leave him free to remain with his present wife if he returned to the Church." He added, "This is a very critical period for him personally."

Father Earls advanced the notion that some of O'Neill's ideas, embodied in his plays, might be the product of a diseased mind. He regarded O'Neill as "a great poet [more] by virtue of his powerful imagination than his technique." Skinner immediately rejected the idea that O'Neill had "shown any symptoms of a diseased mind." He went stoutly to the playwright's defense, saying:

> Practically all of his plays have been heavily burdened with a consciousness of sin and its effects which the truly diseased mind would certainly avoid, excuse, or evade. When we read the intimate experiences of many people who eventually became saints, we learn of the intensity of their preoccupation

with temptation in various forms. I have always had the feeling
that the great saint is potentially an equally great sinner and
that the conquest of the lower self is all the more heroic when
that lower self is powerful and malevolent. As I see it, what
O'Neill has done is to give us a real transcript of the inner
struggles of his soul, and I am no more inclined to call him
diseased for having done this than I would be to call Dante diseased because of the visions of the Inferno which he conjured up.

Skinner again called Father Earls' attention to the fact that
O'Neill's "present wife is doing all in her power to get him to return
to his faith. That is probably the real answer to the good influence she
is supposed to exercise over him. She really understands his inner
need."

Certainly Carlotta wanted O'Neill to return to the Church, but
he refused. "He was always a Christian," she has said in a memo-
randum on deposit at the Yale Library, "in the real sense even though
he never went to church in his adult years. But he practiced Chris-
tianity in his living. I never knew such a just, all-understanding,
forgiving, kind, *good* man! And his patience was amazing. But when
he was lied to and endlessly imposed upon, he was finished and
that was that."

"My husband was not a religious man," Carlotta told Brooks
Atkinson. "He had been born a Catholic, naturally. He hadn't anything in his veins but Irish blood of which he was very proud." In
answer to the question, "Was there any return to religion?" Carlotta
replied very emphatically, "Never, never, at any time, at any moment."

All spring and through the summer of 1932 O'Neill had continued to labor over *Days Without End,* and he completed two drafts.
By September, O'Neill was exhausted from "trying to cram too much
into [the play]," and he decided to take a week off and rest. "He
awoke the next morning," Barrett Clark has said, "with the story,
characters, plot scheme and practically all the details of *Ah, Wilderness!* in his mind clamoring to be put down on paper. O'Neill went
back to work and within a month had completed a first draft of *Ah,
Wilderness!"*

Ah, Wilderness! is a classic example of the boy-meets-girl-boy-
loses-girl-boy-gets-girl formula. Richard Miller, the son of Nat Miller,

the town's newspaper editor, falls in love with Muriel McComber. Richard, who leans toward socialism, is a great lover of poetry, and he makes love to Muriel, in person and in his letters, by quoting some of the world's lushest love poems. Without warning, Muriel writes him that everything is off. Richard, extremely disillusioned, tries to drown his sorrows in liquor and in the arms of a fallen woman, but he becomes sick and his love of Muriel, the "pure" girl preserves his innocence. Later, Muriel tells him that her father forced her to write the renunciation letter, and Richard admits his bad behavior. She forgives him, he forgives her, they embrace, fadeout.

Although the play is somewhat long and the constant poetic quotations grow tedious, there are some excellent moments: Muriel's father telling Richard's father about the boy's letters, quoting the poetry and calling it "vile" stuff; a big Sunday-dinner get-together; Nat Miller as an endearing drunk; and the last scene, when Nat Miller says to his wife, "Well, Spring isn't everything, is it, Essie? There's a lot to be said for Autumn. That's got beauty, too. And Winter—if you're together." These are doubtlessly some of the most cheerfully optimistic lines O'Neill ever wrote.

Why did this play, *Ah, Wilderness!,* unlike any other play O'Neill ever wrote or was to write, well up so suddenly and so clearly in his unconscious? Bessie Breuer has said that it was probably because the play was outside of himself—outside of the self-examination with which he was always tormenting himself. O'Neill has called the play "a dream walking" and "a comedy of recollection." He said it was an attempt "to write a play true to the spirit of the American large small-town at the turn of the century. Its quality depended upon atmosphere, sentiment, an exact evocation of the mood of a dead past. To me, the America which was (and is) the real America found its unique expression in such middle-class families as the Millers, among whom so many of my own generation passed from adolescence into manhood."

In the light of what was happening to O'Neill's relations with his son, Shane, Richard Dana Skinner's remarks are revealing:

> Quite aside from the general importance of *Ah, Wilderness!* there is a very special significance in the emphasis laid on the father and son relationship. It is the first O'Neill play in which the father has not been a pale, stiff shadow or a narrow, stern object of hate and jealousy. What the sudden tender under-

standing amounts to is the development of the full-grown man in the poet's own make-up, of a man willing and eager to take up creative responsibility in life and able at last to see his own father as another individual, respected and apart, loved and admired and—no longer an object of jealousy.

So far as O'Neill was concerned, he had, besides his spiritual struggles, worries about money. Some of his closest friends were asking him for money that fall. The depression was at a new low. O'Neill was feeling the pinch himself and had very little or nothing to give.

Electra, he explained sadly, was shut down. He was praying that when it reopened it would stay open. However, the money he was expecting to get from it was mortgaged for the first few months to "next year's direful income tax." He was also, he said, paying alimony to Agnes and tuition for his childrens' schools and didn't see how he could get on his feet again financially for a year and a half. As for his capital assets, he had real estate that could not be sold for what it was mortgaged for and securities that, if sold, would bring only four-fifths to nine-tenths of the original investment. His story, as far as money was concerned, was "the story of everyone today." Furthermore, he had no plays ready for production. There was one hope; *Strange Interlude* had been made into a "talkie" and if successful it might encourage the film people to buy some more of his plays. *Anna Christie* was the only other play they had bought—that and a one-act play for which he got nothing. The film people, he said, were "scared to touch my stuff."

Among the people to whom he could give little or no financial help were his New London friend Art McGinley and George Tyler, the producer of his early plays and a friend of James O'Neill. Tyler said it was "humiliating" to have to ask for money. O'Neill replied that he should not feel badly but simply feel he was asking a nephew for something for which he had a perfect right to ask. He explained that foreign rights were bringing little. Just recently, Madden sent word of a shabby proposal (to produce an old play) which had come from England. Positively no, O'Neill replied, because the English were not paying any money. If Monte Cristo ever heard that his son gave the "cursed English" even the tiniest break, he would rise up from the grave and beat his younger son with a blackthorn stick.

Early in October, 1932, O'Neill sent word to Barrett Clark that he had drafts of two plays which had nothing to do with each other. He wasn't ready to submit them to the Guild or even to say what their titles were. (They were *Days Without End* and *Ah, Wilderness!*) A few weeks later he complained to Clark that he was having "to bat my brains out" on *Days Without End*. At the moment he was at "the becalmed stage." The theme was most difficult. He yearned for the good old days when he was satisfied to be either "simple-minded or foggily mystical," whereas now his aim was to be "clearly psychological and mystically clear, etc." It was a tough ambition!

In December, O'Neill was in touch again with Art McGinley, who told him he was getting fed up with his newspaper job. O'Neill advised him to hang on to it as a man who had a job in these depression days was just about a millionaire. He commented that it was "a hell of time to be living." They talked about their fathers. McGinley remembered the trouble he had given his father before settling down, and reminded Eugene of a row he [O'Neill] had once had with James O'Neill. The "Old Man" and he, O'Neill explained to McGinley, had become good friends and had learned to understand each other the winter before he died. In the days McGinley was speaking of, O'Neill admitted, he was full of "a secret bitterness about him" and had not stopped to realize that the "Governor" had taken a great deal from his younger son and "kept on smiling."

Bennett Cerf, the president of Random House, flew to Sea Island to confer with O'Neill in the spring of 1933. O'Neill's publisher, Boni and Liveright, had failed, and nearly every publishing house in New York was trying to sign him to a contract. O'Neill said that if Cerf would hire Saxe Commins (his editor at Boni and Liveright), then he would be willing to come over to Random House. Cerf agreed— a decision that proved to be of the greatest importance not only for O'Neill and Commins, but for Random House and American letters as well. For Saxe Commins, who at one time wanted to be a dentist in Rochester, New York, became editor-in-chief at Random House, the editor for Nobel Prize winners Sinclair Lewis and William Faulkner, and the friend and advisor of a great many other fine writers. Only a writer with the prestige and power that O'Neill had in 1933 could have made the extraordinary demand that gave Commins his opportunity.

Lawrence Langner and his wife also visited Casa Genotta in the spring, along with an intimate friend of Carlotta's, Fania Marinoff,

the actress wife of Carl Van Vechten. Again Langner was charmed
by Carlotta, found her "one of those rare women who was born
beautiful and will remain so all her life." He noted that all her talents
and efforts went into making an attractive home and surroundings
'in which Gene could have privacy for his work, and to this she
dedicated herself with almost fanatic fervor." He said of his own
wife, "Armina always returned from the O'Neills' with a feeling of
inferiority, and would say, in despair, 'I'll never run a household as
smoothly and successfully as Carlotta.'"

At the end of that spring O'Neill was still distressed over *Days
Without End,* which he feared was controversial, "especially in its
Catholic aspect." Langner, who had persuaded the playwright to
submit the two plays to the Theatre Guild, sent word that the Guild
had accepted both *Days Without End* and *Ah, Wilderness!* and suggested the latter be put on first. O'Neill, however, had doubts about
which play should be produced first.

It was about this time that the O'Neills decided that Sea Island
was not exactly a year-round place to live; the previous summer had
been murderously hot and uncomfortable. Carlotta asked Ilka Chase
to suggest a place for them to go to that summer. Ilka suggested the
Adirondacks; she even knew some friends who would be happy to
rent them their house at Faust, New York. There Carlotta and Eugene passed the summer of 1933.

According to his work diary, O'Neill had completed the final
draft of *Days Without End* before spring, but his letters reveal he was
still worrying about it. He now told Langner he wanted *Days Without
End* to be produced first. In August he changed his mind and wrote
Langner from the Adirondacks that the play would undoubtedly
arouse "much bitter argument" and would be "well hated by the
prejudiced." This might be fatal to *Ah, Wilderness!* In another letter,
he said there were arguments on both sides as to which play should
be first; he couldn't trust himself to judge.

It was Langner who made the decision. He began casting *Ah,
Wilderness!* with George M. Cohan as Nat Miller, although O'Neill
had meant the part of the sensitive son to be the starring role. Cohan
was not overimpressed with the O'Neill play. He remarked that the
humor in *Ah, Wilderness!* was mostly old vaudeville jokes which
had been done over and over.

O'Neill and Carlotta came down to New York from the Adirondacks late in the summer of 1933 to attend rehearsals of *Ah,*

Wilderness! They stayed again at the Madison in a forty-dollar-a-day suite. At the end of the rehearsal period it was decided to try out the show in cities outside New York. O'Neill refused to go on tour with the show, but after much urging he did make a trip to Pittsburgh to see the tryout there.

When Langner asked him why he wouldn't go to a performance of his own plays, O'Neill said it was because he couldn't stand being present in a crowded theater, could not just sit still and watch. On the other hand, Langner noted, he did not mind spending hours in crowded arenas watching prize fights or six-day bicycle races. The difference, perhaps, was that a theater struck some unnamed terror in him. Perhaps it was memories of his father playing Monte Cristo, or of his mother's aversion for the theater, or even more possibly it was fear that the play might fail. He refused to attend the dress rehearsal of *Ah, Wilderness!* in New York.

Ah, Wilderness! opened at the Guild Theatre on October 2, 1933, and ran 289 performances. It yielded O'Neill some $75,000, received generally excellent reviews and created a sensation on two scores. Its characters did not come to the usual disastrous O'Neill endings, and the people assumed that the great tragic dramatist had had a happy childhood after all and had written about it in the play.

Nothing, O'Neill said, could be further from the truth. "It was" he told Hamilton Basso, "a sort of wishing out loud. That's the way I would have *liked* my boyhood to have been."

Days Without End, which went into rehearsal immediately following the opening of *Ah, Wilderness!*, was "a damned difficult play to produce," O'Neill told Art McGinley. He said he had been busier than ever before, attending rehearsals every day with no time out for lunch, just eating a sandwich at the theater. In the cast were Selena Royle, Earle Larimore and Ilka Chase. Advance publicity notices described it as "a modern miracle play" which depicts "a conflict between atheism and religious faith in which the faith is triumphant."

The play was tried out in Boston during Christmas week and opened in New York at the Henry Miller Theatre on January 8, 1934. The critics panned it as much as they had praised *Ah, Wilderness!* One of them said that it was the sort of shoddy theatricality one might expect from the son of James O'Neill of *Monte Cristo* fame. O'Neill was furious when he read this review, saying that critics had a right to attack a play of his but not to attack his dead father. Langner has said that "Gene was bitterly disappointed with the reception of the

lay," which ran only fifty-seven performances—just long enough for
iuild subscribers to be taken care of.

Some Catholics thought that O'Neill had become a Catholic
gain. One critic called on all Catholics to urge people to see *Days
Without End* because it "proves with high conclusiveness that the
eturn to the bosom of the Church was a very necessary step in the
rtistic life of Eugene O'Neill, the Irish boy who is reclaiming his
irthright." But it did not receive the approval of the Church, which
efused to put it on its white list. Suggestions reached O'Neill that
: would be acceptable if he inserted a line making it clear that the
eroine's first husband, whose infidelity had so upset her, was dead,
ot merely divorced. The idea was abhorrent to O'Neill for two
easons: It involved his artistic integrity, and it struck at his own life,
or both he and Carlotta had been divorced, not once but several
imes.

O'Neill was bitter, but he thanked Langner for the fine produc-
ion. He blamed "the Amusement Racket" which New York "vain-
loriously calls The Theater." But he thanked God that some of those
or whom the play was written had heard what he had to say in *Days
Without End.*

There is an ironic postscript to this play. Some years after
)'Neill's death, the play received Vatican approval and was produced
n Italy by Catholic Action, a lay organization of the Church. In
ugust, 1957, Sister Mary Madeleva, President of St. Mary's College
t Notre Dame, Indiana, from which O'Neill's mother had been
raduated three-quarters of a century before, read both *Long Day's
ourney into Night* and *Days Without End.* Sister Madeleva wrote
his writer, "I am sure Eugene O'Neill was profoundly Catholic in
ind and heart. They [the two plays] are parts of the same story of an
xtraordinary soul almost childlike in its attempt to spell God with the
rong blocks."

CHAPTER

TWENTY-TWO

ಬಡ

THE CURSE AND

THE PATTERN

O'Neill returned to Sea Island, where he lived until the fall of 1936. In a sense, he had retired from "the theater of his time," in which he had once said a playwright must live. For a time he worked on a play about "the notorious Madame Jumel who caused no end of excitement in New York society over a hundred years ago." Contemporary accounts had described her as a "beautiful blonde with a superb figure and graceful carriage." As the wife of a wealthy wine merchant in New York City, she had held forth in the Roger Morris house. Her second husband was Aaron Burr.

O'Neill had titled his play *The Life of Bessie Bowen*. (Madame Jumel's maiden name had been Eliza Brown.) It has never been produced. According to *Vogue,* which published at this time a full-page regal portrait of O'Neill and his wife, Carlotta had given O'Neill considerable help on *The Life of Bessie Bowen*. "Mrs. O'Neill is an assiduous and perspicacious collaborator," the *Vogue* caption said, "in her husband's professional career." The statement was presum-

240

ably approved by Carlotta; her friend, Ilka Chase, was a daughter of
the late Edna Woolman Chase, then editor of *Vogue.*

But O'Neill abandoned the idea of completing this play and
embarked, instead, on the composition of a cycle of plays, eleven in
number, designed to take in the whole sweep and story of the United
States from the early 1700s. He filled hundreds of pages with the
scenarios of these plays. He also discussed his monumental cycle with
some of his friends, telling Lawrence Langner that the characters in
the plays were to be in their youth in one play and would be parents
and grandparents in later plays. The main stories would be based on
the lives of their children and their childrens' children. It reminded
Langner of John Galsworthy's *The Forsyte Saga.* As O'Neill described how he was tracing the effect of the grandparents on the
children and their grandchildren in the scenarios for the cycle plays,
it brought into Langner's mind the "Biblical prophecies as to the sins
of the parents being visited upon their children unto the third and
fourth generations." "I marveled," Langner wrote in his *The Magic
Curtain,* "at the scope of the work he was attempting."

Talking to Clark about the cycle, O'Neill said he was going back
to his "old vein of ironic tragedy." He was adding psychological depth
and insight. He said he had abandoned the simple and affirmative
views of life expressed in *Ah, Wilderness!* and *Days Without End,*
which he now regarded as too conventional. What he was feeling and
thinking and saying in those two plays was an interlude. But now he
had found again his true god—psychological fate—the god to whom
he had made obeisance in *Electra.* But in *Mourning Becomes Electra*
he had treated only two generations of the cursed Mannon family;
now he would show, in family after family, for a hundred and fifty
years, the same psychological fate dogging parents, children, grandchildren, great-grandchildren, on down through time. This recurring
theme, this constantly repeated pattern, would appear over and over
again in all the plays he would write henceforth. It would be as the
brush strokes in Van Gogh's paintings, the drumbeats in *The Emperor Jones,* the fire music in *Siegfried,* the moaning of the chorus
in the ancient Greek plays.

O'Neill felt, as he had said in *Marco Millions,* that God is "only
an infinite, insane energy which creates and destroys without other
purpose than to pass eternity in avoiding thought." He was overcome
with the "immense pessimism" of which Kenneth Macgowan and
Dr. George Hamilton had written in the conclusion of their book,

What Is Wrong with Marriage? Their pessimism was "despair over the way in which the sins of the fathers are visited upon the children. In this respect the family circle seems a vicious circle. It seems indeed the greatest vicious circle ever conceived; for its circumference has become the straight line of descent from parent to child, world without end."

What, precisely, O'Neill had in mind when dealing with "psychological fate" is not easy to define. In *Dynamo* and in *Strange Interlude,* he had said it was love for the parent of the opposite sex, hate for the parent of the same sex. In *Mourning Becomes Electra* it was the Puritan conviction of the sinfulness of sex. In *Desire under the Elms,* and in other plays the psychological fate was carried out in the corruption of character by materialistic greed. Most of these examples could, perhaps, be classified under the general heading of sins—although O'Neill did not call them that. Doris Alexander has described his "psychological fate as simply the influence of parents upon their children in the most important of all relationships—love."

There was yet another psychological fate O'Neill was thinking about in his great cycle—a curse on the misbegotten members of a family. He had talked about such a curse in *Strange Interlude* when he said that "a romantic imagination has ruined more lives than all the diseases—other diseases, I should say! It's a form of insanity." A man who looked beyond the horizon, a dreamer of dreams, courted the black vultures who would claw him to death.

But, O'Neill said, such a man has "a touch of the poet." In one cycle play, which uses just that phrase as a title, a son in the aristocratic Harford family has been cursed with this "touch." His mother tells the tavernkeeper's daughter that her son Simon, who plans to write a book denouncing the evil of greed and possessive ambition, will never write it, but it was already written on his conscience. "The Harfords never part with their dreams," the mother says, "even when they deny them. They cannot. That is the family curse."

The parents of a friend of Shane's took him to see *Ah, Wilderness!* in New York. One scene in particular, concerning the happy home life of the Miller family, struck the boy. After Nat Miller had finished giving his son, Richard, a bumbling, yet tender talk on the pitfalls of life, the son impulsively kisses his father, then hurries out on the porch to watch the moon. The father turns to his wife and says, huskily, "First time he's done that in years. I don't believe in kissing between fathers and sons after a certain age—seems mushy and silly—but that meant something." In Shane's fantasies, this was the kind of relationship he really had with his father. He did love him, but somehow never could find the right time or place to tell him. And, then, when he thought he was going to be able to speak to him about such things, nervousness and shyness made the words end up in silent mumbles.

Agnes was increasingly concerned about him. She was well aware that any fourteen-year-old boy needs a father; on the other hand, many boys in the same situation managed better than Shane. She began to feel that there must be some physical explanation. He was often ill with colds—so frequently that it worried her because his father had had tuberculosis and her own father had died of it. Shane's erratic performance in his studies puzzled Agnes still more because she knew her son had a good mind. He seemed impervious to advice and criticism; he just smiled and went on doing whatever he had intended to do. She saw that he had a curious inner stubbornness almost identical with his father's.

"I noticed then," Agnes said, "that Shane had an extremely interesting mind. He was creative and had an original outlook. His mind had infinite possibilities." The boy loved to draw, and he seemed to have a real talent. He was very good at drawing horses.

Shane was turning out to be an extremely good-looking young man. The fact that he remained thin—with not an ounce of superfluous fat on him—made him seem all the more handsome. Agnes noted that he possessed the same trembling shyness that had characterized his father, whom he resembled more and more.

Agnes finally convinced herself that much of Shane's failure to do well at Lawrenceville was the result of a hip injury received while playing football. An orthopedic surgeon in Philadelphia was inclined to agree. He told Agnes to get the boy to a warm climate. This, of course, entailed transfer to another school. In the end, she decided to send Shane to the Florida Military Academy at St. Petersburg. First of all, she reasoned, the Florida weather would provide the warm climate the doctor ordered for Shane's injured hip. In addition, a military school, she felt, would maintain closer supervision of the boys, and Shane would do better perhaps if subjected to a stronger discipline. So, like Eugene junior, Shane was outfitted with a uniform while still an adolescent. Actually he seemed to do better at the

Florida Military Academy in 1934 than he had at Lawrenceville. His marks were "exceptionally fine."

In his four years at that academy, Shane, in the words of Agnes, "went Southern." He became a hail-fellow-well-met, a "character." He fell in with the prevailing philosophy that girls and drinking were *de rigueur* for a Southern officer and gentleman, and it was there that he lost his faith, in very much the way his father had withdrawn from the Catholic Church while at Betts Academy in Stamford, Connecticut.

Shane spent another summer at Point Pleasant. He wrote to ask his father for an outboard motor. O'Neill upbraided Shane for not being more serious about his life and wasting his time on trivial things. It puzzled the boy. "I think my father loved me," Shane has said. "He sent me to expensive schools. But he didn't seem to like it when I asked him for things."

In 1934, O'Neill worked so hard that, as a result, he had "a close shave from a complete breakdown" which necessitated a six months' rest.

His "Blessed Isle" was turning out to be a cursed isle. He complained that the water in which he swam was generally sandy colored and soupy, the place was humid and hot in summer; there were swarms of insects; special bronze had to be used on the hardware in the house because ordinary metal rusted away from the salt-laden air. One afternoon, Langner noted that all the bushes in Casa Genotta's patio had been clipped close to the ground. "Why?" he asked Carlotta.

"That," Carlotta said, "is so we can see if there are any snakes under them." She went on to say that the island was full of rattlesnakes. O'Neill was listening and commented that rattlesnakes were relatively harmless compared to the little pink coral snakes which likewise were everywhere.

The summer of 1936 at Sea Island was scorching. It was so hot and oppressive that O'Neill and Carlotta were setting a new "World's and Olympic sweating record," he told a friend, "We just drip and drop and drip and drop." At the end of the summer, O'Neill was in such bad health that the doctor "ordered" him to leave Sea Island and get "a complete change of climate, to relax and forget" his cycle of plays for a while. O'Neill said he had run himself "nerve-ragged."

His "Blessed Isle" had turned out to be just another place where he didn't belong—or perhaps didn't want to belong. Later that summer O'Neill definitely decided to settle in the West. His old restlessness was again asserting itself. He wrote Shane that he and Carlotta would like to have him come to Casa Genotta for a last visit on his way back to school. As he was moving west it might be a long time before they could meet again. O'Neill left the details of arranging the trip to Carlotta, for he was not fully recovered from his "close shave" with a nervous breakdown a year ago.

Shane still remembers the very exact and specific instructions Carlotta wrote him about the journey. First of all, he should be sure to buy a ticket straight through to St. Petersburg. He should specify that he wanted the ticket to permit a stopover at Thalmann, which is about twenty miles from Sea Island. Freeman, their chauffeur, would meet him on the 7:09 P.M. train on Saturday night, September 29. He would be taking the same train for St. Petersburg the following Wednesday night. She suggested he talk this over with his mother and be sure to get the through ticket. She also said that she was writing this letter for Gene because he "rarely wrote letters himself."

Shane was met exactly as scheduled. He had a talk with Carlotta about the business of her writing letters to him and Oona for Gene. O'Neill, she said, was too busy to write. Shane, always agreeable, said it was all right with him. Carlotta said that apparently Oona took a different view. She had received a letter from Oona, who suggested that Carlotta was interfering with Oona's correspondence with her father. "If that girl knew," Carlotta told Shane, "how I loathe writing letters to you children on behalf of your father, she would think otherwise. I write such letters only to be courteous. I will not do it any more."

Otherwise, it was a pleasant visit. "I spent a quiet time," Shane has said, "getting to know my father and Carlotta again. My father spent his mornings working, so I did not see him until the afternoon. Breakfast was sent up to my room. I liked that. I have such a hard time getting up. Late in the afternoon my father and I would go fishing and swimming.

"The main thing was the living room. After dinner we'd sit around, Carlotta and my father and myself, and listen to records. There were some classical and some jazz. Sometimes, in the afternoon, we'd go for drives around St. Simons Island. There were all sorts of forts and things. It was very interesting. Then they showed me some sort of marshes—the Marshes of Glynn (the subject of Sidney Lanier's famous poem) or something."

But when Shane left Casa Genotta he still did not feel close to his father. And a month later, Eugene O'Neill was in flight again. "Coastal Georgia was no place for me," he said. "Working through two long successive stifling summers down there did more than any other thing to bring on my recent complete crack-up." In a sense, when O'Neill left Sea Island he left much of his life behind him. He was leaving his children, the coast that he had drawn upon for so much, and the city (New York) that was the home of his profession. O'Neill never again actively participated in the life of the American theater. And when he returned to the East years later, he returned to a different world.

CHAPTER

TWENTY-THREE

ɷɷ

THE PATTERN

CONTINUED

Having put Casa Genotta on the market, the O'Neills took the train to Seattle, where they arrived on November 3, 1936. On the fir-bordered slopes of Puget Sound they subleased a furnished, oblong, English-style house, in which the playwright's study was quickly established in a room that faced the sea. From it he could also see the Olympic Mountains.

O'Neill wanted to obtain material for some of the plays in his octology, as the cycle was now being called, and in Oregon and Washington he planned to acquire background and settings for the period between 1857 and 1880. A visitor found him intensely curious about his new surroundings. O'Neill told him he planned to visit Bonneville and Grand Coulee Dams. When he first arrived in Seattle he drove over the winding road to the glacier-crusted ramparts of Mount Ranier.

His stay in Washington seemed to renew his enthusiasm for living. He put on old clothes, chiefly sweater and slacks, and skimmed over the choppy waters of Puget Sound in a motorboat borrowed from a friend. On a fishing expedition on the Columbia River he caught a seventy-five-pound Chinook salmon.

The weather was chill that fall and O'Neill often sat in front of the huge fireplace. "It's good to hear the logs crackle again," he told a young magazine writer, Richard L. Neuberger, later to become United States Senator from Washington. "After the heat of the South, I don't even mind this fog."

On Tuesday, November 10, Richard Madden, the play agent, called O'Neill from New York to tell him that the *Times* man in Stockholm had heard that the Nobel prize for literature was to be awarded to O'Neill, Paul Valéry, the French poet, or F. E. Sillanpää, a Finnish author. O'Neill said he didn't put any store in the rumor—there had been similar rumors in years past.

On the following Thursday morning, Professor Sophus Keith Winther of the University of Washington telephoned Carlotta and told her that the Associated Press bureau man in Seattle had told him that O'Neill had definitely been awarded the prize, which carried with it a cash award of some forty thousand dollars. The reporters were on their way out to the O'Neill house, he added.

Dressed in a sweater and slacks, smoking a pipe, and with Professor Winther sitting beside him, O'Neill received the reporters. Marie Van Allender of Universal Service asked the traditional question, "What was he going to use the money for?"

"I'll use it to pay taxes!" O'Neill exclaimed. This and alimony were his two perennial peeves. Income taxes were then comparatively small.

O'Neill kept answering the superficial and sometimes meaningless questions. How did he feel? "I feel somehow humble before this recognition." Yes, he was quite surprised, because he had been sure that Theodore Dreiser was to have been this year's recipient. "He deserves it," O'Neill commented. Then, suddenly, he realized that he had had no formal notification. "All I have to go by," he said anxiously, "is what you newspaper folk tell me. Two years ago I even received telegrams of congratulations!"

Although he told the reporters he would go to Stockholm to receive the prize in person from King Gustav, two days later he cabled the Swedish Academy he would be unable to arrive in time. He would, instead, take a freighter in February from Seattle to Sweden via the Panama Canal. Carlotta, from the start, had been unenthusiastic about making the trip, but by February the question was taken out of the way when illness struck and O'Neill was unable to leave his bed. He wrote the committee a gracious letter—Hamilton Basso called it "the only known example of O'Neill's full-dress style—to be read at the presentation ceremonies:

> It is difficult to put into anything like adequate words the profound gratitude I feel for the greatest honor that my work could ever attain. . . . This highest of distinctions is all the more grateful to me because I feel so deeply that it is not only my work which is being honored but the work of all my colleagues in America—that the Nobel Prize is a symbol of the coming of age of the American theatre. For my plays are merely, through luck of time and circumstance, the most widely known examples of the work done by American playwrights in the years since the World War—work that has finally made modern American drama, in its finest aspects, an achievement of which Americans can be justly proud. . . . For me, the greatest happiness this occasion affords is the opportunity it gives me to acknowledge, with gratitude and pride, to you and to the people of Sweden, the debt my work owes to that greatest genius of all modern dramatists, your August Strindberg. It was reading his plays when I first started to write, back in the winter of 1913–14 that, above all else, first gave me the vision of what modern drama could be, and first inspired me with the urge to write for the theatre myself. If there is anything of lasting worth in my work, it is due to that original impulse from him, which has continued as my inspiration down all the years since then—to the ambition I received then to follow in the footsteps of his genius as worthily as my talent might permit, and with the same integrity of purpose.

Following the news of the Nobel award, O'Neill received a tremendous amount of mail and telegrams from all over the world. He felt compelled to reply to each one. Pressure on him to go out socially and to give interviews increased, and he and Carlotta fled to San Francisco, keeping their address a secret. He told friends that "the Nobel was great stuff, a help to nerve relaxation and work-forgetting" but he was feeling "pretty punk" and would probably go on feeling this way until the publicity wore off.

The vultures must have been soaring over O'Neill even as the reporters talked to him. A severe pain in the abdomen brought about his removal, shortly before Christmas, to the Merritt Hospital in Oakland, a suburb of San Francisco. The ailment was diagnosed as appendicitis, but before the appendix could be removed it burst O'Neill said it "so poisoned me that they had to inject everything but TNT to keep me from passing out for good."

The ruptured appendix, removed the day after Christmas, seemed to start O'Neill off on "a continuous variety of ailments." He complained to a friend that as soon as one ailment died out another started, "like chain smoking." Carlotta meanwhile came down with a bad cold and was confined to a hospital room adjacent to his. When he was feeling well enough at the end of January to receive visitors, the trembling of his hands seemed more noticeable. He had lost considerable weight, and his hands appeared unusually small and slender. But in his blue pajamas, which he kept buttoned neatly up to his neck, his graying hair and mustache carefully brushed, he was as handsome as ever. On January 27, lying in bed and surrounded by an assortment of detective novels, he received reporters and photographers from the San Francisco newspapers. He mentioned his plans for settling in northern California. The most beautiful place he had seen was in the Napa Valley. "I was thinking," he said, "that I might buy a sheep ranch there and evict the sheep but that all depends on how ranches come." He apologized for Carlotta's not receiving the press with him; "she has a bad cold," he explained, "and she looks it. She doesn't want to see anyone."

Most of his talk was about his cycle of plays that would tell the story of five generations of "a far-from-modern American family." The first play was finished and he had done the first draft of two more. He preferred not to discuss the theme of the cycle, saying "To say too much about that is to give it away and to say too little doesn't mean a damn thing." The cycle would constitute about twenty hours of drama, but each play would be a conventional length. "The plan is to withdraw the first play before the second starts, even if it is a success. It [the cycle] will be noncommercial."

He praised the Federal Theater Project, which was "bringing the drama to places where the drama had been forgotten." The theater "on the Continent is dead," he said. "The only two Englishmen who amount to anything are two Irishmen, Shaw and O'Casey."

Representatives of King Gustav headed by the Swedish consul in San Francisco brought the award to O'Neill in the hospital. O'Neill got out of bed long enough to receive the gold medal and a diploma. Witnesses noted O'Neill's trembling. The consul made no formal speech of presentation and remarked that "this is one time when custom must give way to emergency." O'Neill made no speech in reply, but merely thanked him.

The comments on O'Neill's new honor were enthusiastic, but perhaps the most interesting remarks had already been made by Sinclair Lewis when he received the Nobel prize in 1930. "... And had you chosen Mr. O'Neill who has done nothing much in American drama save to transform it utterly in ten or twelve years from a false world of neat and competent trickery to a world of splendor and fear and greatness, you would have been reminded that he has done something far worse than scoffing—he has seen life as not to be neatly arranged in the study of a scholar but as a terrifying, magnificent, and often quite horrible thing akin to the tornado, the earthquake and the devastating fire."

One of the people who wrote to congratulate O'Neill was Mary Clark, his nurse at the Gaylord sanatorium so many years before. He replied that "one of the nicest things the prize brought me" was hearing from her, and went on to say that she was one of the "very very few" of his "old friends" who had written. Most of them, he commented sadly, were dead or "estranged" for one reason or another.

Although O'Neill's physical ailments were ostensibly cleared up, that spring in San Francisco he was feeling "hopeless." He was so depressed that he felt he would never be able to work again and referred to this period over and over as "my recent complete crackup." The darkness in O'Neill's spirit stayed with him from the spring into the fall. When Casa Genotta was sold in December, he and Carlotta were again homeless.

In the terrifying state he was in, it is perhaps understandable that O'Neill was unable to answer Shane's letters that spring of 1937. But Shane, now eighteen, was convinced that he would be able to go out to California in the summer to visit his father despite the fact that he had not heard from him. As June approached, he wrote and asked when it would be convenient for him to come out. Prematurely, as it turned out, he wrote to his mother that he would not be coming back to Point Pleasant for a while; he was going to the West Coast to visit his father. Agnes replied that it would be all right to go, but he had better make sure that Carlotta wanted him to come.

"I wanted to talk to my father," Shane has said, "about being a writer. I thought he could advise me. I wanted to tell him about what I had been doing." But he was not asked. "You were right about Carlotta," he later wrote to his mother. "She says she has friends visiting her and I can't come. The expenses for the trip are quite high."

There was an abrupt change in Shane's behavior following this disappointment. "I think that a hard-boiled attitude," the headmaster of the Academy wrote Agnes, "is the only thing to use with Shane because I have tried the more gentle methods with rather poor results."

A fellow cadet known as "Pepper" addressed the following verse, both pathetic and prophetic, to Shane:

> *Here's to a guy with a gut of iron;*
> *He doesn't use a funnel but he thinks he should;*
> *He drinks and drinks, but it doesn't affect him,*
> *But some day he'll drink lye instead of rye,*
> *And then good-bye and good luck, Shane O'Neill.*

Shane had found that drinking eased his painful shyness. In a free verse poem about himself, he wrote:

> *Loneliness*
> *That draws*
> *The very blood*
> *Out of Life*
> *And leaves a hollow shell of a*
> *Man*
> *A shell with nothing*
> *Inside*
> *To equalize the*
> *Bitter world without.*

For some time, Shane had thought he might like to be a writer.

Back at FMA in the fall, he continued to be one of the most popular members of the school and one of its chief hell-raisers. Although Shane was a senior, Agnes decided to send him to still another school where he would not have to live up to his profligate reputation. She chose the Ralston Creek School, a ranch-type preparatory school at Golden, near Denver, Colorado. Shane had now decided to emulate Eugene junior and go to Yale. Shane liked the school, but his performance there, as elsewhere, was uneven. In the fall he was reported as doing extraordinarily well, but after Christmas the headmaster reported that he "had to check him for a general let-down in effort."

Late in February of 1938, Agnes learned that Shane was entertaining the idea of staying out West and becoming a cowboy. He also wrote that he was going to visit his father and that, furthermore, his father was going to pay his way out to the coast.

Agnes wrote Harry Weinberger a long letter at the end of March asking him to "pass on to Gene" that "Shane seems to have fallen in love with the ranch life and to have gone Western—exactly as he did in the Southern life." His father should understand that this was not a bad thing and "probably a phase." She wanted O'Neill to be sure *not* to encourage Shane "to give up college and stay out there and become a cowboy." She hoped that he would get at least two years of college and then, if he wanted to spend his life in the West, he would be in a better position to make such an important decision.

"It is in his father's hands," she wrote, "to encourage Shane to work hard and get into Yale. . . . Shane is going to be very easily influenced right now. Shane, as a lot of good men have been, is a little immature for his age. He really hasn't decided on what he wants to do."

On March 25, 1938, O'Neill wrote Shane a typewritten note signed "Father." It simply suggested that he buy a round trip, "intermediate ticket," from Golden, Colorado, to Oakland, California— this would enable him to ride part of the way in a berth. The cost of the ticket and berth would be fifty-five dollars, and he was adding five dollars for meals. Carlotta joined him in love to him and O'Neill said that it would be grand to see him again. Carlotta wrote a postscript thanking him for his letters and added their telephone number "if anything goes haywire."

"I am glad I am going to see my father," Shane wrote to his mother, "because I will get a chance to talk to him about my future (and things). I will write you how things come out later." He said he had thought twice about the matter of studying and decided it would be foolish to stop. Once again Shane was looking to his father for advice and guidance; he was, in fact, pathetically eager to establish a close relationship with the man he admired most in the world.

CHAPTER

TWENTY-FOUR

ನಿ

"THE RIGHT WAY

OF LIFE"

O'Neill and Carlotta decided to build once more. Their new home, thirty-five miles from San Francisco, was located on 158 acres of woodland halfway up a mountain overlooking the San Ramon Valley in Contra Costa County. From the building site one could look across Walnut Creek at Mount Diablo, which rose like a spire above the Pacific Ocean. They called their new home "Tao House." O'Neill explained that the name signified the peace, restfulness, and contentment of the Taoist religion. Roughly translated, Tao means "the right way of life."

The house was Chinese in inspiration, and Carlotta, who had been partial to Chinese things ever since her trip to the Far East, was both architect and decorator on the project. Prohibitive costs made it impractical to build with authentic Oriental materials, but the concrete blocks which were substituted had been specially designed to resemble Chinese earthen blocks. The result was not an accurate re-creation of a Chinese house, but it was quite charming.

Before it was completed, O'Neill told a friend that this would be "a final home and harbor" for him. The view from the house was the most beautiful he had ever seen. He loved California, and the climate was one in which he was sure he could work and keep healthy. There was one compromise.

Tao House was not within easy reach of water to swim in, and swimming was O'Neill's only athletic activity. (Langner once said that Gene would be content only when he moved to a place that afforded swimming all year round.) To repair the deficiency, the O'Neills built a swimming pool. From its rim one could look down over the whole valley; but from within the pool one could see only the empty space above the valley. O'Neill found the effect disconcerting; he complained to friends that it gave him an eerie feeling to have this wide stretch of nothing alongside when he swam.

Gene and Carlotta had collected many beautiful Oriental *objets d'art,* and after they moved into Tao House they bought still more. They also furnished the house throughout with Chinese-style furniture. The interior walls were left rough and unpainted, and against them the delicate pieces of ornament and furniture created an impressive contrast. To complete the *décor,* Carlotta, who loved gardening, set to work making a Chinese garden. O'Neill added a bucolic touch by installing a flock of chickens.

The O'Neill estate became a rather large establishment, and Carlotta assumed the burden of management. She and Gene enjoyed their home more than any they had had. But when war came to the United States and defense industries claimed all the manpower that was not taken by the armed forces, the job of running Tao House became too great a burden for the couple. Nevertheless, they lived there longer than they lived at any other home, and when they quit it, it wasn't discontent that motivated either of them.

Although O'Neill began to feel better after he moved into Tao House, he was able only to "flirt" with his cycle again. His trembling continued. Then there came a new illness—neuritis—which afflicted his right arm. All through the winter of 1937–38 he found it virtually impossible to get a night's sleep. He told friends he had spent "a rotten bad winter." Despite his illness, he and Carlotta did some entertaining. The artist, Miguel Covarrubias, and his wife, two of their most intimate friends, came to stay. Covarrubias made ink caricatures of both, which were immediately framed and hung in the upper hall of Tao House.

When he resumed work on his cycle, O'Neill followed the same writing schedule as at Casa Genotta from eight-thirty in the morning until one-thirty in the afternoon, seven days a week. He wrote in pencil and, although each letter was perfectly formed, his trembling caused him to make his writing smaller and smaller. Carlotta, at a separate desk, served as his secretary and typed his copy; she had to use a magnifying glass to read his script. For each play, O'Neill made drawings of the sets and a complicated diagram representing the development of the plot.

O'Neill and his wife had long since given up trying to have lunch together. Like most writers, he would very often just be hitting his stride when lunch hour arrived. He would be absorbed in the play on which he was working, in dialogue problems, in timing, in themes. Naturally, he did not feel talkative. Carlotta, wanting to make sure not to interrupt the creative process, would remain silent. The result was that she was made nervous and he became nervous seeing her nervous. The problem was solved by having the maid bring a tray to O'Neill's study. He could nibble or not, as he saw fit. Sometimes after his lunch he would lie down.

By dinnertime, O'Neill was generally ready to stop working; sometimes he was free in the middle of the afternoon. Usually, he did not work after dinner. If, however, he was in the middle of some speech or scene and was afraid he would lose the feeling, he would return to his study and work.

More often, in the evening, O'Neill liked to sit by the fire and read. Both he and Carlotta were avid readers. Sometimes, he would read aloud something he particularly liked. Like many good prose writers he continually read poetry—good poetry. He was particularly partial to the Irish poets; Yeats was his favorite.

At times, O'Neill was extremely funny. Apparently he had inherited more than he thought from his actor father because he could be a first-rate mimic. And yet when he was ill or depressed, his silence was almost oppressive as he brooded in darkness.

Carlotta took pride in caring for O'Neill and their homes. As Brooks Atkinson has said, one of Carlotta's great contributions to the work of O'Neill was that she "kept a good house." Carlotta was particularly proud of the manner of life to which she believed she had introduced him. As she told friends, she made it possible for him to "live like a duke." However, Agnes Boulton told this writer that

O'Neill lived rather well during the later years of their marriage, and, to prove her point, she has shown tailor bills, hotel bills, and bills from stores that are generally known for their expensive wares. In any case, O'Neill's life with Carlotta was far different from anything he had experienced previously. And occasionally O'Neill would talk to Carlotta of his former life and comment almost ruefully upon how far he had come.

O'Neill and Carlotta were well settled in the routine of their new life when Shane came to visit them during his spring vacation. Shane left Golden, Colorado, on Friday, April 8. Herbert Freeman, the O'Neill chauffeur, met him at the station in Oakland in a big new Lincoln limousine. Shane was amazed to learn that he was driving on a mile of his father's own private road leading to the house. He was delighted to see, on the way, that his father was raising white Brahma chickens. Freeman let Shane out at the brown wooden gate adorned with metal characters spelling out Tao House in Chinese. He heard a dog barking and twelve-year-old Blemie came bounding up to him to be petted. A Negro couple looked after the O'Neills, and the man took Shane's bags. Besides Freeman and the Negro couple, there was a laundress, a house maid and a gardener.

When O'Neill came down from his study to greet him, Shane saw at once how much his father had aged since he had last seen him in Georgia. He looked fit but he also looked fragile. His shy smile still "lighted up his face and he seemed completely happy." As he said, he was "full of hope" despite the fact that he had noted "the way the world wags." It looked to him as if man had decided to destroy himself. This would be the only wise decision, O'Neill commented, man had ever made.

Father and son talked of the news which was filling the papers. There was fighting between the Japanese and Mongolian troops on the border of Manchukuo. Hitler and Mussolini were signing a military alliance. Nazi troops had begun to occupy Czechoslovakia. But though there was plenty that was impersonal to talk about, as always O'Neill was an uneasy father. Shane tried to talk about attempting to write, but he got the impression his father didn't want him to be a writer. With Carlotta, things were different. She had lots of things to say to him, especially urging him to study hard and go to college.

"It will help you in many ways," she told him, "later on in life. Learn all you can about any and all things. You never know *what* branch of learning might be your bread and butter in the future." She talked a good deal about being independent, about "standing on your own feet."

"I got to know Carlotta on this trip," Shane has said. "I liked her. I still like her."

But he came away from his visit with the same familiar loneliness. Once more, his verse reflected this:

> *Loneliness makes geniuses*
> *And idiots*
> *All men—good men, bad men*
> *But never*
> *Happy men*
> *Beware it lurks*
> *And seeks you out*
> *You shout, see it approach*
> *But it has you*
> *You can't escape.*

CHAPTER

TWENTY-FIVE

ಬಬ

KISMET IN THE VALLEY

OF THE MOON

Eugene O'Neill, like so many people who settle in the San Francisco area, quite suddenly took up Oriental philosophy. He confided to his friend Nathan that he was planning "an heroic drama of ancient Chinese locale." Tao House itself, his "final home and harbor," as he termed it, stood in the locally named Valley of the Moon, with Mount Diablo (Mountain of the Devil) in plain view.

O'Neill was also fascinated by Kismet, the Arabic concept of fate or destiny. "There is a feeling around," O'Neill told a friend at this time, "or I'm mistaken, of fate. Kismet, the negative fate; not in the Greek sense.... It's struck me as time goes on, how something funny, even farcical can suddenly, without apparent reason, break up into something gloomy and tragic ... A sort of unfair *non sequitur,* as though events, as though life, were to be manipulated just to confuse us. I think I'm aware of comedy more than I ever was before—a big kind of comedy that doesn't stay funny very long."

In the summer of 1939, it would seem that the effect of Kismet was felt in the Valley of the Moon. The year also happened to be a time of oncoming tragedy for the whole world.

O'Neill was to say, later on, that his stay at Tao House was the most pleasant existence he had had in his entire life. Work on his great cycle was moving rapidly ahead in 1939. He estimated that about two more years of work would see the completion of this lifetime project.

There had been up to that time, nine plays in the cycle. The first and second of these, however, had grown in scope, and O'Neill had already begun to fill in his outline with provision for dividing the material in each of these two into two separate plays. Thus, in effect, his cycle now consisted of eleven distinct dramas. The overall title was *A Tale of the Possessors Self-Dispossessed,* and the nine plays in the not yet altered outline were:

1. *The Greed of the Meek*
2. *And Give Me Death*
3. *A Touch of the Poet* (later produced)
4. *More Stately Mansions*
5. *The Calms of Capricorn*
6. *The Earth's the Limit*
7. *Nothing Is Lost Save Honor*
8. *The Man on Iron Horseback*
9. *The Hair of the Dog*

A Touch of the Poet, which was produced on Broadway October 2, 1958, is the story of Irish-born Major Cornelius "Con" Melody, a tavernkeeper living on the outskirts of Boston in 1828. He is pretentious, keeps a thoroughbred mare, and likes to speak of having served under the Duke of Wellington and having fought at Talavera. Con is not accepted by the New England Yankees, partly because he is a faker and his wife is obviously a peasant, but also because he is in trade—and worse, a tavernkeeper. And yet, he regards his own kind as "Irish scum." The bridge is built between the two worlds when Simon Harford falls in love with Con's daughter, Sara. Simon, a Harvard boy, lives, like Thoreau, beside a pond, and he is writing a book.

The Harfords oppose the marriage and, when Con goes to protest, a Negro manservant beats him up. Con returns to the tavern, his dreams and his pretensions shattered, and he shoots the mare,

the symbol of his pride. He says he will change, disturbing his wife
and daughter, who love him the way he is. In the last act, it turns
out that Sara, following the guidance of her father, has seduced
Simon. Thus boy gets girl after all and the Melodys are reunited in
happiness.

Although this is not one of O'Neill's best plays and the plot
and motivations are somewhat oversimplified, yet one is still moved
by Con and his family. The dialogue is sometimes awkward and the
play lacks the usual O'Neill intensity, but *A Touch of the Poet* is both
entertaining and interesting. Con lives on his illusions, much as the
characters in *The Iceman Cometh* exist on their "pipe dreams." And
finally, the play is better viewed and considered in context with the
entire cycle; it was O'Neill's intention to deal next with Simon and
Sara's children—a new family is born, the blending of shanty Irish
with New England Yankee.

While each play was an individual full-length drama, it was
related to the others as an essential link in the entire chain. One drama
authority pronounced it "probably the most stupendous task ever
undertaken by a modern playwright," but only one of these plays has
ever been produced, and the several others that O'Neill had completed
in first draft he destroyed shortly before his death. The theme of the
cycle was, in Hamilton Basso's words, the "dominant theme of
O'Neill's mature philosophy—the corruption of character by materialistic greed." Another play which O'Neill considered for inclusion on
the cycle he called at the time *Give Me Liberty And*—. Although
O'Neill later destroyed this play, he told the plot to Basso, who recorded it:

> [It] deals with America during the French and Indian War.
> Its hero is an Irishman who has joined the British Army to
> escape the slavery of agricultural life in Ireland. It is his idea
> to desert as soon as he gets to America and to go into the wilder-
> ness, where, liberated from the economic and social bondage of
> the Old World, he can live as a truly free man. Once in this
> country, he strikes out for the wilderness. On his journey, want-
> ing food and shelter, he stops at a frontier farm. It is only a
> clearing in a forest, but it is nonetheless the most fertile and
> promising soil he has ever seen.
>   The farm is run by a young widow who badly needs a man
> around the place, and who, as O'Neill saw it, also needs a man.

The Irishman, caught between his dream of freedom and his hunger for land, and attracted by the woman's physical allure, finally abandons his dream and settles for the land. The bleak mood of the play was summed up in its title. According to O'Neill's scheme, the seed of greed that had thus been planted was to grow and flower throughout the cycle.

In the summer of 1939, O'Neill suddenly began to feel that he had gone stale on his cycle. Not only did he have serious doubts about the plays he had written but he began to question whether the whole plan of the cycle was not faulty. One of his new decisions about the plays was that they should deal with two families and not just one.

O'Neill was distressed both by the war news from Europe and by the news of Shane. The boy had returned to Ralston that spring convinced he should go to college. Although he loved the West and wanted to own a horse and attend the University of Colorado, he returned East and made plans to re-enter Lawrenceville in September. Shane fell in love during the summer, but he was drinking too much and despite the girl was restless, lonely and depressed.

Shane did not do at all well at Lawrenceville and was dropped at the end of the winter term. He had succeeded in only one course and that was an art class, where he was able to combine his two loves by drawing pictures of horses he had observed at the school's stables.

After leaving Lawrenceville, Shane began taking courses at the Art Students League. He enjoyed the classes and made friends with the students, many of whom were habitués of the bars and the apartments of Greenwich Village. Shane started going about with them. His feeling of being without a goal and without an identity, except as the son of Eugene O'Neill, still pursued him, and he wrote his father for guidance.

> My interest in art, as do all my other interests, points toward one thing—horses. If I am to go on with it, my aim is to do illustration work such as Paul Brown, Lionel Edwards or Frederic Remington did.
>
> The other thing which is perhaps a surer way of achieving my goal is to take a veterinary course, as I have always felt I would like to since horses became my one interest. I would of course like to raise them for myself, but this is out of the question because of the large amount of capital it takes to start a horse raising business, and the uncertainty of it once it is started.

The veterinary course would take about five years, but I feel that when I had finished it I would be in line for the kind of a job I would like, and I would be more certain of being able to make a success of it than I would of illustration. Illustration is a fine line, but it is very hard to break into, unless you have real talent. You are either a good illustrator or else not an illustrator at all. There is no place for a fair man in that line. If you would like to see any of my drawings I can send them out. I wish you would give me any advice you can on this, keeping in mind that whatever I do, my main interest is horses, and I want to be connected with them as much as possible.

Shane was now shuttling between West Point Pleasant and New York, where his mother and Oona were spending the winter at the Hotel Waylin on Madison Avenue. Agnes O'Neill was busy with a daughter who was turning out to be both beautiful and popular. Oona and her classmates at Brearley were already talking, not only about boys, but about coming out before New York society. Oona had decided she would like to study art, too, and joined Shane in some of his classes at the Art Students League. Both children were invited to visit Tao House that summer, but not together. O'Neill and Carlotta seemed to prefer to have his children make their visits separately. Oona was fifteen and Shane was going on twenty.

When Shane went to the West Coast that summer he showed his father some of the drawings that he had done. O'Neill told him his judgment was not worth much in such things but he would say they "indicated you had a latent talent that would be worth trying out."

O'Neill's advice to his son was to go on with his study at the Art Students League until he felt he had proved to himself exactly how much talent he had. But taking a veterinary course would be a long waste of time. He should put horse raising out of his head for the moment because he would get nowhere trying to aim for two goals at the same time. He should concentrate on one objective.

The trouble with Shane, his father told him, was that choosing to run a horse farm was taking the easiest way. Apparently, Shane wanted to start at the top with his own farm and horses just as if he already knew the business without ever taking the trouble to learn it.

O'Neill told Shane, as he had told him before, that he "hated bawling him out." All he really wished was to give him advice for the immediate future. Illustrating was, after all, a good career and Shane might have the right stuff to succeed at it. In any case, he wanted him to know that he would be extremely interested to see what Shane would do with his drawing. It might be the answer Shane was looking for.

Herbert Freeman, the chauffeur, noticed that Shane seemed to be lost at Tao House and decided that he knew just the thing to cheer him up, the Golden Gate Exposition in San Francisco. "It seemed to Freeman," Saxe Commins has said, "that Shane was having a terrible time on that visit. Freeman was a swell guy and began taking Shane on visits to the Exposition."

Oona went out to Tao House that summer but returned rather abruptly. She seemed amused rather than hurt over the incident that terminated her visit. On the train to the Coast she had picked up some sort of itch, perhaps a heat rash—she was never sure—and she confided in Carlotta. Obviously, Oona reasoned, this was something to be discussed only between women. Carlotta immediately became alarmed and put Oona on the next eastbound plane. Apparently, O'Neill never knew what had taken place.

O'Neill may have thought, that summer of 1939, that he and his children were—like the Mannons in *Mourning Becomes Electra* —driven by some psychological fate. There is no doubt that he was deeply troubled.

"When he was very worried and nervous," Carlotta has said, "he would call to me to come in and talk to him. He didn't sleep well. Or, he would come in and he would talk to me about his work and about the terrible thing of whether we were going to have a World War again. It seemed to upset him no end. He was terribly disturbed that mankind was so stupid. To go through it, he said, only meant destruction for everybody. It did something terrible to him."

There is something infinitely touching about O'Neill, now cut off from his family and the outside world, waking in the night, calling to Carlotta, and telling her of his fears for humanity.

Carlotta noted in her diary for June 21, 1939, that it was a hot sleepless night. Gene, she wrote, "talks to me for hours, about a play (in his mind) of his mother, father, his brother and himself." Another time she heard him mutter—perhaps he was half asleep—". . . an ache in our hearts for the things we can't forget."

At Provincetown the twenty-fifth anniversary of the founding of the Provincetown theatrical group was to be celebrated with a

production of *Ah, Wilderness!,* with Sinclair Lewis in the lead. It was
to be done in the old Wharf Theatre where *Bound East for Cardiff*
had first been played. "Only the combination of my own anniversary
and the chance of seeing Lewis as an actor can get me to come back
to Provincetown again!" O'Neill said. But when the time came to go
east, he sent his regrets. The anniversary was held without him.

Early in September, 1939, after the German invasion of Poland,
O'Neill turned, not to his cycle, but to his own past, to his Jimmy
the Priest's and Hell Hole days. In despair about the world situation
and convinced that the future could only be more dismal, O'Neill
turned to the wretched lives of his old friends, in search for some
meaning in life. He gave dramatic expression to that search in *The
Iceman Cometh.*

The play has a surface plot of utter simplicity. In Harry Hope's
saloon the habitués are getting ready for a party. Every few months
a hardware salesman, Theodore Hickman ("Hickey"), goes on a
bat and treats all his friends. This time, when Hickey turns up he
acts rather strangely. He preaches a new message in which he tells
the assorted failures, the prostitutes, Harry and the audience that
they are living on pipe dreams. They are kidding themselves that
everything will come out all right tomorrow. Occasionally, Hickey
talks of his wife, saying she is at home in bed with the iceman. After
the salesman has reordered all the characters' lives, got them to give
up their pipe dreams and thoroughly depressed everyone, he gradually
admits that he has killed his wife and left her dead in bed. Hickey is
taken away by the police, the characters return with relief to their
drunkenness and their pipe dreams, and the audience staggers out
of the theater exhausted, depressed and yet somehow enriched and
enlightened.

Like so many of his major and deeply moving works, *The Iceman Cometh* is far too long, contains several arid stretches, and makes
its point over and over again. But, for all that, it is one of
O'Neill's really fine plays; it is a triumph of characterization and feeling, if not intellect. Hickey and Harry Hope are two of the most
completely "rendered" gentlemen in modern literature. They and the
the whole aura of jaunty seediness that the play exudes remain with
one long after the performance, for the best of Eugene O'Neill is
not so much seen as experienced.

O'Neill told Lawrence Langner that in *The Iceman Cometh* he
was *not* trying to dredge up nostalgia for the "dead old days on the

bottom of the sea." He did feel, however, that there were moments
when the play "strips the secret soul of a man stark naked—not in
cruelty or moral superiority but with an understanding of life and of
himself." Such moments, O'Neill said, were for him "the depths of
tragedy with nothing more that can possibly be said."

The Iceman Cometh was produced in 1946; it was the first
O'Neill play to be presented on Broadway after the war. In 1956
it was revived brilliantly by José Quintero, and its off-Broadway production not only considerably enhanced the play itself, but was also
greatly responsible for the current O'Neill revival and the revival of
off-Broadway theater in New York.

At work again, he was happy for a time. By January, 1940,
having finished The Iceman, he immediately started another play. He
told a friend he was "feeling fine—better than during any winter since
we have been on the West Coast."

Shane, meanwhile, was spending more and more time in Greenwich Village. In a sense the Village was like home to him. That's where
his father had spent so much time; that's where his father had met his
mother. His own "Hell Hole" was the Old Colony, a bar on the
north side of Eighth Street, whose habitués were rather more cosmo-
politan than his father's barroom associates. When it got around that
he was Eugene O'Neill's son, people continually bought him drinks.

"Shane never mentioned that he was O'Neill's son," a friend
who knew him then has said, "but if you asked him if it were true,
or told him you liked his father's plays, he was always pleased."

Shane himself has said that "people in the Village liked me for
myself. They didn't talk about my father or ask me questions about
him." Not long before his twenty-first birthday, Shane fell in love
again. Marjory Straight (fictional) came from the Middle West.
She resembled Agnes somewhat, in that she had the same build and
the same bony structure to her face. She was also, like Agnes,
beautiful, gentle, shy and sensitive. A love of painting was one of
the bonds between Shane and Marjory, who was a good artist.

In September, 1940, Oona and Shane tried to think of something to send their father to let him know they were thinking of him.
Shane remembered his father's interest in jazz and his pride in his
collection of jazz records. They pooled their resources and sent him
one of the new avant-garde jazz records. Their father sent word that
the record had arrived cracked in half.

Later, in the summer of 1940, Shane went again for a visit to

Tao House. Both O'Neill and Carlotta were, as O'Neill described it, keeping their ears glued to the radio. They heard descriptions of the Nazi sweep into Belgium, into the Netherlands, and then into the Loire valley. "To tell the truth," O'Neill said at that time, "like anyone else with any imagination I have been absolutely sunk by the world debacle. The cycle is on the shelf and God absolutely knows if I can ever take it up again because I cannot foresee any future in this country of anywhere else to when it could spiritually belong." The O'Neills listened as news came of the fall of town after town in the vicinity of the Château de Plessis. "I felt," O'Neill told Shane, 'as though the ranch next to ours had been occupied. I loved France and was happy there."

Shane was not as much interested in the world situation as he was in what he should do with his life. He again tried to get guidance from his father.

"You must find yourself," O'Neill told his son, "and own yourself. You've got to find the guts in yourself to take hold of your own life. No one can do it for you and no one can help you. You have got to go on alone, without help, or it won't mean anything to you."

O'Neill was of the opinion that Shane should try to get a job in a shipyard where he could eventually work into ship designing. His talent for drawing would be an asset. His father pointed out to him that he'd be twenty-one on October 30. O'Neill repeated many times to Shane that he hoped his pending twenty-first birthday would be "a real day of birth of the man in you!"

By the time Shane returned east, he was convinced that he'd better get some kind of job—any kind—to earn money, and let his artistic career go for a while. He would try to write in his spare time; he was again nurturing the aspiration to be a writer. He and a friend from Point Pleasant applied at Camp Dix, in New Jersey, and got jobs as carpenters' helpers, building barracks for the Army. Meanwhile, following his father's suggestion, Shane sought employment at various shipbuilding yards near Philadelphia but without success. After delay, he wrote all this to his father, laboring long and hard over this letter as he did with all his letters to his father. He also sent his father a birthday present and another letter shortly before O'Neill's birthday on October 16.

O'Neill thanked Shane for his birthday letter to him but added that the present had not arrived. He said he would be delighted to have the present, whatever it might be, as proof of his remembrance. Not having received any letters from Shane in so long a time, O'Neill said, he was wondering whether Shane had hesitated to write because he could not report progress along the road to independence and was merely following the same old rut. But it was certainly good to know that Shane did have a job. He hoped this meant that Shane had started "to find himself and own himself." He didn't want to do any more advising, he had said all that could be said when Shane visited him last. It was now up to him.

"You will be twenty-one in a few days," he told Shane, "It will be a good day for you to spend a few hours alone having a frank talk with yourself and considering this, that and the other. A better day than New Year's to make some good resolutions—and then keep them!"

After a lot more advice, O'Neill ended by saying he was sending him a check for fifteen dollars in honor of coming of age. "May it be," he said again, "a real day of birth of the man in you!" He said Carlotta joined him in much love, as ever. Shane didn't cash the check for a long time although he needed the money. Marjory Straight recollects that he finally lost the check.

Shane achieved a temporary prosperity in the fall of 1940. Cleon Throckmorton, a successful stage designer, gave him a job painting "flats" or stage scenery. Shane earned stagehand's union wages amounting to some two hundred dollars a week. He lived in New York with Oona and his mother at the Hotel Weylin. Oona was then sixteen and in her junior year in high school. In another year she would be ready for Vassar.

That fall Shane acquired a new friend. One of Agnes' relatives brought a young writer, Marc Brandel, from Greenwich Village uptown to the Weylin to meet the family. The two young men struck up an instant friendship. Brandel remembers that Shane seemed anxious about doing well, very well, as a writer.

"Of course," Shane told Brandel, "I can never hope to equal my father."

"Agnes and Oona and Shane, sitting there in the living room of their apartment," Brandel has said, "seemed to me one of the most attractive families I had ever seen. Even then Oona was extraordinarily beautiful. Shane was well-dressed and well-groomed. He was handsome, shy, and girls fell all over him. After I got to know him, I realized he was extremely talented. He was always writing

poetry or making sketches. He wanted to write short stories. Both
Oona and Shane were very proud of their father. Once, I mentioned
to Oona that I had been reading her father's plays and told her how
much I admired them. Her face lighted up. She seemed pleased and
proud."

Shane and Brandel did a good deal of drinking together, much of
t at the Old Colony. There, Shane often talked to Brandel about
"taking off somewhere." Laughingly, he would suggest, "Let's take
a slow boat to China."

"I very definitely had the feeling," Brandel has said, "that
Shane's wanting to go out and see the world was part of his wanting
to relive his father's life. He was a most engaging companion and I,
too, thought it would be nice to go somewhere and see the world. It
seemed to be going to hell fast, so why not?"

Early in December, Shane learned about an agency which
provided people driving to various parts of the country with passengers who would take turns at the wheel and share gasoline costs.

"Shane had saved some money. So had I," Brandel said. "We
found we could get to Mexico cheap. We took off the week before
Christmas."

The car in which they headed south was owned by an attractive
actress who promptly fell in love with Shane. Shane, however,
didn't respond, "Shane had a real, old-fashioned, almost Victorian
outlook about women," Brandel said. "He believed in absolute fidelity. He was extremely romantic and idealistic about women. He
wouldn't give the actress a tumble."

They parted company with the actress at Juarez and immediately
proceeded to get roaring drunk. Finally, they checked into a cheap
hotel and fell asleep. In what they thought was the middle of the
night, they awoke to find one of their twin beds on fire, probably
from a cigarette. After quenching the fire they threw their things
into their bags and cleared out. It was Christmas Day. They walked
out into the streets of Juarez to wait for the dawn, but instead of
getting lighter it got darker, and they realized that it was night, not
morning—they had slept around the clock. Shane and Marc took a
bus to Chihuahua, got drunk again, spent another night, and took
the train to Mexico City, arriving in the capital with no money. But
somehow they got by. People bought them drinks or took them to
dinner. Finally a check came (they don't remember from which
family) and they were again solvent.

They didn't do much adventuring in Mexico City, just read, got drunk, and went to the movies. "Shane was a very restraining influence on me," Brandel remembers, "He didn't want to shack up with girls or get drunk too often."

They decided on "a real trip." Shane remembered how his father had gone to Honduras prospecting for gold when he was his age. They'd go down to Acapulco and walk along the shore to Panama. They'd survive by fishing and hunting and sleep on the beach. They spent their remaining funds buying guns, fishing tackle, camping equipment and two hundred boxes of matches, took a bus to Acapulco and began walking. The nights were cold and uncomfortable. They didn't have much luck shooting game or catching fish. Finally, Shane cut his foot on a rock. An American, married to a Mexican woman, took them in for a while. Then they resumed walking south but gave up and returned to Acapulco when their last fishing line snagged on the rocks.

Shane sent off a telegram to his father, asking for the exact bus fare back to New York which amounted to about forty dollars. Shane told Brandel confidently that his father would probably send along enough for both of them with something to spare.

Shane received something of a jolt when his father's telegram came. It included a draft, but the sum was only enough, to the penny, to get him home by bus. Brandel remembers that the telegram said, in effect, "You've done it this time and we're letting you get away with it but don't ever do this again." On the surface, Shane took it as a joke. When he cashed the draft, he asked to have it in silver dollars. He and Brandel carried the dollars to a saloon and made them into little piles on the bar. One of the things they bought was marijuana cigarettes; they were easy to get. At first Shane didn't like smoking it because it made him slightly sick, but after a few more tries, he liked it. This was his first real experience with any form of narcotics.

When the money was gone, Shane sent word to his mother that he was broke. Agnes was annoyed but she sent them money to pay their way home.

Though few guests of the O'Neills ever saw his children, or learned anything about them, a member of the family they had learned to reckon with through the years was Blemie. The O'Neills had bought him in London in 1928 when he was only a puppy.

"Blemie was very definitely a personality," Dorothy Gish, a close friend of the O'Neills, has said. "He was a very important part of their life together."

By 1940, the dog had grown so feeble and so fat that he could hardly walk around. He died in December of that year, to the great distress of O'Neill and Carlotta. They agreed that they would never have another. "We had loved him so much we could never love another one," Carlotta said. At Blemie's death, O'Neill wrote out a will for him which observed, among other things, that dogs didn't fear death as men do because they accepted it as part of life and not as a terrible destroying force. Dogs did not worry about what comes after death because nobody knows the answer to that. Blemie asked, in the will, for peace and eternal sleep for his weary old heart and head, for rest in the earth he loved so much; and he commented, "Perhaps death was best of all."

Carlotta regarded Blemie's "will" as "one of the best things he [O'Neill] ever wrote." She sent copies of it to a number of her friends.

In the first months of 1941 O'Neill was frequently ill. He was finishing *Long Day's Journey into Night* but at a tremendous price. The trembling of his hands was violent at times, apparently growing progressively worse.

"He came in and talked to me all night," Carlotta has said, "which he frequently did when he couldn't sleep. He was thinking about this play, you see, in his youth. He explained to me then that he had to write this play. He had to write it because it was a thing that haunted him and he had to forgive whatever caused this in them [his mother and father and brother] and in himself." Carlotta remembers that after his day's stint, O'Neill would come out of his study gaunt and sometimes weeping. His eyes would be all red and he looked ten years older than when he went into his study in the morning.

Thus the play was written—it was a very large part of him. His whole life and thought were influenced by those early years. "I think he felt freer when he got it out of his system. It was his way of making peace with his family, and himself."

Carlotta has said she typed the play twice after O'Neill finished it in 1941. "I wept most of the time," she said, "which made it very difficult."

For their twelfth wedding anniversary, O'Neill inscribed a copy of the manuscript of *Long Day's Journey into Night* to her.

The inscription follows:

For Carlotta on our 12th Wedding Anniversary

Dearest; I give you the original script of this play of old sorrow, written in tears and blood. A sadly inappropriate gift, it would seem, for a day celebrating happiness. But you will understand. I mean it as a tribute to your love and tenderness which gave me the faith in love that enabled me to face my dead at last and write this play—write it with deep pity and understanding for all the four haunted Tyrones

These twelve years, Beloved One, have been a Journey Into Light—into love. You know my gratitude. And my love!

GENE

Tao House
July 22, 1941

O'Neill wrote the inscription on the original manuscript and he left strict instructions, she has asserted, that she could publish and have the play produced when and if she saw fit. He did not want anyone to write an introduction to *Long Day's Journey*. He felt the inscription adequately presented his reasons for writing the play and his feelings about it.

Long Day's Journey into Night is autobiographical drama. As O'Neill says in his dedication, he is coming to peace with his haunted family. The play opens shortly before it is discovered that Edmund Tyrone (young Eugene O'Neill) has tuberculosis. His father, James, is parsimonious and not anxious to pay for his son's stay at a good tuberculosis sanatorium. Edmund's mother is addicted to drugs and his brother, Jamie, is an alcoholic. They all fuss at one another with seemingly endless energy, and the theater is filled for three hours with their taunts and recriminations. The father, an old actor, tells of the hardships of his boyhood, his struggle to win acclaim as an actor, and finally his defeat, his "selling out" by doing Monte Cristo year after year—for the easy money. The mother reveals that she has married beneath her, talks of her lonely life on the road, remembers her marriage and her dead baby. Jamie drunkenly admits that he is trying to destroy his younger brother. In the end, the characters stand self-revealed, and the audience knows and feels that this family is bound together by ties of love and hate and need. Perhaps they all understand each other a little better.

The play is essentially plotless. It is not so much a story as an experience. It is autobiographical, yet O'Neill has imaginatively heightened his material and rendered a genuine artistic experience. *Long Day's Journey* is undoubtedly too long—one long scene seems almost irrelevant; there is too much quoting of classic poetry; and the deliberate formlessness of it all is enervating. Still, it is a dramatic achievement of the first order, a play that will survive, a play that may well be O'Neill's greatest single work.

(When O'Neill sent the manuscript to Saxe Commins in New York, he told him that under no condition was the play to be produced or published until twenty-five years after his death. Commins and Bennett Cerf read the script and then placed it in the Random House vault with Commins's notation, "Not to be opened until twenty-five years after author's death.")

After completing *Long Day's Journey into Night,* O'Neill turned again to the cycle. He still was dissatisfied with every one of the nine partly completed drafts he had on hand. Two of the plays, *A Touch of the Poet* and *More Stately Mansions,* and one scene in *The Calms of Capricorn,* could be salvaged, he decided, and on those he did some work. The other plays he put aside in order to "clear the decks" until he could again get down to sustained work on the cycle. Meanwhile, he blocked out still another series of eight plays to which he gave the over-all title, *By Way of Obit.* They were, he told Nathan, "an imaginative technical departure from his previous work." He completed the first play of this series and titled it, *Hughie.* It is set in a cheap New York hotel and contains only two characters, Ernie Smith, a small-town gambler, and a night clerk. In a long monologue, Smith reveals his own life and that of Hughie, the previous night clerk, recently deceased. The period was approximately the same as in *The Iceman Cometh,* the summer of 1912. *Hughie* was given its world première in Stockholm on September 18, 1958. In explaining why he kept on working even though he had gone stale on his cycle, O'Neill said you can't "keep a hophead off his dope for long." He had turned to writing scenes from his past on the ground that events had made him feel there was not enough recognizable future on which to go. He didn't want to be working on a cycle play which might take four or five years to complete. He felt an urgency to write plays which he had wanted to write for a long, long time and which he knew he had time to finish.

O'Neill took a great interest in the gloom enveloping the world. In May, President Roosevelt declared "an unlimited state of national emergency." In the following months the United States closed down the German consulates. Greece fell to the Nazis. O'Neill told friends that the world as he had known it was falling apart. How, he asked, could he go on writing when there were so many assumptions which were no longer valid? The assumptions would have to pass the test of the present debacle, but the basic truths about life remained the same.

For a time. O'Neill thought of putting the current world-shattering events in a great play. The trouble, he decided, was the rise of fascism, and he did "some work off and on" on what he called an "antitotalitarian state, anti-instrumentalist philosophy play" which he titled *The Last Conquest*. It would be a symbolic fantasy of the future and show the last campaign for the final destruction of the spirit.

In the East, Shane and Marc Brandel arrived back in Manhattan. Brandel rented an apartment on West Eleventh Street, and Shane moved in with him. They went out for weekends to Point Pleasant, and Brandel helped Agnes with a final revision of her novel, *The Road Is Before Us*. For part of the summer, Shane worked on the charter boats and dreamed of getting a boat of his own. He also continued his writing, at which, Brandel remembers, he "showed great sensitivity, poetic imagination." Later Shane and Brandel obtained jobs as civilian employees on a Navy transport ship docked in Brooklyn.

Shane, at this time, was seeing more and more of Marjory Straight, who was living with another girl artist on Christopher Street. When it came time for the girls to go to bed, Shane would look so forlorn, so appealing, that they'd insist that he spend the night.

"He was gentle, boyish, and hated any kind of restriction," Marjory remembers. "For example, he never sat *in* a chair; he sat *on* it. You always had the feeling he might, at any moment, run away or just disappear. Both my roommate and myself were devoted to him. He had something rough and sexual about him that never quite came to the surface. I think women liked him because they felt a cruelty in him that was never apparent."

Once, Marjory told Shane that she found him puzzling. "All

O'Neills are confusing," Shane said without amplifying the statement.

He talked little about his father but "he had an almost fanatical devotion to Eugene O'Neill," Miss Straight has said. Whenever Shane had a cold, he would be very concerned about it and ask Marjory if she had anything to cure it. "I must be very careful about catching cold," he'd say. "TB runs in my family." Then he'd add, "You know, my father had TB and had to go to a sanatorium to be cured."

One evening Shane came to the girls' apartment bringing two sticks of marajuana, which he laughingly called "tea." Everybody in the Village was taking it, he said. But he didn't seem to mind when Marjory made him hand them over and dropped them in the toilet.

Three days after Pearl Harbor, on Wednesday, December 10, 1941, Shane and Marc went down to the Navy offices at Church Street and obtained seamen's papers entitling them to sign on aboard an American merchant vessel. "I'm an able-bodied seaman," he told Marjory, with feigned nonchalance. Then he added, "You know my father was an able-bodied seaman."

CHAPTER

TWENTY-SIX

ಬಬ

THE CURSE OF

THE MISBEGOTTEN

The Langners were on the West Coast in the spring of 1941, and Carlotta invited them to spend Decoration Day at Tao House. They were met at the garden gate. Langner noted that "Gene [was] thinner than he had been but he seemed to be working well although his spirits were definitely depressed." This was due not only to several personal factors, but also to the condition of the world. After lunch, O'Neill took Langner into his study, which was just off the drawing room, and showed him the manuscripts of the cycle. Langner noted that O'Neill's handwriting was getting smaller and smaller.

That summer Oona visited Tao House again. She had wanted to fly but had to go by train, she said, because "Daddy wanted me to see the country." Oona, who had just passed her sixteenth birthday, was proud of the fact that she had "been going to the Stork Club since I was fifteen." She had one more year to spend at Brearley before entering Vassar. In the words of an acquaintance that summer she was a "starry-eyed schoolgirl filled with giggling good humor."

In high heels she was five feet four inches tall, and she weighed 125 pounds. O'Neill had a professional photographer take pictures of himself and Oona in and around Tao House and took her on visits to San Francisco. He showed her one of his newly written plays; later Oona casually mentioned to friends that she had really noticed only the title, *Long Day's Journey into Night*. She was much more interested in Rosie, the player piano. Although Oona made a big hit with her father, she and Carlotta did not get on at all well. Carlotta felt that Oona was altogether too giddy.

Throughout 1941, O'Neill was again in a state of deep depression. He said that the early part of the year had been the worst period since his "crack-up in 1937." The times, he complained, were not auspicious for dramatists—it just didn't seem to matter whether a play was produced or not. He wanted to stay on at Tao House; the thought of New York, he said, gave him "the pip." But the steady erosion of his way of life at Tao House disturbed him. His ivory tower was in the middle of what he called "the greatest war industry and armed-service sections in the United States." You "couldn't get help any more." One by one, his servants went to work in defense plants or were drafted or enlisted. Finally, the O'Neills were left alone. Carlotta had never cooked before, she has said; O'Neill told friends that she had to start from scratch and had proceeded to "do a grand job, and one thing I can't complain about is indigestion."

He tried to help with the dishes after the meals. But his trembling was getting worse and worse. Despite his difficulty, he boasted, he hadn't broken a single dish. Carlotta's arthritis kept pace with the terrible trembling and rigidity in O'Neill's hands and arms. When neighbors, probably friends of the help ("not the rich estate people of the countryside"), came in and helped the stranded couple, O'Neill was amazed. Overnight he became the champion of the small-town business men, small farmers, the in-between guys—"the forgotten class." Barrett Clark is convinced that the contact O'Neill established with his neighbors in the Valley of the Moon "somehow helped restore the man's essential faith in a world which his reading and contemplation had, in a way, distorted." There was a kinship of quality, O'Neill discovered, between his neighbors around Danville and his old friends of the Hell Hole and Jimmy the Priest's. Money couldn't buy what these people were doing for him, he insisted.

Pearl Harbor came and went, but the impact of the war had already spent itself in O'Neill's mind. He was busily engaged in writing *A Moon for the Misbegotten,* the last thing he ever wrote.

In New York, Shane told Oona that he and Marjory Straight expected to get married. Oona was anxious to meet Marjory, not only because she was Shane's girl but because she was a real working artist. The two girls soon became good friends. Oona, not quite seventeen, and in her senior year at Brearley, was strictly an uptown girl at this time. She was strikingly beautiful; her hair was luxuriously black and very straight, her mouth was wide and her lips full, and her frequent smile displayed two rows of perfectly formed teeth. Her eyelashes were dark and her eyes had a slightly Oriental cast about them. She, like all the O'Neills, had the "black Irish" look. Physically, she had matured early. Not for her were the callow youths from Groton and St. Paul's and Choate— already she was being squired about by "older men" in their thirties or even forties. She had wanted to go along with Shane and Marc Brandel to Mexico, but her mother wouldn't let her, insisting that she finish school. Now Shane was going out into the world and into the war, the greatest adventure of all. She wished she didn't have to go to Vassar.

Early in March, Shane received sailing orders. He made out his allotment and his insurance to Marjory. He also gave her a picture taken on the beach at Provincetown. It showed Shane as a child of three, standing naked beside his father in a bathing suit. On the back he wrote, "Look at my beautiful little savage self." Shane was well aware that his father had given Carlotta a photograph of himself as a newborn baby, inscribing it, "To my love and my life, Carlotta (who sometimes thinks this infant never grew up) from me, this above, her husband. . . ."

Shane's first voyage lasted two months. When he returned he walked into Marjory's studio early in the morning. He reached into his pocket and threw all his money on the kitchen table. The voyage had been a dangerous one and the crew had received extra pay. The trip, he told Margaret, had given him many short story ideas.

Uptown he found Oona more restless than ever about remaining in school; it looked as if she wouldn't go to Vassar. Shane told her that he had been teased by some of his friends about her being elected Number-One Debutante for the 1942–43 season. Stories had ap-

peared in all the papers. At one big press conference Oona was handed
a large bunch of red roses and a reporter, not knowing whose daughter
she was, asked her what business her father was in. Oona had giggled,
then said, "He writes." What view, she was asked, would her father
take of her being elected Debutante Number-One? She said she
didn't know and she wasn't going to ask; she would let her father find
out for himself.

It was apparent that Oona was a girl who knew pretty much what
she was doing and where she was going. She brushed off successfully,
many who tried to probe how deeply she had read into her father's
plays. Sometimes she'd say she had read only *The Emperor Jones* or
Ah, Wilderness!; at others that *The Great God Brown* was her favorite.
She would add, "I read them when I was very young." At her press
conference, one of the reporters observed that obviously, she was as
Irish as Paddy's pig. Did she, now, regard herself as lace curtain Irish
or shanty Irish? Oona was caught off balance, but only for a moment.
She had never heard the expressions. The reporters eagerly explained.

"Put me down as shanty Irish," Oona said. At the end of the
interview, another reporter said, "Boys, we naturally got to ask her
about world affairs. Miss O'Neill, what do you think of world affairs?"
At the time, Corregidor was under bombardment by the Japanese.

"It would seem very funny," Oona said, with commendable taste,
"for me to sit in the Stork Club and express my opinion of world
affairs."

Actually, Oona found that being the daughter of Eugene O'Neill,
the playwright, could be something of a drawback. Her teachers were
annoyed at the fact that she was receiving publicity—especially
publicity in the Stork Club. This was unseemly for a Brearley girl,
and some of Oona's schoolmates indicated they felt the same way.
Oona was included in many of Manhattan's exclusive club dances,
cotillions and junior assemblies, but she was included in spite of being
O'Neill's daughter. Agnes had had to do a good deal of lunching with
her Social Register friends and relatives to offset that.

Although going out with a college undergraduate was almost
exceptional for Oona, who preferred older, more sophisticated men,
in the spring she was asked to Yale's Junior Prom. Eugene junior was
teaching at Yale that year, and one of his students tarried after a
lecture to chat with him.

"Sir," he said. "I am having your sister, Oona, up for the Junior

Prom. I thought you might like to see her. Would it be all right?"

Eugene didn't explain that Oona was his half sister, but he did say that he hadn't seen her since she was about two.

"Tell her," Eugene told the student, "that I'd love to see her again after so long. Tell her that I'll be at my apartment at five and would you, sir, be good enough to bring her around and join me for a drink?" The student said he would be pleased and honored. Eugene waited at his apartment all evening, but Oona never came. Later, he told friends that he was deeply hurt at what seemed to him a studied snub. He was never to see his half sister again.

It may have been Oona's salvation that she seemed to sail untouched and unperturbed through the maelstroms into which members of the O'Neill family were always being drawn. "Oona had a sharply developed sense of self-preservation," one of her friends who knew her from childhood has said. "Even as a child, she seemed to have an eye always alert for security." Another family friend has said, "Oona was born knowing how the world operated. When she's with a man of sixty, you'd think he was twenty-five and she was sixty, she manages things so well. She gives the orders."

Marjory Straight observed, with pained amazement, the sight of these lonely members of the same family, strangers to one another in some ways, charming yet disturbed, moving inevitably to their individual tragedies. One day, after she'd met Eugene junior, she told a friend, "That man has the look of a man who might kill himself."

Between voyages, Shane outdid, in drinking and being "on the bum," anything his father had ever done. Marjory always felt that his insecurity, only slightly assuaged by drink, was somehow bound up with his attitudes toward his father.

Shane's voyages were on ships that formed, in the war years, the great supply lines to England and Africa. On one trip, Shane became friendly with a member of the Navy gun crew stationed on his ship. One evening he noticed that there was an emergency medical kit provided for the crew. Included in the supplies were syringes; there were also morphine tablets. Shane tried one, "to see the effect on me," and found that it helped to "equalize the bitter world without."

Shane and Marjory had a regular routine when he returned from "out there," as he called being at sea. She'd show him the pictures she had painted and he would tell her which ones he liked best. It seemed to Marjory that most of the pictures she was painting were of Shane. Some were of herself and Shane.

Of this period in their lives, Miss Straight has said: "There was little ugliness in either of us, and there was no great strength or force, either. Even though Shane seemed to be doing all the things his father had done—bumming through a foreign country as he had done in Mexico or going off to sea—these things were not part of him."

Early in December, 1942, Shane was again, as he liked to put it, "on the beach." But his sailing orders came before Christmas. The holiday had never meant much to the O'Neills, he said, but maybe he ought to send presents to his mother and father and sister. He would surely hear from his father if he wrote.

"You do it for me, baby," Shane said to Marjory. "Send my father something and Carlotta, too. I haven't written to him in a long time." He gave her the money, and Marjory sent the presents. She took a certain pride in wrapping them.

At Tao House that year, O'Neill was talking to a friend, who had youngsters Shane's and Oona's ages, about raising children. O'Neill said that he had learned a great deal from his eldest child, and that young Eugene had knowledge of much about which he, O'Neill, was profoundly uneducated. "We learn from each other," O'Neill said, "and I think that is the most valuable asset in a father and son relationship." But he talked very little about Shane and Oona.

About two months after Christmas a letter addressed to Shane arrived from Tao House. Marjory forwarded it to Shane and then sat down and wrote O'Neill a long letter. She said she assumed the letter which had arrived was to thank Shane for the Christmas presents and she was forwarding it, unopened, to him. She said Shane had asked her to bring his father up to date on what he was doing, and she told of his trips to sea, into the war zones. Shane was growing up in the war into a fine man, she wrote.

A reply to Miss Straight's letter came almost immediately. The letter, addressed to her, was in Carlotta's handwriting. Miss Straight, it said, should know at once that it was Mr. Eugene O'Neill's wife who had written the letter thanking Shane for his Christmas gift. After considerable, and believe her, deep consideration, she felt that it would be all for the best if Mr. O'Neill did not have the letter Miss Straight had written about Shane's experiences at sea. She felt that it would be much better if Shane himself wrote to his father of such things. After all, it was wartime and such news, secondhand, might upset her husband and make him unable to work. She was sure that Marjory would agree that Mr. Eugene O'Neill's work was of the utmost importance to him, to her [Carlotta], and, indeed, to the whole world. She signed herself, Carlotta Monterey O'Neill.

When Shane arrived in New York, Marjory told him about the letter from Carlotta and said, "Who does she think she is—Saint Peter opening and closing the gates? What's wrong with your father that he allows such a thing to happen? You are his son. Doesn't he have any moral responsibility for his children? Does she open all his mail? Can't your father speak for himself?"

Shane let her run on, smiling tolerantly. "That's the way Carlotta is," he said finally. "She's always been like that. Maybe it has something to do with her not liking Mother. Though she doesn't hate father's first wife, Kathleen. . . ." Shane began to chuckle, suddenly, almost to himself. "Your letter must have been a good one," he said, "so naturally she wouldn't give it to Father. God, I wonder how many of the letters that we, his children, have written to him, he has received."

In the fall of 1943, Shane made his last voyage to sea. He looked so bad and was in such a state of nerves that Marjory urged him to stay home and take it easy. The bombings, the sight of the sailors jumping from their sinking ships into the water and drowning or burning in the flaming oil had broken him. Once, off the coast of England, he had helped pull a Norwegian sailor aboard. "I can't get the words of the man out of my mind," Shane told Marjory when he returned from the voyage. "He kept repeating over and over again, 'I come from Flekkefjord. I come from Flekkefjord.' That was all he could say."

Perhaps, Marjory thought, he could do the writing that he had been wanting to do; she would work. Because she didn't want to miss the daylight painting hours, she worked at night, as a hat-check girl in a night club. Shane spent some days in a hospital for merchant seamen, being treated for shock. After he was discharged, he held various jobs—in a button factory, with a little-theater group, moving scenery and doing other menial chores—but he didn't keep them. Nothing seemed to interest him. Soon, he was back at the Old Colony, drinking steadily. The emptiness inside him gnawed deeper and deeper. He wrote:

> *Can we then fill that space*
> *With liquor?—no*
> *Work—no*

> *A movie?—no*
> *A whore?—no*
> *And laughter comes bitter and*
> *Talks up in space—Hollow.*

Often, when Marjory came home in the early hours, she found
im unconscious from drink. Sometimes he would not come home until
norning, when she was up and working at her easel. There were times
when he didn't come home for several days. Once, he borrowed her
ent money and spent it at the bar. When they were threatened with
viction, Shane went to see his father's lawyer, to ask for a loan. He
lidn't get it. In telling Marjory about his failure to get the money,
e said, "This is terrible. Don't ever let me have any money again."

Twice, Marjory arrived home to find the gas jets all open. Both
imes, she was able to revive Shane by dragging him into the hall-
vay. When he came to, he looked at her and said, "I've made a mess
f everything." After the second try, she and friends prevailed on
Shane to see a psychiatrist. He attended the sessions for a while and
hen took to arriving late for them. For each session he would arrive
ater and later, until soon he was arriving a minute before the session
vas supposed to end. After a while, he didn't go at all.

CHAPTER

TWENTY-SEVEN

ΙΟΟΙ

EXIT OONA

Throughout 1942 O'Neill continued working on *A Moon for the Misbegotten,* the story of his brother, Jamie. Lawrence Langner came to visit that summer, but most of O'Neill's talk concerned plans for producing his plays after the war was over. His sharply developed sense of timing told him that *The Iceman Cometh* should be done a year or so after the war, so as to reflect the disillusionment that was sure to set in. He thought that Eddie Dowling, who was at that time playing in William Saroyan's *The Time of Your Life* in San Francisco, should play the role of Harry Hope, the saloonkeeper in *The Iceman.*

In the course of his visit, Langner noted how ill O'Neill seemed and what "mental suffering he was undergoing." He and his wife left Tao House feeling "quite depressed about Gene's health. Nevertheless, O'Neill continued to work and before the year ended he had completed his final draft of *A Moon for the Misbegotten* and had sent it off to his editor, Saxe Commins. Like *Long Day's Journey into*

Night, which Commins had put into the Random House vault, the new play gave an intimate view into the privacy of the O'Neill family, but Jamie, its central character, was dead and Eugene himself was only very slightly represented; the play was, therefore approved for publication. In *Long Day's Journey* O'Neill himself was more fully represented and the play was a more complete exposure of the interrelationship of all the members of the family.

There was something troubling O'Neill during 1942, other than the strain of the war and living at Tao House without servants, and other than the anxieties and distress of his ill health and Carlotta's arthritis. Whether he was fully conscious of it or not, he was in the process of alienating himself from his only daughter. The history of this rejection—if rejection it was—has never been made entirely clear. The situation between Oona and the Eugene O'Neill household was complicated by Carlotta's attitude.

The real rift between O'Neill and his daughter had begun in the spring of 1942, when pictures and items about the photogenic Oona began appearing in the newspapers. She was now moving prominently in café society and taking part in war work. Pictures of her at the Stage Door Canteen for servicemen appeared in the newspapers. She was photographed at a Russian War Relief benefit held at the old Lafayette Hotel in Greenwich Village, and the picture was nationally syndicated. This upset Carlotta, who was violent on the subject of anything Russian.

Then, before school was out Oona suddenly decided that she wanted to go on the stage. The publicity she had been receiving brought her many offers from film studios, modeling agencies, press agents, and picture magazines. Perfect strangers wanted to be her business manager. A night club wanted to underwrite a thirty-thousand-dollar coming-out party for her. Agnes resisted all this as much as she could. O'Neill, in correspondence with Oona, objected vigorously to her notoriety, and both he and Agnes insisted that she should go on to college. Oona stayed in school but she had to take her biology examination twice before she received her diploma. She refused, however, to go to college. O'Neill told her that he still held some parental authority and reminded her that he was her legal guardian until she was eighteen. He said that she was not to embark on a movie career at her age. But the tempting offers continued. Max Reinhardt wanted her to try out for his Repertory Theatre. M-G-M was casting a film of the South Sea islands in technicolor

and wanted a bronzed girl whom they could photograph withou
make-up. Jerry Levin, a press agent, proceeded to go after the jo
for Oona and promised to get her into the Screen Actors Guild. Ac
cording to Ruth Reynolds of the New York *Daily News,* Oona wa
offered parts in other films, but O'Neill spoke to his friend Hun
Stromberg, a film producer, and arranged for Oona's movie caree
to come to a sudden end.

She turned to the theater, with her mother's reluctant consen
"If you want to go on the stage," Agnes finally agreed, "I sup
pose it's all right." She herself was going to Hollywood to do th
adaptation of her novel, *The Road Is Before Us.*

Oona got a small part in *Pal Joey,* then in rehearsal, with Vivienn
Segal in the lead. She made her stage debut on July 17 at the Maple
wood Theatre in Maplewood, New Jersey, but this version of *Pal Joe*
was a failure and Oona left New York to join her mother i
Hollywood. Miss Segal later recalled Oona at this period. "She wa
a delightful, friendly child. I remember she insisted on going bare
foot. She was like some wild Irish sprite. Her charm, her smile, he
lovely teeth and hair made her a remarkably beautiful girl. We al
loved her."

Later that summer, Oona and her friend Carol Marcus, Willian
Saroyan's wife, were in San Francisco with Saroyan's play *The Tim
of Your Life,* and Oona got a small part in it. She telephoned Ta
House but was unable to reach her father. With Carol she drove ou
there, but they were refused admittance. Oona was given to believe tha
her father wanted nothing to do with her.

In October, the *Daily News* in New York published a double
page feature under the headline:

> OONA O'NEILL GOES HOME
> TO HER FAMOUS FATHER—
> TO GET MOVIE JOB OKAY

The writer, again Ruth Reynolds, had talked extensively with Oona
who said that her father had definitely decided he did not want he
to be an actress; then, smiling enigmatically, Oona added. "He's m
guardian until I'm eighteen. I'll be eighteen next May. A girl ough
to earn her own living."

To Carlotta, who frequently talked of what she called "chea
publicity," all these articles must have been infuriating.

"When Oona got older and started getting publicity as

debutante," Agnes has said, "and when she indicated she wanted to go into show business and started associating with show people, O'Neill cooled toward her." Agnes also thought O'Neill was under the illusion that "Oona was trading on his name."

Oona was welcomed into the most interesting Hollywood circles. Clifford Odets, who knew Oona well at this period, has said that he "scented something very vindictive" in O'Neill's rejection of Oona. It seemed to Odets "as if O'Neill could not forgive his children because *he* had abandoned them! All around, it was very sad and murky, not human. And yet one could not help feeling that if one or two or three little moves had been made, O'Neill and his children would have come together."

During the winter of 1942–43, Oona was much in the company of Charles Chaplin, and it was generally believed that the great comedian was courting her. At this time Agnes, who had received word that her mother had suffered a stroke, had to travel back east. Oona seemed to be getting on well in Hollywood, and Agnes did not demand that she go back east with her. But before she left Agnes had a long and serious talk with her about Chaplin. Agnes reports that "when she told me of her plans to marry him, I asked her if she realized what she was letting herself in for. After all, Chaplin was fifty-four—three times as old as she. She was a very popular girl, you know, and had many young men interested in her—some far, far wealthier than Charlie.

"I'll never forget how she answered me. Looking me straight in the eyes, she replied, 'Mother, I will never love another man in my life.' "

Agnes has expressed a view which has occurred to many others. "Perhaps her love for an older man developed because she missed growing up with a father. She was just a baby when Gene and I separated in 1927."

Shortly after her eighteenth birthday Oona signed for a part in *The Girl from Leningrad*. A month later, on June 16, 1943, Oona and Chaplin were married in the greatest secrecy. They turned up at the County Clerk's office at Santa Barbara a half hour before the official opening at 9 A.M. It was Chaplin's fourth marriage; his previous wives, all actresses, were Mildred Harris, Lita Grey, and Paulette Goddard. He had grown-up sons older than Oona. One of the reasons for the secrecy of the marriage was that public attention had recently been focused on Chaplin as a result of a protracted paternity suit brought against him by a twenty-three-year-old aspirant to a film career.

After receiving their license to marry, Chaplin and Oona drove several miles to the home of Justice of the Peace Linton P. Moore. Their only attendants were a local newspaper columnist, Harry Crocker, and Chaplin's publicity representative, Mrs. Catherine Hunter, who served as best man and matron of honor. Reporters telephoned Agnes at Point Pleasant and asked her for her comment.

"I am very happy about it," she said. "The only reason I was not present at the ceremony is that it was necessary for me to be in New York." Out on the Coast, reporters tried to reach Tao House by telephone to ask Oona's father for comment. O'Neill refused to come to the phone. Eventually he did comment, but only in a letter to his daughter. According to a friend of Oona's who was with her when she received it, O'Neill wrote his daughter "a very harsh and severing letter on her marriage to Chaplin." Oona never heard from her father again.

According to Nathan, O'Neill was bitter about Oona's marriage and resented any reference by his friends or acquaintances to his only daughter and his new son-in-law. "There is enough wry comedy in life as it is," O'Neill remarked.

He told Nathan that he undersood it was "Chaplin's supreme wish to play Hamlet. That's all right with me, but I would not want to play in the same cast, whatever the role." But Saxe Commins has expressed the opinion that O'Neill had nothing particularly personal in his resentment of Chaplin as a husband for his daughter, and that O'Neill "just disliked everything about Hollywood, in general."

Talking to his friends, O'Neill liked to refer to Hollywood as "the City of Dreadful Nonsense." He had received many offers to write for the movies. One producer offered to let O'Neill name his own price if he would write a scenario for Jean Harlow. O'Neill's reply to the overture was a telegram consisting of the word "no" repeated twenty times. A year after Oona married Chaplin, O'Neill gave a friend a more reasoned view of why he had refused to write for the movies.

"I have never even been in Hollywood or Los Angeles," he said. "This doesn't mean I have any prejudice against pictures. It merely means that the screen has never interested me as a medium. So why work at something which doesn't interest me when I have always had work on my hands which does interest me and has always paid me well? It is as simple as that—common sense—although some people seem to regard it as a mad—even inexcusable—eccentricity."

It seems a pity that O'Neill and Chaplin never met. Chaplin, too, was contemptuous of the nonsense that most Hollywood producers turn out in the name of entertainment or with the excuse that "it's what the public wants."

O'Neill's letters refer only indirectly to his distress following Oona's marriage, and he steadfastly refused to make any comment for the newspapers. He told friends that he was "on the nerve-ridden ragged edge." During most of August, he was laid up in bed with the flu, and Carlotta's severe arthritis distressed O'Neill almost as much as it did Carlotta. He found it impossible "to write letters or do anything else." More and more at this time of trouble he looked backward with nostalgia.

Oona, living in Hollywood, appeared happily married and soon became pregnant. The Chaplins dined a great deal with the Clifford Odetses. On several occasions, the short-story writer, Katherine Anne Porter, was present. "I remember her [Oona] only as a very small, young-looking creature," Miss Porter has said, "in a jet-black Chinese coat, knitting away steadily on a baby jacket, in the deepest silence and stillness. Now and then she glanced around and took in the scene with an expression that seemed to me to be full of acute observation, some instinctive malice, and natural wit—an interesting face."

The end of O'Neill's and Carlotta's life at Tao House came late in 1943. Both he and Carlotta were in increasingly poor health. Then Herbert Freeman, their chauffeur, went off to war. Because of the shaking of his hands, O'Neill had not driven a car in years and Freeman's departure stranded them. They stored their furnishings in San Francisco and put Tao House on the market.

The O'Neills sold their home with great reluctance; they had been very happy there, but without servants or staff Carlotta simply had been unable to maintain the place. The house contained twenty-two rooms, and the estate covered 158 acres. There were O'Neill's swimming pool and his chickens; Carlotta had to take care of them and O'Neill and cook the meals. It became impossible for her. She was not completely well herself, and they were running low on money. They had been living on her savings.

In San Francisco, O'Neill and Carlotta settled in a three-room apartment in a family hotel known as Huntington Arms, located on Nob Hill.

Although O'Neill was unable to do any writing in San Francisco, he kept up some of his correspondence. In discussing a possible production of *Lazarus Laughed,* he pointed out that the play contained a "spiritual warning and hope" which could be "important today." He talked with Barrett Clark about Clark's children, who were thinking of embarking on theatrical careers. O'Neill said that he wished that at least one of his own children would turn out to be a bacteriologist or anything else. If one did have a theatrical career, the principal thing was to stay away from the City of Dreadful Nonsense in the southern part of the State of California. He was keeping his San Francisco address a guarded secret because the newspapers were trying "to get me cornered for comment [which] would be embarrassing, to put it mildly." O'Neill and Carlotta were prepared to leave for the East at any time. Both of them, O'Neill said bitterly, had had enough of the Coast.

Then Carlotta fell "seriously ill." She had not been well before the moving began but "the packing and getting out were the last straw for her, and the reaction was that she went to pieces," O'Neill said.

Carlotta had hardly begun to recover when O'Neill suffered a paralytic stroke. He not only was laid up in bed for six months but required around-the-clock nursing. The stroke left him with "an increasing and uncurable palsy."

Carlotta said, some years later, "He couldn't write at all. He couldn't dictate, and he simply—well, he died when he could no longer work—spiritually died and was dragging the poor diseased body along for a few more years until it too died."

Thus Eugene O'Neill had suffered two crippling deprivations. He lost, in a very real and physical sense, his ability to write, perhaps his only reason for living, and he lost his only daughter. Sadly, O'Neill had never established a close relationship with Oona. Actually there was no relationship at all. In its way, this was the real tragedy for O'Neill. He did not lose a daughter, for he had never really had one.

CHAPTER

TWENTY-EIGHT

ကက

RETURN TO THE

CITY

Throughout the winter of 1944–45, O'Neill was too ill to do anything at all. He told a friend just before Christmas that he hadn't done any work in a long time. There was much to do, but somehow he could take no interest in writing plays. His mind was often occupied with thoughts of destruction and death. He reflected on how closely related to the times was his play *Lazarus Laughed,* when death and "the meaning or meaningless of life" were so close to us. He compared "the murder, madness and death realism of Tiberius and Caligula" to Hitlerism. But in the spring the mood of defeatism in the world changed— The Allies already had their enemies on the run, and O'Neill was cheered sufficiently to think about the production of his plays.

Lawrence Langner took *A Moon for the Misbegotten, The Iceman Cometh* and *A Touch of the Poet* back to New York. But first he stopped in Hollywood to look for actors and actresses—particularly for "an Irish giantess." He and O'Neill were in accord that *A Moon for the Misbegotten* should be the first of the three plays to be produced after the war was over, then *The Iceman Cometh,* and later *A Touch of the Poet*. Although O'Neill was still weak and traveling conditions were difficult and getting worse, he made the decision to cross the continent. Carlotta was able to obtain space on an eastbound train through the press representative of the railroad.

She had been put to a great deal of difficulty to obtain the tickets; then, just a few hours before train time, O'Neill suddenly changed his mind. It is not really known why he did not return East at this time. Perhaps he did not feel well enough to undertake the long train trip. At any rate, Carlotta was unable to secure reservations for them again until the latter part of 1945.

The end of the war in Europe did not impress O'Neill as much as the end of the war in the Pacific. He was well enough on August 14 to take part in the V-J Day celebrations in San Francisco. Later, in New York, he took pleasure in recounting details of the hysterical and wildly celebrating crowds.

In October, 1945, Carlotta was able to obtain train reservations on her own, at the end of the month they arrived in New York, where they took a housekeeping suite of rooms at the Hotel Barclay. They tried to keep their arrival a secret, but a reporter for *The New York Times* learned that O'Neill was in town and asked him for news of his future plans. O'Neill said he was in New York "only for a brief stay" and that he was not contemplating the production of any of his plays.

One of the first people O'Neill got in touch with was his elder son, who was living in New York. Father and son had kept in communication with each other by mail. Eugene junior was only thirty-five, but he was already considered an authority on the disputed Homeric authorship, a field full of controversy. He had taken his doctorate in Greek at Yale and had become an assistant professor there. His father's publishers, Random House, had brought out two volumes of Greek plays translated by him and Whitney Oates. The only flaw in an otherwise impressive record was his marital career—there had already been three marriages, all ending in divorce.

In 1944 he had drifted down to the Village, where Shane had welcomed him. But the pattern of their childhood roles persisted; Shane remained the kid brother and Eugene always "took over" when he was in a social group. Physically, Eugene was taller and huskier than Shane. He had inherited the melodious voice of his grandfather, James O'Neill. Sporting a Vandyke beard, he cut an impressive figure in any of the many circles in which he moved, even in eccentric-hardened Greenwich Village.

"Eugene didn't talk to you," Marc Brandel has said, "he lectured you. He was always talking to Shane about 'our father.' The idea was that Shane should not do this or that on account of 'our father.'"

Marjory Straight was amazed at the difference in the two sons. "I was awed by his knowledge, humbled by my own ignorance. I became one of his great listeners," Marjory has said of Eugene. She was fascinated by his behavior with girls. "It was as if," she said, "he wooed and maintained his manhood by his talk of books. He would hold a girl's hand with Dryden, embrace her with Proust, and kiss her sweetly with John Donne."

Eugene, apparently, did not feel his name to be a burden. "Eugene junior would walk into a room," Joy Nicholson, a young actress and director, has said, "practically announcing he was the son of the great O'Neill. It seemed to me, at the time, that he was perfectly adjusted to being known as the son of Eugene O'Neill."

Gene brought Shane news of their father. He told Shane that O'Neill senior had not been happy about Oona's marriage. He said that he had read his father's new play, *The Iceman Cometh*. It was about people in a Greenwich Village bar and was very good.

Eugene junior had tried desperately to get a commission in the Navy but had failed because of his allergies. Then he was drafted, only to be turned down by the Army doctors because of a permanent injury he had suffered in his bicycle accident at fourteen. He took this rejection very hard and stepped up his drinking, which was already impressive. During the war he took a leave from Yale to work in a cable factory in New Haven.

As the war began to draw to a close, Eugene dreaded more and more going back to teaching at Yale. He wanted a broader audience for his talents. He had thought of going into newspaper work, or into the theater, or perhaps the new television industry. His father sent him to see his old friend, Art McGinley, who was working as sports editor of the Hartford *Times*. McGinley sent Eugene to the manager of Station WTIC in Hartford, where young Gene got a job as an announcer. He had insisted that he wanted the job on his merits and did not want to exploit his father's name. Nonetheless, the publicity announcement of his employment said that "the playwright's son, under the name of Gene O'Neill," was working for Station WTIC.

The wartime Greenwich Village that Shane lived in and to which Eugene junior had come was much altered from the Village of the 1920s, of candlelight poetry readings, and of Edna St. Vincent Millay. It was rough now and brassy, filled with men in uniform, and at night it tended to be honky-tonk. Young people—both men and women—wore blue jeans. Few of them were concerned with contribution to the arts. In O'Neill's day there had been some kind of honest enthusiasm for art in the Village, in particular a struggle for the creation and recognition of American art. Now futility was the fashion. Nothing mattered except the moment. Nothing was worth believing in. There was talk of Kafka and Sartre. Or there was no talk, just raised eyebrows, shrugs of shoulders, gestures, and the question, "Are you hep?" Drinking was getting to be slightly old hat, too. There were other things— Benzedrine, for example. You could buy an ordinary Benzedrine inhaler at a drugstore, remove the wick, soak it in water, and drink the solution. It gave you a "charge."

Then there were "sticks of tea"—marijuana cigarettes—which drifted down from Harlem at anywhere between twenty-five cents and a dollar a cigarette, or reefer. "Tea" parties were held in apartments after the bars closed. Shane was invited to such affairs. He liked the sensation, he liked the release from the misery and depression always hounding him. "It was a social thing," Shane has said. "It was a thing you did with others. I started it because everybody else seemed to be doing it. I didn't want to be different, to be a wet blanket." Perhaps it made him feel he belonged.

"Tea" stepped up a devotee's enjoyment of jazz. It enabled the musician himself to break loose from reality into a world of ecstasy. Shane tried a few musical instruments and found that he could play them naturally. His colleagues in his new world of "tea" and jazz tended to be more or less ineffectual personalities. Other things they had in common were broken homes, domineering mothers or fathers, and vague desires—which were seldom acted upon—to take some part in artistic creation.

The smoking of marijuana followed a kind of ritual. The reefers were passed around and Shane, with the others, would inhale noisily, taking in air with the smoke. He would hold the smoke in his lungs as long as possible, to get the full effect. After the second or third reefer, would come euphoria—the feeling of well-being, of being "real cool." Time always slowed down; it seemed that Shane could hear and feel and enjoy every note of the music on the phonograph.

The feelings of those who were smoking were entirely passive. Nobody danced or made sexual overtures. Their talk was about "tea" and where to get it. Marijuana smokers felt superior to ordinary people, who were "squares."

"We all smoked marijuana in those days," Marc Brandel has said. "It was the thing to do. The idea was to get yourself feeling anything but natural. The thing is, most of us outgrew it. Shane didn't."

Shane and Marjory were still together; but "sometimes," she wrote in her journal, "I think we are enemies." A friend invited them to come to her cottage on Martha's Vineyard. "Come," wrote the friend, "it will give you a chance to find each other." Shane was for going. "I've always lived by the sea—like father. He always takes a house beside the sea. It makes me feel almost at home. I know what I think when I hear the waves. Let's go and consolidate our forces."

They went. They settled in the friend's cottage, and walked along the water's edge, picking up shells and driftwood. In the evenings, Marjory sketched while Shane and the friend played gin rummy. Shane read a great deal. One night he read something aloud to Marjory, a passage from Thomas Wolfe's *Look Homeward, Angel:*

"If a man has a talent and cannot use it, he has failed. If he has a talent and uses only half of it, he has partly failed. If he has a talent and learns somehow to use the whole of it, he has gloriously succeeded and won a satisfaction and triumph few men ever know."

They talked of their future. "Let's just stay here and not worry," Shane said. "But we must do something, Shane," Marjory answered. A letter came for Shane from a friend. "Am staying here in Province-town," it said. "Lots of jobs here on fishing boats. The men are all drafted. The pay is good. Come soon."

Shane told Marjory that he would get a job on a boat and she could stay in Provincetown and paint. No more Greenwich Village. The wheel was coming around, in a strange way, to a full cycle in his life. Provincetown was where his father had married his mother, and where Shane had been born in the home of a Portuguese fisherman.

The alarm went off at five o'clock to enable them to catch the early morning ferry to the mainland. Shane was in one of his death sleeps. Marjory shook him. He woke momentarily, long enough to rain the little glancing blows with his fists which always shot out from him when he was awakened. She dressed and packed, meanwhile call-ing him from time to time. He sat up as she was about to leave. She said she would go ahead and try to delay the ferry for a few minutes to give him time to get aboard. He nodded.

At the dock she waited with her suitcase until the passengers were all aboard. Then she walked up the gangplank and found the captain. She said her husband would be there in a few minutes and would he delay the ferry a little? Together, she and the captain stood at the ship's railing looking at the now-empty pier. Soon, the whistle blew. Bells sounded. The engine rumbled in the hold.

Just as the captain was telling her that he couldn't delay the ferry any longer, Shane came hurrying up the pier, carrying the little blue canvas suitcase which held just about everything he owned in the world. Then, suddenly, he turned around and walked in the direction from which he had come. "Never mind, Captain," Marjory said. "I guess there is no need to wait." She watched the pier grow smaller and gradually disappear.

Shane was unable to remember quite what went on in his mind when he turned around that morning on the pier. His seemingly impulsive decision may have altered the course of his life. Marjory returned to the city. She left Greenwich Village and moved uptown. Recognition as an artist came rapidly. Her life with Shane was over.

Shane lingered on the island for several days. He would hold life in suspension—perhaps forever. He continued to read Thomas Wolfe at night by kerosene light. Which of us has known his brother? Which of us has looked into his father's heart? Which of us has not remained forever prison-pent? Which of us it not forever a stranger and alone? During the day he walked by the edge of the sea.

When Shane returned to Greenwich Village from Martha's Vine-yard in the spring of 1944, he moved into Marc Brandel's apartment at 149 West Fourth Street. One of his poems, Brandel remembers, was built around the line, "People don't care." Why Shane continually felt so alone puzzled Brandel. Shane had many friends who were devoted to him. He had a group to which he could feel he belonged—the friends who still gathered in the Old Colony. One of them was Cathy Givens.

Cathy, who became Shane's wife, was, like him, a rebellious child. She was an extraordinarily pretty girl, with a slightly disdainful and insolent look about her, who had been educated at private schools. Her presence in Greenwich Village indicated no overpowering artistic drive. Cathy and Shane were astonishingly alike physically, seeming at first glance almost like brother and sister. Thin and Irish, she resem-bled Shane also in a lack of competitiveness. Both seemed indifferent about their very survival; but still, Cathy wanted a husband, a home and children, and she got them.

Cathy lived with another girl in the Village and worked as a sales-woman at various department stores. Shane took a job at a window display studio run by Tommy Rowland and her husband, Dick. Most of its employees were young people who lived in the Village and wanted to be painters or sculptors. There were no regular hours and little supervision. Employees came and went as they pleased, simply signing in and out. Shane discovered that he possessed an unusual talent for making things with his hands. He improvised striking papier-mâché figures of horses. He also made figures of horses and dogs out of straw. In his notebook, at this time, he wrote these lines:

> *No*
> *You can't go home again*
> *Or fight loneliness*
> *Unless you have the*
> *Weapon—*
> *A friend.*

On the morning of July 31, 1944, Shane, Marc Brandel, and other friends gathered at the Old Colony, before setting out for Norwalk, Connecticut, where Cathy was staying with her mother. Cathy had been brought up as an Episcopalian, but the marriage service was performed by a justice of the peace. Shane gave his occupation as merchant seaman, his age as twenty-four. Cathy's age was twenty.

By the end of the afternoon, Shane and Cathy were back in New York, drinking at the Old Colony and receiving the congratulations of their friends. Shane wrote to his mother in Hollywood that he was married. He did not write to his father because he assumed that his father, having severed his relationship with Oona, had also severed ties with him.

Later in the evening of their wedding day, Cathy and Shane remembered that they had no place to stay. Marc Brandel suggested that they stay at his apartment, while he would stay with a friend. A few nights later, Cathy and Shane shifted to the apartment of another friend. Their gypsy honeymoon continued for several weeks. They stayed wherever they could find a haven. One evening in the San Remo café, they chatted with Jimmy Light's ex-wife, Susan Jenkins, an old friend of Agnes and Gene's from their Provincetown days. She was now married to William Slater Brown, a writer, World War I ambulance driver, and the "B" of E. E. Cummings' *The Enormous Room*. She had not seen Shane since he was a little boy in Provincetown and was upset to learn that he was just married and had no place to live. They could have, she said, an apartment she had been using as a stopover in New York. It was in the southern part of the Village at 49 King Street. Gratefully, Cathy and Shane moved there that night.

"Shane looked like a miniature edition of his father," Mrs. Brown has said. "Both he and his wife seemed homeless and forlorn. Shane was growing a little mustache like his father's. Later, when I came to take my things out of King Street, I noticed he had a newspaper color photograph of his father among his belongings. I could tell he worshiped his father. I had the feeling that he was trying to emulate him."

Early in 1945, Cathy and Shane decided to go out to the West Coast. Agnes wrote that they could visit her in Hollywood. They lent their apartment on King Street to Eugene junior. Shane and Cathy were in California well into the spring. Oona and Charlie Chaplin had them to dinner a number of times and invited them to parties. Shane thought Oona seemed very happy.

"I liked Chaplin," Shane has said. "He told me so many things that interested me. One day, at the beach, we were watching some people off in the distance. He showed me how much you can tell about people and what they're saying and thinking from just watching their movements. You don't have to hear what they're saying. Chaplin made me understand how to show character in pantomime. It was interesting. I learned a lot."

Shane did not look up his father in San Francisco.

When Shane and Cathy returned to New York late that spring of 1945, they moved back into their King Street apartment, and Eugene rented another in the same house.

Young Gene was shocked, as were so many of those close to O'Neill, when he saw his father in New York that fall of 1945. His father's eyes startled him, and he recalled that someone had once said that O'Neill's eyes looked like "the crow's nest of his soul." Now his forearms were shaking almost as violently as his hands.

Barrett Clark, who visited him at about this time, was also "shocked" at his appearance. O'Neill seemed gaunt and shrunken, and his hands trembled so violently that he had great difficulty lighting a cigarette. "This was clearly not nervousness alone," said Clark. "He has told me in his letters of long and strenuous attacks of illness, but I was not prepared to see a man who looked as though he should be in a hospital."

O'Neill told his elder son that he had stopped writing because he no longer could use pen or pencil, and he could not abide a typewriter.

Dictating to a secretary was also out of the question. "Imagine," he said, "trying to dictate a play like *Mourning Becomes Electra!*" At the moment, he was trying out a dictaphone.

Six physicians had examined O'Neill in an attempt to find out what was ailing him. Three of them diagnosed his illness as Parkinson's Disease, which generally affects the use of the muscles, causing tremor and weakness. The other specialists said the illness was not Parkinson's Disease, and there was talk of its being some hereditary nervous ailment. O'Neill now recalled that his mother's hands had trembled. Coffee helped steady his hands at times. He was puzzled as to just how much the trembling had to do with his nerves.

Yet in many ways, Eugene noticed, his father seemed happier than he had been when he had seen him in California. He showed his elder son bound copies of his plays which had been sent to him from all over the world. *Days Without End,* he said with a grin, was banned in Soviet Russia because officials thought O'Neill was an apologist for the Catholic Church. The talk turned to the recent war. Eugene told his father the Navy had rejected him because of his allergies and the Army would not have him because of the injury to his head. O'Neill didn't say anything for several minutes. Then he remarked, "You have escaped now, but it will get you in the end."

Later, commenting to a friend on the significance of the remark, Eugene said, "I think it was that Greek thing in him—the idea that the Furies always catch up with you. The Greek tragedies, the concept of fate in the Greek sense, had a tremendous influence both on his work and on him."

Eugene told his father that he was living in Greenwich Village, under the same roof as Shane. O'Neill said, "Tell Shane to call me. I'd like to see him."

Shane and Cathy had not even known that O'Neill was in New York and were surprised when Eugene dropped into their apartment one evening and said, "Our father is in town. He says to call him." Because Cathy was in her final month of pregnancy, it was agreed that it would be better if Shane went up to see his father for the first time without her.

Shane's reunion with his father took place several weeks before the birth of his baby. They had not seen each other for five years. When he returned from dinner with his father and Carlotta at the Barclay, he was laconic in his descriptions of the meeting. "We got along well together," he told Cathy. But they were still shy with each other. As the playwright Russel Crouse, one of O'Neill's friends, has said, "Gene seemed deeply attached to Shane—in a detached way—if you can picture that. I don't know how else to express it."

Shane too was shocked at his father's physical appearance. Although Shane's own hands sometimes shook, they didn't shake nearly so much as his father's. Carlotta had been nice, Shane said, and was interested when he told them that Cathy was soon to have a baby; he had explained that this was the reason he had not brought her along. Carlotta asked Shane what arrangements he had made and what hospital Cathy would go to. O'Neill said he was anxious to meet Cathy.

On November 19, 1945, Shane telephoned his father that Cathy had given birth. It was a boy, he said, and they had named him Eugene for his grandfather. They neglected, however, to add the descriptive III both being rather vague about such matters. O'Neill was pleased and said he would like to see the baby. A day or two later, Carlotta called on Cathy at French Hospital on the lower West Side, bringing a china figurine of an angel, a pretty plant, and a big box of candy. Cathy was impressed with how fashionable, how stylish, Carlotta was.

"She talked a mile a minute," Cathy has said. "She was very anxious to know exactly where Agnes was. She said it was important that Gene and Agnes should not meet. In fact, that was the reason Gene had not come down to the hospital with her to see the baby. Also, she said he was not well. She said if I met Gene I must make sure and not mention Agnes. It would be embarrassing. It might upset him."

Carlotta called later at King Street and brought a complete layette for the baby. She again explained that Gene was too ill to come.

"We had a nice long talk," Cathy remembers. "She said that the important thing in life was to have ideals. She was obviously uncomfortable about our cold-water flat and its meager furnishings. She said that it was important for a young couple to stand on their own feet. She said she was having Shane and myself up for dinner soon so I could meet Gene. Again she cautioned me not to mention Agnes."

About three weeks later, Cathy and Shane were asked to dinner at the Hotel Barclay. Shane was working uptown at an electrical-fixture factory and arrived before Cathy. When Cathy knocked on the door to the O'Neill apartment, she heard Carlotta saying, "Easy now, Gene, take it easy." O'Neill opened the door. He seemed "very calm, very gracious." Also, Cathy noticed, very shy. He did not kiss her.

"My immediate impression of him" Cathy has said, "was that

here was a very elegant man. I'd sort of expected the old sailor, the saloon guy I had read about. He was extremely well-dressed and had an Old-World air about him. He was very gallant, had beautiful manners.

"I'll never forget his first words to me. I was especially surprised because of Carlotta's repeated cautioning. He looked me over and then, smiling, and looking directly into my eyes, said, 'Why, you look just like Agnes.' Carlotta and I were both somewhat taken aback."

O'Neill, after inquiring about the baby, asked Cathy what books she enjoyed reading. She said she liked the works of Yeats and Edna St. Vincent Millay. At some point in the evening O'Neill remarked that Cathy reminded him of Emily Dickinson. Later the talk turned to jazz. Shane remarked that he liked the music of Louis Armstrong and Benny Goodman. O'Neill said that he had a complete set of Goodman records and they would play some of them soon. He turned out to have an extensive knowledge of jazz. Carlotta took the view that jazz was "savage" music and Cathy asked her what she meant.

"She replied that jazz was the music of Negroes," Cathy remembers, "and that they go by their instincts. She did not believe jazz was true art. None of us commented much on her views of jazz."

It was a pleasant dinner served in the O'Neill's suite by a hotel waiter. Carlotta chose a special wine, but O'Neill only sipped at his glass. He was "in temperance," as he called not drinking. Carlotta said that drinking wine with one's meal was the only civilized way to drink and appeared to know a good deal about French wines. Carlotta gave Cathy a Chablis of a "very good year" to take home.

Shane saw more of his father that winter of 1945–46 than he had since O'Neill left Bermuda in 1927. O'Neill was doing no writing, and for the first time in many years he had time to spare. Shane told him he was still interested in writing.

"In a way, I don't think my father wanted me to write," Shane has said. "For years, during my visits with him, I had tried to talk to him about learning how to write. He didn't seem interested. He always tried to discourage me. I think it was because he thought I'd be happier if I did something else. He said it was a hard thing being a writer.

"We got to talking about writing when he said he had seen some short stories in the *Daily News* signed by a Shane O'Neill. I told him it was not me. Then I remember, another time, he said, 'Of course, if you want to write you will write regardless of what I tell you. If you really are a writer, you will write regardless of anything. Nothing will stop you.' "

One evening, while father and son were playing some of O'Neill's jazz records, Shane became unusually articulate. He spoke of what the modern jazz composers were trying to do, the difference in the various kinds of jazz, and what some of the more progressive musicians and composers were up to.

"I was quite surprised," Shane said, "when suddenly my father said, 'Why don't you write about jazz music?' He said he found the things I was telling him very interesting and that I had told him a lot of things he hadn't known. Actually he knew a great deal about jazz himself and had one of the finest collections of jazz records I had ever seen."

O'Neill reminisced with Shane a good deal that winter, talking about his past life, his parents and Jamie, about going to sea, about the early days of Provincetown Players. He said he did not have much money. Shane should understand that he would not be able to leave him much in his will. Actually, he said, what he was leaving him was embodied in the separation agreement he had made with Agnes at the time of the divorce. Shane would get half the proceeds from the sale of Spithead if and when it was sold. So, he said, in a sense, Spithead would be his legacy.

On Monday morning, February 11, 1946, Shane went uptown, as usual, to the factory where he worked. Cathy got up a few minutes later and went over to look at the baby. He was sleeping on a pillow which had been placed at the bottom of a bureau drawer. Like his grandfather, this Eugene O'Neill was spending most of his early days in a makeshift crib. The baby looked much too still. Cathy touched his forehead. It was cold. Quickly, she picked up the baby and ran to Leroy Street, two blocks away, where her sister Gogo lived. Gogo telephoned Shane and told him to come at once to St. Vincent's Hospital. At St. Vincent's, doctors pronounced the little Eugene O'Neill dead on arrival. The baby's body was taken to Bellevue, where an autopsy was performed. The verdict was "Postural asphyxia from bed clothes. Accidental." The baby's age was listed as two months and twenty-four days.

O'Neill did not attend the funeral of his namesake—Shane afterward was told that his father had not been well enough. Eugene junior was out of town. Agnes and Oona, who were on the West

Coast, talked to Shane on the telephone. It was Agnes' idea that Shane and Cathy should go away for a while. She wired to Harry Weinberger and asked that Gene give the couple enough money to go to Bermuda; he could deduct it from her alimony, she wrote. O'Neill agreed.

The night before they left for Bermuda, O'Neill had Cathy and Shane in to dinner. "Carlotta was ill," Cathy has reported, "and there were just the three of us at dinner. I noticed that Gene, as I was calling him by that time, seemed more relaxed than when Carlotta was with him. Shane and his father did most of the talking," and they talked mostly about Bermuda. O'Neill spoke of how much he had loved Spithead, and of the times that he and Shane had had there."

The young couple sailed for Bermuda at the end of February. They stayed in the cottage next to the big house at Spithead, and for four months they enjoyed a vacation and a welcome respite from their problems. O'Neill paid for their passage and sent them a hundred dollars a month while they were there; and he deducted the whole amount from Agnes' alimony.

When they returned to New York they took a room in a hotel just off Washington Square. They didn't want to go back to the apartment where little Eugene had died. O'Neill, meanwhile, had moved from the Hotel Barclay to an apartment somewhere in the East Eighties. He was in the middle of the long and complicated arrangements for the casting and production of *The Iceman Cometh*.

Shane was unable to find a job immediately and, in a few days, he and Cathy found themselves without funds. On top of this, Shane came down with a bad case of flu. He did not know exactly where his father was living, for O'Neill and Carlotta had checked out of the Barclay without leaving a forwarding address. Cathy and Shane knew they were still in town, however, because O'Neill had granted Earl Wilson, a syndicated columnist, an interview. Wilson did not reveal O'Neill's address but described the scene of the interview as "the sun-sprayed patio of a high-up apartment in the east 80's—an apartment rich with 10,000 books."

Cathy obtained O'Neill's unlisted telephone number from one of the cast of *The Iceman Cometh*. The first time she called, Carlotta answered and told Cathy flatly that O'Neill did not want to see her or Shane. There was no explanation. The conversation was not pleasant and Carlotta terminated it. Cathy called a second time and Carlotta was highly indignant. She said she had explained that O'Neill did not want to see them. Finally, after several more calls, Carlotta told Cathy that O'Neill, even if he wished, couldn't come to the phone because he was taking a bath. According to Cathy, she heard O'Neill's voice in the distance saying, "I'll talk." It was obvious, Cathy has said, that he was very annoyed.

"How did you get this number?" he asked her.

"A friend told me," she answered. "I can't tell you—it isn't any of your business anyway."

"What do you want?" O'Neill asked.

"Shane is not well," Cathy told him. "He has the flu. We need help."

"All right," O'Neill said, "I'll send Aronberg down in the morning." Winfield E. Aronberg had succeeded the late Harry Weinberger as O'Neill's lawyer.

That evening friends of Cathy and Shane insisted that they come to their apartment for a steak dinner. Although Shane was still feeling shaky, he was also hungry and went along. Just before they left for dinner, another friend, named Seymour, dropped by to welcome them back to the city. He had had a few drinks, he said, and was dead tired. Cathy told him to lie down on their bed and take a nap.

While they were gone, Aronberg arrived with a physician. The lawyer had never met Shane and he assumed that the man on the bed was the patient. The doctor told him to take his shirt off and listened with his stethoscope to Seymour's breathing. Finally, the doctor gave the groggy Seymour a shot of Vitamin B. This did it. "I'm not Shane," Seymour said.

The affair was reported to the manager the next morning. Somehow he got the impression that there was something sinister about two men coming into a room at that hour. He told Shane he and Cathy would have to leave the hotel. Just then Aronberg called up.

"What did you do a terrible thing like that to your father for?" he asked Cathy. "Gene asked me to go down there and help Shane. He thought he was sick and dying. I come down with the doctor and Shane isn't even there."

"And what's the idea," Cathy replied, "of you two coming down here looking like a couple of toughs? So tough that the manager has thrown us out of the hotel!"

Though the incident possessed certain comic elements, it ended in anything but comedy. For this was the last communication of any nature between Shane and his father.

O'Neill, always an uneasy father, was gradually achieving his release from the role. First Oona, now Shane—and yet he probably could feel that that release was being forced upon him by his children.

CHAPTER

TWENTY-NINE

১৩৩

PAST AND PRESENT:

THE ICEMAN COMETH

The apartment to which the O'Neills moved in the spring of 1946 was a penthouse at 35 East Eighty-fourth Street. It had been the home of Edward Sheldon, who had just died after a tragic lifetime of bed-ridden invalidism. Carlotta had the apartment entirely remodeled and redecorated at a cost of approximately $25,000. As she had done so many times before, she supervised the architecture and interior decoration, areas in which she appeared to have considerable talent and originality. The walls were redone in bright, cheerful colors and furnished with many of the things O'Neill and Carlotta had bought on their trip to the Far East. Hamilton Basso, who visited the apartment many times, noted a predominance of Chinese art objects, especially "a vaguely catlike animal mounted on a block of marble, who greets visitors with a look of innocent lechery as they step from the elevator." The cat was fashioned in stone by a Chinese sculptor centuries before Christ. O'Neill's library was full of French books, Basso noted, including complete sets of Zola, Hugo, Balzac. After talking with him, Basso concluded that O'Neill "knew French literature very well, especially Zola." He was well read also in the works of Stendhal, being particularly partial to *The Charterhouse of Parma.*

O'Neill's bedroom was a big, sunny room. On the walls were six reproductions of paintings of clipper ships as well as an oil painting of Broadway at the theater rush hour. O'Neill pointed to the clipper ships and to the painting and then said sadly to Basso: "It's the whole story of the decline of America. From the most beautiful thing man has ever made, the clipper ship, to the most tawdry street in the world."

For the first time, there was no dog; instead, in O'Neill's bedroom, there was a canary named Jeremiah, a gift from Carlotta. Rosie, the bawdy-house player piano, remained stored in San Francisco. In its place there was a phonograph with a large collection of records. O'Neill listed his preferences as Beethoven, Schubert, Cesar Franck and Irving Berlin.

One by one, O'Neill resumed his friendships in the East—that is, with friends who managed to penetrate the protective screen that was set up around him.

Barrett Clark came on March 17, St. Patrick's Day, and found O'Neill in good humor, speaking "with complete clarity, to the point [with] almost complete lack of self-consciousness." He noted, in O'Neill's conversation, "a sort of tolerantly humorous attitude toward life that was somewhat at variance with his ideas as they were worked into his plays." O'Neill, despite his illness, was alert, curious, had an interest in material things, concern with books and people, the theater, politics. For a while the two men talked together as fathers. Oona was not mentioned, but O'Neill told Clark that he enjoyed "my eldest, Eugene." O'Neill again observed that "this was an ideal relationship between a father and a son."

Clark advised O'Neill to re-establish his contact with the theater because, as he afterwards wrote, "we needed him, possibly he needed us." O'Neill took this with good grace. He was enthusiastic about the casting of *The Iceman Cometh.* It had now been decided that this, of the recent trio of plays, would be the first to go into production. The casting problems of *A Moon for the Misbegotten,* originally scheduled to be produced first, were proving extremely difficult.

O'Neill was loud in his praises of *The Iceman Cometh*. Clark would like it, he said, though he agreed there was not much action in the play. "Mere physical violence—mere bigness," he said, "is not important. You'll see that *The Iceman* is a very simple play—one set. I've certainly observed the Unities all right, characterization, but no plot in the ordinary sense; I don't need plot—the people are enough."

Band music from the St. Patrick's Day parade drifted into the windows of the O'Neill penthouse. "And why is it," Clark asked, "that a man bearing the name O'Neill is not marching?"

O'Neill flashed the wonderful smile that had endeared him to so many people. This was one O'Neill, it was understood between them, who would never march with the rest. This O'Neill always walked alone.

Readings of *The Iceman Cometh* began in May. James Barton was cast in the role of Harry Hope. O'Neill was impressed with Barton's sensitive reading of the part. It was now a new play to O'Neill; it was always this way when he heard one of his plays read for the first time. Throughout the summer of 1946, the Theatre Guild, the cast and the playwright worked on the rehearsals. Everyone knew that in a sense the play would constitute a kind of reopening of the Broadway theater after the war. It would be like old times —another O'Neill play on Broadway.

There was more pressure exerted on O'Neill than ever before to get him to cut the play. Langner gave him a copy of the play with passages marked where, in the producer's opinion, cuts were very much indicated. In a blue pencil O'Neill wrote boldly the word "no" opposite most of them. When he wrote "yes" it was in a tiny, faltering script. On the cover of the manuscript he handed back to Langner, he wrote: "The hell with your cuts! E.O'N."

In September, as the rehearsals came closer to being finished performances, Paul Crabtree, one of the actors, studied the script and figured out that O'Neill had made the same point eighteen times. He showed the fruits of his research to Langner who, he reckoned, would have the nerve to raise the point—or rather, the eighteen repeated points—with O'Neill. Langner has set down O'Neill's exact reaction: "Gene looked at me and replied in a particularly quiet voice, 'I intended it to be repeated eighteen times!' " Langner then observed that *The Iceman Cometh*, like Shaw's *Saint Joan*, would never be properly produced until the copyright had expired. Again O'Neill smiled. "It will have to wait," he said, "for just that."

Often the rehearsals of an O'Neill play would degenerate into a series of running battles between the playwright and the producer, the director and the actors. Invariably, O'Neill was able to stand his ground against them all.

A typical dispute during the rehearsals of *The Iceman Cometh* concerned the play's length, which seemed inordinate to several members of the company. When all other arguments failed, someone came to O'Neill and told him that the play was running at least twenty minutes too long and that a cut would have to be made. Why? O'Neill asked. It was then patiently explained to the author that the last commuting trains would have left Grand Central Station before the audience even got out of the theater.

O'Neill indicated succinctly that he was interested only in the play, not in whether the audience caught their trains. It was his play, and it would be done his way.

But as the rehearsals proceeded, the cast's affection and respect for O'Neill mounted. He knew the theater and he knew his play, and the actors were aware that he was part of America's theatrical heritage. Most of the time, O'Neill sat next to Eddie Dowling, the director. Dowling, O'Neill felt, tended to encourage the players to overplay their parts. The cast wanted to get the full implications of the play, its shadings and meanings, and O'Neill was always ready to explain his characters for the actors.

"Raw emotion," O'Neill said, "produces the worst in people. Remember, goodness can surmount anything. The people in that saloon were the best friends I've ever known. . . . Their weakness was not an evil. It is a weakness found in all men."

O'Neill tried to explain to the cast the meaning behind the extraordinary behavior of the habitués of the saloon—the meaning behind their deeply troubled words.

"Revenge," he said, "is the subconscious motive for the individual's behavior with the rest of society. Revulsion drives a man to tell others of his sins. . . . It is the Furies within us that seek to destroy us.

"In all my plays sin is punished and redemption takes place.

"Vice and virtue cannot live side by side. It's the humiliation of a loving kiss that destroys evil."

An eager, aggressive actor asked O'Neill where he stood on "the labor movement." (Two of the characters in the play are disillusioned radicals.)

"I am a philosophical anarchist," O'Neill said, smiling faintly, "which means, 'Go to it, but leave me out of it.' ".

At the end of September, the strain of the rehearsals began to tell on O'Neill, and he came down with flu. Karl Schriftgiesser, of *The New York Times,* who had only recently rewritten O'Neill's prepared obituary, called at the O'Neill penthouse and found the playwright dressed in corduroy slacks, blue sports jacket, and dark-red carpet slippers. Schriftgiesser wrote later of O'Neill's "deep, brooding eyes" which "now and again seem to lighten his thin, almost haggard face." O'Neill was chain-smoking an expensive brand of Egyptian cigarettes. In a cloud of blue smoke "an excitement suddenly lifted his voice" as he talked about the old days and the friends he had when he was living at Jimmy the Priest's and at Wallace's Hell Hole.

"I knew 'em all," O'Neill said. "I've known 'em all for years. All these people I've written about I once knew. I do not think you can write anything of value or understanding about the present. You can only write about life if it is far enough in the past. The present is too much mixed up with the superficial values; you can't know which thing is important and which is not.

"The past which I have chosen in the *Iceman* is one I knew. The man who owns this saloon, Harry Hope, and all the others—the Anarchists and Wobblies and French Syndicalists, the broken men, the tarts, the bartenders and even the saloon itself—are real.

"It's not just one place perhaps, but it is several places that I lived in at one time or another—places I knew, put together in one.

"What have I done with this setting? Well, I've tried to show the inmates of Harry Hope's saloon there with their dreams. Some, you see, have just enough money from home to keep them going; but most of 'em keep from starving with the aid of the free lunch. This old Tammany politician who runs the place lives with his dreams, too, and he loves these people for he is one of them in his way.

"You ask, what is the significance, what do these people mean to us today? Well, all I can say is that it is a play about pipe dreams. And the philosophy is that there is always one dream left, one final dream, no matter how low you have fallen, down there at the bottom of the bottle. I know because I saw it."

As O'Neill talked, he paused between sentences, editing his sentences as he spoke them. After a particularly long pause, he said, "It will take man a million years to grow up and obtain a soul." This theme was now recurrent in his conversation.

"I think I'm aware of comedy more than I ever was before," he said, "a big kind of comedy that doesn't stay funny very long." Yet before and after the production of *Iceman* he was in a jocular, uncharacteristically optimistic mood. "I'm happier now than I've ever been," he said. "I couldn't ever be negative about life. On that score, you've got to decide Yes or No. And I'll always say, Yes. Yes, I'm happy."

Then his tone turned gloomy and bitter. "I hope to resume writing as soon as I can . . . but the war has thrown me completely off base and I have to get back to it again. I have to get back to a sense of writing being worthwhile. In fact, I'd have to pretend." He was, he declared, enduring life "with enraged resignation. Outwardly, I might blame it on the war. . . . But inwardly . . . the war helped me realize that I was putting my faith in the old values and they're gone. It's very sad but there are no values to live by today. Anything is permissible if you know the angles."

In the light of the many provocative but conflicting statements the dramatist was making, it was scarcely any wonder that Marguerite Young, a reporter for the *Herald Tribune,* asked O'Neill if he didn't agree that he was "full of paradoxes."

"What did Walt Whitman say?" O'Neill asked. "He said, 'Do I contradict myself? Well, I contradict myself.' "

When Earl Wilson, the "saloon reporter" for the *New York Post,* called on O'Neill, the dramatist rose to the challenge. He regaled Wilson with tales of Jimmy the Priest's, describing it as "a hangout for broken-down telegraphers. I was always learning the international code from them. But it was always too late in the evening for me to be very receptive. So I never remembered it the next day."

O'Neill told Wilson that a juke box company had offered him one of its products on hearing how much he wanted one, but "someone" would not let him have it. Carlotta was occupied elsewhere in the penthouse, and O'Neill apologized for her not joining them, saying, "She's terribly busy killing cockroaches in the kitchen." Later, when Carlotta heard what her husband had said, she was furious. She telephoned Wilson and said there were no cockroaches in the O'Neill penthouse, and she had been occupied with cataloguing her husband's books.

When Wilson got O'Neill on the subject of *Long Day's Journey into Night,* a matter of the greatest curiosity to the theater world since presumably it would not be produced until twenty-five years after the author's death, O'Neill told him, "It is a real story, laid in 1912. There's one person in it who is still alive."

Instantly, Wilson wanted to know if it was O'Neill himself, and whether the play was his autobiography.

"I won't say a word about it," O'Neill replied.

But he permitted Tom Prideaux of *Life* to publish a passage from the play (which O'Neill then referred to as *The Long Day's Voyage into Night*). It was a passage of which he was apparently quite proud. Edmund Tyrone, the stage replica of Eugene O'Neill, is talking of his memories aboard a square-rigger while at sea. The passage ends with Edmund saying he will always be "a stranger who never feels at home, who does not want and is not really wanted, who can never belong, who must always be a little in love with death."

There were now so many requests for interviews with O'Neill that Joseph Heidt, the press agent for the Theatre Guild, decided to stage a mass interview at the Guild offices. It was the last time O'Neill ever talked to a group of reporters. The writers and reporters who turned up at the interview, many of them seasoned veterans, seemed far more nervous than O'Neill. In fact, it was O'Neill who put the group at ease by apologizing for speaking indistinctly. "Even my own family complains about it," he said.

One of the first questions brought up the matter of O'Neill's big cycle. Previously, O'Neill had described it as "a psychological drama of a family against the background of the drive toward material progress and the spiritual degeneration of the American people."

"I'm going on the theory," he now said, "that the United States, instead of being the most successful country in the world, is the greatest failure. It's the greatest failure because it was given everything, more than any other country. Through moving as rapidly as it has, it hasn't acquired any real roots. Its main idea is that everlasting game of trying to possess your own soul by the possession of something outside of it, too. America is the prime example of this because it happened so quickly and with such immense resources. This was really said in the Bible much better. We are the greatest example of 'For what shall it profit a man, if he shall gain the whole world and lose his own soul?' [Matthew 16:26] We had so much and could have gone either way.

"I feel, in that sense, that America is the greatest failure in history, but we've squandered our soul by trying to possess something outside it, and we'll end as that game usually does, by losing our soul and the thing outside it, too.

"Some day, this country is going to get it—really get it. We had everything to start with—everything—but there's bound to be a retribution. We've followed the same selfish, greedy path as every other country in the world. We talk about the American Dream and want to tell the world about the American Dream, but what is that dream, in most cases, but the dream of material things? I sometimes think that the United States, for this reason, is the greatest failure the world has ever seen. We've been able to get a very good price for our souls in this country—the greatest price perhaps that has ever been paid—but you'd think that after all these years, and all that man has been through, we'd have sense enough—all of us—to understand the whole secret of human happiness is summed up in that same sentence (from the Bible) which also appears in the teachings of Buddha, Lao-tse, and even Mohammed.

"If the human race is so damned stupid, that in two thousand years it hasn't had brains enough to appreciate that the secret of happiness is contained in [that] simple sentence, which you'd think any grammar school kid could understand and apply, then it's time we dumped it down the nearest drain and let the ants have a chance.

"I had a French friend, one of the delegates at the San Francisco Conference [of the United Nations] who came to see me. I asked him, 'If it's not betraying any great secrets, what's really happening at the Conference?' He shrugged his shoulders and said 'It's the League of Nations, only not so good.' And I believe it. Of course, I may be wrong. I nearly always am."

His home he regarded as New England and he added that "the battle of moral forces in the New England scene is what I feel closest to as an artist."

A woman reporter asked O'Neill how one could learn to be a playwright. O'Neill looked intently at her, and after a pause said: "Take some wood and canvas and nails and things. Build yourself a theater, a stage, light it, learn about it. When you've done that you will probably know how to write a play—that is to say if you can."

He said that Sean O'Casey was the "greatest living playwright." (Part of O'Neill's adulation for O'Casey may have sprung from the latter's remark, "You write like an Irishman, you don't write like an American." Nothing could have pleased O'Neill more.)

Another woman reporter at the interview asked about his having been quoted by Earl Wilson as saying the *Iceman* "consists of fourteen men and three tarts." O'Neill who often assumed a Victorian correctness and gallantry in the presence of the opposite sex, replied, "Fourteen men and three—uh—ladies." Asked what he was going to do opening night, he replied, with a gleam in his eyes, "If I weren't in temperance I'd get stinko."

There were glasses, ice and whisky on the sideboard. Heidt invited the reporters to have a drink when the interview was concluded, but nobody did.

The afternoon of the dress rehearsal, I interviewed O'Neill for a long piece I was doing for *Picture News, PM*'s Sunday magazine section. I found O'Neill on the darkened stage of the Martin Beck Theatre. Although I had interviewed many of O'Neill's friends in New London and was a personal friend of Eugene junior, I had never met the playwright before this time.

Around us were the sets by Robert Edmond Jones, O'Neill's old friend from his Provincetown days. We sat on a bench and talked about his early life. O'Neill seemed old and sick, but I disagreed with a recent description by a writer from *Time* who said, "his *paralysis agitans* involved his whole emaciated body in one miserable stammer."

He looked sharply at me as he talked, and his face was one that was difficult to put out of mind. He was well-groomed and expensively and quietly dressed in a double-breasted blue suit, but he gave the impression of a down-and-out man who had been completely outfitted the day before by some well-meaning friend.

He was still handsome. His hair was only slightly graying, a distinguished iron gray. He was thin and slightly bent over. His eyes were deep-set and sad, and occasionally he cocked his head as he eyed me. His jaw was lean and forceful.

When I told O'Neill that I was a friend of Eugene junior, and regarded him highly, a pleased look, half proud father and half grateful child, spread over O'Neill's face. He got up and walked over to a stage bar, pulled up a stool and sat there, motioning to me to join him. As O'Neill made himself comfortable at the bar, the conversation switched to the subject of the American Dream, a concept greatly advertised that year.

"Of course, America is due for a retribution," O'Neill said suddenly. "There ought to be a page in the history books of the United States of all the unprovoked, criminal, unjust crimes, committed and sanctioned by our government since the beginning of our history—and before that, too."

The trembling of his hands stopped. His eyes took on a new glow, a fierce intensity, as he continued. "There is hardly one thing our government has done that isn't some treachery—against the Indians, against the people of the Northwest, against the small farmers."

As he talked he seemed in the tradition of all great half-drunken Irishmen who sound off in bars all over the world, extravagant, rambling, full of madness and violence, but studded with enough essential truth, and insight to force you to listen with troubled fascination.

"This American Dream stuff gives me a pain," O'Neill went on. "Telling the world about our American Dream! I don't know what they mean. If it exists, as we tell the whole world, why don't we make it work in one small hamlet in the United States?

"If it's the Constitution that they mean, ugh, then it's a lot of words. If we taught history and told the truth, we'd teach children that the United States has followed the same greedy rut as every other country. We would tell who's guilty. The list of the guilty ones responsible would include some of our great national heroes. Their portraits should be taken out and burned." He was fondling a prop whisky glass and a prop bottle with water and caramel syrup in it.

As his words took on more and more vigor I realized that one could say of him then what his boss on the New London *Telegraph* had said of him in 1912— "He was the most stubborn and irreconcilable social rebel that I had ever met." He wrote about oppressed workers (*The Hairy Ape*) and about the tragedy of color discrimination (*All God's Chillun Got Wings*) long before they were fashionable subjects. I got the feeling that O'Neill's social views sprang from the very depths of his soul, from a deep abiding love of humanity, from a deeply cherished dream of what the world could be.

"The great battle in American history," he said, "was the Battle of Little Bighorn. The Indians wiped out the white men, scalped them. That was a victory in American history. It should be featured in all our school books as the greatest victory in American history."

O'Neill brought his fist down on the top of the bar. "The big business leaders in this country! Why do we produce such stupendous, colossal egomaniacs? They go on doing the most monstrous things, always using the excuse that if we don't the other person will. It's impossible to satirize them, if you wanted to."

The actors and stagehands began drifting back onto the stage. Two "grips" came to move the bar and we walked to the side. The conversation shifted to religion. Had he, I asked, returned to Catholicism, as one biography had implied he might? A look of sadness came into O'Neill's eyes. "Unfortunately, no," he said. "The *Iceman* is a denial of any other experience of faith in my plays. In writing it, I felt I had locked myself in with my memories."

The Iceman Cometh had an advance ticket sale of $262,000, and opened not once but twice. The first performance started at 5:30 P.M. on October 9, 1946, adjourned for an hour-and-a-half intermission, during which the Theatre Guild gave a dinner at the Astor, and ended well after eleven. The second "first night" was almost as elaborate a production. All in all, it was perhaps the greatest opening in Broadway history.

There was as much interest in O'Neill himself as in his new play. Both *Time* and *Life* assigned braces of writers, researchers, and photographers to get materials ready for big stories on the playwright. Reporters from papers all over the country, foreign correspondents, local New York feature writers, besieged the Theatre Guild's press agent for special interviews with O'Neill and for biographical details about him.

All this was not difficult to understand. O'Neill's return to New York was that of a man who had preached a message long years before and then had faded into limbo. So much had happened since the world had seen an O'Neill play produced—the depression, F.D.R. and the New Deal, the terrible years of World War II. As Samuel Grafton wrote, it was as if O'Neill had waited patiently in the wings for our little period of joy and hope to spend itself; now he comes out as one reminding us, almost with a leer, that life is a formless mess to be tempered, if at all, with alcohol and illusion."

There was one unfortunate occurrence on opening night which came close to being disastrous. James Barton, who played Hickey the salesman, entertained a party of friends in his dressing room. They included Babe Ruth, the baseball player, and his family. Barton's part was most taxing, especially in the last act. He should have been resting and especially he should have saved his talk for over the footlights. In the last act, Hickey tells the habitués of the saloon why he murdered his wife. He couldn't bear to have her forgive him over and over again for his sins. He never wanted her to wake up from her pipe dream that he, Hickey, would turn out all right. The speech, probably the longest in the history of the American theater, dominates the last act. Barton had little or no voice left when the time came to deliver the speech. At one point, he seemed to have forgotten his lines and a stage manager prompted him—a fact which he bitterly resented.

Nevertheless, at the final curtain it was apparent that the audience was deeply moved, and there was a great ovation. O'Neill, as was his custom, did not go to the opening. Langner reported to him by phone during the intermissions. After the show, Carlotta had the Langners and a few friends in for a light supper.

The reviews were extremely favorable. Brooks Atkinson said that although "Mr. O'Neill is detached from the modern theater, he is our most dramatic dramatist." Although Atkinson had some reservations and found the play difficult, he felt that O'Neill had forcefully reasserted the high standards of contemporary American theater. Rosamond Gilder of *Theatre Arts* saw the ultimate meaning of the play expressed by the line: "This lie of a pipe dream is what gives life to the whole misbegotten mad lot of us, drunk or sober." Miss Gilder was undoubtedly correct.

Eugene junior saw little of his father during this period and was not included in any of the social affairs surrounding *The Iceman's* opening. Cathy and Shane were not being received at all by either O'Neill or Carlotta. Cleon Throckmorton, who had done so many of the sets for O'Neill plays at the Provincetown Theatre, and who was seeing a good deal of Shane and Cathy at the Old Colony, decided they ought to see the play and took them as his guests.

Cathy was surprised that it was a success because it seemed "old-fashioned" to her. Shane said he thought he knew what his father was trying to say. It was somehow summed up in some things that Hickey said to his fellow down-and-outers at Harry Hope's saloon.

"I've never known what real peace was until now," were Hickey's words. "It's a grand feeling, like when you're sick and suffering like hell and the Doc gives you a shot in the arm and the pain goes, and you drift off. You can let go of yourself at last. Let yourself sink down to the bottom of the sea. Rest in peace. There's no farther you have to go. Not a single damned hope or dream left to nag you."

Shane's health declined steadily in the winter of 1945. He worked irregularly and, as a result, was continually borrowing small sums of money. His hands trembled, and he kept losing weight. Young Gene tried to talk to him, to give him advice; Shane would listen but would seem unconcerned. At cocktail parties in the Village it was observed that he didn't drink. On the other hand, he always looked as if he had a hang-over. Some people thought he acted "kind of queer." Joy Nicholson, the actress, once invited Cathy and Shane to a cocktail party and Shane spent his time there sitting inside the fireplace, his head part way up the chimney. It was rumored he was using other things than alcohol and "tea" to summon his particular pipe dreams.

Agnes, who had rented a house at Litchfield, Connecticut, to look after her mother, was in serious financial straits. Her alimony was considerably diminished now that Oona and Shane had come of age. Under the terms of the separation agreement, alimony was to continue even after O'Neill's death; but a year before, Winfield Aronberg, O'Neill's lawyer, had expressed the view it might be a good idea to work out a flat financial settlement because, as he expressed it, "alimony prevents wives from getting married." For the sum of $17,000, Agnes signed, in 1947, a release freeing O'Neill from any further obligation to her. After Agnes had settled her mother in the house at Litchfield, she asked Cathy and Shane to visit her, hoping the country and the change might improve Shane's health. It was a happy reunion, and while the couple were visiting there, Cathy learned she was pregnant for the second time. Agnes was overjoyed. "I felt as if God," she has said, "was sending a baby to replace little Eugene O'Neill."

But Shane's depressions continued. He was not earning any money now and had no savings. The prospect of having another baby intensified his anxiety. Meanwhile, Agnes told Cathy and Shane that she was going to be married to Morris Kaufman, a man she had met in New York and had known for several years. Kaufman, by this time a Hollywood producer, flew east, and they were married by a Justice of the peace at Elkton, Maryland. Kaufman immediately returned to the West Coast because of his work, and Agnes decided to give up the house in Litchfield and take her mother to California.

Before leaving, however, she had to attend to endless details in connection with Spithead in Bermuda. An old pre-O'Neill mortgage had to be paid off. Under the terms of the separation agreement possession of Spithead had now passed into the hands of Oona and Shane. Offers for the whole place, including the waterfront, the boat house, a cottage, and the great mansion, were as high as $125,000. But it was decided to sell the cottage separately and to continue leasing the main house. Oona and Shane divided the proceeds, about $9,000 apiece, and Oona turned her share over to Agnes.

During the time Agnes was negotiating for the flat settlement which freed O'Neill from paying her any further alimony, she read *The Iceman Cometh.* In the early scenes, Agnes saw about what she expected. There was the "Hell Hole" where she and Gene had met. There was a little of John Wallace, the Hell Hole proprietor, in the character of Harry Hope. Larry Slade was clearly the Terry Carlin of long ago. He had often stayed with Gene and Agnes at Peaked Hill. Agnes saw that Hugo Kalmar was Hippolyte Havel, and recognized the big Negro, Joe Mott, as the leader of the Negro community in Greenwich Village. The girls also recalled people she and Gene had known. Then came the last act and Agnes felt, as she heard Hickey making his great speech, that O'Neill could have been speaking directly to her.

"God, can you picture," Hickey was saying on the stage, "all I made her suffer and all the guilt she made me feel and how I hated myself! If she only hadn't been so damned good—if she'd been the same kind of wife I was a husband ... it isn't human for any woman to be so pitying and forgiving."

Agnes saw something of what Rosamond Gilder saw in the play. There is a force in the world, like the love that Hickey's wife bore her wayward husband, which mingles understanding and forgiveness. Does man find such love suffocating? In the saloon, Hickey was saying, "I couldn't forgive her for forgiving me. I caught myself hating her for making me hate myself so much."

A playwright is more than popular when he has a successful play on Broadway. Attempts were made to lionize O'Neill during the winter of 1946–47, but he had little heart for the fashionable circles to which he and Carlotta were invited. Carlotta enjoyed the company of Ilka Chase, Fania Marinoff, the Gish sisters, and a sprinkling of New York society people, but that winter O'Neill longed more than ever for the Hell Hole and his old friends.

At one party he was introduced to Irving Berlin by Russel Crouse, playwright and a former Theatre Guild press agent. O'Neill asked Berlin if he remembered a song called "I Love A Piano." Berlin went to the piano and started to play the old tune. O'Neill sang. It was then nine-fifteen, and Berlin did not get up from the piano until two the next morning. O'Neill became so excited he couldn't sleep that night.

But most of the time O'Neill was worried and anxious. He was at the peak of his powers and could not set to paper the great plays which were written in his brain and in his heart. He tried again and again to dictate to stenographers, to dictating machines. Nothing worked.

His leisure, tortured though it was, gave him more time to spend with his old friends. Then too, Freeman had returned from the wars and was acting as a combination butler and chauffeur. Sometimes he took O'Neill to see the prize fights or to the postwar "swing" joints. Young Eugene was seeing a lot of his father in New York that winter, but his relations with Carlotta grew increasingly edgy. She didn't like the publicity the son was getting; she felt that it reflected on the O'Neill name. During a Sunday lunch at the O'Neill apartment there was a discussion of the various articles which had recently been appearing on Eugene O'Neill and his work. The writer of one of the articles was a friend of Eugene's and a fellow Yale graduate whom Eugene had helped with advice and research. Carlotta denounced the article and the writer, largely because the publication in which the article appeared preached a liberal political philosophy. This man, she said, had tried to get her husband involved in politics. Politics change. Art never changes.

"My husband," she said, "is an artist. He should have nothing to do with politics."

Eugene rose from the table. "I have respect for scholarship," he said. "I will not listen to my friend's being spoken of in this fashion."

He went to the front door to leave, followed by his father, who pleaded with him to stay. Would he not, for the sake of their seeing each other, forget this? Carlotta was his wife. For the sake of peace? It was a sad and awkward moment.

In the end, Eugene decided it would be best if he left the city.

O'Neill's daughter, Oona, and her family in 1952

In Woodstock, New York, there was a piece of land which was adjacent to the home of a friend of his and afforded a magnificent view of the Catskills. Eugene asked his father to lend him eight thousand dollars to buy it with. He would build a house on it, put down roots and find serenity in the wild beauty of nature. O'Neill said that he would sign a note at the bank, but his son must keep the transaction a secret, especially from Carlotta. He said that he understood his son's wanting a place in the country, a place where he could feel he belonged.

In February, 1947, Eugene's stepfather, George Pitt-Smith, for whom he had a deep affection, died; he had been an invalid most of his life. A year later, Eugene's grandmother, Mrs. Katherine Senneth-Porter Jenkins, also died. The two deaths coming so close together, a friend of Eugene's has said, added to the sense of doom he felt was overtaking him.

He had been very close to his grandmother. During some of his early years he had lived with her on the upper West Side. She had told him stories of his family, of the courtship of his mother by Eugene O'Neill, of his descent from proud Corsican aristocrats. To her he had brought one of the first copies of his *Complete Greek Drama,* in which he had inscribed "To My Dearly Beloved Nana."

He was particularly distressed by the fact that his mother had no other relative in all the world but him. Furthermore, her only income was derived from her work as an editor on a Long Island weekly newspaper. What if he, Eugene junior, were to die? He brooded about this and finally took out a $25,000 life insurance policy, payable to his mother.

At times it seemed to Eugene that he was in direct competition with Carlotta for the favor of his father. When visiting at the penthouse he found himself wondering if he was in his father's house or in Carlotta's. Too often the evening ended with bickering between stepson and stepmother. At the end of one such evening, O'Neill walked to the door with this brilliant son of whom he was so proud.

"It's a strange thing," O'Neill said, "of all the women I treated badly—and there were many—I treated your mother the worst. And she was the one who gave me the least trouble."

There was nothing Eugene or anyone else could respond to that. Perhaps O'Neill required nothing but the saying of it, the saying of it to the son who gave him so much love and so little trouble.

CHAPTER

THIRTY

ຉຌ

THE LAST PLAY:

A MOON FOR THE

MISBEGOTTEN

The last play Eugene O'Neill wrote and the last play produced in his lifetime was *A Moon for the Misbegotten*. This laying bare of his brother's tortured soul has been called a requiem for James O'Neill II. When casting began early in February, 1947, a young actress named Mary Welch told the Theatre Guild people that she wanted to play Josie, the Irish giantess. She was not encouraged. Mary Welch, a dedicated actress, was a tall, handsome, strapping girl in her early twenties; she was of Irish descent and had an Irish pug nose to prove it. Her only failing was that she needed at least fifty more pounds to qualify for Josie. In 1946, she had played in Philip Barry's *The Joyous Season,* and was, as she said, "full of youthful arrogance."

Josie is a "great mother-earth symbol," one of the casting directors told her, "and the actress who plays her should have a range from farce to Greek tragedy."

Mary Welch insisted, and she was introduced to O'Neill, whom she regarded as the greatest playwright who ever lived. "He seemed more bone than flesh," she has written. "I liked him immediately; I like the look of men who carry no excess baggage."

The part of Josie, however, was written for a woman who carried plenty of excess baggage. Josie "is so oversize," O'Neill wrote in his casting directions, "that she is almost a freak—five feet eleven in her stockings and weighs around one hundred and eighty. Her sloping shoulders are broad, her chest deep with large, firm breasts, her waist wide but slender by contrast with her hips and thighs. She has long smooth arms, immensely strong, although no muscles show. The same is true of her legs. . . . She is all woman. . . . The map of Ireland is stamped on her face." O'Neill required that all members of the cast must be of Irish descent.

Miss Welch felt "purified" when she saw O'Neill staring at her. "Are you Irish with that pug nose?" he asked her. "What per cent? From what part of Ireland are your people? I want as many people as possible connected with my play to be Irish. Although the setting is New England, the dry wit, the mercurial changes of mood and the mystic quality of the three main characters are so definitely Irish."

Miss Welch replied that she was one hundred per cent Irish— "County Cork." O'Neill gave her the play to study and told her to come back and read. Two weeks later she read the part and one of the Guild officials commented that Miss Welch was "too normal for Josie's problem of feeling misbegotten." Another said she was not enough of a giant.

"That doesn't matter to me," O'Neill said. "She can gain some more weight, but the important thing is that Miss Welch understands how Josie feels. These other girls, who are closer physically to Josie, somehow don't know how tortured she is, or can't project it. The inner state of Josie is what I want. We'll work the other problem out in clothes and sets. I think the emotional quality is just right."

Apparently O'Neill was much taken with Miss Welch. He had her summoned to his penthouse before the final reading. "Hello Miss Welch—Mary," she reported him as saying. "I thought we'd just have a chat and a cup of tea before the final inquisition." He showed her his new television set, given him by a friend "so I can watch the fights."

He appeared to wish to impress her with his liberal views. (To have been anything but very leftish in the theater at that time was almost a social error.) His face took on a bitter and forceful expression, Miss Welch has said, "as he recalled how some of the New York professional crowd" had received his early plays about the Negro problem.

"They didn't really understand what I was writing. They merely said to themselves, 'Oh, look! The ape can talk!' " O'Neill said, with what Miss Welch thought was "true bitterness." She construed the outburst as an attempt by him "to furnish [me with] the pride and arrogance I lacked in meeting the demands of the part of Josie."

At the initial reading, under the direction of Arthur Shields, James Dunn read the part of Jamie Tyrone, and when he came to the part where the drunken Jamie had a prostitute in his stateroom on the train which was bringing his mother's body back east, he began to cry. Mary Welch also cried. O'Neill walked over to comfort her.

"Oh, here we go again!" he said. "I wept a great deal over Josie Hogan and Jamie Tyrone as I wrote the play."

The reading and the weeping continued until, according to Langner, Dunn said, "We're all crying now. I guess it will be the management's time to cry later." He spoke the truth.

During most of the three-week rehearsal period O'Neill was too ill to attend. He managed to get out of bed and to the theater on three occasions, to give the cast notes. Invariably, when he was not on hand to supervise his plays, it seemed that something happened to them. Something was wrong now, and Langner insisted that the play be tried out in the Middle West. O'Neill didn't like the idea, but he consented. He came to say good-by to the cast and talked a long time with Mary Welch.

"I know you will play Josie the way I want it," O'Neill told her.

"We embraced," Miss Welch told this writer, "and I told him some of the personal reasons why the part meant so much to me—things I have told no other person." Miss Welch noted after one meeting with O'Neill that "this man compels me to behave at my best level, to express the absolute core of whatever is my soul. I can only be me—honest, sincere, no matter how revealing."

After her long, intimate talk with O'Neill, Miss Welch felt "an unaccustomed relief on shedding all the layers of convention I had felt it necessary to assume for contact with other people." On opening night, he sent her a dozen red roses with a note reading, "Again, my absolute confidence."

In *A Moon for the Misbegotten,* Jamie is shown at the end of his days. His mother has died and he is doing his best to drink himself to death. Jamie comes to visit a farm left him in his father's estate and to see the old Irish tenant farmer and his mountain of a daughter, Josie. She soon loves Jamie. The father is afraid Jamie wants to throw him off the farm; he knows that a wealthy neighbor, an Englishman, wants to buy the place because the old man's pigs keep getting into his pond. (O'Neill drew upon his memories of a similar family and a similar situation in the New London of his boyhood, when he wrote this scene.)

The old man tries to get Josie to seduce Jamie, so that they can blackmail him into letting them keep the farm. At the end of the second act, Jamie comes, long after midnight, to keep a date with the big farm girl. He is drunk and prepared to treat her like a whore. Suddenly, thinking about the waste of his life, he quotes Keats:

> *Now more than ever seems it rich to die*
> *To cease upon the midnight with no pain,*
> *In such an ecstasy!*

The last words in the second act are Jamie's muttered opinion of himself: "You rotten bastard!" Above the set a full moon shines for this most misbegotten member of the misbegotten O'Neill clan, and Jamie falls asleep in Josie's arms.

Jamie reveals that he has had no intention of turning them off the farm, and Josie, who has loved him all the while, resolves that no advantage will be taken of him. In a most moving last scene, she bids him good-by. "May you have your wish and die in your sleep, Jim, darling. May you rest forever in forgiveness and peace." There is the final suggestion that the old man's design has been inspired only with the best interests of his daughter in mind. He wanted her to marry Jamie, and he was willing to lose her, all he had left in the world, if she could be happy.

Lawrence Langner thinks *A Moon for the Misbegotten* is "one of the greatest plays O'Neill has ever written . . . one of the few truly great tragedies written in our times." This is probably an overstatement but, given the weird components, *A Moon* is a strikingly effective play. Again it is too long, and again O'Neill indulged himself in too much of other people's poetry, but the play's early scenes are as funny and as broad as anything he ever wrote. And it is surprising how tender are the scenes between Jamie and Josie, a drunk and a freak. Only a very great writer could take these two and make them so sympathetic and so important to the audience.

When the play opened in Columbus, Ohio, on February 20,

1947, a number of people in the audience left the theater at the end of the second act. Langner asked the doorman why they were leaving. "I don't know," the doorman said. "They just said they were Irish."

Langner had feared that the robust, earthy language of the bogtrotter Connecticut Irish farmer, Josie's father, might offend them; lace-curtain Irish-Americans often took a dim view of the Irish characters in O'Neill's plays. Several cities later, the matter of the play's language arose to smite its producers.

In Detroit, the police ordered the play closed for obscenity. Armina Marshall—Mrs. Langner—who was acting as the associate producer of the show, met with the police officer who had issued the order. His principal objection was that the words "mother" and "prostitute" had been used in the same sentence.

"You've allowed *Maid in the Ozarks* to play here," Mrs. Langner said, "and yet you will not allow a play written by Eugene O'Neill, the greatest playwright in America, who won the Nobel Prize?" *Maid in the Ozarks* was a patently salacious play about the romance between a moonshiner and a slightly soiled waitress. It was advertised as "the worst play in the world."

"Lady," the police officer said, "I don't care what kind of prize he's won, he can't put on a dirty show in my town." He explained that he had "helped rewrite that play [*Maid in the Ozarks*], and we finally let it stay here." He lectured the cast of *A Moon* on what they could and could not say. Mary Welch noted down one of his edicts— "You can't say tart but you can say tramp."

The play closed in St. Louis on March 29, 1947. It was not until 1957 that it was presented on Broadway; then it had Franchot Tone, Wendy Hiller and Cyril Cusack in the major roles.

In that spring of 1947 O'Neill was ill at frequent intervals. The Guild said it would engage a new cast and reopen *A Moon,* but O'Neill said no. "Gene asked us," Langner has said, "to defer this until he was feeling better, and he also asked us to postpone the production of *A Touch of the Poet* for the same reason." And so *A Touch of the Poet* was not produced.

During the late spring, the summer and the fall, O'Neill cooperated with Hamilton Basso in assembling material for a three-part profile of himself for *The New Yorker.* This was the last time O'Neill was to work with a biographer. Beginning in June, Basso saw O'Neill in his apartment for a full afternoon every week until the end of

December, 1947. Basso, a scholarly and gentle Southerner, was a great admirer of O'Neill's work.

Basso told O'Neill that, twenty-one years before, he had passed the dramatist in Times Square. It was in the spring of 1926. Basso had just attended a performance of *The Great God Brown,* and was enthusiastic about it. Walking out of the theater into the balmy spring night he repeated to himself a line from the play which had particularly struck his fancy. It is in the last act, when Cybel, the mother, says, "Always again! Always, always forever again!—Spring again!—life again! but always, always, love . . . again." When Basso reached the subway entrance, he shouted the lines at the top of his voice. Suddenly he noticed that a man with deep-set eyes was staring at him; there was a faint smile on the man's face. It was Eugene O'Neill. The story pleased the playwright because it fitted in with one of his beliefs—that much of what happens to us in life is the result of accident.

Basso made voluminous notes during his interviews, some of which have survived. In his notebook occurs one of the best contemporary impressions of O'Neill, under the date, July 9, 1947.

"When I saw O'Neill this time," Basso wrote, "he seemed more subdued than on my previous visit when, discussing mutual remembrances and mutual friends, he was very cheerful and animated. He had a bad case of the New York blues, for he doesn't like the city and misses California a great deal. It's sad to hear him tell about the house he had out there. Being confined to his apartment and unable to work and without anything to occupy himself with, inevitably makes for a feeling of depression.

"It was one of those hot, muggy July days in the city and we sat in the living room of his apartment instead of out on the terrace."

"Although he is only in his late fifties, he looks like a man approaching seventy, at least. Remembering how he looked when I first saw him, over twenty years ago, and recalling the stories I had heard of his rather strenuous physical activity (he was an expert swimmer, for one thing) I was reminded of a clipper ship on the rocks." Basso noted that despite the playwright's infirmity, "he is still a handsome man; a thin, straight six-footer with a quiet air of authority. He is the only person I know whose face, in repose, wears an expression of almost unbelievable intensity. This largely comes from his eyes."

But, to offset this, Basso noted, O'Neill possessed a wonderful smile. "It lights up his whole face. If you want to go as far as Buck (Russel) Crouse (as I wouldn't) it lights up the whole room."

Over the months, Basso observed that the rigidity and shaking in O'Neill's hands and arms were now worse, now better. Generally, it gave him the appearance of "a man with palsy. He can hardly strike a match and, when it's very bad, impossible for him to lift a glass without spilling its contents all over."

O'Neill told Basso that "the severe racking palsy" was a violent aggravation of something he had had "all his life." Even when he was a young man, his hands trembled slightly. His mother's hands trembled in the same way, O'Neill said, and the failing may have been inherited. "But I'm sure," O'Neill told Basso, "I didn't help it any by drinking as much as I did."

It distressed Basso when O'Neill showed him his desk which was kept in readiness for the day when the trembling would stop and he could write again. "When I am writing I am alive," O'Neill had said. "I don't have to take vacations. For me writing is a vacation from living."

The desk was modern, of a light-colored wood. "There is something very sad about that desk," Basso wrote in his notebook. "O'Neill keeps his notebooks in the drawer and showed them to me. They are bound in red leather and contain the synopsis of his intended cycle of plays, now abandoned. His writing before his present illness was microscopically small. It is very beautiful handwriting."

At one of the last interviews, O'Neill talked about how it feels to be a playwright. A late autumn dusk was descending on Manhattan. He had never, he said, attended a performance of any of his plays. He satisfied himself with staying with them until the final dress rehearsal, offering suggestions and advice on matters of acting, directing, costuming, lighting and stage design. Then he let them go their own way.

"After you've finished a play," O'Neill told Basso between long silences, "and it goes into rehearsal it begins to go from you. No matter how good the production is, or how able the actors, something is lost—your own vision of the play, the way you saw it in your imagination."

"I don't think acting is as good as it used to be," O'Neill continued. "Type casting is a bad thing. You don't get actors and actresses by asking them to go out on the stage and play themselves. You just don't. It's not a good thing either for playwriting. The playwright comes to depend on the physical presence of the actors to fill out their characters for him, instead of writing his characters into the script. Whether my plays are good or bad—though I hope some of them are good—I've tried to do that, anyway. I've always tried to *write* my characters out. That's why I've sometimes been disappointed in the actors who played them—the characters were too real and alive in my imagination."

The talk of the two writers turned to length. It was always a problem in writing novels, but perhaps not as much so as in writing plays, Basso thought. "As for length—well," O'Neill said, "if you can't hold an audience for three minutes, three minutes is too long. If you can get them to listen to you for three hours, three hours may not be long enough."

Toward dinner time, Carlotta came into the apartment. She had been out shopping. "But Gene," she asked, "why are you sitting in the dark? Why don't you turn some of the lights on? It's so *gloomy*." As she went from lamp to lamp Basso watched O'Neill's face emerge from the shadows.

"I'm supposed to be a gloomy fellow," O'Neill said. "Hadn't you heard?"

"You can be gloomy enough, sometimes," Carlotta answered. "But why do they always have to exaggerate? Nearly everything that has been said about you is all wrong. Have you had coffee? Oh, Gene, you never think of anything! I'll get it for you."

"What Carlotta just said is true," O'Neill said, snuffing out his cigarette in an ashtray. "Nearly everything that has been said about me *is* all wrong."

Basso noticed that two shelves of books back of O'Neill were given over to English and American poets, and the talk turned to poetry.

"Richard Dana Skinner has written a book about me," O'Neill said, "It's called *Eugene O'Neill: A Poet's Quest*. I don't agree with many things he says, but that just about sums it up. It has been a poet's quest."

The smell of percolating coffee drifted into the living room.

"It's very hard right now," O'Neill said, "not being able to work. I want to get going again. Once I get over this thing—these shakes I have—I feel I can keep rolling right along."

It was Basso's last visit. Before the time came for his next session, he received a telephone message that O'Neill was ill and would be unable to continue the interviews. Fortunately, Basso had enough material to complete the profile, which was published in *The New Yorker* the following February and March after the manuscript had been sent to O'Neill for approval.

The illness that abruptly terminated the interviews was the indirect result of an unhappy event in the life of O'Neill and Carlotta. One afternoon, they were sitting in their living room entertaining friends. The phone rang and Carlotta, as usual, answered.

"Gene, it's for you," Carlotta said, with an edge to her voice. "It's one of your old friends."

There was some reason for her sarcasm. Ever since their return to New York, two years before, old friends ranging from school friends and Hell Hole companions to old Provincetown Players had been trying to reach him—wanting money, a favor, or just to see him.

O'Neill walked to the phone, and one of those present that afternoon heard him say:

"Why yes, Fitzy. Oh. . . .

"Certainly, Fitzy, will one hundred be enough?

"I'll mail it to you right away. Where?

"Oh. Yes. Mount Sinai Hospital."

The person calling that afternoon was more than just an "old friend." She was M. Eleanor Fitzgerald, who, with Robert Edmond Jones, Kenneth Macgowan and O'Neill, had opened the Provincetown Playhouse in New York in 1921. "It was Fitzy who kept us all working together," Macgowan said when she died in New York in 1955, "in some sort of harmony . . . Everyone loved Fitzy and Fitzy loved everyone but she took no nonsense from any of us." Edmund Wilson has said that Miss Fitzgerald "though practical, was a pure idealist . . . everybody . . . who knew Fitzy was touched by an essential nobility that seemed proof against bitterness and disappointment."

It is doubtful whether Carlotta grasped all this. There were bitter words between O'Neill and Carlotta after O'Neill had hung up. Her jealousy of all O'Neill's old friends became uncontrolled when he defended Fitzy and the others. Finally Carlotta left the apartment. She did not return that night or the next day. O'Neill tried in every way to find out where she was; he even hired private detectives to locate her. Later, in January, he had still not found her. His *paralysis agitans* grew alternately better and worse. Sometimes it was partly remedied by his drinking hot black coffee. Saxe Commins, Walter

"Ice" Casey, and Bill Aronberg came to his apartment as often as they were able. One night, while only Walter Casey was present, O'Neill slipped and fell in his bedroom, and fractured his right arm. Casey called Dr. Shirley Carter Fisk, who in turn called Saxe Commins. Dr. Fisk said O'Neill, who was in great pain, would have to go at once to the hospital. Saxe Commins went along to Doctors Hospital with O'Neill in the ambulance and signed his admitting papers. O'Neill's arm was set and put in a cast but because he remained in frightful pain, Commins spent the night at his bedside. A spokesman for the hospital told *The New York Times* that, in addition to his broken arm, "Mr. O'Neill was facing a nervous breakdown." It was also rumored at the time that O'Neill had gone off the water wagon for the first time since his spree in Shanghai in 1928. Whatever the exact truth, O'Neill was to remain hospitalized for fifty-three days.

Carlotta has offered some explanation of O'Neill's violent behavior toward her at this time. She has said that O'Neill, who was thinking of death a great deal during the late 1940s, was so disturbed that he could not work. This was enough to drive him to irrational acts.

Agnes noticed early in their marriage that O'Neill possessed a marked sadistic streak in him. On several occasions he struck her. Carlotta told friends that his mood changed, sometimes, with the moon. His outbursts of sadism continued, as might be expected, into his third marriage. Ordinarily he was gentle, almost childlike, softspoken. Then in a flash he could change, and his behavior has been described, by those who witnessed it, as savage. Afterward would come the overwhelming guilt and no man was more miserable than O'Neill when guilt provoked his self-torture.

Both Carlotta and Agnes have expressed the view that O'Neill, like many sensitive people, was capable of extreme cruelty. A really sensitive person, they feel, can move in opposite directions simultaneously, expressing joy and sorrow, hate and love, cruelty and tenderness, almost in an instant. Others have suggested that O'Neill's great attraction for women was just this curious mixture of cruelty and tenderness.

Eugene junior went to see his father at Doctors Hospital. After talking about what had taken place between himself and Carlotta, O'Neill said: "Go find her! Carlotta is many things but I cannot live without her."

But even before O'Neill left the hospital he and Carlotta were reconciled. Apparently she became ill herself, and she took a room next to his. She had been staying at a hotel not far from their penthouse. On April 19, 1948, O'Neill was discharged, and he and Carlotta resumed their life together. When Shane came to call, the doorman announced him on the house phone and then said Mr. and Mrs. O'Neill were not in. Shane refused to believe this. He went upstairs and knocked on his father's door. No answer. He paced up and down in the hall for several hours. Aronberg, his father's attorney arrived and told Shane that he would have to leave, that his father did not want to see him. There was a mild scuffle but, in the end, Shane went away.

O'Neill and Carlotta now definitely decided to leave New York. The playwright said he was more than ever convinced that he hated the place. He felt sick and run-down. Late in April he went to Boston to be treated at the Lahey Clinic. He and Carlotta stayed at the Ritz-Carlton in rooms overlooking the Boston Common. They took every precaution to keep their whereabouts a secret but that did not prevent Langner from visiting in the summer of 1948 in hopes of getting an O'Neill play into production again. O'Neill told Langner that he was glad to be out of New York and talked about how much he enjoyed living in Boston; it was like home, for he had once spent a year there when he was studying at Professor Baker's Workshop. But he did not feel like having any of his plays produced.

On August 10, 1948, a telephone call was received at the O'Neill apartment in the Ritz-Carlton. It was from Aronberg. Shane had been arrested and imprisoned in New York City by the Federal authorities for possessing heroin.

CHAPTER

THIRTY-ONE

ဆ

SHANE'S PIPE DREAMS

Stammering, O'Neill once said, is the "native eloquence of we fog people." Perhaps he was thinking not only of himself but of Shane. If ever there was a child of the fog it was Shane, conceived by the sea and born by the sea. As an infant, Shane could hear the bells tolling their warning, the sea lashing at the Provincetown coast line. "The fog was where I wanted to be," his father once wrote. "I was a ghost belonging to the fog, and the fog was the ghost of the sea."

After Agnes, with her dying mother, went to the Coast to join her new husband, Shane sank deeper and deeper into one of the depressions that periodically plagued him. At last, he and Cathy decided that it might be a good idea to leave New York, for a long time. They left it, but not for long. The place they chose to go to was appropriate to Shane's mood—Key West, a haven for wandering artists and writers by the sea. It was not long before Agnes had to send them money. Cathy was pregnant again, and she and Shane made their way north to St. Cloud, Florida, not far from Orlando, where Cathy's mother lived. There Shane's third child was born on February 15, 1948. They named her Maura. The new baby brought some comfort to Cathy; to Shane she brought the terrifying realization that, once again, he had given a hostage to fortune.

As soon as Cathy was well enough to travel, she and Shane returned to New York. They sublet a cold-water flat on Ninth Street near First Avenue. It was located in the gashouse district above the lower East Side. Shane went back to work for Rowland's display studio in Greenwich Village. It was not long after this that he fell in with a group of people who were on "horse," or "H," as they called heroin.

"Shane got in with this bunch," Cathy has said, "who were taking the stuff. I didn't know it. I did know that I didn't like them. There was one guy in particular, named Jamie, that Shane saw a lot of. I guess he was a junkie."

It was during the spring and early summer of 1948, that Shane's addiction to heroin grew to alarming proportions. The cost of feeding this habit was, of course, ruinous. He spent all the money he had been able to obtain from his mother. He borrowed money wherever he could. Soon, he was disposing of every salable object in his apartment.

Exactly when Shane became addicted to drugs, or why can be answered only partly by available facts. Authorities in this field do not know precisely why one sick person can take drugs to relieve pain with impunity, whereas another, taking an equal amount, becomes an addict. Shane, of course, was close to being an alcoholic when he began smoking marijuana. Although marijuana is said not to be habit-forming, it is quite common for those who come to use it heavily to "go on to other things." Shane went "on to other things" in 1942, when he shipped aboard a merchant marine vessel and started taking morphine pills from the first-aid kits. He was twenty-four then.

In recent years, psychiatrists have been suggesting that there is often some defect in an addict's personality which makes his self-destruction so thorough and violent that his chances for complete recovery are meager. In the light of many of their findings, it is not difficult to see wherein lay the seeds of Shane's addiction. One authority, for example, found that in more than half the cases he studied "there was evidence of psychosis, neurosis, or alcoholism in near relatives." Viewed in context with the facts of Shane's life, a statement by Dr. James A. Lowery, head of the United States Public Health Service Hospital at Lexington, Kentucky, is significant.

"The personal history of many of these patients [at Lexington]," the statement reads, "shows the absence of the father, or a weak father or mother, during the patient's childhood."

Shane attributes his final descent to association with other addicts. He said he smoked marijuana because all his friends were smoking it. Later on it was heroin. "It was a social thing. It's something you do with other people. I was going with a group of people who all took heroin. Not taking anything made me feel embarrassed, out of place. I felt that unless I took something I'd be a poor sport. So I tried it and I liked it."

It was not long before he became an out and out "junkie." He let his clothes become dirty and rumpled. He did not eat and he grew thinner and thinner. He acquired the language and social attitudes of the junkies, who were then building up a language and a kind of depraved folklore of their own.

The fact that Shane was Eugene O'Neill's son soon became known to his fellow junkies. "It had its advantages," Shane has said, "and its disadvantages. Some of the pushers were afraid to let me have any buys [packs of heroin] because they figured if I got caught, there'd be a lot of publicity and they might get into serious trouble. Some of the guys, on the other hand, thought that, on account of my father, I might have good connections for getting H."

Shane's earlier retreats from life—in liquor, in marijuana, in morphine—were largely a matter of providing himself with relief from the depression that had plagued him most of his life, but his addiction to heroin provided him with something more than escape from the pain of living.

"Taking it," he has told a friend, "gives you something to live for. You have a goal in life—getting the stuff and earning enough money to pay for it. I know people who make fifteen, twenty, twenty-five thousand dollars a year just so they can earn enough to keep using H."

By the middle of the summer of 1948, Shane was hopelessly addicted. The cost of his habit, when he was able to obtain the money, had reached thirty dollars a day. The more "caps" he used, the more he needed. Consumption of heroin does not remain static.

He and a friend named Jimmy wandered through the city together or holed up in furnished rooms with other addicts. Cathy remained in the apartment caring for Maura, but sometimes Shane and his addict friends would come back and stay. Shane and Jimmy obtained most of their buys of heroin from a pusher whose area was Greenwich Village. On Tuesday afternoon, August 10, Shane obtained enough money to buy three capsules of heroin, but was unable to establish contact. Jimmy said he had a connection on the waterfront. It happened that the waterfront pusher was at the time under surveillance by agents of the United States Treasury's Bureau of Narcotics.

Shane and his friend arrived at the appointed place a few minutes ahead of time. When the pusher turned up, Shane gave him four dollars and a half for a packet containing three capsules, then he and Jimmy hurried away, followed by T men. Other T men followed the pusher.

As soon as the agents nabbed Shane and his friend, Shane threw the packet on the sidewalk, just as other addicts had cautioned him to do in the event of arrest. The agents retrieved the evidence and took the two friends downtown to the Federal Building at 90 Church Street. There, they were searched and questioned. Neither would reveal the names of any of the dealers who had been supplying them with heroin. Although Shane's friend remarked that one of the three "caps" was for him, this fact in itself was not deemed sufficient evidence to hold him. He was released and went immediately to Shane's apartment to tell Cathy the news.

Meanwhile, Shane was booked, fingerprinted, and placed in a cell at the Federal Detention Headquarters. When an agent volunteered to make a telephone call to his family, Shane gave him the name and address of his father's lawyer. Aronberg said that O'Neill was in Boston but he would telephone him and find out what he wanted to do. He called back to say O'Neill would have nothing to do with the case. Shane was on his own.

The next morning Shane was questioned in the office of the United States Attorney; afterward, his bail was fixed at five hundred dollars and he was held for the Grand Jury.

Cathy set about finding out what she could do to get Shane out of jail. The next day she, too, called O'Neill's lawyer. He told her O'Neill was ill and could do nothing. He said they didn't want him to know about Shane. Several days went by and Shane was still in jail. Eventually, a friend of the Shane O'Neills' made arrangements with Harrington Harlowe, an attorney, to take Shane's case. Harlowe went down to the Federal Detention Headquarters and talked with Shane. He then went to see Cathy.

"Cathy and the little baby, Maura, were a forlorn sight," Harlowe has said. "There was practically no furniture in the apartment. She told me of some people I might call to get in touch with O'Neill. I finally got his Boston apartment on the phone. I talked to a woman who, I think, was Mrs. O'Neill. She told me she would speak to Mr. O'Neill and to call back later. I did and was told to see O'Neill's New York attorney. I went around to see him and he said he would find out what O'Neill wanted to do and let me know. The next day we met again and he told me, in effect, O'Neill was going to have nothing to do with the boy. I got the impression that O'Neill had pretty definitely washed his hands of the whole thing."

A week later, on Tuesday, August 17, Shane was brought before the Federal Grand Jury and was indicted. Meanwhile he underwent the onset symptoms of being suddenly without drugs. His flesh became heavily goose-pimpled, a withdrawal symptom which has given this traumatic illness its name—"cold turkey." Beads of sweat appeared all over his body. His muscles jerked. Tears flowed from his eyes and his nose ran. Cramps doubled up his body, and, from time to time, he vomited. His temperature and blood pressure rose. Finally, an ambulance surgeon was called and Shane was administered a shot of morphine with a hypodermic needle. The shots of morphine were repeated so that he was not subjected to a protracted withdrawal period.

Eugene junior, reached by telephone in Woodstock, told Aronberg that there wasn't anything he could do. He did not have the money for bail, and he said that there was nothing to be gained by his coming down to New York. He had his own problems.

Cathy visited Shane in jail and talked to him through a heavy wire mesh screen. She told him that there was no way of arranging bail. He was bitter that no one seemed to love him enough to help him.

"I remember Shane didn't seem to mind the jail too much," Cathy has said. "He talked about the other prisoners, all kinds of thieves and what not. He said he liked the guys inside."

Harlowe, who worked on Shane's case without fee, learned that the government would drop the prosecution of Shane if he agreed to go to the hospital at Lexington for a minimum of four months, or until discharged as cured. This would require Shane to plead guilty to the charge of possessing "approximately three grains of heroin on or about August 10, 1948." Harlowe explained that he recommended this because he had seen addicts who had gone there voluntarily and had been able to stop taking drugs. Shane agreed to follow Harlowe's suggestion.

The case of the United States of America versus Shane Rudraighe O'Neill was called on Friday morning, August 20, 1948, before Judge Harold R. Medina. There were no friends or relatives of Shane's or Cathy's present in court.

"At the time Shane O'Neill was brought before me," Judge Medina has said, "I was serving in the criminal division of our district court and I can tell you I didn't like it. I hate judging my fellow man."

In this instance, Judge Medina's duty was even more painful. The judge is a Princeton alumnus, and his two sons are Princeton men. Judge Medina was a sophomore at Princeton when O'Neill senior was a freshman.

"It was a shock to see the boy," Judge Medina has said, "when he was brought before me. He looked terrible, down and out, disheveled, dirty, dressed in rags. I could only feel the deepest sorrow for him, he looked so lost, so bewildered. I got that feeling I so often got when I was serving in the criminal division—there but for the grace of God go I. I wanted to help him. I wanted him to feel I wanted to help him. I knew that going to Lexington doesn't always help these addicts. I knew that an institution is not the best place in the world. I tried to think what I could say that would let him know there was someone who wanted to help him. I tried to think of something to say that would build up his morale."

Judge Medina turned to Shane and said he had a suggestion to make to him. "You have got a real chance here," he said, "and it may, as these things go, be your last chance. Now take advantage of it and you may find, when you get down there, some things that may be hard to take, all the way down the line, but if you just make a resolution that you are really going to take advantage of this it will fix you up for life and you will be all right. Now try to do it."

Shane listened intently to Judge Medina. "Thank you, sir," he said, "I will attempt to."

Judge Medina thereupon remarked, "I want you to know while

you are down there any time you have something on your chest that is worrying you, you can write to me as you would write a friend and I will treat it just that way."

Shane spent Friday, Saturday, and Sunday in his apartment at 151 First Avenue with Cathy and Maura. He said he was not surprised that his father had refused to do anything about his trouble. His father was not well, he pointed out. He was still bitter, however, that no one had produced his five-hundred-dollar bail. The ten days he'd lain in jail, alone and forgotten, had seemed like a lifetime to him. Even criminals made bail, he said. He was philosophical about going to Lexington. He said he was determined to be cured of his addiction.

Cathy told him she would make out all right. He should get cured and not worry about her and Maura. She would stay with her father in Stamford for a while and then probably go on down to her mother's in Florida.

Early Monday morning Shane reported to the United States Marshal in the Federal Court House and, with other addicts, was taken in a bus to Lexington. Afterward, he said, "It's a tremendous place, wonderful food. I met several people right off I knew." He adjusted quickly and was given a job on the hospital farm milking cows and doing odd jobs. One thing that made his stay at Lexington easier, Shane feels, is that he did not have to go through a withdrawal period. He had been through that at the Federal prison in New York. He liked working on the hospital farm because he had always liked caring for animals.

Left to shift for herself and her baby, Cathy again called on O'Neill's lawyer to ask whether there would be any possibility of getting assistance from Shane's father. According to Cathy, the lawyer said, "Gene is so sick, we don't want him to know about this."

Agnes and her husband reached New York about Christmastime and went on to Bermuda to recondition and rent Spithead. They were there when they learned that Shane was in Lexington. Agnes was distressed to learn that Eugene had been informed of his son's predicament and had done nothing to help him. But O'Neill's apparent inability to face the problem of drug addiction in this instance was, perhaps, understandable in the light of his earlier experience with it. His first and perhaps only genuine reaction was horror, the horror that he had felt regarding his mother's addiction. And it has been suggested that he was burdened with a powerful guilt feeling arising from the notion that the pain of his birth caused his mother's addiction. The horror and the guilt are both unforgettably dramatized in *Long Day's Journey into Night,* but his re-creation of these emotions did not signify his mastery of them. Besides, by 1948 Eugene O'Neill was indeed seriously ill and had aged horribly—both physically and spiritually. He was no longer master of his own destiny.

CHAPTER

THIRTY-TWO

೧೪

THE VULTURES IN

FULL FLIGHT

The image of O'Neill that emerges at this time is that of a man isolated from his children and insulated from the world. How much of this was due to his own desires, and how much to the maneuvers of those who wished to guard him from further shocks, may never be known. One thing is certain: He was a sick man, without hope or belief that he would get well. It seemed that he was yielding himself completely to his lifelong, if sometimes dormant, "infatuation with oblivion." It may be, too, that he did not wish to get well if it meant survival with his affliction and, in consequence, inability to resume his career.

He once told this writer why he had always sought solitude: "I kept writing because I had such a love of it. I was highly introspective, intensely nervous and self-conscious. I was very tense. I drank to overcome my shyness. I could scarcely write, if at all, and live in the city. I would pick a place out of the ordinary run of places to do my writing. When I was writing, I was alive."

In 1948 he had once again begun to dream of finding a permanent home, and the first prospective new location he had looked at was Provincetown. What might have moved him in that direction, he never said; but evidently he did not find it, and he did not stay there long. The Provincetown he knew no longer existed; the fishing village he once loved had become a seaside resort, it seemed to him.

By midsummer he and Carlotta had found a modest, one-and-a-half-story white clapboard summer house in an exclusive section of Marblehead, on the Massachusetts coast. It was right on the sea—"with my feet in the Atlantic," O'Neill reported. Carlotta, who bought the place out of her "reserve fund" was less enthusiastic and referred to it as "dinky . . . one of those summer cottages." Nevertheless she put the house, which was located on Point o' Rocks Lane, in her name and proceeded to do it over at considerable expense.

O'Neill said that he felt as if he was coming home at last. He was even hopeful for a little while that he was going to write again. He told Bill Aronberg, who came up to see him, that this was the first piece of waterfront property to be sold in this neighborhood in years. The house was built in 1880 and was like the house his father had bought his mother in New London. Here in New England beside the sea, O'Neill said, he felt that he had roots. Perhaps that had been his mistake—leaving the edge of the sea. Spithead, too, had been at the very edge of the sea, but it was a safe sea protected by Hamilton Harbor. He spoke of Point o' Rocks to Saxe Commins as "our last home."

(Bessie Breuer, O'Neill's old friend, has suggested that if he had lived he would have ended up right back in New London. "It was as if, like a bird, he had been circling the whole world," she has said, "each time coming closer and closer to the town in which he and his family had lived for so long.")

Soon O'Neill was feeling well enough to write letters to friends in New York. The words, though distinguishable, still looked as if they were made by a seismograph. He said he guessed he was stuck with some kind of tremor for the rest of his life. But the world, too, was in a tremor, so he supposed he shouldn't mind.

But when he was not writing, he was not "alive." In 1948 he joined the Euthanasia Society of America, whose purpose was to legalize the "act or practice of mercifully ending the life of an incurable sufferer." Later, he became so convinced of the importance of the work of this society, founded by the aristocratic Boston divine, Charles Francis Potter, that he accepted membership on its "American Advisory Council."

During the winter of 1948–49, O'Neill and Carlotta seemed to find peace again. "I made that place into a beautiful little house," Carlotta has said. The privacy that O'Neill said he wanted was readily available. It is a tradition in the little New England town that "Marbleheaders keep to themselves." The O'Neill neighbors remained close-mouthed about them. The Yankee postman allowed that the O'Neill mail was "very heavy."

O'Neill actually seemed to be getting better in 1949. Drugs appeared to alleviate the trembling of his hands, and visitors at Point o' Rocks reported that he was showing "remarkable improvement." He even went occasionally to the local movies with Carlotta. He had started to work on a new play which had nothing to do with his cycle. Richard Madden, his agent, said that the dramatist "was very much improved. Furthermore his whole tone and attitude over the phone are very bright indeed." Madden corroborated the report that O'Neill was able to write again in longhand.

But the optimistic reports of O'Neill's recovery turned out to have been premature. On November 4, 1949, when Carlotta was asked how he was making out with his writing, she replied, "He hasn't worked for three years, and God knows if he ever will be able to." She said he had tried to compose a play by dictating to a secretary but "discovered he couldn't work that way. It's terrible. It gets worse. The hands tremble and then the feet." Once, about this time, when he was told that a friend had died, he commented, "There's a lot to be said for being dead."

In June, 1950, Aronberg called O'Neill and told him that some of his early plays, deposited in the Library of Congress, had been discovered and, being without copyright, were regarded as in the public domain and publishable by anyone. O'Neill did not want them published, but he was too ill to do anything about it. He said he didn't think the plays were any good and were "not worthy of publication."

Despite a statement to this effect, which Aronberg issued on O'Neill's behalf, the Fathoms Press, otherwise unknown to literature, issued a volume titled *Lost Plays of Eugene O'Neill*, which consisted of one long play called *Servitude* and four one-acters—*Abortion, The Movie Man, The Sniper,* and *A Wife for a Life.* Their unauthorized publication distressed many people and raised the question whether an author cannot exercise control of writing he has done years before.

When Langner came to visit again in Marblehead, he begged to be allowed to produce *A Touch of the Poet* with "a certain director of whom O'Neill approved."

"I don't believe," O'Neill said, "I could live through a production of a new play right now." When Langner presented new arguments, O'Neill said, "No! That's my last word on the subject."

Neighbors now reported that O'Neill had stopped going to the movies. It was gossiped that "even old friends who come from far away rarely get to see him." Dr. Frederick B. Mayo, a Swampscott physician, was said to be making repeated visits, and rumor had it that both O'Neill and Carlotta were very ill.

In Hollywood, Oona had had her third baby, O'Neill's fifth grandchild. But he was estranged from Oona, as he was from Shane. Shortly after Shane's release from Lexington, he and Cathy and Maura had flown down to Bermuda where they stayed two years, at first living with Agnes and Mac at Spithead, then later in a small cottage on the hillside. Cathy was pregnant again and, when Agnes and Mac returned to the United States to look after Agnes' mother, the Shane O'Neills were left alone. On the evening of December 20, 1949, one hour after the doctor had said that the baby was not due for six hours, Cathy gave birth to a girl, whom they later named Sheila. The doctor had gone, and Shane assisted in the delivery. "I was really flustered," he has said. "Fortunately, Cathy directed me what to do."

As for Eugene junior, his life had been out of control for some years now. Along with his teaching schedule, young Eugene had continued to pursue his career in radio and television, and also did readings for "Talking Books" for the blind. He was a regular panel member of CBS's "Invitation to Learning," chairman of a series called "Children's Classics," and from time to time he was a panelist on "Author Meets the Critics." Martin Stone, the producer, remembers that Eugene was generally broke during this period. They used to meet late in the afternoon at the Yale Club taproom. "I remember in particular that he never talked about his father," Stone has said. "He was always worried about money. He used to order a beer and let the cocktail hour tidbits serve as his dinner—that's how broke he was. I figured he had a great future. He was talented and I was glad to put him on the show."

Early in March, 1947, Eugene destroyed in a few minutes all hope of a successful career in television. At first, he would carefully prepare for each of his appearances. He was well-informed, articulate; his resonant voice and his clear diction were impressive. Whatever the subject under discussion, he was able to comment intelligently. His beard, his good looks, his lively intelligent eyes, his agreeable manner, gave him a unique, almost unforgettable appearance.

The night Eugene O'Neill, Jr., wrecked his career, he was scheduled to appear as a critic of a book, *It Took Nine Tailors,* by Adolphe Menjou. Several days before the program, Stone had asked Ruth Lander, a close friend of Eugene, to make sure to have Eugene dress reasonably well for this appearance. Ruth knew that getting Eugene to dress well for *anything* was a matter to be handled with care, and she worked hard at it.

On Sunday evening, March 23, Eugene turned to Ruth and said, "Let's see. Tonight we're reviewing the movie actor's book." He stressed the word movie. "He is the best-dressed man in America, they say. Well, then, I shall be the worst-dressed." Eugene carefully picked out a rumpled suit and a shirt with a frayed collar. At dinner, he drank two Martinis. He complained of a cold.

"He felt terrible," Ruth has said. "He was getting some kind of flu. I think he had taken a lot of aspirin or something. The Martinis seemed to go straight to his head."

When they arrived at the studio, Martin Stone took one look at him and said, "Oh, God!" It was too late to do anything about replacing him. Word flashed around among the studio executives, "O'Neill junior is drunk." Menjou was smooth and polished. Eugene scowled at him. The cameraman kept the camera off Eugene as much as possible. Only once or twice was he able to get in a comment. He was thick-tongued. Menjou put on a brilliant performance as did the other panelists, and a minimum amount of damage was done. But in television a performer appears drunk only once.

In 1947, Eugene adequately filled his teaching post at Princeton for the first term. During the second term, he failed to appear for some of his lectures. When he did turn up for classes he often looked unwashed, unshaved and generally disheveled; he was either drunk or suffering from a terrible hang-over. He was not asked to return.

For the next two years, he tried to make a life for himself and Ruth Lander. In Woodstock he set himself a regular writing schedule, by which he rose at six in the morning, cooked his own breakfast, and then chopped wood for two hours. "Then I put in four or five hours of intellectual work in my study," he once told Mary Braggiotti. "My desk faces a large window and the minute I lift my eyes I have one of the most beautiful views in New York State before me—green valleys and wooded mountains. It is always relaxing and, somehow, reassuring." He worked at one of his father's old desks and had in his library two thousand books, many of them signed copies of his father's works.

His major income came from teaching or lecturing at several small colleges. On Tuesdays he went to Rutherford, New Jersey, to lecture at Fairleigh Dickinson College. He taught a course called "Sources of Reason and Unreason" at the New School for Social Research in New York. Another subject on which he lectured was titled, "Is Peace of Mind Necessary or Is Guilt Necessary?"

But, as the fall of 1950 approached, Eugene enjoyed less and less peace. Ruth was finding him increasingly difficult. He was drinking heavily. At times, he was quite violent. One evening, when she was making arrangements for her separation, he noticed that she had picked up a copy of *The Iceman Cometh* which O'Neill had given her. It was inscribed "To Ruth Lander with all the best of good wishes. Eugene O'Neill." Eugene junior snatched the book away and scribbled in it, "My father wrote this in ignorance of the real nature of this woman. Eugene O'Neill, Jr."

During the summer of 1950 he saw much of a teacher and writer from New York named Flora Rheta Schriber, and also of Elyse Whitney, an art collector. Both women tried to help him. Miss Whitney tried to straighten out his hopelessly entangled checkbook. She insisted that he write checks at once for the most pressing bills, including electricity and telephone, which were in danger of being turned off. Miss Schriber, a successful magazine writer, tried to help him apply his talents to making the money which he so badly needed. They talked about marriage in August. She introduced him to her parents. At times, she felt, "his main interest in me was in acquiring a mother and father."

Sometimes, in discussing his family with her, Eugene was bitter. "You might as well know," he said, "what it's like to be a member of this family." He spoke of his being cut off from his father. Even now, he had a note coming due at the bank and he was afraid of losing his precious piece of woodland on which he had hoped to build a home. He had written to his father, asking if he could come up to Marblehead for a visit, and O'Neill had replied that he would be glad to see his son but that "under the circumstances" he thought it would be advisable that "we meet in Salem." Perhaps O'Neill senior did not feel up to risking another conflict between stepson and stepmother. Whatever the reason, Eugene junior was furious. "If I do not see my father in my father's house," he wrote him, "then I do not see my father."

He told Miss Schriber of Shane's going to Lexington for drug addiction and how his father had apparently done nothing for him. He spoke of Oona, rejected by her father because of her marriage to a man three times her age and now an expatriate. He spoke of his own mother who faced old age with no funds in reserve, no pension, nobody but her only living son to care for her.

One pleasure remained to him that summer. He acted in several amateur theatricals in Woodstock; in one, he was the narrator in Thornton Wilder's *Our Town*. On Monday, September 18, he and Miss Schriber agreed to meet again the following Monday. During the ensuing week, however, he talked with Ruth Lander and begged her to marry him and resume their life together. On Friday night he took Ruth and some friends to a roadhouse on the outskirts of Woodstock. He ordered champagne for his party and announced that he and Ruth were to be married. Ruth had not agreed to this, but she knew it was futile to argue. His talk became increasingly irrational during the weekend. He kept declaiming, from Shakespeare, "There's a divinity that shapes our ends, Rough-hew them how we will."

Ruth talked with him again on Saturday. He talked wildly. "I was frightened by a certain look in his eye," she has said. "I told him that we should wait and see how things were. That look I saw terrified me."

On Saturday night, Eugene had dinner with old friends, Frank Meyer and his wife, Elsie. They felt he was not himself, not well. At nine Sunday morning he called Ruth and told her to feel free to come up and take any of her things that she had left in the house.

On Monday morning, Elsie Meyer saw his jeep still parked outside his house; she knew that he would ordinarily be on his way to New York to meet with his classes that night at the New School.

He also was scheduled to meet his mother for dinner. Mrs. Meyer called Ruth Lander and asked her if she had heard from Gene. Both women became anxious. Mrs. Meyer said she would not go into the house alone. At one-forty-five in the afternoon, accompanied by friends, she pushed open the front door of Eugene's house. They saw his lifeless body lying just inside. His hand was stretched out as though he had been trying to reach for the doorknob or asking for the help that had eluded him all his life. He had bled to death. Later, a state trooper found a note under an empty whisky bottle in the bathroom. It read: "Never let it be said of an O'Neill that he failed to empty a bottle. *Ave Atque Vale* [Hail and Farewell]."

It was not too difficult to piece together what had taken place on the morning of his death. Eugene junior shaved with a straight razor. Knowing that it is easier to bleed to death when one is immersed in hot water—an ancient Roman custom—he stepped into the bathtub and cut his wrists and ankles. Then, perhaps, he changed his mind about dying. He got out of the tub and went to the telephone; it had been cut off. Blood was on it and on the furnishings and on many of his books. He didn't make it to the front door.

On Monday evening, September 25, 1950, Saxe Commins received word that Eugene junior was dead. He immediately called Aronberg and asked him what he thought should be done. Commins, who loved O'Neill, was terribly distressed. He was a close friend of Eugene junior and he was the editor of Eugene O'Neill and Whitney Oates's volume of Greek plays.

Aronberg sensed at once that Commins did not want to call his old friend. "I'll telephone Gene," he said. "This is a matter that should be handled by a lawyer."

Accounts of the ensuing telephone conversation differ widely. Naturally, Carlotta was deeply disturbed. Although O'Neill was sitting in the same room, she did not have him come to the phone; she thought he was too ill to take the news. But somehow the playwright knew that Eugene junior was dead. He asked, with pathetic and awful simplicity, when and how his eldest son had died. It was almost as if he knew and had expected the terrible event. After Carlotta told him what she knew, O'Neill remained silent. He never mentioned his son's name again—except to say that now that Eugene was dead, *Long Day's Journey into Night* could be published.

If O'Neill ever blamed himself for the death of his son or for any of the things that happened to his children, he blamed himself in silence; he never spoke of them to anyone.

In Bermuda, the next morning, a friend told Shane about young Eugene. Shane was stunned, and yet he seemed almost to have expected the news. "I wonder what was troubling him?" Shane mused. "He seemed so strong, so able to take care of himself. He was a nice fellow. He liked to give us advice. But I liked him."

O'Neill remained unavailable to reporters who tried to reach him for comment. Carlotta said that she was taking him on an automobile trip, with their physician, through New England. Meanwhile, at Campbell's funeral parlor on Madison Avenue, New York City, Eugene junior's fellow Skull and Bones members took charge. The only blood relative present was his mother, Kathleen. O'Neill had sent a floral piece with a card attached reading, *"Father."* There was a separate piece from Carlotta.

Eugene O'Neill lived three years and two months after the death of his eldest son. They were the most wretched years of his tragedy-scarred life. It was "on or about the first of February, 1951," to quote the bitter words of a legal document, that Carlotta charged O'Neill with being "guilty of cruel and abusive treatment" at that time, as well as on "divers occasions."

It was generally known in the neighborhood of Point o' Rocks, as the winter of 1951 wore on, that both O'Neill and Carlotta were unwell and that dissension had split their household. Dr. Mayo made continued visits to the frame house and was keeping both husband and wife under sedation. On Monday evening, February 5, Dr. Mayo was scheduled to drop by the O'Neill home after dinner. His arrival was delayed. When he did reach the house, he found O'Neill lying on the rocks outside in the front yard. His right knee was fractured and he was unable to rise.

Dr. Mayo called an ambulance and O'Neill was carried on a stretcher to Salem Hospital. Carlotta went along. When he had been put to bed, with no one allowed in his room, she began shouting in the lobby. Hospital attendants were alarmed, and they called the police. Later Dr. Merrill Moore, a psychiatrist (who by an odd coincidence, was a cousin of Ralph Barton) was summoned to attend to Carlotta at the Salem Police Station. After medical examination by the physician, she was admitted to McLean Hospital, a state institution for the mentally ill at Belmont, Massachusetts.

Word of the illnesses of O'Neill and Carlotta spread through Boston. Reporters besieged Salem Hospital for news. Hospital officials referred them to Dr. Mayo who refused comment except to say that O'Neill was a "medical patient" and was "not on the hospital's danger list." He added that both O'Neill and Carlotta "have been adamant about refusing to disclose his ailment." The next day, February 7, Dr. Mayo revealed that O'Neill was suffering from Parkinson's Disease in addition to a fractured leg." He said that "O'Neill's wife is under treatment," but would not reveal the nature of her illness. Dr. Mayo called Saxe Commins, and Bill Aronberg in New York and both came at once to Salem.

Carlotta, in her account of the events leading up to O'Neill's hospitalization, has said that he broke his leg as a result of his insistence on going out of the house into the darkness. Apparently there had been a disagreement between them, and O'Neill had thrown an overcoat over his lounging clothes and had stalked out of the house. In his haste to get out he had neglected to take his cane, and on the sharp protruding rocks at the front of the house he slipped and fell. It appears that he lay there a long time before he was discovered, for, in addition to suffering a fractured kneecap, he developed pneumonia, according to the physician who attended him. Versions of the detailed circumstances vary.

Dr. Moore advised O'Neill, as well as O'Neill's friends Aronberg and Commins, that the dramatist and his wife should be separated. He believed that Carlotta was not at all well. On March 23, O'Neill signed a petition in which he contended that Carlotta was "incapable of taking care of herself." (At the time the petition was signed O'Neill was convalescing from his illness.)

At McLean Hospital, authorities decided that Carlotta was capable of taking care of herself. They agreed, however, that she was upset. They retained Dr. Harry Kozol, an expert in legal psychiatry, to examine Carlotta and to protect her rights. He concluded that her behavior was the result of "delirium from bromides." Released, she took a room in a Boston hotel and filed a petition for separate support. Carlotta said, through her attorney, Robert W. Merserve, that "on or about the first day of February, 1951, and at divers other times prior thereto my husband has been guilty of cruel and abusive treatment of your petitioner." She added that O'Neill had failed to support her and that she was now living apart from him for "justifiable cause." O'Neill's attorney answered by contesting the petition "for want of jurisdiction."

On March 31, 1951, O'Neill accompanied by a trained nurse, came to New York by train. Saxe Commins, Bill Aronberg and

Lawrence Langner brought O'Neill to Doctors Hospital. Although an effort was made to keep his arrival and hospitalization a secret, Earl Wilson learned that O'Neill was in "a New York hospital" and stated that he weighed only eighty-four pounds. Wilson added that O'Neill was *not* in a critical condition, *not* sad, but ate very little, and was confined to his bed. He had requested "pretty nurses" and told hospital attendants, "I don't want to be taken care of by any old witches." His right leg was still in a cast.

Old friends from O'Neill's Provincetown Players days and from the Broadway theater began coming to see him. When Jimmy Light, who loved him perhaps more than any of the others, arrived, the two men looked at each other for a long time unable to say anything. O'Neill took a cigarette and with great effort lit it himself despite the terrible trembling of his hands. Light took this to mean O'Neill wanted Light to know he was not helpless. O'Neill insisted on being brought up to date on all the things Light had been doing. He wanted to know what had happened to all his old friends. Why had they not kept in touch with him? Light did not tell him that most of them had tried without success. Several pretty Broadway actresses visited him. O'Neill enjoyed seeing them but, as he told Bill Aronberg, "What can I do about them? Look at me. My hands shaking. My leg in a cast. I am too old. I'm not a young man any longer."

Aronberg sent his secretary, Jane Burnside, who was in her twenties and was very pretty, to visit with O'Neill on a number of afternoons. Miss Burnside has recalled that some of the time O'Neill talked, but sometimes he remained silent and seemed far away. She let the direction of the conversation come from him. O'Neill was talking at random about things in the past. Some of the things he spoke of were sad things. Some of his memories made both of them smile.

Then all at once he said, "I had three children." He was looking directly into her eyes. "I lost the one son," O'Neill said, "my eldest." He talked at length about Eugene. He told about how brilliant he had been, how he had done so well at Yale, and how he had become a great Greek scholar.

"He seemed to be so proud of Eugene junior," Miss Burnside said. "But he seemed completely puzzled as to why he had committed suicide, although he did not talk directly about what had happened. Then he said, 'And there is Shane.' It is hard to remember his exact words. He said he felt awfully sorry for Shane. He thought Shane was a mixed-up kid and didn't seem to know what he wanted to do.

O'Neill said he didn't know what he, his father, could do about it, though."

Then Miss Burnside made an observation that has been made by others who have talked with O'Neill at this time: "I could tell that he loved his children very much. It was just that he felt helpless to do anything about them."

One night, Bill Aronberg and Merrill Moore took Ruth Lander to dinner; afterward, all three went to Doctors Hospital. Moore went into O'Neill's room and talked with him alone for a while. When he came out he told Ruth that O'Neill remembered meeting her at the time of *The Iceman.* "He thinks you were married to Eugene." Moore said. He took Ruth into O'Neill's room.

"He was standing there," Ruth has said, "looking at me with those big eyes. His arms were outstretched to me and he was saying, 'I remember you, Ruth, when we met backstage at *The Iceman.* I loved you then and I love you now.' Ruth took O'Neill in her arms and he sobbed on her breast.

"I know," Ruth has said, "that it was not really me that he cared about. I felt that in embracing me he was saying good-by to Gene. It was his way of saying farewell. He was weeping for his dead son."

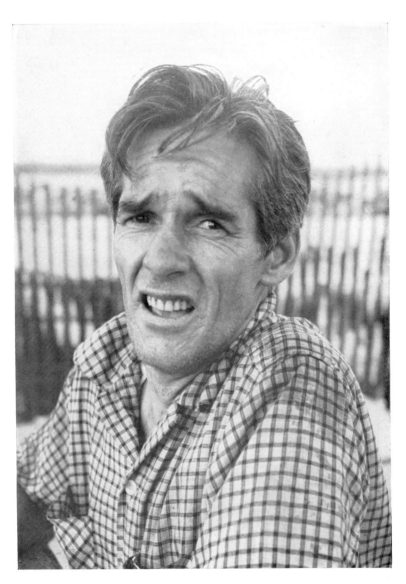

O'Neill's son, Shane, today

CHAPTER

THIRTY-THREE

ಬಬ

DEATH OF THE O'NEILL

Toward the middle of April, Carlotta, at the Shelton Hotel in Boston, was able to reach O'Neill by telephone. A friend of O'Neill's has recalled that one afternoon he arrived at his hospital room and "Gene was all smiles."

"Carlotta has called," O'Neill said, "and everything is all right. She wants to take me back."

Carlotta told a reporter for a national magazine that O'Neill was writing love letters to her and sending her red roses. She said that she loved him and felt that he needed her more than anything else. Both Dr. Kozol and Carlotta were confident that there would be a reconciliation within three weeks. They were eager to tell the story which would "set the public straight on what all the trouble was about."

The deadline for the legal skirmishing which had been going on between O'Neill and Carlotta was set for April 23. Carlotta's lawyer told reporters that she might sue if the "Guardianship of Insane" action were not withdrawn; she would charge O'Neill, his lawyer, and Dr. Moore with conspiracy against her.

In New York, O'Neill told his friends he would be going back to Carlotta. She would take care of him. He had nobody else but her. Legal threats were stilled, and an agreement was reached.

The week of May 14, O'Neill began saying good-by to the old friends he had not seen for so long and whom he knew he would never see again. One of his most difficult good-bys was with Saxe Commins—who had named his son after O'Neill. Commins wanted to take his old friend to the train but O'Neill insisted on saying good-by in the hospital room. When the time came for Commins to leave, O'Neill made only this explanation. "It is my destiny that I go back," he said.

Then, as the two men embraced, O'Neill said, "Good-by, my brother."

Aronberg, O'Neill's attorney, went to the station with him. "We never talked literature and stuff like that," Aronberg has said. "Gene and I liked to go out and have a good time together. 'Way back, we went to the six-day bike races. We used to go to tracks. Gene was a two-dollar bettor. It was the fun of the races he liked. Lots of evenings we went to swing spots together. I have an entirely different view of O'Neill than writers and people like that have. He was a friend, a pleasant companion. He was a swell guy. He liked a good time."

"Well, Gene," Aronberg said when he and his friend parted, "this is the last I'll see of you."

"What do you mean, Bill?" O'Neill said. "Of course I'll be seeing you again. Why do you say that, Bill?"

"Because Carlotta doesn't like me, that's why," Aronberg said.

"Ha," O'Neill said banteringly, "she doesn't like anybody. That doesn't mean anything."

"You wait and see," Aronberg said, "after you get up to Boston, I won't be your attorney any more. She'll fire me!"

"Over my dead body," O'Neill said. "You'll always be my attorney. You're my friend."

"No," Aronberg said as he put out his hand, "this is the last I'll be seeing of you, Gene. The best of luck."

O'Neill's nurse, a Canadian girl, wheeled his 117 pounds aboard the Yankee Clipper. He would never again return to the city of his birth.

Newspaper accounts said that Carlotta was disposing of their "$100,000 home at Marblehead" and the couple would move into a Boston apartment hotel to "avoid the servant problems that contributed to their difficulties." Aronberg announced that "all legal actions brought by the couple have been dropped."

Several days later Aronberg received a letter, signed by O'Neill, that told him he was no longer to serve as his attorney.

Eleven days after O'Neill left Doctors Hospital he signed a new will. It was far different from the will he had previously signed when Aronberg was his attorney. Carlotta was "nominated and appointed" executrix. All of his estate "of whatever nature" he gave, devised and bequeathed to Carlotta. His burial instructions ignored the O'Neill family plot in New London, where he had erected an imposing stone. The document was signed in a very shaky hand by O'Neill. Dr. Kozol, the psychiatrist, was a witness.

Shane and Cathy had moved back into Spithead, which had been rented for a while. Shane was not working; in fact, he again was drinking heavily and smoking marijuana. They were out of money by this time, and it was abruptly decided that Shane should leave the island. He arrived in New York early in June, 1951, just one jump ahead of a proposed newspaper story in Bermuda which would have said that he and Cathy were holding marijuana parties at Spithead. Shane did not send any money back to Cathy and she had to sell the entire contents of Spithead to a secondhand-furniture dealer. Cathy and the children arrived in New York in July.

Both Shane and his mother were without funds the following fall. Agnes, in caring for her mother during her last months, had used up all the money from her settlement with O'Neill. Shane agreed that they must sell Spithead. Because of the run-down condition of the house and its being entirely without furnishings, the best price she could get was thirty thousand dollars. Shane's share was fifteen thousand.

Cathy had gone to Florida to stay with her mother and Shane later joined her. There, early in 1952, she gave birth to another baby, a boy, who was named Ted. By the summer of 1952, Shane and Cathy and their children were settled on the top floor of an apartment building on Twenty-second Street near Lexington Avenue, in New York.

One afternoon, in the middle of September, Oona and Charlie Chaplin, on their way to Europe for a six-week visit, came to see them. The première of Chaplin's new film, *Limelight,* was being held while they were in New York, and Shane and Cathy were asked to attend and come to a party afterwards. It had been almost seven years since Oona and Shane had seen each other.

The party after the opening was given by Lillian Ross, a writer for *The New Yorker,* in her apartment on the upper East Side. Oona asked her to include, besides Cathy and Shane, Agnes and her husband, Mac Kaufman, and some of her friends from her school days. Miss Ross was at that time working on a profile of Chaplin.

The party's gaiety was somewhat marred by the news from Washington that the Attorney General was going to look into Chaplin's alleged subversive activities before allowing him to return to the United States. Chaplin told some of the guests that he had always loved the United States, and he pointed out that he had sold millions of dollars worth of war bonds in order to aid the war effort.

The next afternoon, Cathy took her three children to the Chaplin suite in the Hotel Sherry Netherlands. Oona had arranged a children's party with ice cream and cake and presents. She gave Maura and Sheila beautiful fairy princess dresses and there was a Teddy bear for little Ted.

The Chaplin family sailed on September 23, 1952, aboard the Queen Elizabeth, traveling in style with a large entourage of servants. An enthusiastic crowd greeted them at Waterloo Station. Oona heard a cockney news vendor call out, "Hello Charlie boy." Chaplin cheered up considerably. At the Savoy Hotel, where he took his family, seventeen policemen had to hold back the cheering admirers. Tears came to Chaplin's eyes, according to Clifton Daniel, correspondent for *The New York Times.*

"It's wonderful," Daniel heard Oona say, "it's wonderful. I had no idea it would be like this. It's really marvelous."

It was her first trip abroad and Chaplin took her to the roof of the Savoy and pointed out the sights of London, where he had been born in poverty. It was also the city to which her father had come nearly a quarter century before, when he had left her and Shane and Agnes in Bermuda.

Seven months later, when Chaplin changed his plans and announced that he would not return to the United States, Oona dropped her United States citizenship and became a British subject.

In the summer of 1952, O'Neill allowed *A Moon for the Misbegotten* to be published, because he was hard pressed for cash. He had to have a trained nurse eight hours each day. Carlotta told the widow of Barrett Clark that she was nursing O'Neill the other sixteen hours. She said she only hoped her money and her strength held out.

In publishing *A Moon* before it appeared on Broadway, O'Neill broke a precedent he had set for himself. In a prefatory note he said, "I cannot presently give it the attention required for appropriate presentation." He said there were no plans for its production.

Reporters tried to reach O'Neill for comment. Carlotta turned them away. "We do not want to be bothered by any more cheap publicity," she told them. She was bitter about the stories which had reported their troubles and separation and charged that more space was given to the separation than to the reconciliation.

For two winters after leaving New York, O'Neill stayed in his room at the Shelton, living in a hotel room, as in his childhood. Carlotta has said that she had to bathe and dress him and then carry him piggy-back to the window so he could look out on the Charles River. In good weather he could see the Harvard oarsmen rowing their sculls. He would stay up a few hours, and then she would put him back to bed.

During the winter of 1952–53, Agnes and her husband went to Mexico to live. Both were writing. In the late winter they received word that somebody had broken into Old House at Point Pleasant. The police investigated and found that Cathy and Shane and the children had moved in; they had run completely out of money in New York. Shane had sold everything he owned. The $15,000 from the sale of Spithead was all gone. Once again Shane and Cathy and the children, seemingly destined to wander like gypsies, never staying in any place long, always poverty-stricken, were without a place to live.

On June 25, 1953, the police in Point Pleasant, acting under a New Jersey State law, registered Shane as a convicted narcotic addict. He gave his age as thirty-three, his permanent address as 30 East Twenty-second Street, in New York, and said that he was employed as an assembler at the Edison Price Electric Company on Center Street in New York. He told the police that he no longer used drugs.

Almost two months later, Cathy and Shane received a letter from Oona, telling that she had had her fifth child and second son on August 24, 1953. She said she was naming him Eugene, but she did not otherwise refer to her father.

Shane spent his time wandering back and forth between Point
Pleasant and New York. Often he walked around Manhattan all
night long. Sometimes he was picked up by police and, because he
seemed confused and unable to explain where he lived, was sent to
Bellevue.

O'Neill's distress over the things that were happening to his
children was apparent only to those who knew him best. He expressed
neither complaint nor criticism, and though he became more and more
ill and more and more unhappy, he said nothing.

In the last year of his life, during their stay at the Shelton Hotel
in Boston, he and Carlotta destroyed at least six of his cycle plays.
He had devoted a part of his life to these plays and had completed
at least a second draft of each, but apparently he knew that he would
not live to finish them.

"It isn't that I don't trust you," Carlotta has quoted O'Neill as
saying to her, "but you might drop dead or get run over or something,
and I don't want anybody else finishing up a play of mine." All of
the plays had been completely written, Carlotta has said, but they
still required some cutting and revising.

"We tore them up bit by bit, together," she later revealed. "I
helped him because his hands—he had this terrific tremor, he could
tear just a few pages at a time. It was awful. It was like tearing up
children."

When she was asked whether she had tried to dissuade O'Neill,
Carlotta emphatically replied that she had not. To have done so, she
said, would have been presumptuous. Then, as if to clarify, in her own
mind as well as her listeners', her unique relationship with O'Neill,
she said with finality that he was a *writer* and he was the *man*—as if
nothing more could be said.

There was no advance warning late in November, 1953, that
Eugene O'Neill was about to die. He began to sink on the evening of
Thursday, November 26. His nurse stayed at his bedside. Carlotta
sent for Dr. Kozol. Toward three o'clock, his pulse grew weaker, his
breathing more troubled. Finally, a little after three, in the morning
of November 27, 1953, his pulse stopped altogether. His tired heart
was at last at rest. At his bedside were his wife, his nurse and his
wife's psychiatrist.

Joseph Heidt, the Theatre Guild press agent, was asleep at his
Long Island home early that morning when his telephone rang; it

was Doctor Kozol. Carlotta had asked him to call Heidt and tell him that O'Neill was dead. The doctor told Heidt some of the details of O'Neill's condition at the end. The official cause of death, the doctor said, was bronchial pneumonia. "But you know, Heidt," Dr. Kozol said, "O'Neill didn't have to die. But he didn't seem to want to live. He just lay down and died. He stopped trying."

O'Neill's children were not notified. They learned the news from radio broadcasts and the newspapers.

The obituaries and the tributes said little that had not already been printed in his lifetime. Perhaps his best epitaph was written by John Mason Brown, who said that "If O'Neill wrote tragedies, he lived them, too . . . the loneliness of his last years and his ultimate inability to write at all . . . [he] had something of the titan in him."

Carlotta ordered an autopsy performed on O'Neill's body at Massachusetts General Hospital. Not only Carlotta, but the scores of doctors who had treated O'Neill for so-called Parkinson's Disease wanted to know the exact nature of his illness. Carlotta clung to her belief that the hardships he endured as a young man were responsible for his illness. "He drank too much an inferior liquor, and wore his body and soul out, without proper food or even a bed at night." The autopsy was not made public but Carlotta has said that the findings indicated a hereditary nervous disease.

Actually, Parkinson's is not a disease that has an entity itself, like smallpox or measles. It is a syndrome, a combination of symptoms, given the title Parkinson's. O'Neill had the classic symptoms: the "pill-rolling tremor," his basal ganglia were affected. He also had arteriosclerosis. One of the physicians who treated him still insists it was Parkinson's Disease. O'Neill himself seemed to prefer to believe it was a hereditary nervous disease and told Hamilton Basso of this diagnosis six years before his death. One physician also noted that O'Neill had a certain mystic view of his illness, that he somehow felt it was a part of his fate, his own peculiar destiny. Perhaps it was.

Carlotta announced that funeral plans would be kept "a family secret." She said it was her husband's wish that neither the time nor place of his funeral be announced. She issued strict instructions at the hotel, at the funeral home, to servants, to friends, to doctors and nurses, that no information whatsoever was to be given to anyone. On the following Wednesday, Shane read an Associated Press dispatch from Boston, in which a Dr. Harry L. Kozol, "physician to Mr.

O'Neill's widow" said that he had attended the funeral with Mrs. O'Neill.

"Mrs. O'Neill wishes you to know," the doctor said in a prepared statement, "her husband was buried in Forest Hills Cemetery in exact accordance with his wishes and instructions to the very end."

Later, in an interview, Carlotta shed some light on the mystery that had enveloped the death and burial of her husband. It had been O'Neill's wish, she explained, that there be no publicity or public ceremony at his funeral. In fact, he had specified that at his death no newspaper or person was to be informed what funeral parlor he was in or where he was to be buried. "He wished nobody to be at his funeral," she said, "but me and his nurse. And he wished no religious representative of any kind."

Apparently O'Neill had decided not to be buried in the family plot in New London. Carlotta and her lawyer selected a cemetery near Boston. It was the playwright's wish that his wife be buried beside him, and some time before his death he drew a design for their gravestone. On this design were only the dates and places of their births, two lines left open for the dates of their deaths, and lastly the words, "Rest In Peace."

Carlotta described the cemetery in which her husband is buried and where she will rest some day; it is a beautiful place, with great old trees, large rhododendron and blooming dogwood. She finds it a comforting place and, like many other widows, she feels a little less lonely when she visits there. Carlotta continues to observe the anniversary of her husband's death.

On Christmas Day, Friday, December 25, 1953, Shane opened *The New York Times* and read a headline that said:

SON AND DAUGHTER CUT OFF
BY EUGENE O'NEILL IN WILL

O'Neill's will, which had been signed by him in Boston on May 28, 1951, just eleven days after he was released from Doctors Hospital in New York, named Carlotta as executrix and sole beneficiary. The fourth paragraph of the page-and-a-half will stated:

"I purposely exclude for any interest in my estate under this will my son, Shane O'Neill, and my daughter, Oona O'Neill Chaplin, and I exclude their issue now or hereafter born."

Shane was not surprised. He said to Cathy, "My father told

me he felt he had provided for me and Oona when he left Spithead to us at the time of the separation. He told me that he didn't think he would have much to leave anybody.

"You know," Shane added, almost to himself, "he had that wonderful collection of jazz records. I wonder what will become of them. I would like some of the records."

The following year, Agnes and Mac returned from Mexico. They moved into Old House with Shane and Cathy and the children. For a time, things worked out. Mac got a job on a fishing boat. He persuaded the skipper to give Shane a job, too. After a few voyages, the skipper didn't rehire Shane. He thought Shane acted "kind of queer." Shane had insisted on growing a beard while at sea and sporting a red stocking cap with a tassle.

Agnes helped Shane and his family out. Oona sent on a hundred dollars a month to Cathy. Shane continued to look for jobs, but he would hold them only for a few days. It was becoming known in Point Pleasant that he had been a drug addict. His eccentric behavior, although normal for him, convinced people that he still was an addict.

By a great effort of the will, he was managing to stay away from heroin, but, like so many former addicts, he took a great many Benzedrine pills every day. "Benzedrine," Shane has said, "makes life just bearable. You can get by. I was sorry to give up taking heroin because taking it gives you something to live for."

Late in the winter, Shane finally received formal word regarding his father's death. It was in the form of a letter from Carlotta's attorneys which informed Shane that he had been "purposely excluded" from the will of his late father, that the will had been filed for probate in the Suffolk County Court in Boston, and that the deadline for any objection was February 4, 1954. Shane read the letter and tossed it aside. He seemed indifferent. A number of his friends suggested that he contest the will. In some states, he was told, a father cannot cut off his children. Shane would listen and nod, but he did nothing. Lawyers wrote suggesting this and that course of procedure in the matter of claiming his inheritance. Sometimes he would cut someone short when the matter was brought up. "It is my business," he snapped. "It can be of no interest to anyone but me. It is a family matter."

On October 2, 1954, a Point Pleasant police officer found Shane lying in a ditch in the hot sun and dressed in a heavy overcoat. When questioned, he seemed dazed and was unable to give a satisfactory account of himself. He was arrested, found guilty of being a disorderly person, and placed in the county jail in Toms River where he was held for a time "under observation." Authorities concluded that he had taken too much Benzedrine.

The living arrangements at Old House proved less than satisfactory, and later in the fall Cathy and Shane and the children took an apartment over a store in the downtown section of Point Pleasant.

Cathy had her fifth baby, her third girl, on Washington's Birthday, February 22, 1955, and the O'Neill's named her Kathleen. She had very blue eyes and very blond hair. There were now four children at the Shane O'Neills'.

On a hot night the following summer, the chief of the Point Pleasant police drove to Cathy and Shane's apartment. He had bad news to deliver. Word had come over the state police teletype that Cathy's mother, Charlotte De Oca, had been murdered in Saint Cloud, Florida. Cathy knew that her mother had married a fourth husband a year or so before but that lately she had been separated from him. His name was Robert Nonts De Oca and he was said to possess both Spanish and Indian blood. He was given to violent bursts of temper and was irrationally jealous. Arrested, he was judged insane and was sentenced to life imprisonment in the state penitentiary for the criminally insane at Chatahootchie. Cathy was sole beneficiary of her mother's estate. It amounted to a trust fund of sixty thousand dollars. And so, still another footnote of violence, sudden death and grinding tragedy was written into the tale of the house of O'Neill.

EPILOGUE

 හ

THE HAUNTED

On June 21, 1955, Yale University announced that "Carlotta Monterey O'Neill, widow of the Nobel-Prize-winning playwright Eugene O'Neill, has given the University the American and Canadian rights of Mr. O'Neill's unpublished play 'Long Day's Journey Into Night.' The Yale University Press will publish the new play next February 20, 1956." The announcement went on to say that the deed of the gift to Yale provides that income from publication of the play is to be used for "the upkeep of the Eugene O'Neill Collection in the Library, for the purchase of books on the drama, and for the Eugene O'Neill scholarships in the Yale Drama School."

The announcement immediately raised the question, what happened to the playwright's stipulation that *Long Day's Journey* was not to be published or produced until twenty-five years after his death? The answer was made public a year later when Carlotta revealed that her late husband himself had suggested an earlier release of the play. The provision for withholding the play had been made, she told *The New*

York Times in June, 1956, "because he had been urged to do so by his son Eugene junior for his son's own personal reasons. Some time after his son's death, which took place in 1950, my husband told me that he could no longer see any reason for withholding production or publication of the play, and we had many discussions before my husband's death looking toward its early release."

When *Long Day's Journey into Night* appeared in the bookstores, a friend lent Shane a copy. Later, when the friend asked him what he thought of this tale of his O'Neill grandparents, his Uncle Jamie and his own father, Shane said, "I found the book very interesting but I can't understand why it should be of interest to anyone except a member of our family. It's very personal."

Shane's nocturnal wanderings around Point Pleasant caused complaints to be registered with the police. He sometimes walked along the street talking to himself. On one occasion, the early morning of May 2, 1956, an elderly lady in Point Pleasant told the police that she had been awakened by noises outside her ground-floor bedroom window, and in the moonlight she had seen Shane's gaunt face peering into the room. He was again booked on a charge of being a disorderly person, and he was sentenced to twenty days in the Ocean County jail.

Dr. W. G. Hayden, the prison doctor, examined him. Shane at this time would occasionally go for days without eating. One by one his teeth had fallen out, and he had let his hair grow long and bushy. "He was a complete physical wreck," Hayden said. "He had several hundred Benzedrine tablets on him when he was picked up. I have no doubt that his taking Benezdrine caused his difficulty." The doctor thought that Shane should be committed to a mental institution.

Agnes intervened and for a time it appeared that a way might be worked out for Shane to get medical and psychiatric help while remaining at home. Shane, however, objected so vigorously to getting any sort of help that the doctors decided to proceed with his commitment. He was admitted to Ancora State Hospital (for the mentally ill) on May 21. "He is suffering from malnutrition and vitamin deficiency . . . shows mental deterioration because of long indiscriminate use of drugs," his report read. "Insight and judgment poor. Has visible tremors of the hands and mouth. Appears depressed and discouraged." Shane was specifically committed for "treatment as a Benzedrine addict."

In June, Cathy received some of her inheritance in cash and she bought for $9,000 a small house with a two-car garage several blocks away from Old House. "I figured," she said, "that I'd fix it so that at least we'd always have a place to live."

Shane's health improved steadily at Ancora. He put on weight rapidly, partly the result of being outfitted with a set of false teeth. Agnes and Cathy came to visit him once a week, although it was a long trip from Point Pleasant. By the end of the summer he was able to come home for a temporary visit. He loved the home that Cathy had bought and begged her to help him get released from Ancora. Cathy talked to one of the psychiatrists at the hospital and he told her, she says, that there was "nothing really wrong with Shane." He added, of course, that it was important to his physical and mental health that Shane give up all drugs, including Benzedrine. Shane was released September 12, 1956.

That fall, Carlotta wrote to José Quintero and asked him to call at her suite at the Hotel Lowell on Sixty-eighth Street just off Madison Avenue. Carlotta and José had tea together.

"We were talking," Carlotta has said, "and I said, 'José, would you like to put on *Long Day's Journey into Night?*' I thought the man was going to faint. I really did, he was in such a state. I said, 'yes, I ask you this because you deserve it for what you did [with *The Iceman Cometh*]. You took a play that had been badly produced and revived it in New York where that is poison . . . Now I trust you, I have talked to you enough, I know you well enough, your subtlety; you know O'Neill, you know what he says, what he means by what he says and nobody else that I know of in this business does. . . .' He [Quintero] stumbled out and said, 'I'm a wreck.' But he did deserve it."

Quintero has described Carlotta that day in her apartment as "a lady of medium height, her black hair pulled back and cut short at the back of the neck. The dark penetrating eyes were arresting in the steadiness of their gaze. She was dressed in black, which she wore with distinction." He has said she talked about her husband's work almost as though he were in the room. There were pictures of him everywhere—when he was young, lean, handsome—and of him and Carlotta on their honeymoon in Paris. On the bookshelves were three or four copies of each of his plays. She spoke feelingly of her husband's dedication to his work. She said, almost sadly, that the only thing he really cared about was his work.

"I left the apartment," Quintero has said, "almost believing that permission to do the play had come from the dead dramatist himself. It was less a permission than a sacred charge."

The American première of *Long Day's Journey into Night* was given in Boston on October 16, 1956, Eugene O'Neill's sixty-eighth birthday. (The world première had been given in Stockholm the previous February.) After *Long Day's Journey* opened in New York, Brooks Atkinson of *The Times* pointed out that O'Neill's "mother's drug addiction is the dramatic focus of the play . . . the characters are victims of fate. They cannot control dark forces that shape their destinies . . . The creative contribution . . . is the sense of doom that emerges from all parts of the story." In summing up, Atkinson wrote: "Let's agree it is a masterpiece . . . nothing he wrote has the size, perspective, patience and mercy of *Long Day's Journey into Night* . . . The pity, the understanding, and the forgiveness spread like a kind of sorrowful benediction and bring a relentless drama to a magnificent conclusion."

In addition to winning for the late playwright his fourth Pulitzer Prize for Drama, the play was voted by the drama critics the best play of the year. The play launched a new Eugene O'Neill revival. Plans were set in motion to revive *A Moon for the Misbegotten.* A musical comedy version of *Anna Christie,* to be called *New Girl in Town,* was put in rehearsal.

Shane and Cathy, without a telephone and seldom reading the newspapers, were almost unaware that his father's fame was once again in the ascendancy. The *New York Post* received a tip that Eugene O'Neill's son was "somewhere in New Jersey" and assigned Helen Dudar to get the story.

Miss Dudar spent almost an entire afternoon with Cathy and Shane in their Point Pleasant living room. To repeated questions as to whether he was bitter at the way his father had treated him over the years, Shane replied, "I don't bear him any resentment." He said he had "licked" his drug addiction. Why his father had stopped seeing him, he said he had never been able to figure out.

"I've thought a lot about it—maybe he got mad because I didn't write. I wanted to write—I wanted to write him about his plays—I thought I understood what he was saying."

Miss Dudar saw Shane as "tall, gaunt almost to the point of emaciation as he sits rocking nervously in his living room . . . choking out his words . . . his hands and his eyes betray defeat in some inner struggle. . . . Shane's hands tremble. He clutches one of his children's dolls to hide the tremor, but his speech will not hold still. He converses, not as if he wanted to, but as if he must in order not to incur displeasure. The words tumble out in disjointed, broken sentences, as uncertain as his own view of life." Shane had misplaced his false teeth that afternoon and Miss Dudar noted that "the deep crevices created by his missing teeth, the downward slope of the sad eyes, gave his face the look of an elongated Greek drama mask of tragedy." Miss Dudar saw him as she drove away "in the gathering twilight, the tall, shivering figure looks like a hesitant stranger, newly arrived, not quite at home."

One afternoon Carlotta asked Quintero to take her to the Helen Hayes Theatre where she could watch, unobserved, a rehearsal of *Journey*. She came dressed completely in black, Quintero has said, her intense dark eyes looking straight before her as she entered the theater. As the rehearsal progressed, she sat erect. She held her back like a ramrod, not even touching the back of her chair. Once or twice she relaxed and put her foot on the balcony rail.

When the rehearsal was over, Carlotta sat for a long time without saying a word and then asked one of Quintero's partners, "Do you think it would be proper for me to go backstage and speak to the actors?"

As the widow came on the stage with the assembled actors, there was a stunned silence. It lasted for what seemed like a long time.

"I don't know what to say," Carlotta said, "how to express it."

She walked over to Fredric March, and very solemnly shook his hand. Then she kissed Florence Eldridge, his wife. (The Marches played the parts of James and Mary Tyrone.) For a moment or two Carlotta looked from face to face among the actors.

"Where's my baby?" she said. "Where's my Gene?" Bradford Dilman, the young actor who had played the part of Edmund Tyrone, was standing near the stage door. She walked over and, according to Quintero, "embraced him with great tenderness."

After the cast had said good-by and left, Carlotta chatted some more with Quintero. Finally she took his hand and slipped a plain gold ring on his finger.

"Wear this," she said. "It's Gene's wedding ring. Wear it. It will bring you luck."

In July of 1957, Shane received a typewritten letter from the Wall Street law firm of Cadwalader, Wickersham and Taft.

"Dear Mr. O'Neill," the letter said, "We are writing on behalf of our client, your late father's widow, Carlotta Monterey O'Neill, in connection with a number of your father's United States copyrights in which you have or may have an interest." The letter stated that Shane, under a new court decision concerning another case but setting a precedent, was entitled, together with Oona, to $14,497.40 in accrued royalties earned by *Strange Interlude* and *Dynamo*. In March, 1958, he and Oona would have another $5,000 to divide. This meant also that in the future, Shane and Oona would share in *Mourning Becomes Electra* when it came up for copyright renewal in 1961.

Shane read the letter but threw it aside, entirely indifferent to his good fortune. Later, on urging from Cathy and his mother, he said he was willing to do whatever Oona wanted to do. He bought what he thought was "a pretty colored postcard" which he intended to send to Carlotta. He wrote her that he hoped she was well and happy. He carried the card around in his pocket for a long time and then lost it.

Late in the winter of 1958, Shane took a walk along the New Jersey shore with this writer. "I'm bored," he said, "with all this talk about me and my father. It doesn't interest me. I think people are bored with me. Now look over there at those fishing boats. They're beauties, perfect for lobstering. And there's the *Caroline E* and she's for sale. That's because she's old. I used to work on her fifteen years ago. I'd like to sail on her again.

"I don't understand this civilization. Sometimes I think we should export all the children to the Himalayas and develop a new, a superior civilization." His eyes turned toward the sea and fell on a fishing boat bobbing up and down on the horizon. "I'd like to go to sea again," he said. "I liked it out there."

On the way back to the house, I asked Shane if he didn't think he ought to pay some attention to money matters on account of Cathy and the children. No, he said, they would be taken care of. It didn't matter what he did or anyone did; things turned out just the same. You got by or you didn't.

"Things might have been different in the past," he said. "I would like to have kept Spithead, but everybody wanted to get something out of it.

"But it doesn't matter. What's done is done. What happens to me doesn't make much difference. Maybe I'll get a good job and keep it. In any case, it doesn't matter. It's of great indifference to me."

As Shane and I walked in the twilight along the marshes, a flock of ducks rose with a whir, beating their wings against the sky. Shane looked up, pleased and happy.

"I'm sure they have some language of their own," he said, "some way of speaking to each other."

PREMIÈRES OF O'NEILL
PLAYS IN AMERICA

Bound East for Cardiff. Produced by Provincetown Players. Wharf Theatre, Provincetown, Mass., summer, 1916.

Thirst. Produced by Provincetown Players. Wharf Theatre, Provincetown, Mass., summer, 1916.

Before Breakfast. Produced by Provincetown Players. The Playwrights' Theatre, New York, Dec. 1, 1916.

Fog. Produced by Provincetown Players. The Playwrights' Theatre, New York, Jan., 1917.

The Sniper. Produced by Provincetown Players. The Playwrights' Theatre, New York, Feb. 16, 1917.

In the Zone. Produced by Washington Square Players. Comedy Theatre, New York, Oct. 31, 1917.

The Long Voyage Home. Produced by Provincetown Players. The Playwrights' Theatre, New York, Nov. 2, 1917.

'Ile. Produced by Provincetown Players. The Playwrights' Theatre, New York, Nov. 30, 1917.

The Rope. Produced by Provincetown Players. The Playwrights' Theatre, New York, April 26, 1918.

Where the Cross Is Made. Produced by Provincetown Players. The Playwrights' Theatre, New York, Nov. 22, 1918.

The Moon of the Caribbees. Produced by Provincetown Players. The Playwrights' Theatre, New York, Dec. 20, 1918.

The Dreamy Kid. Produced by Provincetown Players. The Playwrights' Theatre, New York, Oct. 31, 1919.

Beyond the Horizon. Produced by John D. Williams. Morosco Theatre, New York, Feb. 2, 1920. With Richard Bennett and Elsie Rizer.

Chris Christopherson. Produced by George C. Tyler. Atlantic City, March 8, 1920.

Exorcism. Produced by Provincetown Players. The Playwrights' Theatre, New York, March 26, 1920.

The Emperor Jones. Produced by Provincetown Players. The Playwrights' Theatre, New York, Nov. 3, 1920. With Charles Gilpin and Jasper Deeter.

Diff'rent. Produced by Provincetown Players. The Playwrights' Theatre, New York, Dec. 27, 1920. With James Light.

Gold. Produced by John D. Williams. Frazee Theatre, New York, June 1, 1921. With Willard Mack.

Anna Christie. Produced by Arthur Hopkins. Vanderbilt Theatre, New York, Nov. 10, 1921. With Pauline Lord, Frank Shannon and George Marion.

The Straw. Produced by George C. Tyler. Greenwich Village Theatre, New York, Nov. 10, 1921. With Margalo Gilmore and Otto Kruger.

The First Man. Produced by Neighborhood Playhouse. Neighborhood Playhouse, New York, March 4, 1922. With Augustin Duncan and Margaret Mower.

The Hairy Ape. Produced by Provincetown Players. The Playwrights' Theatre, New York, March 9, 1922. With Louis Wolheim.

Welded. Produced by MacGowan, Jones and O'Neill with the Selwyns. 39th Street Theatre, New York, March 17, 1924. With Doris Keane and Jacob Ben-Ami.

The Ancient Mariner. Produced by Provincetown Playhouse. Provincetown Playhouse, New York, April 6, 1924. With E. J. Ballantine.

All God's Chillun Got Wings. Produced by Provincetown Playhouse. Provincetown Playhouse, New York, May 15, 1924. With Paul Robeson and Mary Blair.

S. S. Glencairn. Produced by Barnstormers. Barnstormers Barn, Provincetown, Mass., August 14, 1924. With Sidney Machet.

Desire under the Elms. Produced by Provincetown Playhouse. Greenwich Village Theatre, New York, Nov. 11, 1924. With Walter Huston and Mary Morris.

The Fountain. Produced by MacGowan, Jones and O'Neill with A. L. Jones and Morris Green. Greenwich Village Theatre, New York, Dec. 10, 1925. With Walter Huston.

The Great God Brown. Produced by MacGowan, Jones and O'Neill. Greenwich Village Theatre, New York, Jan. 23, 1926. With William Harrigan, Robert Keith and Leona Hogarth.

Marco Millions. Produced by Theatre Guild. Guild Theatre, New York, Jan. 9, 1928. With Alfred Lunt and Margalo Gilmore.

Strange Interlude. Produced by Theatre Guild. John Golden Theatre, New York, Jan. 30, 1928. With Lynn Fontanne, Earle Larimore and Glenn Anders.

Lazarus Laughed. Produced by Pasadena Community Playhouse, Pasadena, Cal., April 9, 1928.

Dynamo. Produced by Theatre Guild. Martin Beck Theatre, New York, Feb. 11, 1929. With Glenn Anders, Dudley Digges and Claudette Colbert.

Mourning Becomes Electra. (A trilogy: "Homecoming," "The Hunted" and "The Haunted.") Produced by Theatre Guild. Guild Theatre, New York, Oct. 26, 1931. With Alla Nazimova, Alice Brady and Earle Larimore.

Ah, Wilderness! Produced by Theatre Guild. Guild Theatre, New York, Oct. 2, 1933. With George M. Cohan and Gene Lockhart.

Days without End. Produced by Theatre Guild. Guild Theatre, New York, Jan. 8, 1934. With Earle Larimore and Stanley Ridges.

The Iceman Cometh. Produced by Theatre Guild. Martin Beck Theatre,
New York, Sept. 2, 1946. With James Barton and Dudley Digges.
Long Day's Journey into Night. Produced by Leigh Connel, Theodore
Mann and Jose Quintero. Helen Hayes Theatre, New York, Nov.
7, 1956. With Frederick March and Florence Eldridge.
A Moon for the Misbegotten. Produced by Carmen Capalbo and Stanley
Chase. Bijou Theatre, New York, May 2, 1957. With Wendy Hiller,
Franchot Tone and Cyril Cusack.
A Touch of the Poet. Produced by the Producer's Theatre. Helen Hayes
Theatre. New York, October 2, 1958. With Helen Hayes, Eric
Portman, Kim Stanley, and Betty Field.

INDEX

(*Note:* The symbol **O'N** is used throughout the index to designate **Eugene** O'Neill.)

Index

p. 18.

p 312